Communications
in Computer and Information Science 738

Commenced Publication in 2007
Founding and Former Series Editors:
Alfredo Cuzzocrea, Orhun Kara, Dominik Ślęzak, and Xiaokang Yang

Editorial Board

More information about this series at http://www.springer.com/series/7899

Markus Helfert · Cornel Klein
Brian Donnellan · Oleg Gusikhin (Eds.)

Smart Cities, Green Technologies, and Intelligent Transport Systems

5th International Conference, SMARTGREENS 2016
and Second International Conference, VEHITS 2016
Rome, Italy, April 23–25, 2016
Revised Selected Papers

 Springer

Editors
Markus Helfert
Dublin City University
Dublin 9
Ireland

Cornel Klein
Corporate Technology, Software
  and Systems
Siemens AG
Munich
Germany

Brian Donnellan
Innovation Value Institute
Maynooth University
Maynooth, Kildare
Ireland

Oleg Gusikhin
Ford Research and Advanced Engineering
Dearborn, MI
USA

ISSN 1865-0929   ISSN 1865-0937 (electronic)
Communications in Computer and Information Science
ISBN 978-3-319-63711-2   ISBN 978-3-319-63712-9   (eBook)
DOI 10.1007/978-3-319-63712-9

Library of Congress Control Number: 2017950486

Printed on acid-free paper

This Springer imprint is published by Springer Nature
The registered company is Springer International Publishing AG
The registered company address is: Gewerbestrasse 11, 6330 Cham, Switzerland

Preface

This book includes extended and revised versions of a set of selected papers from SMARTGREENS 2016 (5th International Conference on Smart Cities and Green ICT Systems) and VEHITS 2016 (Second International Conference on Vehicle Technology and Intelligent Transport Systems), held in Rome, Italy, during April 23–25, 2016. SMARTGREENS 2016 received 72 paper submissions from 34 countries, of which 11% are included in this book. VEHITS 2016 received 49 paper submissions from 23 countries, of which 12% are included in this book.

The papers were selected by the event chairs of both events and their selection is based on a number of criteria that include the classifications and comments provided by the Program Committee members, the session chairs' assessment, and also the program chairs' global view of all papers included in the technical program. The authors of selected papers were then invited to submit a revised and extended version of their papers having at least 30% innovative material.

The purpose of the 5th International Conference on Smart Cities and Green ICT Systems (SMARTGREENS) was to bring together researchers, designers, developers, and practitioners interested in the advances and applications in the field of smart cities, green information and communication technologies, sustainability, and energy-aware systems and technologies.

The purpose of the Second International Conference on Vehicle Technology and Intelligent Transport Systems (VEHITS) was to bring together engineers, researchers, and practitioners interested in the advances and applications in the field of vehicle technology and intelligent transport systems. This conference focuses on innovative applications, tools, and platforms in all technology areas such as signal processing, wireless communications, informatics, and electronics, related to different kinds of vehicles, including cars, off-road vehicles, trains, ships, underwater vehicles, or flying machines, and the intelligent transportation systems that connect and manage large numbers of vehicles, not only in the context of smart cities but in many other application domains.

The papers selected to be included in this book contribute to the understanding of relevant trends of current research on smart cities, green ICT systems, vehicle technology and intelligent transport systems including: smart grids, monitoring data, Internet of Things, electric vehicles, intelligent transportation systems, transportation planning, and traffic operation.

With the advances of new and innovative technologies, the field of smart and connected cities is expected to grow even further. Topics such as data privacy, Internet of Things, and architecture or business models for smart cities are becoming increasingly important for both researchers and practitioners. At the same time sustainability and energy are two crucial aspects to consider for the advances and applications in the field of vehicle technology and intelligent transport systems as well as smart cities. In the next few years we can expect a range of innovative technologies and research results for these topics in smart cities and intelligent transportation systems such as energy and vehicle analytics and autonomous and connected vehicles.

We would like to thank all the authors for their contributions and also the reviewers, who helped ensure the quality of this publication.

February 2017

Markus Helfert
Cornel Klein
Brian Donnellan
Oleg Gusikhin

Organization

Conference Co-chairs

SMARTGREENS

Markus Helfert   Dublin City University, Ireland

VEHITS

Oleg Gusikhin   Ford Motor Company, USA

Program Co-chairs

SMARTGREENS

Cornel Klein   Siemens AG, Germany
Brian Donnellan   Maynooth University, Ireland

VEHITS

Markus Helfert   Dublin City University, Ireland

SMARTGREENS Program Committee

Javier M. Aguiar	Universidad de Valladolid, Spain
Antonio Fernández Anta	IMDEA Networks Institute, Spain
Carlos Henggeler Antunes	DEEC, University of Coimbra/INESC Coimbra, Portugal
Jorge Barbosa	FEUP, Portugal
Siegfried Benkner	University of Vienna, Austria
Simona Bernardi	Centro Universitario de la Defensa, Academia General Militar, Spain
Dumitru Burdescu	University of Craiova, Romania
Blanca Caminero	Universidad de Castilla-La Mancha, Spain
Davide Careglio	Universitat Politècnica de Catalunya, Spain
Calin Ciufudean	Stefan cel Mare University, Romania
Georges Da Costa	IRIT, Paul Sabatier University, France
Amélie Coulbaut-Lazzarini	Université Versailles Saint Quentin en Yvelines, France
Brian Donnellan	Maynooth University, Ireland
Annarita Giani	Los Alamos National Laboratory, USA
Muhammad Hasan	Texas A&M University, USA
Peer Hasselmeyer	NEC Europe Ltd., Germany
Nikos Hatziargyriou	National Technical University, Greece
Markus Helfert	Dublin City University, Ireland
Lorenz Hilty	Empa, Switzerland

Seongsoo Hong	Seoul National University, Korea, Republic of
Guoqiang Hu	Nanyang Technological University, Singapore
Filip Idzikowski	Poznan University of Technology, Poland
Muhammad Ali Imran	University of Surrey, UK
Pertti Järventausta	Tampere University of Technology, Finland
Jai Kang	Rochester Institute of Technology, USA
Stamatis Karnouskos	SAP, Germany
Mani Krishna	University of Massachusetts Amherst, USA
Marco Listanti	University of Rome La Sapienza, Italy
Shaobo Liu	Marvell Semiconductor, USA
Rabi Mahapatra	Texas A&M University, USA
Sumita Mishra	Rochester Institute of Technology, USA
Daniel Mosse	University of Pittsburgh, USA
Bruce Nordman	Lawrence Berkeley National Laboratory, USA
Barbara Pernici	Politecnico di Milano, Italy
Andreas Pfeiffer	RWTH Aachen University, Germany
Vitor Pires	Escola Superior de Tecnologia de Setúbal, Instituto Politécnico de Setúbal, Portugal
Pierluigi Plebani	Politecnico Di Milano, Italy
Radu Prodan	University of Innsbruck, Austria
Milan Prodanovic	Instituto Imdea Energía, Spain
Gang Qu	University of Maryland, USA
Gang Quan	Florida International University, USA
Eva González Romera	University of Extremadura, Spain
Enrique Romero-Cadaval	University of Extremadura, Spain
Bo Sheng	University of Massachusetts Boston, USA
Norvald Stol	NTNU, Norway
Ryszard Strzelecki	Gdynia Maritime University, Poland
Mark Sumner	University of Nottingham, UK
Dan Keun Sung	Korea Advanced Institute of Science and Technology, Korea, Republic of
Dimitrios Tsoumakos	Ionian University, Greece
Shengquan Wang	University of Michigan-Dearborn, USA
Hung-Yu Wei	National Taiwan University, Taiwan
Igor Wojnicki	AGH University of Science and Technology, Poland
Yinlong Xu	University of Science and Technology of China, China
Ramin Yahyapour	GWDG, University Göttingen, Germany
Chau Yuen	Singapore University of Technology and Design, Singapore
Rüdiger Zarnekow	Technische Universität Berlin, Germany
Sotirios Ziavras	New Jersey Institute of Technology, USA

SMARTGREENS Additional Reviewers

Hannes Kuebel	Technische Universität Berlin, Germany
Vincenzo De Maio	University of Innsbruck, Austria

Abdelrahim Mohamed   University of Surrey, UK
Vasilis Papaioannou   NTUA, Greece
Zohreh Pourzolfaghar   DCU, Ireland
Marcin Rodziewicz   Poznan University of Technology, Poland
Ahmed Zoha   COMSATS University, Pakistan

VEHITS Program Committee

Thomas Adler   RSG, USA
Shlomo Bekhor   Israel Institute of Technology, Israel
Mohamed Benbouzid   University of Brest, France
Sandford Bessler   Austrian Institute of Technology (AIT), Austria
Neila Bhouri   IFSTTAR, France
Zoltan Bokor   Budapest University of Technology and Economics,
                         Hungary
Catalin Buiu   Universitatea Politehnica din Bucuresti, Romania
Yongcan Cao   University of Texas at San Antonio, USA
Gihwan Cho   Chonbuk University, Korea, Republic of
Seibum Choi   Korea Advanced Institute of Science and Technology,
                         Korea, Republic of
Andy Chow   University College London, UK
Francesco Corman   Delft University of Technology, The Netherlands
Koen H. van Dam   Imperial College London, UK
Mariagrazia Dotoli   Politecnico di Bari, Italy
Bertrand Ducourthial   Université de Technologie de Compiegne, France
Mehmet Onder Efe   Hacettepe University, Turkey
Lino Figueiredo   ISEP, Instituto Superior de Engenharia do Porto,
                         Portugal
Gaspare Galati   Università di Roma Tor Vergata, Italy
Fernando García   Universidad Carlos III, Spain
Yi Guo   University of Alberta, USA
Oleg Gusikhin   Ford Motor Company, USA
Markus Helfert   Dublin City University, Ireland
Zhongsheng Hou   Beijing Jiaotong University, China
Hocine Imine   IFSTTAR, France
Fu-Chien Kao   Da-Yeh University, Taiwan
Hakil Kim   Inha University, Korea, Republic of
Xiangjie Kong   Dalian University of Technology, China
Zdzislaw Kowalczuk   Gdansk University of Technology, Poland
Milan Krbálek   Czech Technical University, Czech Republic
Hongchao Liu   Texas Tech University, USA
Wei Liu   University of Glasgow, UK
João Peças Lopes   INESC TEC/Universidade do Porto, Portugal
Zi-Feng Ma   Shanghai Jiao Tong University, China
Youcef Mezouar   IFMA/Institut Pascal, France
Lyudmila Mihaylova   University of Sheffield, UK

Pedro Moura	Institute of Systems and Robotics, University of Coimbra, Portugal
Mirco Nanni	CNR, Italy
Katsuhiro Nishinari	University of Tokyo, Japan
Alfredo Núñez	Delft University of Technology, The Netherlands
Carolina Osorio	Massachusetts Institute of Technology, USA
Dario Pacciarelli	Roma Tre University, Italy
Markos Papageorgiou	Technical University of Crete, Greece
Ioannis Papamichail	Technical University of Crete, Greece
Brian Park	University of Virginia, USA
Paulo Pereirinha	INESC Coimbra/Polytechnic of Coimbra/APVE, Portugal
Hazem H. Refai	University of Oklahoma, USA
Gianfranco Rizzo	Università degli Studi di Salerno, Italy
Claudio Roncoli	Aalto University, Finland
Carla Silva	Instituto Superior Técnico, Portugal
Silvia Siri	University of Genoa, Italy
Uwe Stilla	Technische Universität München, Germany
Todor Stoilov	Bulgarian Academy of Sciences, Bulgaria
C. James Taylor	Lancaster University, UK
Ahmet Teke	Çukurova Üniversity, Turkey
Tomer Toledo	Technion, Israel Institute of Technology, Israel
Balint Vanek	Hungarian Academy of Sciences, Hungary
Kyongsu Yi	Seoul National University, Korea, Republic of
Jianhua Zhang	East China University of Science and Technology, China
Peng Zhang	Shangai University, China
Hengbing Zhao	UC Davis, USA
Nan Zheng	Ecole Polytechnique Fédérale de Lausanne, Switzerland

VEHITS Additional Reviewers

Raffaele Carli	Politecnic of Bari, Italy
Graziana Cavone	Universiy of Cagliari, Italy
Bo Chen	University of Alberta, Canada
Nicola Epicoco	Politecnico di Bari, Italy
Razia Jamil	East China University of science and Technology, China
Jiajun Xia	e cu s t, China
Zhong Yin	University of Shanghai for Science and Technology, China

SMARTGREENS Invited Speakers

Paolo Tenti	University of Padova, Italy
Giovanni Giuliani	HP Italy Innovation Centre, Italy
Barbara Pernici	Politecnico di Milano, Italy
Venkatesh Prasad	Ford Motor Company, USA
Vincenzo Sinibaldi	Comarch, Italy

VEHITS Invited Speakers

Venkatesh Prasad	Ford Motor Company, USA
Danil Prokhorov	Toyota Tech Center, USA
Vincenzo Sinibaldi	Comarch, Italy

Contents

Vehicle Technology and Intelligent Transport Systems

Invited Paper

About Monitoring in a Service World

Barbara Pernici[✉], Pierluigi Plebani, and Monica Vitali

Politecnico di Milano, piazza Leonardo da Vinci 32, 20133 Milano, Italy
{barbara.pernici,pierluigi.plebani,monica.vitali}@polimi.it

Abstract. Monitoring of services is becoming more and more common to ensure the quality of applications and to provide the required level of service. Nowadays, the technology needed for supporting monitoring and, as a consequence, also monitoring data are widely available. On the other hand, new challenges and research issues arise concerning the design of the monitoring infrastructure, to provide the relevant information both to users and service providers, and their use, and in particular the analysis of monitored data. This paper discusses the main aspects of monitoring, and the use of monitoring data, focusing on event identification and the evaluation of the actions and resources needed to maintain the required level of quality of service. Research challenges related to modeling and using monitoring data are discussed.

Keywords: Quality of service · Monitoring · Event identification · Quality requirements

1 Introduction

Services based on information technology are becoming more and more widespread to support different types of applications. The cloud computing paradigm has introduced different levels of services, introducing the concept of Infrastructure as a Service (IaaS), Platform as a Service (PaaS), and Software as a Service (SaaS) [15], and additional layers and service-based approaches are being proposed, such as for instance Business Process as a Service (BPaaS) [5] and many more. Intrinsic to the use of a service-based paradigm, there is the need of regulating the interaction between the service provider and the service consumer. Such interaction requires that a service is provided according the functionality and quality of service levels agreed between the two parties. Such an agreement can be either explicitly or implicitly defined, in terms of expectation from the users of a given service, and it can make the difference between similar alternative services in terms of user acceptance and therefore concerning the success of the service itself.

As a consequence, there is an increasing need of data about the actual conditions is which a service is provided, i.e., Quality of Service (QoS). These data

---

B. Pernici—The present paper presents an extended view from the keynote presentation of the author at SmartGreens 2016.

M. Helfert et al. (Eds.): SMARTGREENS 2016 and VEHITS 2016, CCIS 738, pp. 3–23, 2017.
DOI: 10.1007/978-3-319-63712-9_1

are needed both on the provider and on the consumer side. On the consumer side, data about the functioning conditions of a service are needed to verify if a service is working and if its expected quality properties are the expected ones. This information can be used to select the best available services first, and to verify their functioning conditions during use, and be the basis for formal contractual agreements between service consumers and providers (Service Level Agreements - SLA). On 'the providers side, in addition to establishing contractual conditions, the data about provided services can be useful to take corrective measures in case the level of quality varies or could be improved.

This aspect is particularly important if the number of consumers for a given service is variable over time, in particular when services are on demand, scalability and elasticity are expected, and therefore the service requires a variable number of resources to satisfy consumers requests.

As discussed in [1], monitoring is needed at different abstraction levels: high-level monitoring provides information about the status of the virtual platform, collected by providers or consumers at the level of middleware, application or users, by the parties themselves or by third parties; low-level monitoring is performed at the providers side to collect specific information at the hardware level, operating system, middleware, network infrastructure and the facility supporting the IT infrastructure. As a consequence, probes needed to collect the information can be located in connection of the different layers of the service infrastructure.

Once the monitoring data are collected and analyzed, the information deriving from the monitoring activity can be used to perform three main types of actions:

- *Adaptation actions*: the system can be adapted, reconfigured, using resources in different quantities and in different ways, in order to provide the requested service and at the requested level.
- *Flexibility support*: the system is capable, possibly also with the support of human intervention facilitated by the monitoring infrastructure, of coping with changing requirements and modes of operation, allowing variable loads and variable levels of service according to different contexts of execution.
- *Awareness support*: the system is capable of analyzing data and of presenting the information to customers and providers in a synthetic way, in the form of dashboards that provide an overview of the status of the system, possibly also associated with alarms and specific warning actions.

The use of monitoring data is becoming more and more widespread in a variety of systems in which adaptivity, flexibility, and awareness support are foreseen.

In the following, we give an overview of some relevant scenarios illustrating them with some examples:

- *Adaptive processes*: since the early days of web service technology, context awareness has been the basis for adapting process-based service compositions: in the PAWS system [3], context is specified on the basis of quality of service parameters, used to evaluate the global quality of the service composition, in Process-Aware Information Systems (PAIS) the execution of flexible processes is designed to be variable in different situations [19].

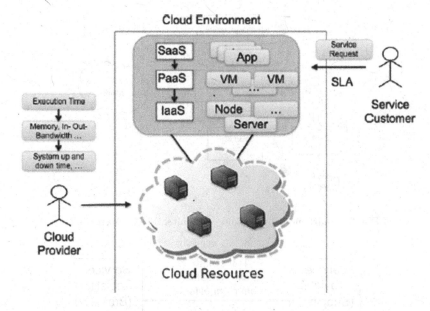

Fig. 1. QoS in services example.

- *User awareness*: several awareness systems, such as, for instance, for utility systems, such as in the case of energy consumption, monitored data are used to inform consumers about their behaviour patterns and to create situations in which consumers are prompted to change their previous behaviour. Tools for facilitation behaviour changes in consumers may be based on serious games and social interaction [4].
- *Cloud service provisioning infrastructures*: as it will be discussed in Sect. 3, monitoring infrastructures are always provided in cloud computing environments, in which QoS is one of the essential elements. In such environments monitoring can present different characteristics in terms of frequency and cost, and it can be used for regulating not only the interactions between providers and consumers, but also the internal use of resources by providers; in Fig. 1, the high-level monitoring and low-level monitoring needs for consumers and providers respectively are shown. Specific uses of monitoring data can be found in methods for improving energy efficiency [10,22] or for reducing the environmental impact of cloud computing [9].
- *Internet of Things*: the availability of monitoring data from sensors is one of the characteristics of the Internet of Things (IoT). Several applications are being developed and others are envisioned for the future. For instance, one application domain can be found in home care, as illustrated in Fig. 2, which shows the architecture for home care developed in the Attiv@bili project [23]. In this case the monitoring data are captured by sensors in smart watches and the infrastructure must guarantee the correct delivery of the monitoring data to all interested applications and interconnected systems.

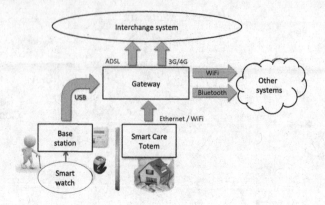

Fig. 2. Smart monitoring devices architecture in Attiv@bili.

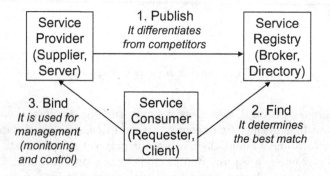

Fig. 3. QoS in a Service Oriented Architecture.

As shown in the previous paragraphs, monitoring can be performed on different types of observed components and for several purposes. In this paper, we discuss some critical aspects of service monitoring and present some research challenges. First of all, Sect. 2 introduces the concept of monitoring as a system that needs to be designed according to the goals to be achieved with the monitoring activity. In Sect. 3, we introduce the main elements at the basis of a monitoring system, including the need of specifying the quality dimensions and measures, and evaluating the quality of the monitoring data. In Sect. 4, we analyze more in detail the different techniques to use the monitoring data and their potential and implications. Finally, in Sect. 5, we present and discuss some research challenges concerning monitoring requirements and analysis and use of monitoring data.

2   Designing Monitoring Systems

As introduced in the previous section, QoS is an important aspect in Service-Oriented Architectures (SOA). Referring to the traditional SOA, quality is relevant in all phases, as illustrated in Fig. 3. The provider of the service has to declare the quality level which can be provided for the service, stored in a QoS-aware service registry [7]. QoS properties can be evaluated during the service selection phase, to determine which is the best service according to the consumer's goals, and Service Level Agreements (SLA) are defined in the binding phase, specifying the conditions for service provisioning that have to be satisfied during service execution.

Once the provider and the consumer agreed on *what* to monitor, the design of a monitoring system requires to focus on *how* to monitor. Without entering into the details of a monitoring infrastructure, as discussed in [21] a monitoring system has to provide two main modules: the interceptor and the logger. While the former is in charge of transparently capture the information exchanged by the service provider and consumer, the latter is responsible for storing such messages. As also proposed in [8], depending on where the interceptor and the logger are deployed, several configurations are possible (see Fig. 4):

- *Monitor in the middle*: the monitoring system is provided by a third party which is in charge of intercepting and storing information about the execution of the service. An API is provided to allow both consumers and providers to access to the information stored. This configuration is mainly focused on monitoring the information exchanged from which some of the QoS attributes can be inferred. For this reason, information about the status of the provider infrastructure on which the service is running are not available.
- *Monitor at the consumer side*: the monitoring system is under the control of the consumer. In this way, it is possible to collect all the information about the QoS that is considered relevant for the consumer. Similarly to the previous configuration, QoS attributes that can be monitored or inferred must be based on the information exchanged. As the data collected by the consumer can be considered private, no API is usually provided.
- *Monitor at the provider side*: the monitoring system is under the control of the provider. In this case, the provider can collect information about the status of the modules and devices on which the execution of the service is based on. Moreover, monitoring information can be customized for the different customers of the same service. This improves the knowledge that a provider can obtain from the service execution but, at the same time, also increases the effort required to store and manage the ever increasing amount of monitoring information. An API is made available to allow the customers to access to the monitoring information of their interest.

For the sake of simplicity, we do not consider additional configurations where the interceptor and the logger are deployed on different sites. Moreover, where not explicitly defined, hereafter the monitor at the consumer side configuration is assumed to be adopted.

As a consequence, monitoring is to be considered in the design of applications, since it is essential for the correct functioning of service-based applications, to ensure that service provisioning satisfies the conditions defined in the agreement between providers and consumers.

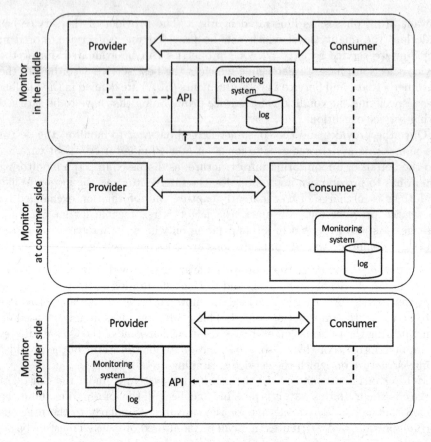

Fig. 4. Monitoring systems configuration deployments.

For instance, in the S-Cube project [2, 20], a life cycle for service-based applications has been defined including two main iteration cycles, as illustrated in Fig. 5: the evolution and the adaptation cycles. In the evolution cycle, service-based applications are designed/re-designed according to requirements, both in terms of functionalities to be provided and in terms of possible adaptation actions to be used at run time in the adaptation cycle during the execution of the adaptive application. Monitoring is an essential component during the execution of applications, as it provides the information needed to identify adaptation needs and eventually the requirements for system evolution. In order to provide the needed information to identify adaptation needs and to select the adaptation strategies, also monitoring becomes an element of the design/evolution cycle, since it is necessary to specify the elements to be monitored in order to have the required monitoring information to take appropriate decisions. Such a service life cycle allows the service provider to maintain the agreed conditions for service, continuously adapting service executions depending on the variable context of

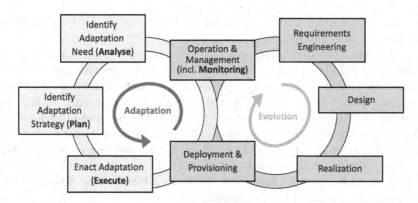

Fig. 5. S-Cube life cycle [2, 20].

execution, and evolving the system when adaptation is not sufficient any more to guarantee the required QoS.

Considering monitoring as an element of design implies that the elements to be monitored must be specified and their relevant QoS characteristics defined. In addition, monitoring must support the evaluation of conditions, to be able to identify adaptation needs in a timely and accurate way.

As a consequence, there is a need for a a systematic approach to monitoring, and in particular in the following of the paper we focus on two main issues to be considered during the development of a monitored service:

- *What*: models to specify monitoring elements, their characteristics, assessing the implications of monitoring choices (Sect. 3).
- *Usage*: how monitoring data can be used to identify adaptation needs, critical situations, considering that the monitoring actions are also an overhead during the execution of the system, and therefore a balance must be found between the need to collect and analyze monitoring data and the amount of resources needed for these activities (Sect. 4).

3 Elements of Monitoring

Service monitoring requires to take into account two main aspects: monitoring the *efficiency* and monitoring the *effectiveness* of the service. In the former case, the goal is to focus on the non-functional aspects of a service, especially focusing on how well a service is providing its functions to the consumer. Performance, security issues, and privacy are typical examples of aspects to be considered. In the latter case, the goal is to focus on the functional aspects of a service checking if the exchanged data are correct; this requires the adoption of *data quality* (a.k.a. information quality) techniques to realize if, when invoking the operations exposed by a service, the results are not as expected or the service is not able to recognize non-valid input data. Efficiency and effectiveness of monitored service usually go under the umbrella of the QoS, with the modeling techniques discussed in Sect. 3.1.

In addition to the QoS, another perspective needs to be taken into account: the *quality of monitoring*. As mentioned in Sect. 2, the monitoring activity is performed by a service, thus being a service, it is important to evaluate its quality, i.e., the quality of the data collected through the monitoring. In fact, the monitoring system produces streams of data from diverse, and often heterogeneous sources. These data are fundamental for figuring out possible misbehavior of the service while it is running. In addition, data could be subject to further analysis to identify patterns and trends that are important to improve the service. Section 3.2 focuses on this aspect discussing which are the attributes that characterize the quality of the monitoring.

3.1 Modeling the QoS

Modeling QoS means providing a tool for the consumer of the monitored service to realize if the service is running as expected. For this reason, we need to specify two aspects: how the service is behaving, i.e., the status of the service, and what the consumer is expecting from the service. In other words, on the one side the consumer specifies the *monitoring requirements*, i.e., the information about the status of the monitored service that he/she is expecting to obtain from the monitoring system. On the other side, the monitoring service is defined in terms of *monitoring capabilities*, i.e., the information that the monitoring service is able to provide. Aligning these two perspectives is often a cumbersome task due to the intrinsic characteristics of the QoS. Indeed, as also stated in the ISO 9216 [13], QoS is a *subjective*, *domain-dependent*, and *multi-dimensional* concept.

Starting from the subjectivity, each consumer of the monitored service could be interested on different aspects about the functioning of the service to evaluate its quality. Some consumer might be more focused on performance, some other on cost. As a consequence, the QoS model needs to be flexible enough to make a custom definition of QoS possible. Moving to domain-dependency, the monitoring requirements for two services living in two different domains, even if they are specified by the same consumer, may result on different definitions of service. For this reason, the QoS model should not include a pre-defined set of dimensions to be used in the QoS definition. On the contrary, the QoS model needs to be extensible, i.e., it should be able to consider additional quality aspects that could be relevant only for a specific domain (e.g., refresh rate for a shared storage service). Finally, QoS is multi-dimensional: it cannot be defined by a single aspect, but it requires the modeling of different perspectives, each of them related to the others. Thus, the QoS model must permit the definition of relationships among the dimensions used to specify the different quality aspects.

To capture all these requirements a QoS model should be compliant to the QoS metamodel proposed in [14] and also reported in Fig. 6. Focusing only on the most relevant elements, the `Service Quality Offer` and the `Service Quality Request` express the monitoring capabilities and requirements, respectively. As they need to be compared to realize if a monitoring system can satisfy the

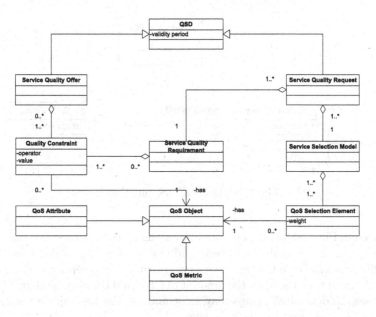

Fig. 6. Service quality meta-model [14].

consumer expectation, they must be based on the same model, i.e., the QoS Definition (QSD), although it is used in a different way. The consumer expresses requests listing and ranking the QoS Objects, where the ranking is obtained using weights expressing the order of importance among the QoS objects. On the other side, the monitoring service lists the QoS objects that is possible to measure making their values available to the consumer. Based on this structure, the QoS object represents a central point in QoS modeling as the requirements and capabilities base their definition on this element. Being a placeholder for the real QoS aspect to be considered, the resulting QoS model ensures the expected flexibility. Indeed, the QoS Attribute and the QoS Metric that could specialize a QoS Objects represent what is really asked/offered by the consumer/provider. More in detail, as shown in Fig. 7, a QoS Attribute defines an aspect that can be relevant for the monitored service (e.g., response time, availability). These attributes can be logically grouped in QoS Categories (e.g., security, performance) that give a high-level representation of how the quality of a service can be defined to also increase the readability of the model. Finally, each attribute needs to be measured and one or more QoS Metrics can be defined. For instance, the availability of a service can be computed using the classical metric that computes the ratio between the amount of time in which the service is available and the total amount of time.

As an attribute is related to one of the aspects defining the behavior of a service, to have a complete view about a service not only many attributes can be requested by a consumer and many could be offered by the monitoring service provider, but also relationships among the attributes may exist. For this reason,

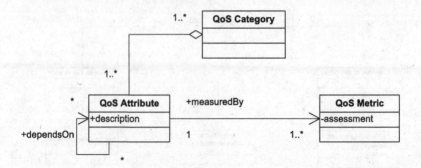

Fig. 7. Monitoring elements [14].

as reported in Fig. 7, dependency relations among attributes must be considered. In some cases, the dependency is clear and exists according to the definition of the attribute itself. For instance, the energy consumed by a service while running depends, among the others, on the amount of CPU and memory used [9]. In some other cases, hidden relationships may exist and, as discussed in Sect. 4.2, some approaches are required to discover them.

3.2 Modeling the Quality of the Monitoring

Data collected by the monitoring system are a valuable source of information for both the provider and the consumer. The former can realize if there are problems while running the service and, in case, space for improvement can be sought. The latter can figure out if the service is working as expected or, comparing the monitoring data, coming from equivalent services, can decide which is the best one.

In any case, it is important that data collected by the monitoring system have a good quality. Indeed, poor data quality may cause false positives and false negatives in detecting anomalous behaviors. Moreover, especially when very little variations for some attributes have significant impact on the evaluation of the service, the accuracy of the data is fundamental.

As any type of quality, also data quality definition – similarly to QoS as discussed before – is multi-dimensional, subjective, and domain dependent. In particular, four main attributes are really important: timeliness, accuracy, completeness, and availability. These attributes are defined in [25] and reported in [6] as:

- *Timeliness* refers to "the delay between a change of the real-world state and the resulting modification of the information system state."
- *Accuracy*: "inaccuracy implies that the information system represents a real-world state different from the one that should have been represented." Inaccuracy refers to a garbled mapping into a wrong state of the system, where it is possible to infer a valid state of the real world though the not correct one.
- *Completeness* is "the ability of an information system to represent every meaningful state of the represented real-world system." Of course, completeness is tied to incomplete representations.

– *Availability* of data is the extent to which data (or some portion of it) is present, obtainable, and ready for use.

Obtaining a good level of quality for the monitoring data according to these attributes depends on many factors. Monitoring QoS attributes requires the installation of probes that are in charge of reading the status of a phenomenon related to the attribute and to convert it into a value. Probes can be implemented as hardware or software. For instance, in a data center the monitoring of the power consumption of a machine requires the installation of PDU (Power Distribution Units) able to detect the amount of power and to send this information to a monitoring system. In this case, possible errors can come from a not proper calibration of the instruments.

Moving to another example, if the attribute to be monitored is the power consumption of a service installed on such a machine, then the data obtained through the PDU is only one of the composing elements [9]. Indeed, as discussed above, the power of a software process (associated to the service) depends on the amount of power consumed by the machine, the fraction of CPU used by the process, the amount of memory and the I/O bandwidth. For this reason, this attribute requires the presence of a software probe that collects all the required information and calculates the final value. Here errors depend on factors like the precision of the probes, the approximations done during the computation, and the reliability of the formulas adopted. Given this complexity, monitoring data are thus prone to systematic errors which affect the quality of the data returned by the monitoring system and the minimization of these errors requires higher costs. High quality probes are more expensive, as well as more precise computations could increase the resource demanding for the monitoring system and thus the cost.

A proper balance between the cost of designing and running the monitoring system and the quality of the monitoring data is crucial. In addition to the aspects introduced above, particular emphasis can be reserved to the cost of storing the monitoring data. Especially when the monitoring system is installed at the provider side, the amount of monitoring data depends on the number of services, the number of attributes for each service, and how frequently these attributes are measured. As an example, Cloudera[1] offers more than one hundred categories of metrics, with a one minute sampling rate, with the possibility to define aggregation functions. Indeed, more attributes and more frequent sampling time result in higher quality of monitoring data and higher costs for storing all these data. For this reason, especially for cloud providers, different monitoring services are proposed with different costs. For instance, Amazon CloudWatch[2] offers both a basic monitoring service where pre-selected metrics are made available at five-minute frequency with no additional cost, and a detailed monitoring where the set of metrics is the same but at one-minute frequency and with an additional cost. Also

---

[1] http://www.cloudera.com/documentation/enterprise/5-6-x/topics/cm_metrics.html.

[2] https://aws.amazon.com/it/cloudwatch/.

Paraleap CloudMonix (formerly known as AzureWatch)[3] offers both the possibility to monitor an unlimited set of metrics but at ten-minutes frequency with no additional cost, and at one-minute frequency with a fee.

Based on this scenarios, taking into account the quality of monitoring data introduces also a new dimension for the service provider selection. Indeed, when the same service is offered by several service providers, the selection is usually based on the QoS. Introducing also a proper evaluation of the quality of monitoring data allows the service consumer to select the service provider that also provides the most reliable and accurate monitoring data that can be useful for ex-post analysis. About this scenario, [12] proposes an approach that optimizes the quality of monitoring considering the accuracy of the quality attributes, the coverage and the extensibility of the monitoring system, while respecting budget constraints of the consumer.

4   Use of Monitoring Data

As mentioned in Sect. 3, the data collected by the monitoring system can be relevant to ensure the quality of the service provided, to identify issues about the service behavior, and to react to undesired situations in order to restore an effective behavior for the monitored service. In a SOA, an agreement is negotiated between the service provider and the consumer, the SLA in which metrics are identified together with their acceptable and undesired values, referred as Service Level Objectives (SLO) or quality objectives as shown in Fig. 6. The monitoring system is the source from which SLOs can be computed and the satisfaction of the SLA can be evaluated. Two phases of the SLA life-cycle are involved in this activity: the SLA assessment and the SLA settlement [14]. In the assessment SLOs are evaluated and compared with reference values and constraints. The assessment has to be executed regularly and has a period of validity. When a SLO is violated, some repair actions can be taken. This operation is part of the settlement phase in which penalties and rewards are assigned according to satisfactions and violations of the SLA, and actions affecting the SLA evaluation outcome are prescribed.

The main issues related to the exploitation of the monitoring data for assessment and settlements are:

- *Events identification*: not all the collected information is relevant, techniques are needed for isolating relevant events that should be considered for enacting repair strategies (Sect. 4.1).
- *Condition evaluation*: identified events have to be compared with reference values in order to determine if an undesired behavior is occurring, and strategies for bringing the service back to a normal behavior need to be selected (Sect. 4.2).
- *Resources and cost*: monitoring has a cost in terms of computational resources and storage space, but also an economic cost changing with the number of collected metrics, their quality and precision (Sect. 4.3).

---

[3] http://cloudmonix.com.

In the following of this section, these three issues will be discussed in more detail.

4.1   Identifying Events

The analysis of the satisfaction of SLOs is usually performed through the evaluation of indicators, usually related to the quality perspective (Key Performance Indicators - KPI), but also to other perspectives (e.g., energy efficiency through Green Performance Indicators - GPI). Indicators are assessed through the computation of one or more metrics, associated to them, starting from the data collected by the monitoring system. A set of thresholds can be associated to each indicator, defining which are the desired and undesired values [11]. When an indicator is outside the desired range of values, something should be done to correct this misbehavior. The approach towards the assessment of indicators can be either proactive or reactive. A *reactive approach* considers as an issue only violation of the desired values range. In the *proactive approach*, violations should be avoided by preventing them observing the trends of the indicators values. In order to do that, an alarm set of values is considered between the violation and the satisfaction zone. An indicator whose value is in the alarm zone is not violated, but it is likely to be violated soon. Figure 8 shows the intervals of satisfaction, violation, and alarm of a generic indicator. Each of these regions is defined by two thresholds. Defining which are the best values for these thresholds is not an easy task. In order to define the set of undesired values, it is possible to use as a reference best practices (e.g., the Green Grid Data Center Maturity Model[4]) and consumer requests through the Service Level Agreement (SLA). Also, changing the size of the alarm zone, the approach to violations can change from a more reactive to a more proactive approach, thus making this decision flexible. The threshold definition issue has been discussed in more detail in previous work (e.g., [18]).

Fig. 8. Identifying satisfaction, alarm, and warning zones for indicators.

Classifying the indicators value in one of the zones described before is not enough, since it is also important to understand the severity of the violation. This can be evaluated performing a normalization of the indicators values [17] where each value is transformed into a value in the interval $[0, 1]$. Thanks to this normalization it is possible to compute a complex metric obtained from

---

[4] http://www.slideshare.net/martinciupa/data-center-maturity-model-white-paper finalv2.

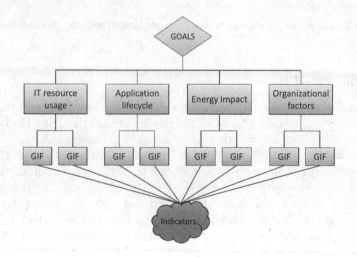

Fig. 9. Indicators aggregation organized in a hierarchical way [17].

the aggregation of several indicators concurring to the satisfaction of a common goal, considering what in Sect. 3.1 was referred to as a QoS category. The aggregation can be performed as a weighted sum function of the selected metrics values, referred as Green Index Function (GIF). Indicators can be hierarchically organized as shown in Fig. 9, in which categories (e.g., IT resource usage, Application lifecycle, Energy impact, and Organizational factors) aggregate indicators through a GIF, and are used to define complex goals.

As shown in Fig. 9, indicators or their aggregation can be considered as goals and can be represented in a goal-oriented model in which goals are indicators satisfaction. An event should be raised when a violation is observed, implementing the adaptation cycle presented in Fig. 5. The adaptation process is composed of two phases: the event creation and the adaptation strategy selection. An event is raised when a significant violation of an indicator threshold has been observed. Not every violation generates an event. In fact, temporary violations can be ignored since they can automatically recover or they can be due to noise. The approach proposed in [16] addresses the identification of significant violations in order to generate events. Through the Integrated Energy-aware Framework (IEF), violations are identified considering their duration over time and their severity, thus generating an event only if the indicator is in the alarm or warning zone for a time exceeding the accepted duration for a violation. An event is thus described by the timestamp in which it has been generated, the value associated to the violated indicator, a direction stating if this value is increasing or decreasing (trend), a significance defining which event occurrences have priority, and a severity computed considering the quantitative importance of the violation.

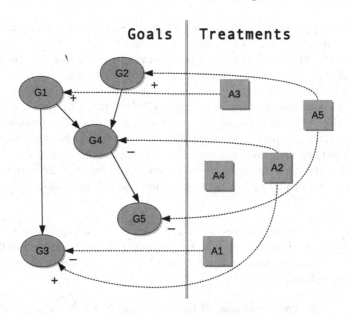

Fig. 10. Modeling adaptation through a goal-based model.

4.2   Condition Evaluation and Selection of Actions

Events are symptoms of misbehavior in the monitored environment and can be used as drivers for adaptation. Evaluation of the conditions over indicators for the generation of events is a complex task. In fact, the evaluation of violations is sensitive to several factors. As discussed before, aggregated indicators can be obtained from the weighted sum of a set of other indicators. In this case we deal with a multi-attribute metric, in which weights can change over time, affecting the evaluation of the aggregated metric. Another factor to be considered is the consumer: different consumers can have different preferences, different stakeholders of the same service can have a different perception of what should be considered as a violation of the constraints. Finally, evaluation can be context-dependent, and some constraints could get relaxed under some circumstances.

Adaptation can be performed by enacting an adaptation strategy, consisting in one or more treatments (or actions), affecting the state of the system. In a goal-oriented approach, it is important to model:

- Which goals are affected by the enactment of an action.
- Which kind of outcome (positive or negative) the action has over the affected goals.

A representation of this action-to-goal model is represented in Fig. 10, where two layers are depicted: a goal layer and a treatment layer.

The goal layer contains the identified goals, modeled as the satisfaction of constraints over indicators. As discussed in Sect. 3 and shown in Fig. 7, direct and indirect dependencies among metrics may exist. In the goal layer of the model, these relations between indicators are also modeled as shown in the left part of Fig. 10. These relations are important for predicting the outcome of a modification and for conducting what-if analysis. Modeling relations between metrics can be a trivial activity if performed manually by expert. As discussed in Sect. 3.1, dependencies can be directly extracted from the definition of the metric, or can be hidden. For discovering hidden relations, automatic approaches can be employed. In [24], a representation of relations between goals of a goal-oriented model is provided using a Bayesian Network expressing causal dependencies among goal states. The network is automatically computed from the analysis of the information collected through the monitoring system using a three steps approach:

- Learning the structure of the Bayesian Network (which goals have a relation).
- Learning the direction of edges in the Bayesian Network (cause vs effect).
- Learning the parameters of the Bayesian Network (conditional probability tables for each node).

The treatment layer contains all the actions that can be used to affect the system state and it models their effects over the goals. The model can be used to decide which is the best strategy to enact when a violation occurs. Since an action can have both a positive and a negative effect over the indicators, it is important to take into account both direct and indirect effects when taking a decision on which action to enact. This decision is strictly dependent on the context, which is the state of all the goals in the considered system. Since services are executed in a complex and dynamic environment, discovering and modeling action-to-goal relations is a complex task. In [16], the selection of an action is always followed by a history-based analysis addressed to recognize patterns and used to validate the current model and to eventually modify or create new relationships. In [24], the action-to-goal relations are acquired through a continuous refinement algorithm (the Adaptation Action Selection - AAS), which starting from scratch observes the outcomes of action enactments and updates the model considering both the current observation and past observations. The action effect over indicators is associated with an impact value, assessing the probability that applying the action the value of the indicator will change. The selected adaptation strategy should maximize positive effects over violated indicators, while minimizing side effects over the satisfied ones. This algorithm enables self-adaptation when an action modifies its outcome over indicators due to some external noise and is not sensitive to the noise caused by other events affecting the environment of execution during the observation.

When evaluating the effectiveness of an adaptation approach several criteria should be considered:

- *Stability*: the decision taken by the algorithm should bring to a stable system for a sufficient amount of time if no external factors occur. Stability avoids that the algorithm keeps prescribing modifications, that in some cases could contradict themselves, in search for an optimal solution that may not exist. An example can be migration: if the performance of a service is not satisfying, it is possible to migrate the service in a host with a better nominative QoS. If after migration a significant improvement is not observed, it is not desirable that the algorithm enacts another migration, since migration is costly and introduces a temporary performance degradation itself.

- *Flexibility*: the solution should be responsive to modifications to the service, to the set of selected indicators, and to the constraints above these indicators without requiring a heavy reconfiguration of the adaptation algorithm.
- *Scalability*: the solution should scale linearly with the increasing number of goals and constraints and with the introduction of new adaptation strategies, keeping the computational time for evaluating the system limited and providing a solution in a reasonable time.

These criteria can be used to compare several approaches and to select the one that fits better in the considered context.

4.3 Resources and Cost

Monitoring is an important step for guaranteeing the quality of the provided service and for assessing the SLA satisfaction. However, collecting monitoring data comes at a cost. The trade-off between the advantage of monitoring and its cost should be considered.

In a cloud oriented environment, the monitoring system is managed by the cloud provider who hosts the service. As discussed in Sect. 3.2, different providers can offer a different quality of service according to their resources, but also a different set of monitored information, at a different quality with a different cost. Also, customization of the monitoring service is important for getting full advantage of the monitoring system. Choosing which is the best cloud provider can be difficult. Several aspects have to be considered:

- *Quality of the service*: different cloud providers can offer a different quality for hosting the service in terms of KPIs such as response time and availability.
- *Monitoring offer*: the amount of available metrics can change, also their granularity can be different. Some providers offer only metrics at the physical level, others collect also Virtual Machine level metrics and application level metrics.
- *Monitoring quality*: quality of the monitoring system depends on the precision of the collected information which depends mainly on the sampling time and on the ability to store old data to perform analysis [12].
- *Monitoring extensibility*: some cloud providers offer the possibility of extending the monitoring system with custom metrics both at the hardware level (through the installation of new probes) and at the software level (through the execution of scripts).

According to their characteristics, the monitoring services offered by the different cloud providers have different costs. It is important that this cost does not overcome the advantage obtained from the monitoring data. Also, the analysis of the monitoring data requires a computational effort which can be directly proportional to the amount of these data. Computational resources have to be employed for this analysis, thus increasing the total cost of hosting the service.

In order to avoid useless costs, the proper set of metrics, together with the correct sampling time, should be selected. How to select which are the metrics that actually depict the state of a service and provide value to the analysis is still an open issue.

5   Challenges and Future Research Work

In this section, we comment about the open issues and discuss challenges and future research work. As mentioned at the end of Sect. 2, the paper has examined two main issues in a systematic approach to monitoring: the "What", i.e., the specification of monitoring elements, and the "Usage", i.e., how monitoring data can be used.

The main question about the *What* issue concerns which monitoring data should be collected. The interesting data depend on the service being provided, for each situation not only the elements to be monitored should be specified, but also which are the available *sources* of monitoring information, possibly more than one; another issue concerns the definition of the *granularity* of monitoring data, and the possibility of viewing the data and analyzing it at different granularities; a third issue concerns the *quality of the monitored data*, which should be assessed to provide a complete information about the available information.

Concerning sources, it should be possible to dynamically create or use new monitoring sources, in particular in services being provided in very variable situations, such as, for instance, in emergency situations. The impact of context for evaluating which monitoring data are necessary, the needed granularity, and the need for further analysis are the elements which need further investigation. In fact, monitoring should not be homogeneous, considering always the same elements, but a focus on situations which need attention should be supported. It is also interesting to provide methods to combine different monitoring sources, to better assess and improve their quality, in particular consistency and completeness. The selection of sources should not consider only data provided by the system being monitored, but also consider information originating from other potentially useful sources. For instance, a process being executed is regularly monitored, but some problems occurring during the process execution may be originated by external causes [23], e.g., bad weather conditions in a delivery service or changed health conditions in a regular home care service. The quest for information from unrelated available sources for additional monitoring data should therefore be further investigated. As a conclusion, we can state that while monitoring systems are a rather mature field, there is still need for research in the field of selection of monitoring variables, both in defining their requirements in a precise way, and with the possibility of coping which changing situations, and also providing support for the identification of external monitoring systems which can provide additional information to the system being developed for providing service. The problem of finding the right sources of data becomes a relevant issue, including the retrieval of sources, associating meta-data to them to be able to correctly interpret the monitoring data, and considering a value-driven source selection. Once monitoring variables are identified in the different sources, it is also important to understand the relationships between variables, as this information can be useful both for filtering data and for relating information from different sources to get additional insight.

When addressing the *Usage* issue, several aspects still require further investigation. First of all, there is a need to coordinate monitoring activities. In fact, monitoring can have phases, and monitoring activities might have to be dynamically selected. There is an intrinsic variability in systems being monitored, which requires a corresponding variability in the monitoring system behavior. In some situations, monitoring is not always necessary or only a light observation is needed, and there is a strong variability of needs between starting up phases (or when adaptation actions are performed [16]), during regular execution, and during exceptional or crisis situations. In general, there is the need to design the monitoring process(es), not only the monitoring system. The monitoring requirements must be specified, defining the monitoring requirements for different goals, the requirements related to different types of events and risks, defining monitoring actions such as the selection of variables, sampling rates, granularity, sources, and so on, in the different situations. It is also necessary to include in the requirements the specification of the quality parameters for monitored variables, such as, accuracy, completeness, and timeliness.

During the adaptation loop, it is necessary to apply the control policies defined at design time. It must be possible to verify if requirements are satisfied in the given context and to be able to identify the best adaptation strategies if adaptation is needed. Therefore, the design of assessment conditions and of adaptation rules are closely associated to the design of the monitoring system. As a concluding remark, we emphasize the need of coordinating monitoring activities, to investigate monitoring as a process, and to study design criteria for monitoring; in addition, for the specification of monitoring requirements research is needed on informal, semi-formal, and formal models and methods.

Acknowledgements. This work was partially developed within the European COST Action IC 1304 Autonomous Control for a Reliable Internet of Services (ACROSS) and partially supported by the Lombardy Region within the Sistema innovativo di Big Data Analytics project.

References

1. Aceto, G., Botta, A., de Donato, W., Pescapè, A.: Cloud monitoring: a survey. Comput. Netw. **57**(9), 2093–2115 (2013). doi:10.1016/j.comnet.2013.04.001
2. Andrikopoulos, V., Bucchiarone, A., Nitto, E., Kazhamiakin, R., Lane, S., Mazza, V., Richardson, I.: Service engineering. In: Papazoglou, M.P., Pohl, K., Parkin, M., Metzger, A. (eds.) Service Research Challenges and Solutions. LNCS, vol. 6500, pp. 271–337. Springer, Heidelberg (2010). doi:10.1007/978-3-642-17599-2_8

3. Ardagna, D., Comuzzi, M., Mussi, E., Pernici, B., Plebani, P.: PAWS: a framework for executing adaptive web-service processes. IEEE Softw. **24**(6), 39–46 (2007). http://dx.doi.org/10.1109/MS.2007.174

4. Arnone, D., Rossi, A., Melodia, E., Mammina, M., Jenkins, S.: Improving energy awareness integrating persuasive game, feedback, and social interaction into the novel ener-scape application. Int. J. Adv. Intell. Syst. **8**(3&4), 437–447 (2015)

5. Barton, T., Seel, C.: Business process as a service - status and architecture. In: Enterprise Modelling and Information Systems Architectures - EMISA 2014, Luxembourg, 25–26 September 2014, pp. 145–158 (2014). http://subs.emis.de/LNI/Proceedings/Proceedings234/article12.html

6. Batini, C., Scannapieco, M.: Data and Information Quality. Springer International Publishing, Switzerland (2016)

7. Bianchini, D., De Antonellis, V., Pernici, B., Plebani, P.: Ontology-based methodology for e-service discovery. Inf. Syst. **31**(4–5), 361–380 (2006). doi:10.1016/j.is.2005.02.010

8. Cabrera, O., Franch, X.: A quality model for analysing web service monitoring tools. In: 2012 Sixth International Conference on Research Challenges in Information Science (RCIS), pp. 1–12, May 2012

9. Cappiello, C., Datre, S., Fugini, M., Melia, P., Pernici, B., Plebani, P., Gienger, M., Tenschert, A.: Monitoring and assessing energy consumption and CO_2 emissions in cloud-based systems. In: 2013 IEEE International Conference on Systems, Man, and Cybernetics, pp. 127–132, October 2013

10. Cappiello, C., Ho, T.T.N., Pernici, B., Plebani, P., Vitali, M.: CO_2-aware adaptation strategies for cloud applications. IEEE Trans. Cloud Comput. **4**(2), 152–165 (2016). doi:10.1109/TCC.2015.2464796

11. Cappiello, C., Plebani, P., Vitali, M.: Energy-aware process design optimization. In: 2013 International Conference on Cloud and Green Computing, Karlsruhe, Germany, 30 September–2 October 2013, pp. 451–458. IEEE Computer Society (2013). doi:10.1109/CGC.2013.77

12. Fadda, E., Plebani, P., Vitali, M.: Optimizing monitorability of multi-cloud applications. In: Nurcan, S., Soffer, P., Bajec, M., Eder, J. (eds.) CAiSE 2016. LNCS, vol. 9694, pp. 411–426. Springer, Cham (2016). doi:10.1007/978-3-319-39696-5_25

13. ISO/IEC: ISO/IEC 9126-1 Software Engineering. Product Quality - Part 1: Quality model (2001)

14. Kritikos, K., Pernici, B., Plebani, P., Cappiello, C., Comuzzi, M., Benrernou, S., Brandic, I., Kertész, A., Parkin, M., Carro, M.: A survey on service quality description. ACM Comput. Surv. **46**(1), 1:1–1:58 (2013). http://doi.acm.org/10.1145/2522968.2522969

15. Mell, P., Grance, T.: The NIST Definition of Cloud Computing. Technical report, NIST, National Institute of Standards and Technology, U.S. Department of Commerce (2011)

16. Mello Ferreira, A., Pernici, B.: Managing the complex data center environment: an integrated energy-aware framework. Computing **98**(7), 709–749 (2016). doi:10.1007/s00607-014-0405-x

17. Ferreira, A.M., Pernici, B., Plebani, P.: Green performance indicators aggregation through composed weighting system. In: Auweter, A., Kranzlmüller, D., Tahamtan, A., Tjoa, A.M. (eds.) ICT-GLOW 2012. LNCS, vol. 7453, pp. 79–93. Springer, Heidelberg (2012). doi:10.1007/978-3-642-32606-6_7

18. Pernici, B., et al.: Setting energy efficiency goals in data centers: the GAMES approach. In: Huusko, J., Meer, H., Klingert, S., Somov, A. (eds.) E2DC 2012. LNCS, vol. 7396, pp. 1–12. Springer, Heidelberg (2012). doi:10.1007/978-3-642-33645-4_1

19. Reichert, M., Weber, B.: Enabling Flexibility in Process-Aware Information Systems - Challenges, Methods, Technologies. Springer, Heidelberg (2012)
20. S-Cube Team: S-Cube Network of Excellence final report. Technical report (2012). http://www.s-cube-network.eu/final-report.pdf
21. Seely, S., Lauzon, D. (eds.): WS-I Monitor Tool Functional Specification v 1.1 (2005). http://www.ws-i.org/Testing/Specs/MonitorFunctionalSpecification_Final_1.1.pdf
22. Vitali, M., Pernici, B.: A survey on energy efficiency in information systems. Int. J. Cooperative Inf. Syst. **23**(3) (2014). doi:10.1142/S0218843014500014
23. Vitali, M., Pernici, B.: PiE - Processes in Events: interconnections in ambient assisted living. In: Ciuciu, I., Panetto, H., Debruyne, C., Aubry, A., Bollen, P., Valencia-García, R., Mishra, A., Fensel, A., Ferri, F. (eds.) OTM 2015. LNCS, vol. 9416, pp. 157–166. Springer, Cham (2015). doi:10.1007/978-3-319-26138-6_19
24. Vitali, M., Pernici, B., O'Reilly, U.: Learning a goal-oriented model for energy efficient adaptive applications in data centers. Inf. Sci. **319**, 152–170 (2015). doi:10.1016/j.ins.2015.01.023
25. Wand, Y., Wang, R.Y.: Anchoring data quality dimensions in ontological foundations. Commun. ACM **39**(11), 86–95 (1996). http://doi.acm.org/10.1145/240455.240479

Smart Cities and Green ICT Systems

Analysing the Impact of Storage and Load Shifting on Grey Energy Demand Reduction

Iván S. Razo-Zapata[1(✉)], Mihail Mihaylov[2], and Ann Nowé[2]

[1] Luxembourg Institute of Science and Technology, Esch-Sur-Alzette, Luxembourg
ivan.razo-zapata@list.lu
[2] Vrije Universiteit Brussel, Brussels, Belgium
{mmihaylo,ann.nowe}@vub.ac.be

Abstract. We present an analysis on the application of load shifting and storage to enhance the use and penetration of green energy while decreasing grey (non-environmentally friendly) energy demand. We use multi-agent-based simulations that are fed with real data to analyse the impact of load shifting and storage on energy consumption as well as energy prices. We show results for scenarios in which storage is placed at different locations. In this way, results suggest that up to 15% reduction in grey energy consumption is feasible during peak times. Nonetheless, if the percentage of distributed renewable resources grows to 50%, higher reductions can be achieved, i.e. up to 50%. Finally, an important finding suggests that distributed storage helps to keep prices for green energy low.

Keywords: Smart grid · Multi-agent systems · Load shifting · Storage

1 Introduction

Engineering smart grids is a challenging task that must deal with new emerging actors, e.g. prosumers (energy consumers that can produce their own power), as well as with complex interactions between people, technology and natural systems [19,23]. Among those interactions, economic and power flows are of utmost importance [23,29]. Although novel mechanisms have been already proposed to not only optimise those flows but also improve the integration of renewable resources [4,7,8,12], they have not analysed the use of load shifting and storage to reduce grey energy demand and improve the integration of renewable sources.

As a way to analyse such potential use, we take NRG-X-Change as an example of a novel mechanism that can benefit from load shifting and storage. NRG-X-Change aims to promote the trade and flow of locally produced green energy within dwellings [12]. It offers to prosumers the possibility to trade their excess of green energy by using NRGcoins, which are virtual coins inspired by the Bitcoin protocol [13]. Unlike Bitcoins, NRGcoins are generated by injecting green energy into the grid rather than using computational power [12].

Although NRG-X-Change promotes the local trade and consumption of green energy between residential consumers and prosumers, it does not guarantee that

© Springer International Publishing AG 2017
M. Helfert et al. (Eds.): SMARTGREENS 2016 and VEHITS 2016, CCIS 738, pp. 27–48, 2017.
DOI: 10.1007/978-3-319-63712-9_2

green energy production fully matches consumption. In fact, when green energy is not enough to cover demand, consumers and prosumers will consume grey (non-environmentally friendly) energy to satisfy theirs needs and maintain a given level of comfort. To soften the dependency on grey energy, i.e. reducing its consumption, load shifting and storage capabilities can be integrated into NRG-X-Change. In this way, "original grey consumption" can be covered using stored green energy or delayed until green energy becomes available. Nonetheless, this integration is far from trivial, since it has been already shown that such capabilities impact energy demand and price [18], which may potentially inhibit trade and/or increase consumption.

This chapter extends previous work on the integration of load shifting and storage to reduce grey energy demand [20]. Compared to our previous work, the main contributions are the inclusion and analysis of scenarios in which storage is placed at different locations. In this vein, we perform numerical simulations using a multi-agent system that replicates the behaviour of main stakeholders, i.e. energy retailers, consumers and prosumers. Moreover, our simulations are fed with real energy consumption and production data provided by a Belgian distribution system operator (DSO).

The results suggest that load shifting and storage can reduce energy demand during *peak hours*. In this way, a 15% reduction can be achieved within a typical Belgian district that is on average composed of 60 households in which 10% are prosumers. Nonetheless, as our results indicate, 50% reduction can be achieved during peak hours if the number of prosumers reaches 50% and retailers as well as prosumers are equipped with storage, which is a plausible scenario for the coming years [21]. Furthermore, an important finding suggests that the use of storage influences energy prices.

The results of our research may help policy makers design appropriate incentives to boost energy storage and reduce consumption of grey energy. In addition, our results can help DSOs decide on the need for investment in storage. Likewise, they can also see the impact of load shifting in different scenarios and therefore allocate the necessary resources into the development of demand response programs.

The next sections are organised as follows. Section 2 presents related work covering aspects such as load shifting, demand response and negotiation strategies for energy markets. Later on, Sect. 3 describes the overall energy market as well as the physical setting. Finally, Sect. 4 shows results, whereas general conclusions and future work are presented in Sect. 5.

2   Related Work

2.1   Modifying Energy Consumption

Different strategies can be applied to modify the consumption of energy. On the one hand, storage capabilities can reduce demand for energy during critical periods by using green energy that has been previously stored when green energy was abundant [18]. On the other hand, demand response (DR) capabilities can be used to reduce customers' normal consumption pattern by shifting a percentage of their demand to off-peak hours [1,5]. Different techniques have been applied to support DR capabilities, which can be roughly classified into three schemes: (1) Price based: in this scheme the price of energy changes over time, which may motivate customers to also change their consumption profile. (2) Incentive or event-based: customers are rewarded for changing their energy demand upon retailer's requests. (3) Demand reduction bids: customers send demand reduction bids to energy retailers [25].

Although several DR techniques and programs have been proposed in literature [1,25] and implemented in pilots [14] respectively, they all agree on an important issue: residential customers offer a lower potential for demand reduction compared to commercial and industrial consumers [1,5]. Likewise, in [5,17], it is also reported that the economic benefits are moderate for residential consumers compared to the required investment. Consequently, as an attempt to better reduce residential demand for grey energy, we aim at enhancing DR techniques by using storage capabilities. This combination will allow not only to shift energy demand to time slots in which green energy is produced but also to slots in which storage devices discharge green energy to be consumed.

2.2   Negotiation Strategies

Several mechanisms have been also proposed to trade energy within smart grids. Nobel [7] applies a market mechanism in which prosumers offer their excess of energy by submitting asks (sell orders) while consumers submit bids (buy orders). They, both prosumers and consumers, submit asks and bids based on predictions about their expected production and consumption respectively. Later on, asks and bids are matched based on price, i.e. a scalar value. Likewise, PowerMatcher [8] uses a market mechanism for matching supply to demand. Nonetheless, bids and asks are not scalar values but price curves. An aggregator is in charge of grouping individual curves so that more supply and demand can be matched. The orderbook then computes price equilibrium to match aggregated asks and bids.

In [4], the authors propose a mechanism in which energy is contracted by individual consumers and prosumers via negotiations. Although no central mechanism rules the price of energy, the energy retailer is in charge of assigning prosumer-consumer pairs for negotiation. In a similar vein, Wang and Wang have proposed adaptive negotiation strategies to trade energy between smart buildings and grid operators [32]. The trade takes the form of a bi-directional process in which a seller, e.g. grid operator, continuously adapts (submits) prices for energy (asks), whereas a buyer replies with counter offers (bids). Bids and asks can be adapted using the Adaptive Attitude Bidding Strategy (AABS) or an improved version that applies particle swarm optimisation techniques (PSO-AABS).

Similar to Nobel and PowerMatcher, NRG-X-Change presents a market mechanism to locally trade energy between consumers and prosumers [12]. It relies on prosumers injecting their excess of green energy into the grid and trading

NRGcoins, which are used to pay for green energy. In this way, prosumers inject-ing green energy are rewarded with NRGcoins, whereas consumers must pay for the usage with NRGcoins [12]. To trade NRGcoins, consumers and prosumers participate in a continuous double auction (CDA) [24], where buyers and sellers apply bidding strategies to submit bids and asks respectively. NRG-X-Change originally uses the so-called adaptive attitude (AA) strategy, which relies on short-term and long-term attitudes for *adapting* to market changes [9,11].

In this work, we use the NRG-X-Change to trade green energy as it offers a novel mechanism that incentives prosumers to inject their excess of green energy while promoting a transparent economic exchange via NRGcoins. To trade grey energy, however, we apply a negotiation approach based on AABS as this type of negotiation mimics retailer's control on grey energy prices, i.e. they establish prices based on their private reservation price. The next section elaborates on these issues as well as on the overall architecture to support load shifting and storage.

3   Energy Trade

Briefly, the electricity system (ES) is composed of all systems and actors involved in production, transportation, distribution and trade of electricity. This ES can be divided into a commodity subsystem and a physical subsystem [29]. The former covers all economic flows resulting from electricity trade, whereas the physical subsystem consists of all equipment that produces, transports and uses the electricity.

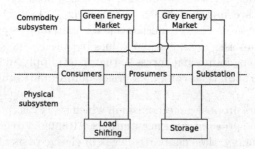

Fig. 1. High level description of our simulated electricity system (ES), elements and relationships are adapted from [29].

In our case, as seen in Fig. 1, we assume that the commodity subsystem is composed of green and grey energy markets, which operate in parallel but use different mechanisms. Moreover, the physical subsystem specifies the overall smart grid architecture as well as the way storage and load shifting operate. The next paragraphs elaborate on each subsystem.

3.1 Commodity Subsystem

Green Energy Market. We use the NRG-X-Change mechanism to allow the flow and trade of green (solar) energy between prosumers [12]. We assume consumers and prosumers are connected to the electricity grid via a substation (see also Sect. 3.2). Excess of locally produced green energy is fed into the grid and is withdrawn mostly by consumers. The billing is performed in real-time by the substation using NRGcoins, which are independently traded on an open currency exchange market for their monetary equivalent.

NRGcoin is a virtual coin inspired by Bitcoin whose main advantage is that it can be exchanged for a specific quantity of green energy at any time. For instance, if a prosumer injects 10 kWh right now, she will earn NRGcoins accounting for that amount of energy, based on the local supply and demand measured by the substation [12]. Later on, e.g. after few years, regardless of the NRGcoin market value, the prosumer can use the same NRGcoins to pay 10 kWh of green energy under similar energy supply and demand conditions as during injection [12].

Unlike the original NRG-X-Change, to trade NRGcoins, we use the Adaptive-Aggressiveness (AAggressive) bidding strategy as it applies a learning approach, which has been shown to be very robust in dynamic markets [31]. AAggressive is composed of four basic blocks: *equilibrium estimator*, *aggressiveness model*, *adaptive layer* and *bidding layer* [31]. Based on historical record of prices, the equilibrium estimator computes the target price for the trader, whereas the aggressiveness model determines the trader's risky behaviour to submit high (low) bids (asks). The adaptive layer implements short-term and long-term *learning* to adapt the behaviour of the trader. While the short-term learning updates the agent's aggressiveness, the long-term learning modifies the agent's bidding behaviour. Finally, the bidding layer implements a set of rules to determine whether the trader must submit bids (asks) or not.

Parameter tuning for AAggressive is done as suggested in [31]. Nonetheless, we specified constraints for bids and limit prices. On the one hand, minimum and maximum allowed bids in the market are as follows. The minimum bid is 0.01 Euro and the maximum bid is 0.215 Euro, which is the estimated average price for residential customers in Belgium during 2014 [30]. On the other hand, limit prices for buyers and sellers were randomly defined in the range 0.01 and 0.215 Euro.

Grey Energy Market. In [12], the authors allow prosumers trading green and grey energy with NRGcoins. In this work, however, to trade grey energy prosumers must pay in Euro. The main motivation is that NRGcoins should be perceived as assets that guarantee provision of green energy only. Similar ideas have been previously explored. For instance, ecolabels that inform customers on whether some products and services are green or eco-friendly [22].

Since prosumers and consumers must consume grey energy whenever there is a lack of green energy, prosumers and consumers use the AABS strategy to negotiate prices for grey energy with the substation [32]. As described in Sect. 2.2, the AABS strategy relies on a bi-directional negotiation in which a buyer (prosumer/consumer) submits bids (price willing to pay for energy) to a seller (substation) that responds with asks (desired selling prices). Once the buyer's bid is equal to or greater than the seller's ask, an agreement has been reached to trade energy among the two of them. The final price for energy is the average between the bid and the ask.

Substation decreases or increases their asks depending on AABS selling strategy and the availability of green energy. If green energy supply is bigger than demand, the price for grey energy goes down, otherwise it goes up. The idea is to discourage consumers and prosumers of using grey energy. This way, if grey energy price is higher than their reservation price, they will try to shift loads. Nonetheless, even if the price is high and green energy is not available, they will have to use grey energy anyway.

To decrease or increase grey energy prices, the AABS' L_2 parameter [32], which is used to modify the substation's reservation price, is continuously adapted using Eq. 1.

$$L_2 = \begin{cases} L_2 - \alpha \times (GS/PwD) & \text{if } GS > PwD \\ L_2 + \alpha \times (GS/PwD) & \text{otherwise} \end{cases} \tag{1}$$

where GS is the supply of green energy, PwD is the power demand and α is a random value between 0.001 and 0.005. The reservation price of the substation is initially fixed at 0.2 Euro, which changes depending on $L2$ and is a bit lower than the maximum price for green energy (see Sect. 3.1). Reservation prices for consumers and prosumers are randomly determined between 0.15 and 0.30 Euro. The rest of AABS parameters are tuned as suggested in [32].

3.2   Physical Subsystem

Overall Architecture. In this work we use real-world data that has been provided by a Belgian DSO. The physical setting contains prosumers that are equipped with solar panels, which allows them to generate their own power. Both, consumers and prosumers have smart meters that report to the substation the amount of energy being absorbed from and injected to the grid. As meters only report the injected energy after prosumers satisfied their own demand, we do not have a full picture of the actual energy being produced. The same applies for the absorbed energy that is reported to the substation, i.e. we do not have information about the overall energy being consumed by prosumers as part of it is satisfied with their solar panels. Consequently, we do not have information about prosumers' internal energy consumption and production but only about energy flows between the meters and the substation. Furthermore, the measurements take place every 15 min, which are standard time slots in the electricity system [3].

Storage. In our setting we assume substation and prosumers are the only ones using batteries. The former can store the excess of green energy production in the grid, whereas the latter can generate their own energy and store their excess after satisfying own consumption.

Prosumers. Although commercial batteries offer storage capabilities in the range of 4 to 13 kWh, we randomly assign prosumers storage in the range of 4 to 7 kWh. E.g. Tesla's Powerwall offers storage of 7 and 10 kWh [28], whereas Bosch's offers storage of 4.4 and 13.2 kWh [2] respectively. Moreover, to the best of our knowledge, only small capacities per prosumer have been properly tested and installed within current pilots. E.g. within the project Grid4EU, home batteries with 4 kWh capacity have been already installed in the French region of Carros [6]. Regardless of the capacity of the battery, we assume they have an efficiency of 90%, for both charge and discharge, which is a lower bound to the efficiency already provided by commercial batteries. E.g. Tesla and Bosch respectively report 93% and 97.7% efficiency for storage solutions that also include power inverters [2,28].

Substation. By the same token, although we are aware of commercial batteries offering different storage capacities [26,27], we define a lower boundary of 50 kWh for the substation's capacity. Tesla's Powerpack offers 100 kWh and Socomec's storage solutions (which were installed within the NiceGrid project [6]) offer capacities from 33 kWh to 100 kWh. Finally, we also assume an efficiency of 90%, for both charge and discharge [26,27].

Load Shifting. As previously reported in [10], loads associated to devices such as washing machines, dish washers, tumble dryers and air conditioners might be "easily" shifted since they not only account for 20% to 30% of the overall consumption [16] but also presented the highest willingness to postpone start according to residential customers [10]. In this way, when green energy is not available, we assume 20% to 30% of consumers' and prosumers' loads can be shifted to reduce consumption of grey energy. Although loads can be shifted to time slots in which green energy is abundant, loads cannot be shifted for an unlimited amount of time. Realistic times to postpone the start of loads are between 30 min to 3 h, i.e. 2 to 12 slots, as reported in [10].

Likewise, we also assume a waiting time before a consumer/prosumer can delay another load again. We randomly assign waiting times to consumers and prosumers in the range of 48 and 96 slots, which means that they will have to wait at least half day before delaying another load. Furthermore, since consumers and prosumers could all try to shift loads at the same time, we need to avoid such case too as it may generate demand peaks at a further stage, e.g. when their time slots expire and they need to re-start loads. To this aim, whenever a consumer or prosumer wants to start the shift of a load, she can only do it with a probability of 0.5. If probability is in her favour at that time slot, she can start shifting the load, otherwise she will have to try again in the next time slot. In this way, we aim at constraining the start of load shifting as well as at spreading controllable devices' loads through a full day.

Finally, to allow load shifting, consumers and prosumers use a "set and forget" approach in which they pre-set the loads that can be shifted (e.g. washing machines, dish washers or tumble dryers) as well as the time they can be delayed, i.e. a number between 2 and 12 slots. In addition, as load shifting depends on whether green energy is available or not, we assume that information about availability could be potentially delivered via internet, sms, or display directly on the appliance [10].

4 Preliminary Results

4.1 Simulation Settings

To understand the impact of load shifting and storage for grey energy demand reduction and energy trade, we use a multi-agent system that is implemented in Repast simphony [15]. The multi-agent system is fed with real consumption and production data provided by a Belgian DSO. In our simulations, consequently, we use a week of real consumption and production of electricity within a typical Belgian district, which is composed of 54 consumers and six prosumers equipped with solar panels and batteries. First, regarding storage, we study three scenarios in which storage capabilities are located at different points.

Scenario 1: Includes storage for all prosumers only. The storage capacities are randomly assigned between 4 and 7 kWh.

Scenario 2: Includes storage being located only at the substation, i.e. prosumers cannot store their excess of energy. The power stored by the substation comes from prosumers' excess of energy, which can be used by both prosumers and consumers to match their energy demand. In other words, the substation battery is not charged with energy coming from outside the district, nor discharged to other districts. Moreover, as explained in Sect. 3.2, the capacity of the substation is set to 50 kWh.

Scenario 3: This scenario represents a combination of the former two scenarios as it includes storage for both substation and prosumers.

Second, regarding load shifting, for all the scenarios load shifting is always applied in both consumers and prosumers. Finally, due to the plausible increase of prosumers within the electricity system, and as an attempt to understand future conditions, we present results for settings containing higher percentage of prosumers for all scenarios [21].

4.2 Energy Consumption

In this section we present plots of the average amount of grey and green energy being consumed by both prosumers and consumers. We show values for a typical

Belgian district, i.e. prosumers account for 10% of households, as well as for futuristic settings in which the percentage of prosumers are respectively 30% and 50%. To achieve these percentages, we fed real consumption and production data of 18 and 30 prosumers respectively in our simulations. These numbers represent the 30% and 50% of households in a typical Belgian district (usually composed of 60 households).

Figure 2(a) shows the average consumption of green energy for different percentage of prosumers for a whole week. As one can see, the more prosumers, the more green energy being consumed. Although main consumption occurs at daytime hours, when prosumers inject their excess of production after covering their own demand, consumption of green energy can also be observed at night time thanks to storage. For instance, as seen in Fig. 2(a), green energy consumption is observed during night hours between the first and second day.

In the same vein, Fig. 2(b) depicts the average consumption of grey energy, which shows that the more prosumers, the less grey energy is demanded during daytime hours. Unlike, green energy consumption, grey energy consumption

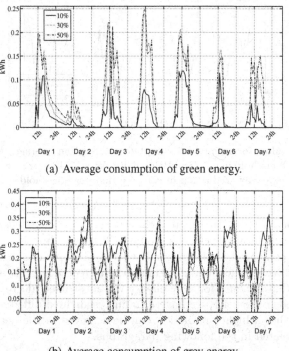

(a) Average consumption of green energy.

(b) Average consumption of grey energy.

Fig. 2. Average consumption of green and grey energy per household for different percentage of prosumers in a district. Note that green energy can also be consumed at night time thanks to storage and load shifting. Note that when the percentage of prosumers is above 30%, consumption of grey energy reduces considerably during daylight hours.

occurs mostly at late afternoon and early morning, when green energy is not gen-erated. Consequently, it is important to reduce the energy consumption during those periods as prosumers and consumers will mostly use grey energy.

4.3 Consumption Reduction

In order to determine whether reduction in consumption can be achieved using load shifting and storage, we have analysed the overall consumption, i.e. green and grey consumption, of a typical Belgian district for a whole week. We measured the average energy consumption when neither load shifting nor storage are available (original consumption) as well as the case when both are available (adapted consumption). Figure 3 shows both measures, original (dashed line) and adapted (solid line) consumption, which represent the average demand the substation is expected to face. Moreover, it also shows the average reduction being achieved (dotted line).

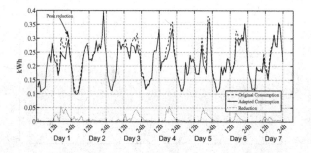

Fig. 3. Average values for original and adapted consumption (storage and load shifting capabilities) per household in a typical Belgian district with 10% prosumers. The dotted line represents the average reduction in consumption per household.

Although peak reduction can be achieved for some days, such reduction is moderate as the highest reduction is around 0.05 kWh, which is approximately a 15% reduction compared to the original consumption. Nonetheless, most of the peak reduction takes place at night time, when green energy is not generated, which implies that demand for grey energy will most likely decrease.

As explained in Sect. 4.1, we have also analysed three different scenarios to determine whether a higher reduction can be achieved in the near future. The results are presented in the following paragraphs.

Scenario 1: Figure 4(a) shows the average reduction when storage is only available for prosumers and the districts contain 10%, 30% and 50% of prosumers. The highest peak reduction is achieved by the district with 50% prosumers and is above 0.12 kWh, which represents a reduction of at least 30% compared to the original consumption.

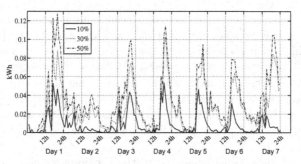

(a) Reduction when storage is only available for prosumers.

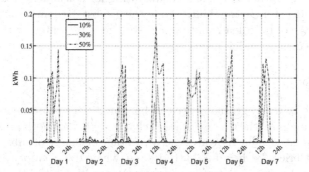

(b) Reduction when storage is only available for substation.

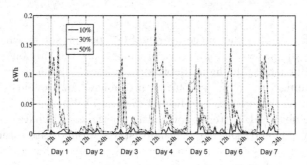

(c) Reduction when storage is available for both prosumers and substation.

Fig. 4. Average reduction in consumption per household using storage and load shifting capabilities for different percentage of prosumers.

Scenario 2: Figure 4(b) shows the average reduction when storage is only located at the substation. This time the highest peak reduction is around 0.17 kWh, which is about 50% of the original consumption. This reduction is achieved again in the district with the highest percentage of prosumers, i.e. 50% prosumers. Unlike the first scenario, however, the reduction achieved by the district with 10% prosumers is very low.

Scenario 3: Figure 4(c) shows the average reduction for the case in which both substation and prosumers are equipped with storage. Like in the previous two scenarios, the highest peak reduction is achieved by the district containing 50% prosumers. Such reduction is also around 0.17 kWh and is approximately equivalent to 50% of the original consumption. The reduction achieved by the district with 10% prosumers is again moderate compared to the first scenario but slightly higher than in the second scenario. This result may suggest that placing storage at both substation's and prosumers' facilities can lead to better reduction in grey energy consumption.

To achieve the reductions presented in the previous scenarios, nonetheless, one must be aware of not only using load shifting for consumers and prosumers but also providing storage capabilities to (either) substation and (or) prosumers. The performance of both load shifting and storage is presented in the following sections, i.e. Sects. 4.4 and 4.5 respectively.

4.4   Storage

To determine how much green energy can be stored after prosumers cover their own needs, we measure the average state of charge (SOC) for both prosumers and substation. The SOC value indicates the percentage of charge of substation's and prosumers' batteries, i.e. how full batteries are, where 0% = empty and 100% = full. Similar to the previous section, we present results for the three described scenarios.

Scenario 1: Figure 5(a) shows the average SOC per prosumer when the substation is not equipped with storage, i.e. prosumers are the only ones capable of storing excess of energy. The figure depicts three lines, one per each setting, i.e. districts containing 10%, 30% and 50% of prosumers. As previously described, the capacity of the batteries can be from 4 kWh to 7 kWh.

As it can be observed, batteries constantly charge and discharge their energy to meet energy demand. Discharge usually starts around late afternoon (the hours when green energy production decreases), whereas charge starts before noon. Furthermore, discharge provides green energy to be consumed at night time as observed in Fig. 2(a). Batteries, in this scenario, only reach full charge during the first day. This aspect should be considered before installing batteries with big capacity as they may not always be filled, which means a waste of storage capacity.

Scenario 2: Figure 5(b) shows the SOC of the battery located at the substation when prosumers are not equipped with storage. As can be seen, when the percentage of prosumers is 10% the battery cannot be charged as all the excess of energy is used by consumers and prosumers. Combined with the low reduction in consumption (see Fig. 4(b)), this may indicate that retailers should only consider adding storage to substations for districts with more than 10% prosumers. In this way, although moderate, the SOC increases as the percentage of prosumers

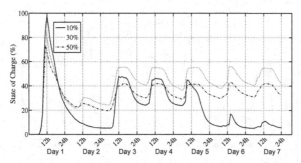

(a) Average SOC per prosumer when storage is only available for prosumers.

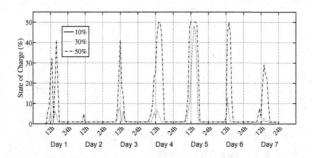

(b) Substation's SOC when storage is only available for substation.

Fig. 5. Average state of charge (SOC) per prosumer for different percentage of prosumers. 0% = empty and 100% = full.

also increases since there is more excess of green energy during daytime hours, which helps to reduce energy consumption as seen in the previous section.

Scenario 3: Figure 6 shows the SOC for both prosumers' batteries as well as substation's battery. Figure 6(a) shows the average SOC per prosumer, which increases during daytime hours and decreases during the evening due to discharges to satisfy energy demand. Unlike in Fig. 5(a), batteries reach higher SOC as storage is also available at the substation. In this way, when green energy is not available, prosumers can withdraw energy from substation's storage without discharging their own batteries.

Figure 6(b) shows the substation's SOC, which is similar to Fig. 5(b) since the substation's battery can only be charge when the percentage of prosumers is above 10%. The overall SOC for the districts containing 30% and 50% prosumers, however, are slightly lower than in Fig. 5(b).

Based on these results, we can discuss two relevant findings. First of all, drops in production (as during the second day) will not allow batteries to be completely filled as they will have to provide green energy at night time. Moreover, since

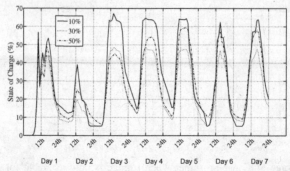

(a) Average SOC per prosumer when storage is available for both prosumers and substation.

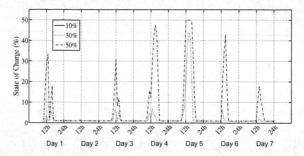

(b) Substation's SOC when storage is available for both prosumers and substation.

Fig. 6. Average state of charge (SOC) per prosumer for different percentage of prosumers. 0% = empty and 100% = full.

green energy is also scarce due to production drops, more loads would be shifted, which forces batteries to provide energy when the associated time slots expire.

Second, load shifting could help to fill batteries as initial consumption can be delayed, which may give time to store green energy. For instance, contrasting scenario 1 and scenario 3, the average SOC during the first day in Fig. 5(a) is higher than during the first day in Fig. 6(a) since there are loads being shifted in scenario 1 as seen in Fig. 7(a). Therefore, it is important to note that since load shifting directly impacts on the charge and discharge of batteries, an optimal planning of storage capacity that takes into account load shifting is also required. Such planning will allow to efficiently use storage (i.e. no waste of capacity) and provide more flexibility for load shifting. Nonetheless, it is clear that storage helps to meet both original and shifted demands. The performance of load shifting is presented in the next section.

4.5 Load Shiftting

Although load shifting aims to curtail energy demand by delaying the start of controllable devices (e.g. washing machines, dish washers and tumble dryers), the delay cannot last for more than three hours, i.e. up to 12 time slots [10]. In this way, our mechanism allows to shift chunks of energy consumption whose dimensions are time and power (watts). Shifted chunks have a time length of 2 to 12 time slots and a power given by the amount of demand being curtailed (i.e. 20% to 30% of the overall consumption). Moreover, regardless of the amount of demand being delayed, a shifted load is always re-started either when green energy becomes available or before the end of its time slot, so they are never delayed more than three hours (12 time slots). In this way, when the chunks of all consumers and prosumers are aggregated, they can provide a considerable amount of curtailment per slot as depicted in Fig. 7. The following paragraphs present and describe the results per each scenario.

Scenario 1: Figure 7(a) shows the total demand being curtailed per time slot for three districts composed of 10%, 30% and 50% prosumers respectively. The highest amount of curtailment is observed in districts with low percentage of prosumers, i.e. 10% and 30%. The reason is that since green energy is scarce, i.e. prices for green energy go up (see also Sect. 4.6), consumers and prosumers try to shift more loads. Furthermore, as can be seen, it is possible to curtail up to 2 kWh within a single time slot, e.g. before third day's noon.

Scenario 2: Figure 7(b) shows the the total demand being curtailed when storage is located only at the substation. Unlike in the previous scenario, the highest amount of curtailment is lower than 2 kWh. Prosumers and consumers, as in the previous scenario, start delaying loads once the price for green energy also increases (e.g. see Fig. 8(b)).

Scenario 3: Figure 7(c) shows the total demand being curtailed when both substation and prosumers have storage. Unlike the previous two scenarios, there are not loads being shifted during the first day since green energy can be obtained from either the prosumers's batteries or the substation's battery. Moreover, because of the same reason (storage available for prosumers and substation), the highest amount of curtailment is also lower than in the previous scenarios. Similar to the previous scenarios, however, the districts with lower percentage of prosumers tend to delay more loads as green energy is scarce.

4.6 Energy Prices

As not only energy-related measures are important to understand smart grids, but also economic aspects, we have also analysed the price behaviour of both green and grey energy. As explained in Sect. 3.1, grey energy prices are negotiated between the substation and both consumers and prosumers, whereas green

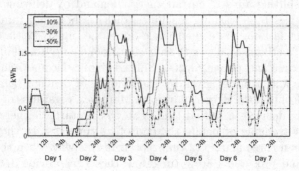

(a) Total demand being curtailed when storage is only available for prosumers.

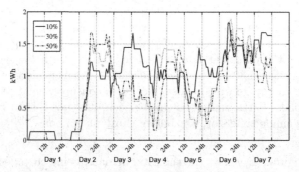

(b) Total demand being curtailed when storage is only available for substation.

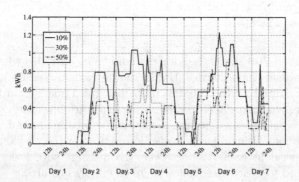

(c) Total demand being curtailed when storage is available for both prosumers and substation.

Fig. 7. Total demand being curtailed per slot over seven days.

energy prices come from a continuous double auction in which the participants are prosumers and consumers (see Sect. 3.1). The analysis of energy prices provides an idea about the expected profits or losses in a given energy market. Besides presenting results for the three described scenarios, we present results for an extra scenario in which storage is not available at all. The main motivation is to show the economic effect of adding storage capacity to the grid.

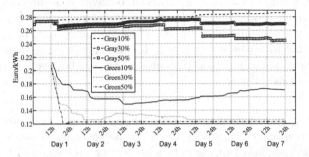

(a) Energy prices when storage is only available for prosumers.

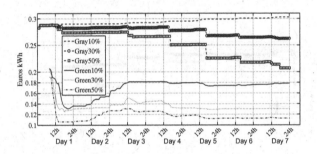

(b) Energy prices when storage is only available for substation.

Fig. 8. Grey and green energy prices during a whole week for different percentage of prosumers.

Scenario 1: Figure 8(a) shows the behaviour of grey and green energy prices when prosumers are the only ones with storage capabilities. On the one hand, the price for green energy shows a clear pattern, the more prosumers in a district, the cheaper the price. For instance, the price for green energy when the district contains 50% of prosumers is almost 0.12 Euro after the first day, whereas the price when the district has 10% prosumers is around 0.16 Euro. Moreover, regardless of the percentage of prosumers, green prices start relatively high and fall as green energy becomes abundant.

On the other hand, as an attempt to discourage the use of grey energy, the substation increases and decreases the price of grey energy based on whether green energy is abundant or not (see also Sect. 3.1). When abundant, the price for grey energy goes down. Otherwise, the price goes up. Consequently, as seen in Fig. 8(a), the grey energy price follows the overall behaviour of green energy prices. It drops when green energy prices drop and increases otherwise, which is the kind of behaviour we want to promote as consumers may be less willing to withdraw energy during those periods.

Scenario 2: Figure 8(b) shows the energy prices when only the substation is equipped with storage. Although the overall behaviour is similar to previous scenarios (the more prosumers, the lower the price for green energy), the price for green energy reaches its lowest point when the percentage of prosumers is 50%, i.e. the price for green energy after the fifth day is lower than 0.12 Euro. The overall prices when there are 10% prosumers are, however, slightly higher than in the previous scenario.

Scenario 3: Figure 9(a) shows the prices for energy when both prosumers and substation are equipped with storage. Like in the previous scenarios, the prices for green energy are lower in districts with higher percentages of prosumers. Moreover, once again, the price for green energy after the fifth day is lower than 0.12 Euro.

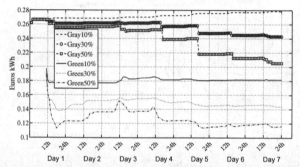

(a) Energy prices when storage is available for both prosumers and substation.

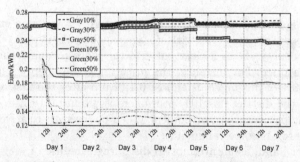

(b) Energy prices when storage is not available at all.

Fig. 9. Grey and green energy prices during a whole week for different percentage of prosumers.

Scenario 4: Finally, we have also analysed the behaviour of green and grey energy prices when no storage capabilities are used. Figure 9(b) shows the behaviour of both prices. Although the overall behaviour is similar to the previous scenarios, there is an interesting phenomenon since the prices for green energy are slightly higher, which may suggest that storage helps to keep the price of green energy low.

Even though this phenomenon requires a more elaborate analysis, retailers as well as prosumers should acknowledge this when investing in storage since they could directly influence energy prices, which may potentially offer a good return on investment. In this way, retailers could try to keep profitable prices, whereas prosumers may try to ensure low prices when buying and high prices when selling energy. Moreover, the impact of storage on energy prices has been observed before [18].

5   Conclusions and Future Work

We use a multi-agent system to analyse the impact of load shifting and storage to reduce grey energy demand. Likewise, we describe an electricity system composed of a physical subsystem that provides the overall smart grid infrastructure (e.g. energy consumption and production, storage, and load shifting) and a commodity subsystem that support markets for green and grey energy. Green energy is traded using NRGcoins under the NRG-X-Change mechanism, whereas grey energy is traded in Euro via a bi-directional negotiation between an energy retailer and users of energy, i.e. consumers and prosumers.

We present results for three main scenarios in which there are different percentages of prosumers and storage is placed at different locations. Within the first two scenarios, storage is only available for either prosumers (scenario 1) or substation (scenario 2), whereas in the last scenario we allow storage to be allocated at both prosumers' and substation's facilities. The results show that reductions in grey energy consumption are possible not only for current renewables penetration rates (i.e. up to 15% reduction when prosumers are 10% in a district) but also for future scenarios in which the penetration of renewables will increase (i.e. up to 50% reduction when prosumers are 50% in a district). Furthermore, such reductions are mainly possible by combining load shifting an storage.

Regarding economic issues, prosumers, DSOs and retailers must be aware of the impact of storage and load shifting. DSOs and retailers must carefully consider investments in batteries at their facilities since when a considerable amount of prosumers is equipped with batteries, such investment may not be beneficial. In contrast, prosumers and consumers benefit from installing storage capacity as it will ultimately lower their electricity bill. Lastly, both DSOs and retailers should develop suitable demand response programs to incentivise load shifting, which may help them to better balance their customer portfolio and save in operational costs.

In this vein, our future work will focus on applying better strategies to optimise the use of load shifting and storage. We envision, for instance, the use of cooperative and coordinated ways to charge and discharge batteries, which can be applied to not only cope with demand but also influence energy prices. Likewise, load shifting can be coordinated among prosumers and consumers. In addition, we also want to improve the NRGcoin and NRG-X-Change concepts since they could potentially offer better economic incentives to stakeholders while promoting energy balancing within microgrids.

To conclude, our main message is that to reduce grey energy consumption while improving the integration of renewables, combination of storage and load shifting programs is worth exploring for economic and environmental reasons [14].

Acknowledgments. This research has been funded by the European Union's Seventh Programme for research, technological development and demonstration under the grant agreement number 324321, project SCANERGY.

References

1. Aghaei, J., Alizadeh, M.-I.: Demand response in smart electricity grids equipped with renewable energy sources: a review. Renew. Sustain. Energy Rev. **18**, 64–72 (2013)
2. Bosch: BPT-S 5 hybrid solar power storage (2016). http://bosch-power-tec.com/en/bpte/produkte/storage_solutions/bpt_s_5_hybrid/vs_5_hybrid. Accessed 11 July 2016
3. Bush, S.F.: Smart Grid: Communication-Enabled Intelligence for the Electric Power Grid. IEEE Press, New York (2014)
4. Capodieci, N., Pagani, G.A., Cabri, G., Aiello, M.: Smart meter aware domestic energy trading agents. In: Proceedings of the IEEMC 2011 Workshop on E-energy Market Challenge, pp. 1–10. ACM, New York (2011)
5. Gottwalt, S., Ketter, W., Block, C., Collins, J., Weinhardt, C.: Demand side management-a simulation of household behavior under variable prices. Energy Policy **39**(12), 8163–8174 (2011). Clean Cooking Fuels and Technologies in Developing Economies
6. Grid4EU: Nice grid demonstrator (2016). http://www.nicegrid.fr/. Accessed 4 Feb 2016
7. Ilic, D., Da Silva, P.G., Karnouskos, S., Griesemer, M.: An energy market for trading electricity in smart grid neighbourhoods. In: 6th IEEE International Conference on Digital Ecosystems Technologies (DEST), pp. 1–6, June 2012
8. Kok, J.K., Warmer, C.J., Kamphuis, I.G: Powermatcher: multiagent control in the electricity infrastructure. In: Proceedings of the Fourth International Joint Conference on Autonomous Agents and Multiagent Systems, AAMAS 2005, pp. 75–82. ACM, New York (2005)
9. Ma, H., Leung, H.-F.: An adaptive attitude bidding strategy for agents in continuous double auctions. Electron. Commer. Res. Appl. **6**(4), 383–398 (2007)
10. Mert, W., Suschek-Berger, J., Tritthart, W.: Consumer acceptance of smart appliances. Technical report, EIE Project Smart Domestic Appliances in Sustainable Energy Systems (Smart-A) (2008)

11. Mihaylov, M., Jurado, S., Avellana, N., Razo-Zapata, I., Van Moffaert, K., Arco, L., Bezunartea, M., Grau, I., Cañadas, A., Nowé, A.: Scanergy: a scalable and modular system for energy trading between prosumers. In: Proceedings of the International Conference on Autonomous Agents and Multiagent Systems, AAMAS 2015, pp. 1917–1918 (2015)

12. Mihaylov, M., Jurado, S., Van Moffaert, K., Avellana, N., Nowé, A.: NRG-X-Change: a novel mechanism for trading of renewable energy in smart grids. In: 3rd International Conference on Smart Grids and Green IT Systems (SmartGreens) (2014)

13. Nakamoto, S.: BitCoin: a peer-to-peer electronic cash system (2008)

14. Niesten, E., Alkemade, F.: How is value created and captured in smart grids? A review of the literature and an analysis of pilot projects. Renew. Sustain. Energy Rev. **53**, 629–638 (2016)

15. North, M.J., Collier, N.T., Ozik, J., Tatara, E.R., Macal, C.M., Bragen, M., Sydelko, P.: Complex adaptive systems modeling with Repast Simphony. Complex Adapt. Syst. Model. **1**(1), 1–26 (2013)

16. Paatero, J.V., Lund, P.D.: A model for generating household electricity load profiles. Int. J. Energy Res. **30**(5), 273–290 (2006)

17. Prüggler, N.: Economic potential of demand response at household level–are central-european market conditions sufficient? Energy Policy **60**, 487–498 (2013)

18. Prüggler, N., Prüggler, W., Wirl, F.: Storage and demand side management as power generator's strategic instruments to influence demand and prices. Energy **36**(11), 6308–6317 (2011)

19. Ramchurn, S.D., Vytelingum, P., Rogers, A., Jennings, N.R.: Putting the 'smarts' into the smart grid: a grand challenge for artificial intelligence. Commun. ACM **55**(4), 86–97 (2012)

20. Razo-Zapata, I.S., Mihaylov, M., Nowé, A.: Integration of load shifting and storage to reduce gray energy demand. In: Proceedings of the 5th International Conference on Smart Cities and Green ICT Systems, pp. 154–165 (2016)

21. Rickerson, W., Couture, T., Barbose, G.L., Jacobs, D., Parkinson, G., Chessin, E., Belden, A., Wilson, H., Barrett, H.: Residential prosumers: drivers and policy options (re-prosumers). Technical report, International Energy Agency (IEA), 06/2014 (2014)

22. Big Room and World Resources Institute: Global ecolabel monitor 2010: towards transparency (2010). http://www.ecolabelindex.com/downloads/Global_Ecolabel_Monitor2010.pdf. Accessed 23 Sept 2015

23. Schuler, R.: The smart grid: a bridge between emerging technologies society and the environment. Bridge **40**(1), 42–49 (2010)

24. Shoham, Y., Leyton-Brown, K.: Multiagent Systems: Algorithmic, Game-Theoretic, and Logical Foundations. Cambridge University Press, Cambridge (2008)

25. Siano, P.: Demand response and smart grids–a survey. Renew. Sustain. Energy Rev. **30**, 461–478 (2014)

26. Socomec: Socomec energy storage (2016). http://www.socomec.com/energy-storage_en.html. Accessed 11 July 2016

27. Tesla: Powerpack (2016). https://www.teslamotors.com/powerpack. Accessed 11 July 2016

28. Tesla: Powerwall (2016). https://www.teslamotors.com/powerwall. Accessed 11 July 2016

29. van Werven, M.J.N., Scheepers, M.J.J.: The changing role of energy suppliers and distribution system operators in the deployment of distributed generation in liberalised electricity markets. Technical report, ECN-C-05-048, ECN (2005)
30. VEA: Vlaams energieagentschap - rapport 2013/2 (2014). http://www2.vlaanderen.be/economie/energiesparen/milieuvriendelijkemonitoring_evaluatie/2013/20130628Rapport2013_2-Deel2Actualisatie-OT_Bf.pdf. Accessed 23 Sept 2015
31. Vytelingum, P., Cliff, D., Jennings, N.R.: Strategic bidding in continuous double auctions. Artif. Intell. **172**(14), 1700–1729 (2008)
32. Wang, Z., Wang, L.: Adaptive negotiation agent for facilitating bi-directional energy trading between smart building and utility grid. IEEE Trans. Smart Grid **4**(2), 702–710 (2013)

Enhancing User Comfort in Demand Response Solutions for Water Heaters: User-Centric Hot Water Management

Alexander Belov[✉], Alexandr Vasenev,
Nirvana Meratnia, and Paul J.M. Havinga

University of Twente, Enschede, The Netherlands
{a.belov,a.vasenev,n.meratnia,p.j.m.havinga}@utwente.nl

Abstract. Demand Response (DR) solutions for tank electric water heaters (WHs) let residential consumers benefit financially, however, a negative impact of DR on personal comfort may force users to reject them. To facilitate DR implementation in practice, there is a need to consider the end-user's comfort. Typically, DR for WHs concerns only the user satisfaction with a variable water temperature. This paper extends the conventional control by considering the tap water flow as a variable during water activities. The main contributions of this paper are (i) a model to relate user comfort with the tap water flow rate, (ii) the control mechanism consisting of the pre-heating control and the flow control to maintain the user comfort. Simulations demonstrate that the proposed control coupled with the suggested user interface can inform about available trade-offs between energy consumption and comfort, and thus can help the user to rationally save energy for water heating.

Keywords: Demand side management · Demand response · Comfort modeling · Tank water heaters · User interface

1 Introduction

Demand Response (DR) as an integral part of Demand Side Management can be identified as a set of initiatives "designed to induce lower electricity use at times of high wholesale market prices or when system reliability is jeopardized" [9]. DR is recognized by the European Commission as an important instrument to enhance energy efficiency and stability of the electrical grid [13].

Improving energy efficiency is impossible without considering residential users involved in the demand response. Final consumption in the residential sector accounted for 26.65% of the total energy consumption in the EU-27 in the year 2010 and continued growing as reported by Eurostat [34]. Therefore, reduction of energy consumption in the residential sector can significantly contribute to decrease of the Union's energy dependency and carbon-dioxide emissions [12].

The adoption of DR programs balances how users perceive possible benefits and shortcomings. By implementing DR, small residential consumers can gain

M. Helfert et al. (Eds.): SMARTGREENS 2016 and VEHITS 2016, CCIS 738, pp. 49–74, 2017.
DOI: 10.1007/978-3-319-63712-9_3

numerous benefits such as reduction of outages, more transparent and frequent billing information, participation in the electricity market via aggregators, as well as energy and financial savings [20]. Notwithstanding, there is still a significant level of consumer resistance to participating in DR projects, mainly because consumers are afraid of losing control of devices in their own household and are sceptical about new electricity rates [32]. Consumers' concerns and uncertainties create a barrier for the wide-scale uptake of DR solutions, which in turn decreases the overall profitability of DR measures [41].

The need for involving consumers in sustainable consumption has been highlighted by the EC Task Force for Smart Grids by stating that "the *engagement* and *education* of the consumer is a key task in the process as there will be fundamental changes to the energy retail market" [19]. The European Communication on smart grids underlines the importance of consumer awareness by stating that "developing smart grids in a competitive retail market should encourage consumers to *change behavior*, become more active and adapt to new 'smart' energy consumption patterns" [8].

Consumers can modify their energy consumption habits based on direct feedback about their energy usage and based on estimates for energy costs [11]. To be of use, this information should be provided in a timely manner and in an easily understandable format [13]. Typically, the task of informing users is handled by means of various user interfaces (UIs) integrated into automated home DR solutions for, among others, room heating, air-conditioning, water heating systems, and other electric loads [21,28,31]. Several off-the-shelf solutions for UIs are available in the market today [23,33].

A number of projects [22,25,37,39] are now focusing on consumer engagement in DR. For example in the *EcoGrid EU* project, consumers armed with demand response-equipped devices and intelligent controllers can react to real-time price signals [25]. The *Ewz-Studie Smart Metering* project aims to assess consumer response to different DRs through use of tools such as in-home displays, expert advice, social competition and social comparison [1]. Other projects like *Consumer to Grid project* intend to measure the behavioral change induced by various feedback mechanisms such as monthly bills, website, smart phone APPs and ad-hoc feedback gadget [22].

Despite all these tools, ready-to-deploy products, and projects, the expressed European view on energy saving schemes indicates the need for further in-depth consideration of improving energy utilization in individual households. Essentially, this concerns how to improve the efficiency of energy usage and how to communicate the related information with the consumer.

1.1   Modeling User Comfort for Domestic Water Heaters

This paper concentrates on the specific problem of "how to improve the efficiency of energy consumption of a domestic electric storage-tank water heater (WH) with respect to user comfort and how to enhance consumers' awareness about their electricity expenses for water heating?". The case of domestic water heaters is particularly relevant to the residential energy consumption because they make up more than two thirds of the total household consumption together with room heaters and air conditioners in European countries [7]. Furthermore, since tank water heating units are still present in a prevailing number of European households and because of their capability to store thermal energy, they serve as a good example of a household loads with flexibility to shift their energy consumption to the off-peak energy demand hours or to periods when electricity prices are low.

Previously, a number of approaches (e.g. [4, 14, 17, 35, 40]) have been suggested to account for user comfort with respect to WHs in order to minimize comfort disruptions and hence to increase attractivness of these DR solutions to the customers. Majority of these works deal with the thermal discomfort caused by uncomfortable tap water *temperature*. They assume that the tap flow rate is *fixed* during the entire water usage and is *pre-determined* by the user.

However, additional savings can be achieved by investigating opportunities to reduce the tap flow rate. Modern water efficient faucets can save water during tasks performed in running water by limiting the flow rate [2] or by interrupting the water flow when it is not needed [10, 42], which in turn reduce the water heater's demand and lead to energy savings.

This paper argues in favor of relaxing the assumption about the fixed tap flow that can open up opportunities for additional electricity savings. A loosely-defined flow rate, suggested by the user and related to the user comfort model, can be subject of sophisticated control. Additionally, by carefully examining the amount of tap hot water withdrawn, the intentions to save energy and water usage can be united. As these objectives are highly relevant for the green energy paradigm, this approach can support smoother transition towards green energy solutions.

In our view, three aspects should be considered to enable efficient utilization of both water and energy for water heating. Firstly, a model should be developed to accurately account for relations between tap water flow rate and user comfort. Secondly, a mechanism to control the WH for this model should be developed. Finally, information about the control possibilities and their impact on energy consumption for water heating and user satisfaction with the tap flow rate should be represented to a user by means of a clear and understandable user interface. Together, these topics highlight multiple intricate interrelations between energy and water savings, user comfort, and possibilities for user control of water events.

Previously, we suggested a system built around the *water activity* (WA) concept where a WA performed by a user has parameters such as a start-up time, duration, the tap water temperature and tap water flow rate [3]. In this paper we extend the user comfort model, that has previously accounted only for a user satisfaction with water *temperature* [4], and introduce a new flow-based discomfort metric. This paper also suggests the way to organize an interface to visualize interrelations between energy, tap flow rate, and user comfort to the end-user.

Therefore, this paper presents four main contributions: (1) a simple approach to obtain estimates of the day-ahead WAs based on the water temperature inside the tank; (2) a comfort model that can link energy consumption for water heating to personal tap flow rate comfort and show their effect on one another, (3) a control mechanism that incorporates the comfort model and consists of two elements significant for provision of the desired tap flow rate and temperature, and (4) an interface via wich the user can interact with the proposed control.

The rest of the paper is organized as follows. Section 2 discusses the existing connection between the tank water temperature and hot water usage as well as our initial considerations on two types of control to support the scenario in which an end-user requests the fixed tap water temperature. The modeling of different components of a domestic hot water system together with the existing model of the user flow comfort are presented in Sect. 3. Section 4 outlines introductory steps to design of an interface with the user. In Sect. 5 we present the possibility for a day-ahead forecast based on the statistical estimations of the tank water temperature and apply a multi-objective optimization to unfold an explicit relation between electricity expenses for water heating and user flow comfort. Role of the user interface and suggestions for its implementation are presented in Sect. 6. Section 7 evaluates a naive approach to estimate day-ahead hot water usage activities, exhibits and discusses the simulation results for the selected water activities. In Sect. 8 we present the potential direction for improvement of statistical estimates of day-ahead WAs. Some directions for the future work are outlined in Sect. 9 and our conclusions are summarized in Sect. 10.

2   Preliminary Discussion

The main focus of this paper is on improvement of energy utilization in a domestic WH by means of a control mechanism that treats the *tap flow rate* as a controllable parameter.

We first discuss in-brief the specifics of domestic hot water consumption concentrating on the scenario of a single-person apartment. Further we highlight the possibilities to enable better energy utilization for water heating.

2.1   Domestic Hot Water Usage

Let us consider a simplified, yet realistic, scenario of a single-person apartment wherein WAs can take place without overlapping in time. The graphs shown in Fig. 1 represent daily hot water usage profiles, retrieved by means of the Load Profile Generator (LPG) software [36] and mapped against the WH's tank water temperature curve.

As it can be seen from the graphs, intra-day water events have a random and sporadic character. In working days, the person tends to consume hot water preferably in the morning and evening. Weekends demonstrate a peculiar over-day hot water usage. Even though water consumption patterns have, in general, very distinctive signatures in the above two plots, the both typical days exhibit some similarities, as for instance the night periods without hot water demand. These night periods are well aligned to each other with some degree of tolerance and followed by a morning hot water usage. One can notice that the WA

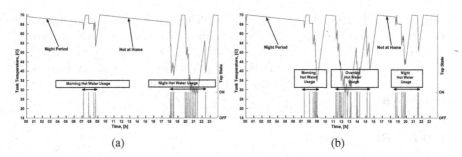

(a)   (b)

Fig. 1. Hot water usage under considered scenario (a) Typical working day, (b) Typical weekend day.

performed by the user the first in the morning causes a rapid drop of the temperature inside the hot water tank. Noteworthy is that the drop of thermal energy inside the tank can be caused by the heat losses to the environment and by the hot water demand, however, the latter factor has much stronger impact on the heat discharge. Hereby, we can conclude that heat losses to the ambient are neglectfully small compared with the heat discharge due to WAs that causes an intense decrease of the tank water temperature [17].

Another important point to mention is the dynamic nature of domestic hot water consumption. From the daily life experience one can note that the tap is frequently opened and closed on demand. Intensive water demand can follow short water events and vice versa, making the tank hot water temperature drop down to uncomfortable levels. Consider the intensive hot water usage that took place in the morning period in Fig. 1(b). Multiple consecutive WAs causes the tank temperature decrease to around 35 °C which signifies that any subsequent user's request for the hot water temperature beyond this level cannot be handled by the WH, and the user will naturally experience uncomfortable temperature.

In view of the properties of the daily hot water consumption patterns, we argue the necessity of analyzing the daily hot water consumption patterns and providing the measures to alleviate the impact on the user, on the one hand, and to moderate electric consumption for water heating accordingly, on the other.

2.2   WH Pre-heating Procedure

To maintain the tap water temperature at the requested level, there might be a need to pre-store additional heat in the WH during the night period, taking into account the constraint for the maximum tank water temperature [24] dictated by safety reasons and the hot water demand in the upcoming morning period. The pre-preheating procedure for household WHs in deregulated energy markets has been proposed by [30]. In contrary to [30], we concentrate on the user comfort issues that might arise due to the regular operation of conventional WHs and specifics of hot water consumption patterns, rather than aiming at purely monetary gains that can deliver such pre-heating. In other words, we speculate about the applicability of this generic approach to ensure the sufficient amount of heat in the WH to undo the potential negative impact on user comfort. Moreover, we impose even stricter requirements for user comfort asking for the *fixed* tap water temperature during a single WA. In other words, this paper focuses on the scenario where a user desires the stable temperature out of the tap during the entire WA.

2.3   Flow Rate Control

As mentioned earlier, this paper concentrates on the scenario of hot water usage where tap water is supplied at the fixed temperature. Significantly, during WAs the water temperature naturally goes down in WHs, leading to a decrease of the tap water temperature. It happens because of (i) the cold water inflow in the tank that creates the pressure in a hot water system to deliver hot water to the tap and (ii) the insufficient power of electric heating elements that cannot cope with the rapid temperature drop of the mixed cold and hot water in the tank.

Normally, the preferred tap water temperature and tap flow rate are manually set by a user, operating the tap mixer. Unlike the common practice, in this paper we consider that only the tap water temperature is manually set by the user, while the *outflow from the tap* is treated as a control variable to fulfill the user request for the fixed temperature. More precisely, the fixed temperature can be ensured by controlling the proportion of hot and cold water flows in the mixing device that can be simply expressed as $\frac{\text{hot water inflow}}{\text{cold water inflow}}$. The analysis of this ratio done in our previous studies [5] highlights the possibility to maintain the user request for the fixed temperature by progressively increasing the hot water inflow, while gradually lowering the cold water inflow in the mixer throughout the WA.

Figure 2(a) shows a case when a user is willing to get tap water at 45 °C. To keep the tap water temperature at the desired level, the flow controller can

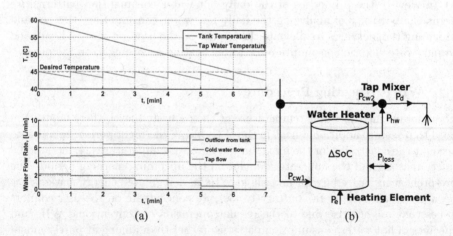

Fig. 2. (a) Flow control, (b) Considered hot water system.

adjust hot and cold water flows in a step-wise manner. From mathematical point of view, the flow control represents the dynamic programming (DP) optimization problem where at every step the solver attempts to find the best combination of the blending hot and cold water flows to minimize the difference between the user desired fixed tap water temperature and the one that is actually provided from the tap.

3 Modeling Hot Water Supply

This section introduces important concepts for modeling the WH operation and end-user comfort to be used in subsequent sections of the paper.

3.1 Water Heater Operation

Most of household electric storage-tank water heaters (WHs) operate in a cyclic manner. This means that the heating elements of a WH are continuously turned on and off to maintain the temperature inside the tank within some temperature deadband. More specifically, the WH remains on, if its internal temperature is below the upper setpoint temperature. When the upper setpoint is reached, the heating elements are shut down till the temperature in the tank drops below the lower setpoint. There is extensive literature on modeling WHs, see for instance [16,27,29]. Contrary to those, in this paper we consider a small-sized WH assuming that *entire water in the tank is at the same temperature, i.e. non-stratified.* In this regard, we adopt the following thermodynamic model of the well-mixed WH described in [15]:

$$MC\frac{dT}{dt} = P_e + P_{cw} - P_{hw} - P_{loss},\tag{1}$$

where M is the water mass in the tank, C is specific temperature of water, P_e is the thermal power supplied by the heating elements, P_{cw} and P_{hw} are cold water inflow and hot water outflow of the tank, and P_{loss} is the heat losses to the ambient.

The mentioned components of the model are indicated in Fig. 2(b).

Energy and mass balance in the mixing device can be expressed as:

$$\begin{cases} P_d = P_{hw} + P_{cw2}; \\ \dot{m}_d = \dot{m} + \dot{m}_{cw}; \end{cases}\tag{2}$$

where P_d is the tap water thermal power demanded by the user, P_{hw} is the power flow from the tank, P_{cw2} is cold water from the main controller, and $\dot{m}_d, \dot{m}, \dot{m}_{cw}$ are the demanded, hot and cold water mass flow rates, respectively.

As discussed in Sect. 2.3, the proportion of the hot and cold water inflows can be tuned in the tap mixer to establish the user-desired water temperature. This proportion determines how fast the temperature in the tank $T(t)$ will fall during the water activity (WA). (2) expresses that the ratio between the hot water and cold water flow rates in the mixer bind together the temperature inside the tank $T(t)$, the demanded temperature $T_d(t)$, and the cold water temperature T_{cw} at every moment of time:

$$k(t) = \frac{\dot{m}(t)}{\dot{m}_{cw}(t)} = \frac{T_d(t) - T_{cw}}{T(t) - T_d(t)}. \tag{3}$$

3.2 Comfortable Tap Flow Rate

It follows from the governing equation of the flow control (3) that the flows $\dot{m}(t)$ and $\dot{m}_{cw}(t)$ are altered over time. Noticing that $\dot{m}(t) + \dot{m}_{cw}(t) = \dot{m}_d(t)$, one can conclude that the tap flow rate can change too and thus can possibly reach the values inconvenient for the user. Therefore, the idea of the flow-adjustable hot water supply with the fixed tap water temperature calls for a careful consideration of impacts on user comfort.

The concept of the flow rate comfort introduced previously in [5] can be illustrated by the following example. Let us consider a person who wants to take a 7-minute shower at the fixed water temperature of 45 °C. The flow control algorithm can return multiple solutions to this control problem, each of which resulting in a different water flow from the shower head. Two of these solutions are shown in Fig. 3(a).

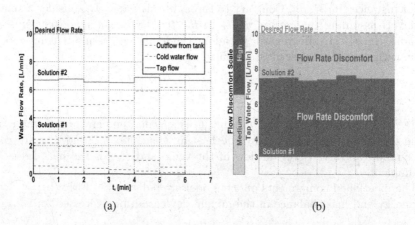

(a)   (b)

Fig. 3. Flow rate discomfort.

As it can be seen from Fig. 3(a), both control solutions lead to the tap water flows uncomfortable for the user. In fact, the user can experience distinct dissatisfaction at every step of control which is caused by the mismatch between the currently provided flow and the flow rate desired by the user (10 [L/min]). To quantify the user inconvenience of having unsatisfactory flow rate for the entire WA, we take instantaneous flow deflections over time as illustrated in Fig. 3(b). Furthermore, we suppose that the time during which the user experiences the undesirable flow is significant for the WA accomplishment. This means that if the duration of discomfort is short enough, the user might still proceed with the WA. Otherwise the user might refuse to continue. Noteworthy, such flow variation considered over time can also indicate the amount of overused/undelivered liters of water. This can be crucial in some scenarios, for example, in filling a bath. To this end, we accumulate all instantaneous deviations of the supplied water flow over the entire duration of a WA. The resulting flow rate discomfort can be then described by the following metric:

$$A_{\dot{m}_d} = \sum_{i=1}^{N} |\dot{m}_{\text{exp}, i} - \dot{m}_{\text{d}, i}| \Delta t, \tag{4}$$

where N is the number of control steps, $\dot{m}_{\text{exp}, i}$ is the desired flow rate at i-th step, $\dot{m}_{\text{d}, i}$ is the tap water flow provided at step i, and Δt is the size of the control step.

To handle the fixed $T_\text{d}(t)$ and $A_{\dot{m}_d}$ at levels acceptable to the user the flow control at every step seeks optimal combinations of $\{T_i, \dot{m}_i, \dot{m}_{\text{cw},i}\}, \forall i \in N$, where T_i is the tank temperature at the beginning of step i and N is the total number of control steps.

3.3 Effect on Thermal Comfort

Apart from the uncomfortable flow rate, the user can also experience a drop of tap water temperature within every step of the flow control as illustrated for a single step in Fig. 4(a). Noticeably, different people typically have different tolerance to cold and hot water due to individual skin sensitivity [38]. To estimate the levels of thermal discomfort the user can experience during the flow control, we employ the thermal comfort model presented earlier in [4].

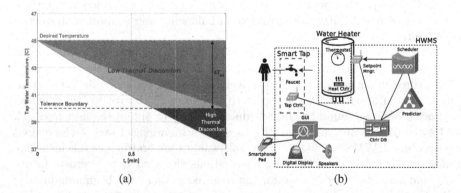

(a)   (b)

Fig. 4. (a) Effect on thermal comfort during flow control, (b) HWMS components (no arrow shows bi-directional links).

4   Hot Water Management System (HWMS)

Pre-storing of heat in the tank can be initiated by means of the HWMS that has an appropriate knowledge about the expected WAs, i.e. user comfort requests and their timing, and is able to inform the user about the options corresponding to different levels of comfort to provide hot water service for the following day.

More specifically, based on a day-ahead forecast of WAs with the *calibrated granularity* (small hot water events might be aggregated in bigger groups) the system can trace the future temperature inside the WH, i.e. its state of charge (SoC). If the SoC of the WH at the beginning of predicted water usage is insufficient to suit the known user comfort request, the system will compute the need to pre-store some heat in order to maintain user comfort at the desired level that is known in advance either through user input or via machine learning.

Since in reality the user might wish to change his comfort preferences (for instance, a user may want to sacrifice some comfort in favor of lowered electricity bill) the acknowledgement from the user is of utmost necessity. Thus, HWMS should be capable to notify the user about the predicted WAs through the user interface. Such message can contain different options to provide the hot water service to the user mapped against the corresponding levels of energy consumption.

Figure 4(b) that illustrates the main components of the proposed HWMS such as the main controller includes component 'GUI', database controller 'Ctrlr. DB' that stores all user preferences and optimization results, prediction module that builds a day-ahead forecast of WAs and the 'Scheduler' that based on the forecast computes the outcomes of the pre-heating control and the flow control and sends the solutions to the 'Setpoint Manager' and the 'Smart Tap' nodes. While the 'Setpoint Manager' is responsible for tracking the tank water temperature on the intra-day time scale and executing the pre-heating control solutions, the 'Smart Tap' module performs the flow control during the actual water usage to maintain the fixed tap water temperature. The 'Setpoint Manager', which has an interface with the thermostat, plays a central role in balancing user comfort with electric consumption for water heating.

The user can communicate with the HWMS through the 'GUI' component that can be realized on diverse user gadgets and digital display. The 'GUI' serves three main purposes (a) to collect the needed for the 'Scheduler' comfort related information from the user, (b) to represent control options (energy-comfort trade-offs) found by the Scheduler, and (c) to obtain the user feedback about the offered options. Once the user has acknowledged one of the offered options, the HWMS tracks the real tank water temperature on the intra-day timescale, then based on the new observations the system re-forecasts future WAs and corrects the estimates for the required SoCs at the beginning of each WA as well as the optimal start-up times for the pre-heating procedures. The steering signals from the 'Scheduler' are fed to the setpoint control manager to change the thermostat current setpoint temperature setting to start/stop heating as well as to the 'Smart Tap' to adjust the flow ratio specified in (3).

At every step of the flow control during WAs the HWMS withdraws a small portion of hot water from the tank and mixes it with cold water to achieve the wanted fixed tap water temperature. Obviously the stronger is the hot flow rate at every step, the (potentially) higher is the tap water temperature. However, a strong step-increase of the hot flow can lead to a rapid WH discharge and thereby to violation of the user-desired fixed tap water temperature requirement. Therefore, additional heat should be pre-stored by means of the pre-heating control. Having a relationship between the flow rate comfort and electric consumption for pre-heating the user can estimate the consequences of current comfort settings on energy consumption, i.e. the user can perform energy-comfort balancing.

5   Uniting Water Pre-heating and Flow Rate Control

Let us elaborate on how the water pre-heating procedure outlined in Sect. 2.2 and the flow rate control discussed in Sect. 2.3 can communicate to enable balancing of energy consumption of the WH with diverse comfort requests of an end-user, i.e. energy-comfort balancing. First and foremost, in order to make the pre-heating procedure possible we put attention onto the ways to attain the information about the day-ahead hot water usage.

5.1   Estimation of Day-ahead Hot Water Usage

As it follows from Sect. 2.1, daily hot water usage charts mapped onto the tank water temperature graphs can give meaningful information about the time intervals characterized by a rapid drop of the tank water temperature and times of stand-by heat losses where the temperature fall is less intensive. By analyzing the daily tank temperature fluctuations across the *sufficient* number of days, one can retrieve the daily hot water usage patterns, i.e. the typical start and end times of daily hot water demand, which, in turn, delivers an essential input for forecasting the daily WAs. WAs can be thought of as instances of hot water events, i.e. tap is open, water usage and tap is closed, (possibly) aggregated into bigger entities over time to reach the stationarity of such random time-series.

In this connection, consider the statistics of the tank water temperature from the 19 working days shown in Fig. 5 under the specified scenario of a single-person apartment.

As it can be seen from Fig. 5 the standard deviations (STDs) for tank water temperature during the night period are represented by relatively short intervals, whereas the morning and evening periods of hot water usage are highly scattered around their mean values. A higher variation of the tank water temperature during the mentioned periods is caused by a random nature of WAs happened. Nonetheless, the first occurrence of hot water usage in the morning and evening periods followed by periods without WAs, i.e. night time and when a person was absent (working hours), demonstrate relatively short dispersion of STDs which points out the possibility to make a prediction of the first WA.

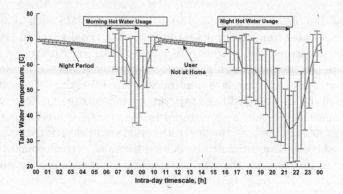

Fig. 5. Statistics for 19 working days.

One can think of a computer program that based on the statistics of the past observations of the tank water temperature tracks short STDs, which during the working days may coincide with the night and working hours as in our data-set, and returns the time of a day once a sudden increase in STDs is captured. That program can be executed the by the 'Predictor' module of the HWMS shown Fig. 4(b).

5.2   Water Heater Pre-heating Control

Armed with the day-ahead WA estimates the HWMS can initiate the pre-heating in advance before a WA will actually take place as illustrated in Fig. 6(a). As it can be seen in Fig. 6(a), the user might end up with a higher energy consumption than usual, if the requested comfort level was relatively high.

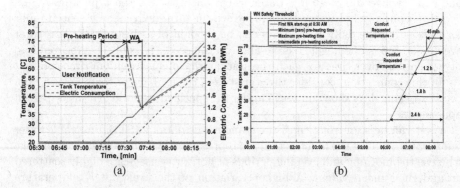

Fig. 6. (a) Dashed lines - WH regular operation, solid lines - WH pre-heating (b) Possibilities to pre-heat the WH.

The information about the retrieved statistics and, in particular, about the first hot water usage that occurs after periods of no-water-usage can be used to draw a conclusion with *some degree of confidence* about the beginning of the pre-heating procedure. More precisely, it makes it possible to identify the intervals without hot water usage long enough to fit there the duration of the pre-heating procedure.

Suppose the first estimated WA would take place at 8:30 AM, then there might be varied alternatives to heat-up the water to satisfy the user comfort request, depending on the SoC of the WH at 12:00 AM as illustrated in Fig. 6(b).

In the worst-case scenario, where the WH has been initially filled with cold water at $T(0) = 15\,°C$ and the user request corresponds to the WH maximum allowed temperature equal to $90\,°C$, the pre-heating procedure will take $2.4\,h$. However, if the initial SoC of the WH has been the same as the maximum thermostat set-point temperature, assuming that in the preceding days the WH had operated regularly, i.e. without the pre-heating control, then the HWMS will compute another start time for the pre-heating. Importantly, the user might have a desire to lower the wanted tap water temperature, which, for example, can comply with the optimal tank water temperature decrease from $90\,°C$ to $65\,°C$. In that case, the HWMS will decide that there is no need for pre-heating, so no extra electric energy will be wasted. The system should account for that option and should notify the user about all possible solutions in the range from the minimum comfort (cold tap water) to the maximum safety allowed temperature (skin scalding for adults occurs at $60\,°C$ after $5\,s$ [43]), whereas the learning mechanism of the HWMS can shorten this range based on the past user choices. The tap temperatures inside this range are in conformity with different levels of electric consumption for water pre-heating.

That is to say, the WH's tank can be initially at any allowed temperature depending on the previous history of water usage $T(0) \in [T_{cw}, T_{wh,max}]$. By solving the differential equation (1) electric consumption for pre-heating E_e for a single WA can be expressed as:

$$E_e = P_e \Delta t_{pre} = \alpha P_e log[\beta f(T(t_{pre.\ str}), T(t_{WA}))], \tag{5}$$

where Δt_{pre} is the pre-heating duration; α and β are the coefficients dependent on engineering parameters of the WH; $T(t_{pre,\ str})$ and $T(t_{WA})$ are the SoCs of the WH in the beginning of the preheating period and at the start-up of the estimated WA respectively.

We assume hereinafter that $T(t_{WA})$ is in the range $[T_{cw}, T_{wh,max}]$ and no WA can occur in the period $[0, t_{WA}]$. To calculate the best time for pre-heating, the HWMS solves the following system of equations:

$$\begin{cases} \Delta t_{pre} = E_e/P_e, \\ T(t_{pre,\ str}) = (\gamma + T(0))e^{\sigma(t_{WA} - \Delta t_{pre})} - \gamma, \end{cases} \tag{6}$$

where E_e is the expression for electric energy from (5); γ and σ are the coefficients dictated by the engineering parameters of the WH.

5.3 Comfort-Efficient Flow Rate Control and Updated Flow Comfort Model

A comfort-efficient flow control should ensure a user preferred fixed tap water temperature and flow rate comfort. The latter requirement calls for the need to couple the flow control algorithm with the user flow comfort model. However, the flow comfort model $A_{\dot{m}_d}(t)$ previously employed by the algorithm and represented earlier in Sect. 3.2 simply represents the area bounded by the user-desired tap flow and the actually supplied flow, and thus can result in the same comfort level for different realizations of the tap flow.

To overcome the above flaw of the model, we update it to account for variations in user perceptions of the water flow by incorporating the tolerance function $F_{\dot{m}_d}$. The tolerance function $F_{\dot{m}_d}$ reflects how deviations of the tap water flow are important to a person in a specific scenario of water usage. Thus this extension adds flexibility to the original comfort model and enables to differentiate between comfort levels of multiple users. We assume that the flow tolerance function establishes a linear relationship between user dissatisfaction and tap water flow deflections at any time step i:

$$F_{\dot{m}_d,i} = \begin{cases} 0 & \text{, if } \dot{m}_{d,\,i} \in \Delta\dot{m}_{d,\,\text{comf}}; \\ \alpha_1\dot{m}_{d,\,i} + \beta_1 & \text{, if } \dot{m}_{d,\,i} \in \Delta_{\text{tol}}^-; \\ \alpha_2\dot{m}_{d,\,i} + \beta_2 & \text{, if } \dot{m}_{d,\,i} \in \Delta_{\text{tol}}^+; \\ 1 & \text{, otherwise;} \end{cases} \tag{7}$$

where $\dot{m}_{d,\,i}$ is the tap water flow rate at step i; $\Delta\dot{m}_{d,\,\text{comf}}$ is the range of flows comfortable for the user; $\alpha_1 < 0, \alpha_2 > 0, \beta_1, \beta_2$ are some coefficients; Δ_{tol}^- and Δ_{tol}^+ are lower and upper flow tolerance zones as illustrated in Fig. 7:

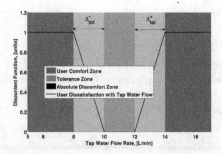

Fig. 7. Tolerance function in the form of user discontent.

Then the updated user flow comfort model can be formalized as:

$$D_{\dot{m}_d} = \sum_{i=1}^{N} F_{\dot{m}_d,i} A_{\dot{m}_d,i}, \tag{8}$$

where $F_{\dot{m}_d,i}$ is the user tolerance level at step i of the flow control; $A_{\dot{m}_d,i}$ specifies the area resulted from the flow $\dot{m}_{d,\,i}$ deviation from the comfort zone $\Delta\dot{m}_{d,\,\text{comf}}$ during step i.

An efficient flow control should take care that only the needed amount of the heat is withdrawn from the WH on the one side, and ensure the user flow comfort on the other side. The latter requirement calls for need to incorporate the user flow comfort model into the flow control algorithm. In order to explicitly incorporate the comfort model into the flow control the relationship between the user flow comfort and electricity expenses should be found.

5.4   Multi-objective Optimization and Pareto Front

Since our final goal is to unite the pre-heating control with the flow control to enable user-driven balancing of electricity expenses for water pre-heating and user comfort, we suggest the following two steps: (i) based on WAs' estimates for the day ahead and information about user-wanted fixed tap water temperatures find SoCs of the WH at the beginning of every WA in the whole range of possible flow comfort outcomes, (ii) compute start times of the pre-heating control and electric energy spent for each of the SoCs from step (i).

We apply a multi-objective optimization approach to resolve step (i) of the above scheme. In general, multi-objective optimization allows to manage multiple goals to be achieved simultaneously subject to a set of constraints. If achievement of one goal has a negative impact on attaining another goal, two goals are said to be conflicting. From mathematical perspective, minimization (or maximization) of conflicting objective functions leads to a number of optimal solutions that make up Pareto front [6]. Pareto front is characterized in the way that switching from one solution to another on the front improves one of the conflicting objectives and degrades the value of another.

In our case, we consider minimizing energy consumption and maximizing user flow comfort as two conflicting objectives. Then the problem can be formalized as follows:

$$
\begin{cases}
min[F_1] = min\Big[\sum_{j=1}^{N_{\text{WA}}}\sum_{i=1}^{N_j} E_{\text{e}}(\Delta T)_{j,i}\Big], & (9) \\[2ex]
min[F_2] = min\Big[\sum_{j=1}^{N_{\text{WA}}}\sum_{i=1}^{N_j} D_{\dot{m}_d}(T,\dot{m},\dot{m}_{\text{cw}})_{j,i}\Big], & (10)
\end{cases}
$$

subject to:

$$T_{\text{cw}} \leq T_{j,i} \leq T_{\text{wh, max}}, \tag{11}$$

$$0 \leq \dot{m}_{j,i} \leq \dot{m}_{\text{d, exp},j}, \tag{12}$$

$$0 \leq \dot{m}_{\text{cw},\,j,i} \leq \dot{m}_{\text{d, exp},j}, \tag{13}$$

where j is the index of an estimated WA; N_{WA} is the total number of estimated WAs; i is the index of the flow control step; N_j is the number of the flow control steps for the j-th WA; ΔT in (9) refers to temperature increase from $T_{\text{pre. str}, j}$ to $T_{\text{WA}, j}$ as in (5), while in (10) T stays for the tank water temperatures throughout the j-th WA; $\dot{m}_{\text{d, exp}, j}$ is the tap flow rate desired by the user for the j-th WA.

The above problem can be solved by using the SoCs before each j-th WA $T_{\text{pre. str}, j} = T_{\text{cw}}$ as a reference for $E_{\text{e}}(\Delta T)$ along N_j-steps. Therefore, the term $E_{\text{e}}(\Delta T)$ in (9) is not a real electric consumption, but rather its maximum estimated value. Actual electricity expenses might be smaller depending on the SoCs preceding the WAs. The solution is then represented by $\sum_{j=1}^{N_{\text{WA}}} N_j$-number of triples $\{T_{\text{WA}, j,i}^*, \dot{m}_{j,i}^*, \dot{m}_{\text{cw}, j,i}^*\}$, where $T_{\text{WA}, j,1}^*$ is nothing but the optimal minimum SoC of the WH before the j-th WA capable to maintain the user-desired fixed tap water temperature and current value of $D_{\dot{m}_d}$. A set $T_{\text{WA}, j,1}^*, \forall j \in [1, N_{\text{WA}}]$ for every comfort request in the range $[F_{2,\min}, F_{2,\max}]$ is in essence the solution for step (i) of the proposed scheme.

After resolving step (i) one can address step (ii) by pluging the obtained values of $T_{\text{WA}, j,1}^*$ into (6) and (5) to find the start times and actual values of electric consumption for pre-heating.

6   Interacting with a User

The necessity of attaining Pareto fronts in our case is mainly dictated by two reasons: (a) its convenience of representing an extensive information about multi-objective optimization results in a compact form that is abstract enough to hide unnecessary details from the user; (b) its capability to plainly illustrate a wide range (possibly infinite) of alternative solutions that the user can accept while pursuing either of the above goals. This means that the user can observe not only a single solution that satisfies his current choice but also a variety of other options that might also influence his actual decision. All in all, it can be assumed that when the user is provided with multiple trade-offs he can make more conscious and justified balancing between energy consumption/costs and personal comfort.

In principal, the system starts operating with checking the available comfort models for the planned activities. If the system starts up freshly or if some of the user comfort parameters from the previous runs are missing, the HWMS is in the *calibration phase* as shown in Fig. 8. In this phase, the Scheduler requests 'Ctrlr. DB' to derive the needed inputs from the user via 'GUI' component. The needed input parameters consist of (a) user comfort preferences for the planned WAs, and (b) updated WAs schedules. The former inputs can be entered in the form of user comfort model parameters, though some of them can be automatically set within the system calibration phase.

As it can be seen in Fig. 8, the important role of the 'GUI' is to check the user feedback about the quality of hot water service provided. The user feedback feature of the 'GUI' is essential for correct provision of hot service with respect to the user's comfort choice and the amount of money (s)he is ready to pay for it. As such in the calibration phase, the 'GUI' can initiate a test program that tends to automatically tune the tap flow rate during the selected WAs, check the user response, and re-adjust some of the comfort model parameters.

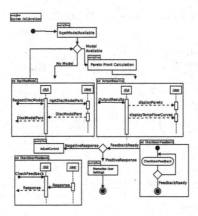

Fig. 8. System calibration phase.

The HWMS and the flow rate control that it implements delegate to the user the responsibility for making a decision concerning how realistic and comfortable the current user flow comfort model is and how much money to pay. Therefore, at this stage the system is fully user-centric and governed by the user's choice. It does not take decisions about how much comfort to provide and at what expense instead of the user, but it rather works out control actions based on the information from the user and offers different control alternatives to the user, assisting him in making a rational comfort-energy choice.

In the system calibration phase the controller utilizes the available user comfort model and information about estimated day-ahead WAs' to provide the user with a clear energy-comfort balancing mechanism, i.e. Pareto front. Pareto front is derived by the 'Scheduler' component of the HWMS by simultaneously resolving the objectives $min[F_1]$ and $min[F_2]$.

7   Performance Evaluation and Validation

Because the designed hot water management system (HWMS) highly relies on the information about the day-ahead hot water usage, we first of all evaluate how well are WAs' estimates extracted from the past observations of the tank water temperature.

Second, we validate how the multi-objective optimization problem represented in Eqs. (9)–(13) could attain the connection between the electricity consumption for pre-heating and flow comfort, retrieving Pareto fronts for several WAs regularly performed at home. The chosen WAs are listed together with their estimated flow rates and volume values [18,26,44] in Table 1.

We build Pareto fronts for the selected WAs with varied duration aiming to estimate the maximum and minimum values of the electric consumption and the resulting flow rate discomfort. The values used in these simulations are listed in Table 2.

Table 1. WAs selected for simulations.

WA	Volume, [L]	Estimated flow rate, [L/min]	Flow range, [L/min]
Wash Hands[a]	0.7 ... 7.5	6	2 ... 9
Dishwashing[b]	38 ... 75	9	6 ... 25
Shower[c]	32 ... 225	15	8 ... 25

[a] Bath tap, running water.
[b] Kitchen tap, running water.
[c] Mains fed.
Note: There is little statistical data on hot water usage per activity available. Some of the missing data per activity is replaced by data per water source location.

Table 2. Simulations of WAs with different duration

Duration, [min]	Comf. flow range, [L/min, L/min]	Flow tolerance, [L/min, L/min]	Temp. tolerance, [°C, °C]
0.5	[10,12]	[8,12]	[40,45]
7			
15			

We further carry out simulations for 7-minute WAs in distinct ranges of tap water temperatures and flow rates desired by the user while setting the fixed lower boundaries for the flow tolerance zones Δ_{tol}^- and Δ_{tol}^+ shown in Fig. 9(a).

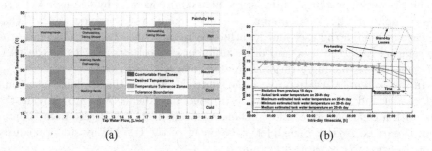

(a)   (b)

Fig. 9. (a) WAs & parameters used for simulations, (b) Estimated day-ahead tank water temperature.

Since the flow rate discomfort $D_{\dot{m}_d}$ depends on the size of the control step (term $A_{\dot{m}_d,i}$ in Eq. (8)), we also estimate the effect of altering the step size on $E_e(\Delta t_{\text{pre}})$ and $D_{\dot{m}_d}$. In addition, we show how $D_{\dot{m}_d}$ affects the thermal discomfort D_T following the discussion in Sect. 3.3.

7.1   Estimation of Day-Ahead Hot Water Usage

Using the solution of (1), we obtained the tank water temperature time-series based on the 1-minute hot water consumption profiles generated by the LPG software [36] for 20 working days. The time-series were downsampled to 20-minute time intervals to lower down the variability of the mean and variance. The statistics for 19 sequential days was derived and the last day was used as a reference for estimation as shown in Fig. 9(b).

The maximum estimated temperature in Fig. 9(b) was built based on the maximum positive STDs at time 00:20 and at 06:00. After 06:00 the slope coincides with the mean-slope obtained statistically from the previous 19 days. The minimum estimated temperature, on the other hand, was plotted based on maximum negative STDs at time 00:30, 06:00 and 07:00. The medium estimated temperature was constructed via the mean value at 00:20 and at 06:00, after 06:00 this temperature was a line through the difference between min and max temperature estimates at 06:20. The start-ups of the pre-heating procedures were calculated on the basis of (6).

7.2   Simulation Results

Pareto optimal solutions for WAs with different duration can be found in Fig. 10. The graphs represent the electric energy consumed for water preheating $E_e(\Delta t_{pre})$ as a function of the flow rate discomfort $D_{\dot{m}_d}$. The discomfort is shown in percentage as a share of the maximum $D_{\dot{m}_d}$ for the current parameters of water usage. The color of each solution on Pareto front refers to the certain range of tap water flows and the time during which the user experiences flow discomfort $D_{\dot{m}_d}$. The bar exhibits these values in the following format $[\dot{m}_{d, min}, \dot{m}_{d, max}], \Delta t_D$, which is the minimum and the maximum flows reached during the WA and the duration of $D_{\dot{m}_d}$. The two sequential solutions from Fig. 10(b) that have different $D_{\dot{m}_d}$ and equal $E_e(\Delta t_{pre})$ are plotted in Fig. 11.

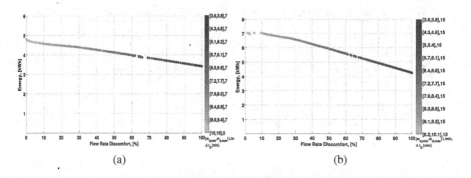

Fig. 10. Varied duration (a) 7-minute WA, (b) 15-minute WA.

The influence of the control step size on the flow discomfort $D_{\dot{m}_d}$ is demonstrated in Fig. 12. The thermal discomfort D_T has been calculated for every solution on Pareto front of the considered WAs. The connection between the thermal discomfort D_T and the flow rate discomfort $D_{\dot{m}_d}$, is represented for the 7-minute WA in Fig. 13(a). Colorful curve illustrates a number of Pareto optimal solutions where each color refers to a certain tap water temperature range $[T_{max}, T_{min}]$ and discomfort duration ΔT_{DISC} specified in the bar. Figure 13(b) shows how the relation between D_T and $D_{\dot{m}_d}$ depends on the control step size.

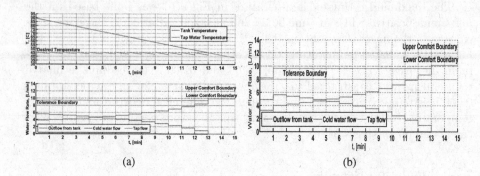

(a)   (b)

Fig. 11. 15-minute WA & fully charged tank (a) $D_{\dot{m}_d} = 10\%$, (b) $D_{\dot{m}_d} = 3\%$.

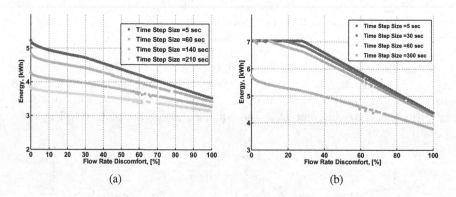

(a)   (b)

Fig. 12. Varied size of timesteps (a) 7-minute WA, (b) 15-minute WA.

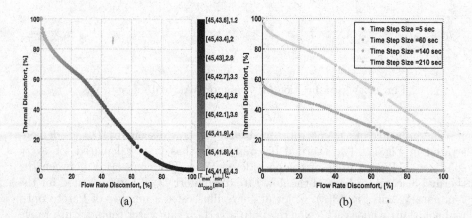

(a)   (b)

Fig. 13. Effect on thermal discomfort for 7-minute WA.

7.3   Discussion of Results

One can see from Fig. 9(b) that the estimated WA for the 20-th day would occur 1.67 h earlier than the actual WA, meaning that the pre-heating procedure would start also earlier. This early pre-heating does not *directly* impact the user thermal comfort during the WA, because the water can be still heated up to the maximum temperature of 90 °C prior to the hot water usage. However, such operation will cause extra heat losses to the ambient which in our case can account for up to 0.1 kWh with the maximum temperature drop in the tank of 1.1 °C. As a result, the user thermal comfort might be *indirectly* deteriorated. The temperature estimation errors within this interval are calculated as the difference between the medium estimated temperature and the actual tank water temperature and vary from 0.19 °C to 9.76 °C.

According to the set of Pareto optimal solutions shown in Fig. 10, the user can reduce $D_{\dot{m}_d}$ at the cost of the increased $E_e(\Delta t_{\text{pre}})$ and vice versa. This indicates a non-linear negative correlation between these functions.

It is noteworthy that in case of intensive water usage, the flow controller cannot handle the user request for the fixed temperature during the entire WA. For example, the tap water temperature inevitably drops within the last 2 min of the 15-minute WA as represented in Fig. 11(a). It can be explained by the limited capacity of the tank. Although the WH is pre-heated to the maximum temperature defined by safety reasons (90 °C in our case), the thermal energy accumulated in the tank is insufficient to provide the user with tap water of the preferred 45 °C along the whole WA.

As it can be seen from Fig. 10(b) minimization of $D_{\dot{m}_d}$ for long lasting WAs can be achieved without maximizing electric consumption. This situation takes place because the WH is fully charged and cannot be further heated. More rigorous examining of the neighbor solutions on Pareto front points out that such decrease of $D_{\dot{m}_d}$ results in a steep jump of the resulting tap water flow rate $\dot{m}_d$ as can be seen from Fig. 11. Such sudden increase of the water flow can bring extra inconvenience to the user and thus should be also taken into account during the flow control.

As it follows from the simulation results illustrated in Fig. 12, long time lags between the flow control actions allow to minimize $D_{\dot{m}_d}$ spending less electricity than in the case of the frequent flow regulation. While the extension of control steps has a positive effect on $D_{\dot{m}_d}$ and $E_e(\Delta t_{\text{pre}})$, it has a negative effect on the thermal discomfort D_T as shown in Fig. 13(b). The longer steps permit the water in the tank cool down to the lower temperature which results in the increase of D_T. Considering the contrary effects of the step size on the two types of discomfort and $E_e(\Delta t_{\text{pre}})$ a compromise between $D_{\dot{m}_d}$ and D_T can be achieved by incorporating D_T as the third objective function for the multi-objective optimization problem and finding the optimal timing for the flow control actions.

The obtained Pareto fronts in Fig. 10 represent a simple, yet efficient way to visualize the detailed information about multiple solutions for flow rate control and their effect on energy consumption and user comfort. By picking any of the suggested solutions on Pareto front via the GUI the user can further demand the indeep information about the expected water usage such as the resulting tap and tank water temperature values, water flow rates in the whole hot water supply system and duration of $D_{\dot{m}_d}$ at every moment of the expected WA, for example, as shown in Fig. 11.

8   Further Improvement of Day-Ahead WA Estimates

The forecasting of the tank water temperature can yield the information about the start times and duration of the upcoming WAs. Whereas the incline of the tank water temperature curve can serve as a good indicator of the intensity of hot water demand. Hence it can contribute to differentiation between intensive and non-intensive WAs. For example, the WA 'taking shower' creates a steep slope because it intensively withdraws the hot water from the tank. In complex scenarios of the flow control, where the variation of the hot water outflow from the WH is high, a daily tank water temperature curve might represent a more sophisticated tracery. Classification of these temperature patterns during WAs might be a step towards the WA identification.

The resulting time error in our naive WA estimation based on the day-ahead tank water temperature is relatively high and might negatively impact the end-user's thermal comfort maintained by the flow control. Furthermore, the high variation of the temperature errors in our naive WAs estimation can hinder differentiation of intense and non-intense WAs. To mitigate these errors, it is worthwhile to consider the autocorrelation of the tank water temperature at different points in time. Thus, autocorrelations for the considered training dataset of 19 working days looks like shown in Fig. 14(a).

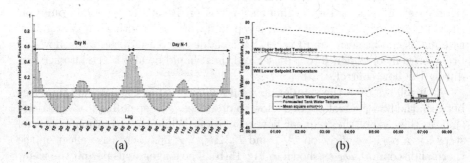

Fig. 14. (a) Autocorrelations, (b) ARIMA model output.

The meaningful autocorrelation lags in Fig. 14(a) signify the influence of the past data on future samples and can serve as an input for an autoregressive integrated moving average (ARIMA) model. The example of the ARIMA model is illustrated in Fig. 14(b). As it can be seen from Fig. 14(b), while the time estimation error has decreased from 1.67 h to 1.20 h, the mean square error of the ARIMA forecast is significantly high (8.95 °C). The potential of the ARIMA model to forecast the day-ahead WAs' timing seems persuasive and needs further investigation.

9   Future Work

The normal operation of the WH implies that the hot water outflow from the tank induces the equal inflow of cold water, which creates the needed pressure to deliver hot water to the tap and causes the insider WH temperature to drop. One might think of the ways to cut the cold water inflow in the WH so that the insider temperature remains fixed during WAs and there is sufficient pressure in the hot water pipe.

In our studies we applied a linear relationship to model how the user tolerates the aberrant tap water flow. The further research can concentrate on obtaining the realistic shapes of individual tolerance functions, which implies the involvement of external users in experiments. Once derived, these functions can be organized in a library that associates personal flow comfort of each inhabitant with a particular type of WAs performed in a house.

Some extra work on UI improvement and real-world testing can be also suggested. Learning Pareto 'curves' in a broad range of scenarios of water usage and organizing them in a knowledge base by different users' preferences and diverse water usage scenarios could make it possible to forsee water individual usage habits over a day and in the future to set the right trade-offs in an automated way without interrogating the user and only based on the obtained knowledge.

The scenario considered in this paper can be also adapted to double-rate tariffs in the future. For example, if the night price is lower than the day time electricity rate (e.g., Economy 7 in UK), then controller can preheat all the water in the period of lower energy cost.

10   Conclusion

In this paper we present a new possibility to balance electricity consumption for domestic water heating and user comfort represented by the personal satisfaction with the tap flow rate. Unlike conventional approaches that commonly treat comfort as a user content with only the tap water temperature, we regard comfort in light of both comfortable tap flow rate and temperature. Based on the scenario wherein the user desires the fixed water temperature, this paper specifically underscores how the flow rate comfort can influence electric energy consumption of a tank electric water heater and views the outflow from the tap as a controllable parameter.

In this light, we propose the control mechanism that consists of the preheating control and the flow control communicated to each other in a single scheme. While the pre-heating control ensures sufficient heat in the tank to enable the fixed tap water temperature requirement, the flow control is responsible for the fulfilment of such requirement during the hot water usage, managing the flows in the tap mixer and the user flow comfort at the appropriate level.

The suggested computational scheme links two controls together using the day-ahead forecast of hot water usage. The paper considers a naive approach to derive the estimates of start-times of the upcoming hot water activities based on the STDs and means of the past observations of the tank water temperature. Although the applied simple statistics has shown to be insufficient to accurately forecast the occurrence of the future hot water events, it has a clear potential for improvement in the form of autoregression models.

We capture the user discontent with the tap water flow through the metric that quantifies end-user dissatisfaction. This metric extends the comfort model presented previously in our works by considering the flow rate tolerance variable amongst different users.

The outcomes of the proposed control scheme represent a set of trade-offs between the electricity consumption and the corresponding levels of the flow rate comfort. It can be expected that based on this information the end-user can consciously limit the tap flow rate in certain scenarios of the hot water usage and thereby can gain energy/money savings. The paper has a special focus on how the available trade-off can be presented to the user. By simulating several home WAs we illustrate a powerful potential of Pareto fronts to meaningfully group and cross-relate multiplicity of different individual solutions.

In addition, the analysis of simulation results reveals that the flow control not only affects the flow rate comfort, but also it influences the thermal comfort at every control step. To reconcile two different by nature types of comfort, the size of the flow control steps should be optimally chosen.

Acknowledgment. We would like to express our gratitude to the Go-Green and JPI IRENE projects.

References

1. Ewz-studie smart metering project (2015). https://www.ewz.ch/smartmetering
2. United States Environmental Protection Agency (2015). http://www3.epa.gov/watersense/products/bathroom_sink_faucets.html
3. Belov, A., Vasenev, A., Meratnia, N., Havinga, P.J.: User interface for manual balancing of comfort and energy consumption of domestic water heaters. In: Proceedings of European Nearly Zero Energy Buildings Conference 2016. Energiesparverband, February 2016
4. Belov, A., Vasenev, A., Meratnia, N., van der Zwaag, B.J., Havinga, P.J.: Reducing user discomfort in direct load control of domestic water heaters. In: Proceedings of the 2015 IEEE Innovative Smart Grid Technologies - Asia (ISGT Asia), pp. 1–6. IEEE, November 2015. Online ISSN IEEE Xplore = 2378–8542
5. Belov, A., Meratnia, N., van der Zwaag, B.J., Havinga, P.J.: An efficient water flow control approach for water heaters in direct load control. J. Eng. Appl. Sci. **9**(11), 2106–2120 (2014)
6. Caramia, M., Dell'Olmo, P.: Multi-objective Management in Freight Logistics: Increasing Capacity Service Level and Safety with Optimization Algorithms. Springer, London (2008)
7. European Commission: Energy efficiency plan 2011, March 2011

8. European Commission: Smart grids: From innovation to deployment', communication from the commission to the european parliament (2011). http://eur-lex.europa.eu/LexUriServ/LexUriServ.do?uri=COM:2011:0202:FIN:EN:PDF
9. Federal Energy Regulatory Commission, et al.: Assessment of demand response and advanced metering (2006)
10. Crosswater Digital (2015). http://www.crosswater.co.uk
11. E.E. Directive: Directive 2009/72/ec of the European parliament and of the council of 13 July 2009 concerning common rules for the internal market in electricity. Offic. J. Eur. Comm. **211**, 55–93 (2009)
12. E.E. Directive: Directive 2010/31/eu of the European parliament and of the council of 19 May 2010 on on the energy performance of buildings. Offic. J. L, 1–35 (2010)
13. E.E. Directive: Directive 2012/27/eu of the European parliament and of the council of 25 October 2012 on energy efficiency, amending directives 2009/125/ec and 2010/30/eu and repealing directives 2004/8/ec and 2006/32. Offic. J. L **315**, 1–56 (2012)
14. Dlamini, N.G., Cromieres, F.: Implementing peak load reduction algorithms for household electrical appliances. Energy Policy **44**, 280–290 (2012)
15. US DOE: Energyplus engineering reference. The Reference to EnergyPlus Calculations (2013)
16. Dolan, P., Nehrir, M., Gerez, V.: Development of a monte carlo based aggregate model for residential electric water heater loads. Electric Power Syst. Res. **36**(1), 29–35 (1996)
17. Du, P., Lu, N.: Appliance commitment for household load scheduling. IEEE Trans. Smart Grid **2**(2), 411–419 (2011)
18. EngineeringToolbox: Average water usage per activity. http://www.engineeringtoolbox.com/water-use-activity-d_1900.html
19. EC Smart Grids Task Force: Task force for smart grids, vision and work programme. European commission (2010). https://ec.europa.eu/energy/en/topics/markets-and-consumers/smart-grids-and-meters/smart-grids-task-force
20. Giordano, V., Gangale, F., Fulli, G., Sanchez Jimenez, M.: Smart grid projects in Europe: lessons learned and current developments. European Commission, Joint Research Center. Institute for Energy, The Netherlands (2011)
21. Giorgio, A., Pimpinella, L.: An event driven smart home controller enabling consumer economic saving and automated demand side management. Appl. Energy **96**, 92–103 (2012)
22. C2G to Grid Project (2012). http://energyit.ict.tuwien.ac.at/projekte/abgeschlossene-projekte/53
23. Honeywell (2015). http://yourhome.honeywell.com
24. InterNACHI: Inspecting water heater tanks in residential dwelling units. Course document. Technical report, International Association of Certified Home Inspectors (2015)
25. Jorgensen, J., Sorensen, S., Behnke, K., Eriksen, P.B.: Ecogrid eua prototype for European smart grids. In: 2011 IEEE Power and Energy Society General Meeting, pp. 1–7. IEEE (2011)
26. Kaye, J.: Action a2a development of concept and offering renew: development of concept and offering. Technical report, Energy Saving Trust Limited, Waterwise Project (2009)
27. Kondoh, J., Lu, N., Hammerstrom, D.J.: An evaluation of the water heater load potential for providing regulation service. In: 2011 IEEE Power and Energy Society General Meeting, pp. 1–8. IEEE (2011)

28. Koutitas, G.: Control of flexible smart devices in the smart grid. IEEE Trans. Smart Grid **3**(3), 1333–1343 (2012)
29. Lane, I., Beute, N.: A model of the domestic hot water load. IEEE Trans. Power Syst. **11**(4), 1850–1855 (1996)
30. Lu, N., Katipamula, S.: Control strategies of thermostatically controlled appliances in a competitive electricity market. In: IEEE Power Engineering Society General Meeting, pp. 202–207. IEEE (2005)
31. Lu, N., Zhang, Y.: Design considerations of a centralized load controller using thermostatically controlled appliances for continuous regulation reserves. IEEE Trans. Smart Grid **4**(2), 914–921 (2013)
32. SETIS Magazine: Demand response - empowering the European consumer, March 2014. https://setis.ec.europa.eu/publications/setis-magazine/smart-grids/demand-response-empowering-european-consumer
33. Nest, P.A.: (2015). https://nest.com/uk/thermostat/meet-nest-thermostat/
34. Bertoldi, P., Hirl, B., Labanca, N.: Energy efficiency status report. Offic. J. L, 1–141 (2012)
35. Pedrasa, M.A., Spooner, E., MacGill, I.: Improved energy services provision through the intelligent control of distributed energy resources. In: 2009 IEEE Bucharest PowerTech, pp. 1–8. IEEE (2009)
36. Pflugradt, N.: Load profile generator - user manual (2015). http://www.loadprofilegenerator.de
37. E.S.M. Project (2011). http://www.esb.ie/main/sustainability/smart-meters.jsp
38. Robertson, V.J., Ward, A., Low, J., Reed, A.: Electrotherapy Explained: Principles and Practice. Elsevier Health Sciences, London (2006)
39. Sæle, H., Grande, O.S.: Demand response from household customers: experiences from a pilot study in norway. IEEE Trans. Smart Grid **2**(1), 102–109 (2011)
40. Sepulveda, A., Paull, L., Morsi, W.G., Li, H., Diduch, C., Chang, L.: A novel demand side management program using water heaters and particle swarm optimization. In: 2010 IEEE Electric Power and Energy Conference (EPEC), pp. 1–5. IEEE (2010)
41. Sharon Mecum, Q.C.: A wish list for residential direct load control customers. Panels of the 2002 ACEEE Summer Study on Energy Efficiency in Buildings (2002)
42. Stepon (2015). http://www.stepon.com.cn/en/ViewPro.aspx?PID=9
43. Viola, D.W.: Water Temperature Control and Limitation. Plumbing Manufacturers Institute, Schaumberg (2002)
44. Widén, J., Lundh, M., Vassileva, I., Dahlquist, E., Ellegård, K., Wäckelgård, E.: Constructing load profiles for household electricity and hot water from time-use data–modelling approach and validation. Energy Build. **41**(7), 753–768 (2009)

Characterizing Smart Grid Events
Using Clustering Methods

Eric Klinginsmith, Richard Barella, Xinghui Zhao$^{(\boxtimes)}$, and Scott Wallace

School of Engineering and Computer Science, Washington State University,
14204 NE Salmon Creek Ave., Vancouver, WA 98686, USA
{eric.klinginsmith,richard.t.barella,x.zhao,wallaces}@wsu.edu

Abstract. Phasor Measurement Units (PMUs) are widely used in smart grid to provide high-frequency, real-time measurements of the electrical waves, enabling wide-area monitoring and control. These devices generate a significant amount of data on a daily basis, which presents challenges for grid operators to leverage the useful information contained in this data. In this paper, we present an empirical study of applying unsupervised clustering on PMU data for event characterization on the smart grid. We show that although the PMU data are time series in nature, it is more efficient and robust to apply clustering methods on carefully selected features from the data collected at certain instantaneous moments in time. Experiments have been carried out on real PMU data collected by Bonneville Power Administration in their wide-area monitoring system in the pacific northwest, and the results show that our instantaneous clustering method achieves high homogeneity, which provides great potentials for identifying unknown events in the grid without substantial training data. In addition, we also present our initial effort in cluster-specific classification, which incorporates supervised learning in the process to classify event types within individual clusters.

Keywords: Smart grid · Phasor Measurement Unit (PMU) · Synchrophasors · Machine learning · Clustering · Event characterization

1 Introduction

The emerging smart grid technology provides opportunities to implement a more reliable, intelligent, and highly automated energy delivery network, harnessing the advances in communication and information technologies. A key component in the smart grid is the *Phasor Measurement Unit (PMU)*, or *synchrophasor*, which measures phase angles and magnitudes of the electrical waves in real time, at a high frequency, ranging from 30 measurements per second to hundreds of measurements per second. Data generated by these devices contain valuable information about the operation status of the power grid. A significant amount of work has been done to detect or monitor certain conditions of a power grid by leveraging information extracted from PMU data. Potential applications include fault

© Springer International Publishing AG 2017
M. Helfert et al. (Eds.): SMARTGREENS 2016 and VEHITS 2016, CCIS 738, pp. 75–96, 2017.
DOI: 10.1007/978-3-319-63712-9_4

detection [12], localization [10], tracking [4], and oscillation detection [14]. A comprehensive survey on various applications using PMU data can be found in [21].

Over the last 5 years, the PMU deployment has been significantly increased in the U.S., from 200 PMUs in 2009 [16] to approximately 1700 in 2014 [1]. However, with the number of PMUs rapidly increasing, the volume of the data generated by those PMUs presents challenges for efficient processing. An installation of 100 PMUs produces data in the scale of 3–4 TB per month, which will quickly become inaccessible for traditional workflow. A more automated and efficient approach for data processing is essential, in order to take advantage of the valuable information in PMU data. The efficiency of the data processing is even more critical for real-time monitoring of the power grid.

Machine learning techniques provide potentials for automated information extraction from large data sources, and therefore become the most widely used approach for address the big data challenge. Among machine learning techniques, clustering [3] is an exploratory approach which can potentially identify unknown signatures by grouping data objects based on their similarities. In this paper, we apply various clustering methods on PMU data streams collected from a large power grid in the pacific northwest. The goal is to explore the applicability of different clustering techniques in identifying known or unknown events which occur in the power grid.

The remainder of the paper is organized as follows. Section 2 reviews related work in applying machine learning techniques on PMU data. Section 3 introduces the dataset we use in this research, as well as the feature selection for the clustering methods. Section 4 presents our work in applying hierarchical clustering on PMU time series, and the experimental results. Section 5 presents a different approach for clustering instantaneous data, as well as experimental results. In Sect. 6, we present our initial efforts in implementing and evaluating cluster-specific classifiers, which incorporates supervised learning for classification purposes. Section 7 concludes the paper and proposes future directions for this research.

2   Related Work

PMUs are widely used to monitor the operational status of a power grid with the aim of enhancing the situation awareness for power system operators. A significant amount of work has been done to detect or monitor certain conditions of a power grid by leveraging information extracted from PMU data. Jiang et al. propose an online approach for fault detection and localization using SDFT (smart DFT) [10]. Liu et al. use Frequency Domain Decomposition for detecting oscillations [14]. Kazami et al. propose a multivariable regression model to track fault locations [4]. Besides voltage and current magnitudes, which are the most commonly used features in detecting faults, phase angle measurements can also be used in detecting outages [22].

Most recently, with the emergence of big data analytics, new technologies are introduced to PMU data storage and processing. Most importantly, a variety of machine learning techniques have been applied to analyze PMU data for the purpose of recognizing patterns or signatures of events. Two widely adopted techniques are classification and clustering.

Classification methods employ supervised learning and therefore, after training, can identify known signatures or patterns. In [15], Nguyen *et al.* develop a decision tree based on the J48 algorithm, for the purpose of detecting line events on the power grid using PMU data streams. Zhang *et al.* propose a classification method for finding fault locations based on pattern recognition [24]. The key idea is to distinguish a class from irrelevant data elements using linear discriminant analysis. The classification is carried out based on two types of features: nodal voltage, and negative sequence voltage. Similar classification techniques are used to detect voltage collapse [7] and disturbances [17] in power systems. Specifically, Diao et al. develop and train a decision tree using PMU data to assess voltage security [7]. Ray et al. build Support Vector Machines and decision tree classifiers based on a set of optimal features selected using a genetic algorithm [17]. Support Vector Machine-based classifiers can also be used to identify fault locations [20], and predict post-fault transient stability [9].

Although classification methods usually can provide high accuracy, they require a substantial amount of labeled data for training. Unlike classification, clustering methods with unsupervised learning do not require labeled training data. Antoine et al. propose to identify causes for inter-area oscillations by clustering a number of parameters provided by PMUs, including mode frequency, the voltage angle differences between areas and the mode shapes [2]. It has been shown that by clustering these parameters, changes in inter-area oscillations can be explained. Clustering methods have also been proven to be effective in identifying different types of disturbances [6].

In this paper, we investigate PMU data collected from a wide-area monitoring system, extract useful features, and evaluate different unsupervised clustering methods on PMU data for the purpose of events characterization. To the best of our knowledge, this is the first work which applies unsupervised clustering methods to real PMU data for this characterizing line events.

3   Datasets and Feature Selection

Our datasets were obtained from Bonneville Power Administration (BPA), one of the first transmission operators to adopt synchrophasor technology. In this section, we describe the datasets we use in this research, as well as the features we extracted for the clustering methods.

3.1   Datasets

BPA has provided two separate datasets to use. The first contains 31 locations from across the pacific northwest. These PMUs measure line and/or bus voltage across all three phases (A, B, and C). They also record positive sequence voltage and current phasors, frequency and rate-of-change of frequency. At each PMU, the data is recorded at 60 Hz. Measurements from this dataset are primarily from 500 KV and 230 KV buses, although a small number of lower voltage transmission lines are also covered. This dataset was collected from the period October 17, 2012 to September 16, 2013 and contains 114 documented faults that occur at a bus or on a transmission line instrumented with at least one PMU. The faults include instances of single-line-to-ground faults, line-to-line faults, three-phase faults, in that order of relative frequency, and no-fault data. The data set used for clustering contains 100 of the 114 documented fault events and 19 no fault events, i.e., 119 events in total. Since not all events or locations on the electrical grid have all the required data for calculating of the features required for our clustering, those events and locations were dropped. On average we gathered data at 56 different locations on the electrical grid for each of the 119 events, resulting in 6676 data points in total. Of the 6676 data points 4935 are Line to Ground faults, 331 are Line to Line, 196 are Three Phase, and 1214 are marked as No Fault.

The second dataset contains 41 locations also within the pacific northwest. They record the same data as the first at the same 60 Hz rate. Measurements are still primarily from 500 KV and 230 KV buses. Data was collected for the entire month of October 2014. Other than the date range in which it was collected the main difference between this dataset and the first one is that all electrical faults on the grid were included, not just the ones that occurred at a bus or on a transmission line instrumented with at least one PMU. Note that this dataset is only used in Case Study 3, i.e., Sect. 6, which requires substantial amounts of data for training purposes. A comparison of the two datasets is shown in Table 1.

Table 1. Overview of PMU datasets.

Dataset	# Locations	Data collection period	# Faults	Size
1	31	10-17-2012 to 09-16-2013	114	34 GB
2	41	10-01-2014 to 10-31-2014	26	1,271 GB

3.2 Feature Selection

In our datasets, the measurements recorded by the PMUs are voltage magnitude and phase angle (positive sequence and A, B, C phases), current magnitude and phase angle (positive sequence only), and frequency (60 Hz). It has been shown in previous work that the per-phase voltage magnitude is an effective measurement to identify different types of line events [12].

Figure 1 shows the per-phase voltage magnitude over time for two typical line events, single-line-to-ground fault, and line-to-line fault. Note that the voltage magnitude values are normalized based on the *steady state voltage*. As shown in Fig. 1, the voltage sags behave differently in different types of events, which provides potentials for separating events into different groups via clustering. This observation serves as the guideline for developing features for our the clustering method.

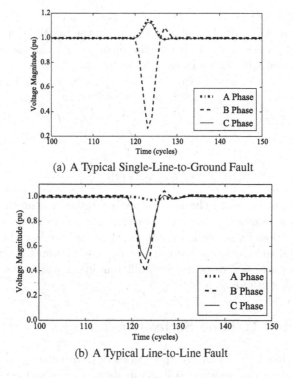

(a) A Typical Single-Line-to-Ground Fault

(b) A Typical Line-to-Line Fault

Fig. 1. Typical line events on a smart grid.

To enable efficient clustering in a two dimension space while retaining all the information contained in the three phase voltage magnitudes, we developed two new features, *RelativePhase2over1*, and *RelativePhase3over1*, by synthesizing the three per-phase voltage values. These two features are calculated in 3 steps. First, we calculate the relative phase deviations (RP) from steady state for three phases, as shown in Eqs. 1, 2 and 3.

$$RP_a = |1.0 - \frac{v_a}{ss_a}| \tag{1}$$

$$RP_b = |1.0 - \frac{v_b}{ss_b}| \tag{2}$$

$$RP_c = |1.0 - \frac{v_c}{ss_c}| \tag{3}$$

In the above equations, v values are per-phase voltage magnitudes, ss values are steady state voltages on the corresponding phases, and the values are normalized based on the steady state voltages. We then sort these relative phase deviations in ascending order, resulting in a tuple, as shown in Eq. 4.

$$[RP_3, RP_2, RP_1] = sort([RP_a, RP_b, RP_c]) \tag{4}$$

Note that sorting the relative phase deviations simplifies the complexity of our feature space. Although by doing that we lose the information about deviations on specific phases, the relative deviation magnitudes among three phases are captured, which still enable us to differentiate fault types.

In the last step, we use the values in the relative phase deviation tuple to calculate the two new features, as shown in Eqs. 5 and 6.

$$RelativePhase2over1 = \frac{RP_2}{RP_1} \tag{5}$$

$$RelativePhase3over1 = \frac{RP_3}{RP_1} \tag{6}$$

These two features retain the information contained in the three per-phase voltage values, yet provide a simplified two dimensional space for the clustering methods. In addition, by normalizing the magnitudes based on the steady state voltages, we eliminate the bias introduced by the absolute magnitude deviations, so that the characteristics, or patterns of different events can be better captured by the clustering methods.

4   Case Study 1: Time Series Clustering

Given the fact that PMU data are time series data in nature, we have applied the time series clustering method [13] to our dataset. The technical details and experimental results are described in this section.

4.1   Data Processing and Distance Metric

Time series clustering takes data on a window of time as one data entry. For our case, one data entry is a time window of data collected by one PMU. This approach provides an opportunity for clustering based on the shape of the event over time, instead of a single data point. However, events with longer duration present challenges in data handling. To simplify the data processing without losing the advantages of time series clustering, we have applied the widely used Piecewise Aggregate Approximation (PAA) [11] to reduce the number of points in each time window. Specifically, each data window is divided into n time slices. Then, the mean of each time slice is calculated. These mean values are used to replace of the actual data collected during the corresponding time slices.

Another challenge in time series clustering is to define a meaningful similarity metric of two data entries. One basic method is to calculate the euclidean distance between the two time series. However, this method can be inaccurate, as the same event can appear at different sites where one site sees the fault a few cycles after the other, which results in the time series of the two sites to be out of sync. Therefore, it is critical to use a method that can take slight offsets in time into account. To this end, we utilize Dynamic Time Warping (DTW) [11], a well researched solution to this problem. DTW aligns the sequences by locally stretching and shrinking one sequence to obtain the optimal fit to the other sequence and then calculates their relative distance given the optimal alignment. This causes the time series to be compared in a non-linear fashion instead of in lock-step.

4.2 Clustering Results

For clustering, we chose the hierarchical clustering algorithm [18], because it is the most suitable method for the time series model, and it allows customized distance metric, for which we used the DTW distance metric described above.

In order to apply the hierarchical clustering method to our data, we need to transform each event into time series data with a fixed window size. Since most of the line events in our dataset last approximately 6 cycles (1/10th of a second), we choose a window size of 10, which gives us extra space to capture steady state data before and after the event. Specifically, we process each event as follows. First, for each event which lasts less than 8 cycles, we add steady state data to both sides until the duration is greater or equal to 8. Second, we perform PAA [11] with a window size of 8 to each event, so that the data is divided into 8 slices, or time steps. Third, we add a steady state data point to each side of the event, forming a time series data with a fixed size 10.

After obtaining the 10 time steps for each event, we calculate the features described in Sect. 3.2 for each time step. Finally we apply the hierarchical clustering method on these data points. Due to the limited space of the paper, we only present the result time step 5. We chose time step 5 because it is located in the middle of the event window, and carries the most representative features of the event. The clustering result for this time step is shown in Fig. 2. Different colors represent different groups of data entries. To associate the groups generated by the clustering method with the event types in our dataset, we have calculated the percentage breakdown of each event type in the 4 groups, and the results are shown in Table 2.

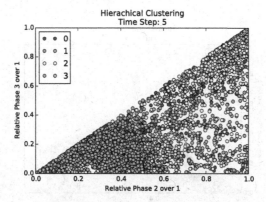

Fig. 2. Hierarchical clustering at time step 5.

Table 2. Time series hierarchical clustering % breakdown.

	LG	LL	TP	NF
0	14.08%	9.37%	44.39%	28.25%
1	14.23%	29.00%	11.23%	29.41%
2	18.70%	38.37%	35.71%	40.94%
3	52.99%	23.26%	8.67%	1.40%

As shown in the results, half of the single-line-to-ground (LG) events are clustered in group 3 while the rest are split among the other three groups. Majority of the Line-to-line (LL) events are split among three groups 1, 2, and 3. Majority of the three-phase (TP) events are split among groups 0 and 2. Finally, most of the no-fault (NF) data entries are split between groups 0, 1, and 2. Overall, hierarchical clustering on PMU time series data does not work well, which can be reflected by the low homogeneity score of 0.156. Note that the homogeneity score [19] is a metric indicating how well data points which belong to the same class are assigned to the same cluster. A perfectly homogeneous solution has a homogeneity score of 1.

Since it has been shown that the combined voltage deviations, as illustrated in Eq. 7, is an effective metric for representing the impact of the event on the PMU site [12]. A greater value of ΔV represents higher impact of an event on a PMU. In order to remove the events which occur at locations that are far away from the PMUs, we filtered our dataset by removing all the data entries with ΔV values less than 0.018, a threshold suggested in [12]. After this filtering process, our dataset contains 2211 data points. That is to say, 4462 data points are filtered out. These data points are signals captured by PMUs which are far away from the location where the event occurred.

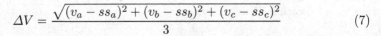

$$\Delta V = \frac{\sqrt{(v_a - ss_a)^2 + (v_b - ss_b)^2 + (v_c - ss_c)^2}}{3} \tag{7}$$

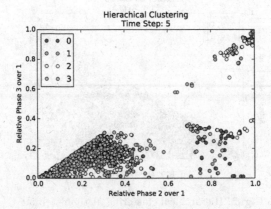

Fig. 3. Hierarchical clustering on filtered data at time step 5.

Table 3. Time series with ΔV filter hierarchical clustering % breakdown.

	LG	LL	TP	NF
0	15.24%	44.36%	0.00%	0.00%
1	19.52%	21.77%	31.43%	0.00%
2	27.80%	15.32%	58.10%	33.33%
3	37.44%	18.55%	10.47%	66.67%

We then carried out the hierarchical clustering on the filtered dataset, and the results are shown in Fig. 3 and Table 3.

The results of the hierarchical clustering on filtered dataset are similar to those on the original dataset, with an even lower homogeneity score of 0.027. This indicates that although PMU data are time series, it is challenging to apply clustering methods on these time series.

5   Case Study 2: Instantaneous Clustering

Besides time series clustering, an alternative solution is to represent each event using one single data point at an instantaneous moment in time, and apply clustering methods on these data points. In this section, we describe our work in this direction.

5.1   Data Processing

In order to apply instantaneous clustering methods to our data, we first need to choose a data point to represent each event. As shown in the typical line events in Fig. 1, the best candidate is the moment when the maximum voltage deviation is reached. However, even though a given site may have a minimum at a given cycle, that does not guarantee that another site's minimum is located at the same cycle. Instead of choosing one site to represent all sites we developed a better method that takes all sites into account. In our method all sites vote on what cycle they say is the minimum cycle of a given fault. The cycle with the most votes from the sites is the one that is chosen. This method allows us to get the point in time where we see the largest deviation for the most sites. Note that in order to take into consideration all three phases, we use the metric ΔV shown in Eq. 7 in the voting process. In other words, for each event, the cycle during which the largest number of sites observe their greatest ΔV value is chosen to represent that event across the grid. We then apply instantaneous clustering methods on these data points.

5.2   Clustering Results

For instantaneous clustering, we choose two widely used methods, k-means [23] and DBSCAN (Density Based Spatial Clustering of Applications with Noise) [8] to perform the clustering on our data points described above, based on the two features presented in Sect. 3.2.

The results of the k-means clustering are shown in Fig. 4. The data points are divided into 4 different groups, each of which is represented by a different color. The percentage breakdown for different even types are shown in Table 4.

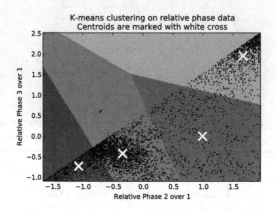

Fig. 4. K-means clustering on instantaneous data.

Table 4. K-means clustering % breakdown.

	LG	LL	TP	NF
Blue	1.72%	0.60%	98.98%	74.79%
Gray	64.84%	7.86%	0.00%	4.53%
Orange	3.49%	91.54%	1.02%	20.02%
Brown	29.95%	0.00%	0.00%	0.66%

In general, k-means clustering performs well in separating different events into groups. Particularly, three-phase (TP) events are well isolated from the rest event types. However, some single-line-to-ground (LG) events are mixed with line-to-line (LL) events, and the no-fault (NF) data points are separated into two main groups. Note that the over all homogeneity score of k-means clustering on the instantaneous PMU data is 0.60, showing a major improvement over the hierarchical clustering on time series data.

We then applied the density-based DBSCAN clustering method on the same dataset, and the results are shown in Fig. 5 and Table 5.

When using DBSCAN the user does not provide the number of clusters. Instead the algorithm breaks down the data into as many clusters as it sees fit. On top of this it also adds an additional cluster for what DBSCAN has determined to be noise in the data. In this case DBSCAN divided the data into 16 groups. Despite the large number of groups, DBSCAN performs well

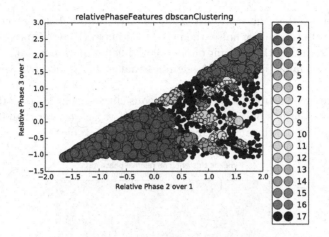

Fig. 5. Relative phase features.

Table 5. DBSCAN clustering % breakdown.

	LG	LL	TP	NF
1	95.16%	8.16%	0.00%	5.93%
2	1.62%	0.60%	98.98%	69.44%
3	0.55%	3.32%	0.00%	0.66%
4	0.00%	4.23%	0.00%	0.08%
5	0.04%	15.11%	0.00%	0.41%
6	0.10%	0.00%	0.00%	1.40%
7	0.16%	8.46%	0.00%	0.66%
8	0.04%	6.65%	0.00%	0.00%
9	0.00%	0.00%	0.00%	0.74%
10	0.04%	0.00%	0.00%	1.32%
11	0.00%	9.67%	0.00%	0.16%
12	0.63%	0.00%	0.00%	1.48%
13	0.00%	5.74%	0.00%	0.00%
14	0.06%	0.00%	0.00%	0.91%
15	0.02%	0.00%	0.00%	0.91%
16	0.10%	0.00%	0.00%	0.33%
Noise	1.48%	38.07%	1.02%	15.57%

in dividing LG and TP from the other two type of events. However, instead of grouping LL into a single cluster, DBSCAN has divided it into 7 groups. Also, most of the LL data are identified as noise. Most of the No Fault data points are grouped in the same cluster as TP, but a good portion of it is also marked as noise. This clustering has a homogeneity of 0.628.

We observed that there is quite a bit of data being labeled as noise. If we could reduce the amount of noise, then that could help DBSCAN preform better. In addition, reducing the amount of noise could help separate no fault data from TP. With most faults a higher ΔV signifies that signal is closer to the location of the fault.

Therefore, we execute the two instantaneous clustering method on the filtered dataset which contains only data points with ΔV values greater than 0.018. The clustering results of k-means are shown in Fig. 6 and Table 6.

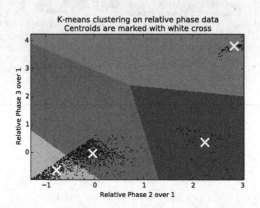

Fig. 6. K-means clustering on filtered instantaneous data. (Color figure online)

Table 6. Filtered K-means clustering % breakdown.

	LG	LL	TP	NF
Blue	37.18%	0.00%	0.00%	0.00%
Gray	0.56%	0.81%	100%	100%
Orange	62.21%	0.00%	0.00%	0.00%
Brown	0.05%	99.19%	0.00%	0.00%

The results here show some improvements over those on the non-filtered data, although LG is still split between two clusters. LL is predominately in one cluster. Interestingly, all of TP is in a single cluster with all NF data points. This is because that after the ΔV filtering, only a small number of NF data points are left in the dataset. The homogeneity score of this method is 0.932, much higher than the results on the non-filtered dataset.

On the same filtered dataset, we have also applied the DBSCAN clustering method, and the results are shown in Fig. 7 and Table 7.

Comparing to the results on the original dataset, this set of results show significant improvement, because the filtering help remove most of the noise. With the filter DBSCAN preformed excellently well, illustrated by its homogeneity

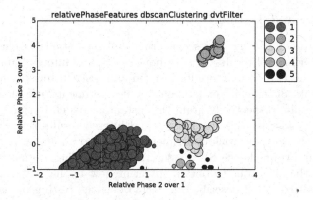

Fig. 7. Relative phase features.

Table 7. Filtered DBSCAN clustering % breakdown.

	LG	LL	TP	NF
1	99.34%	0.00%	0.00%	0.00%
2	0.56%	0.81%	100%	100%
3	0.00%	84.68%	0.00%	0.00%
4	0.00%	6.45%	0.00%	0.00%
Noise	0.10%	8.06%	0.00%	0.00%

score of 0.933. It was able to cluster most of LG in cluster 1, LL in cluster 3 and 4, and all of TP in cluster 2. Similar to the k-means method, No Fault data are mixed with TP in cluster 2, because of the limited number of data samples after the filtering.

6   Case Study 3: Cluster-Specific Classification

The case studies presented in Sects. 4 and 5 demonstrate the effectiveness of clustering methods to categorize PMU data on the smart gird into groups based on a known taxonomy. In this section, we present our effort in applying a supervised learning method on the clustering results for classifying event types within individual clusters. Specifically, we use clustering as a prepossessing step to generate training data for a set of cluster-specific Support Vector Machines (SVMs) [5] to perform the classification task. SVM is a supervised machine learning model that learns a set of vectors within the feature space that separate different class of data. We believe that by doing this we can achieve similar accuracy to that of a single SVM trained on the entire dataset as opposed to cluster-specific classifiers trained on a portion of the dataset. This would demonstrate the clustering's ability to select good subsets for training and ultimately lead to a higher accuracy relative to the training sample size.

6.1   Training and Testing Datasets

In the case studies of time series clustering and instantaneous clustering, we presented experimental results on both non-filtered and filtered data. This case study uses each of these four results to train and test cluster-specific SVMs in four experiments. Specifically, experiment 1 and experiment 2 use the non filtered and filtered results respectively, from the instantaneous clustering; experiment 3 and experiment 4 use the non filtered and filtered results respectively from time series clustering. For each experiment we created a number of SVMs (one per cluster), and trained each SVM using the data residing in its corresponding cluster. Note that in order to obtain sufficient new testing data, in this case study, we used dataset 2 described in Sect. 3.1 as the testing dataset. Within this testing set there are 26 line events. Some signals are not available for every event. On average each event is recorded at about 217 different PMUs on the power grid. In total this test set has 5631 data points, in which 3243 are LG faults, 1956 are LL faults, and 432 are TP faults. There are 0 NF data points in this dataset. For each experiment we collected data from this dataset using the same methods as the training set. For experiments 2 and 4 we also applied the same filter to the test dataset that was applied to the training set prior to clustering. This filtered testing dataset contains 888 data points. 762 are LG faults, 51 are LL, 75 are TP, and 0 are NF. In order for us to test the SVMs, we must split the test set into clusters, so that each SVM could be tested on data that belongs to the same cluster it was trained on. To this end, a nearest neighbor approach is used to determine which cluster a given point belongs to. This is a reasonable approach, because each datapoint in the testing set is very likely to be clustered with the datapoint in the training set that it is closest to. Note that in all four of these experiments a linear kernel was used for all SVMs. We chose not to use parameter fitting methods to avoid potential bias on our results.

6.2   Experiment 1: Classification on Instantaneous Clusters (Non Filtered)

This experiment trained 17 SVMs on the non-filtered dataset from case study 2 and then tested those SVMs on the second dataset detailed in Sect. 3 and further broken down in Sect. 6.1. The non-filtered dataset from case study 2 is made up of 17 clusters, however, 3 clusters could not be used for testing because the testing set does not contain data that belongs to those clusters. Specifically, we are not able to test clusters 12, 14, and 16. The accuracy of all 14 SVMs are given in Table 8. We also created a 15th SVM that was trained and tested on the entire training and testing sets respectively. This SVM's is listed as "All" in Table 8.

As shown in Table 8, most SVMs do not perform well in terms of accuracy. There are a few that do well, resulting in a total accuracy of 69%. The All SVM also gets an accuracy of 69%. However, the All SVM is trained on all the data, while the cluster-specific SVMs are only trained on a fraction of the dataset

Table 8. Experiment 1 SVM summary.

SVM number	Accuracy	# Training points	# Testing points
1	0.88	4795	2928
2	0.67	45	36
3	0.00	1119	531
4	**0.96**	57	585
5	**1.00**	24	90
6	0.80	49	15
7	0.03	46	264
8	0.00	34	15
9	0.00	14	12
10	**1.00**	14	6
11	0.00	22	3
13	0.78	19	54
15	0.00	12	6
17	0.50	390	1086
Total	0.69	6640	5631
All	0.69	6676	5631

(one cluster). It should be noted that some of the most accurate SVMs, specifically 4, 5, and 10, where trained on a relatively small portion of the dataset. This shows that in some cases clustering does provide latent information that may be useful to training SVMs on smaller datasets.

For comparison purposes we also used a pseudo random number generator to randomly split our training and testing data into 17 clusters. We then trained and tested 17 new SVMs on these randomly clustered datapoints. The accuracy breakdown is also given in Table 9. Overall, the accuracy of these SVMs trained and tested on randomly clustered datapoints is 56%, 13% less than the clustered dataset. In addition, the randomly clustered data was much better distributed and some SVMs in this method were given more datapoints to train on, yet cluster-specific classifiers achieved similar accuracy. This shows that cluster-specific classifiers can perform better with less training data. However, there are still quite a few clusters that do poorly under similar, more in some cases, amounts of training data. We believe that this demonstrates that the clustering itself is doing most of the work and that the SVMs in most cases are just classifying test points as the same class as the majority class of the training data. This is interesting, because it informs us that the SVMs that do well demonstrate that data within these clusters in our feature space are very good indicators of a particular class.

Table 9. Experiment 1 random cluster SVM summary.

SVM number	Accuracy	# Training points	# Testing points
1	0.58	393	332
2	0.57	393	332
3	0.56	393	332
4	0.51	393	332
5	0.56	393	331
6	0.58	393	331
7	0.67	393	331
8	0.62	393	331
9	0.57	393	331
10	0.49	393	331
11	0.59	393	331
12	0.54	393	331
13	0.54	392	331
14	0.59	392	331
15	0.57	392	331
16	0.54	392	331
17	0.45	392	331
Total	0.56	6676	5631

6.3   Experiment 2: Classification on Instantaneous Clusters (Filtered)

Experiment 2 uses filtered data from case study 2 to train 3 SVMs. The accuracy for all three SVMs is shown in Table 10. As in the previous experiment, an additional SVM was trained and tested on the entire filtered dataset. This result is also listed in Table 10 under "All".

Table 10. Experiment 2 SVM summary.

SVM number	Accuracy	# Training points	# Testing points
1	0.40	123	129
2	**1.00**	1971	678
3	**0.93**	120	81
Total	**0.91**	2214	888
All	**0.91**	2214	888

This experiment is much more successful at classification than experiment 1, however, this is due to the fact that SVM 2 was trained on a cluster containing a single classification. Therefore, all testing data that belongs to cluster 2 are classified as that class. The high accuracy shows that cluster 2 is very good in identifying that classes, however SVM 1 does very poorly with an accuracy of 40%. While this method gets a generally high accuracy of 91% it may not do well under different circumstances. Again the accuracy of the single SVM over all the data gets exactly the same accuracy of 91%, similar to experiment 1. In addition, SVM1 has a similar amount of training data to that of SVM 3, and yet there is a 53% difference in accuracy. Therefore, we can conclude that the clustering is able to identify good points for training and testing for SVM 3 while it is not optimal for SVM1.

Again, we have also trained and tested an additional 3 SVMs for this experiment on data that has been randomly clustered. A summary of the accuracies is shown in Table 11. These SVMs overall perform similarly to cluster-specific SVMs. Under this method SVM 1's accuracy is improved from 40% to 91% while the cluster-specific method has better accuracy for SVM's 2 and 3. This shows that cluster 1 requires more divers training data in order for an SVM to be an effective classifier while in the case of clusters 2 and 3 clustering can be used to increase classification accuracy, even under fewer training samples which is the case with SVM 3. However again, when we further investigated the testing we found that all three SVMs classify the entire testing set as a given class. This continues to support the idea that the SVMs are not doing any actual work and instead the clustering is achieving a high accuracy.

Table 11. Experiment 2 random cluster SVM summary.

SVM number	Accuracy	# Training points	# Testing points
1	**0.91**	738	296
2	**0.90**	738	296
3	**0.91**	738	296
Total	**0.91**	2214	888

6.4 Experiment 3: Classification on Time Series Clusters (Non Filtered)

The previous two experiments, while vaguely promising, do not perform well. We speculate that the major issue is a lack of diversity in the training sets. DBSCAN does well to split the data into homogeneous clusters, but because the clusters are so homogeneous there is a lack of data from other classes for the SVMs to train on. Therefore, when testing data is introduced that contains data that a given SVM has trained very little on it is not surprising to see those data points being misclassified. In contrast, the time-series clusters are not very homogeneous, this implies that they may make better training sets because of the diversity of classes within the clusters. In addition, the clustering while not homogeneous may have discovered a relationship in the similarity of the data it clustered. Therefore, in the next two experiments we explore if training on time-series data clusters can improve classification. This third experiment specifically trains on the results from the non-filtered clustering of case study 1. These SVMs are then tested on the same testing dataset as the first experiment only this time the entire 10-cycle window is used to determine what cluster the data point is closest to. We used DTW as our similarity metric when categorizing which cluster each testing data point belongs to. SVMs expect data to be organized as a single vector of scalar values. To accommodate this trait we used cycle 5 of the 10-cycle window for training and testing because cycle 5 represents the middle of the window which is the point at which the deviations should be at their maximum. The accuracy breakdown is shown in Table 12.

Table 12. Experiment 3 SVM summary.

SVM number	Accuracy	# Training points	# Testing points
1	0.48	1156	777
2	0.56	1177	1293
3	0.58	1617	1371
4	0.72	2726	2190
Total	0.62	6676	5631
All	0.63	6676	5631

Although the clustering for this experiment has a low homogeneous score, SVMs ultimately perform much better with a total accuracy of 62%. This shows that while the clustering, from a homogeneous stand point, is not optimal, the performance can be greatly improved using a cluster-specific classifier. However, this result is very similar to the single SVM with an accuracy of 63%. Cluster 4 performs well with an accuracy of 72% even though it was trained on a fraction of the data.

In addition, four SVMs were trained and tested on randomly clustered data. The accuracy summaries are given in Table 13. Overall, cluster-specific classifiers are more accurate by 4%. The amount of training data is also very similar. This is due to time series clustering behaving more randomly and therefore performing similarly to that of random clustering. Unlike the previous two experiments the confusion matrices of this experiment do classify testing data as multiple classes. This shows that the SVMs are doing some additional work. This is expected as the training data provided to these SVMs are not dominated by a single class.

Table 13. Experiment 3 random cluster SVM summary.

SVM number	Accuracy	# Training points	# Testing points
1	0.60	1669	1408
2	0.57	1669	1408
3	0.65	1669	1408
4	0.50	1669	1407
Total	0.58	6676	5631

6.5   Experiment 4: Classification on Time Series Clusters (Filtered)

In this last experiment we used the filtered clustering results from case study 1 to train five SVMs. These SVMs were tested by filtering the test set from experiment 3. The overview table is given in Table 14.

Table 14. Experiment 4 SVM summary.

SVM number	Accuracy	# Training points	# Testing points
1	0.72	357	129
2	0.85	447	237
3	0.88	632	207
4	**0.97**	778	315
Total	0.88	2214	888
All	0.88	2214	888

This result is actually the most promising one as it has a total accuracy of 88%. This is lower than that of experiment 2, however, overall it is superior because it does not rely on SVMs trained exclusively on data from one class, therefore, we believe that it can be applied to a broader range of data. The other promising result is that there is no single cluster with a low accuracy, unlike experiment 2 which had a SVM with 40% accuracy. The SVM trained over all the data has exactly the same accuracy of 88%.

Finally, just as in previous experiments, we explore training on random cluster SVMs. The summary breakdown is shown in Table 15. The randomized clustering method was very similar to the non-random approach. Overall it is only a 1% improvement making it practically the same. This result is very similar to experiment 2 in which the total accuracy of both the random clustering and non random clustering methods resulted in nearly the same accuracy. Again, time series clustering results in a similar amount of training data in comparison to random clustering. In addition, a majority of the SVMs do classify test data into multiple classes. Therefore, the SVMs do additional work in classifying the testing dataset, yet they perform no better than random clustering, especially when considering the amount of data used in training.

Table 15. Experiment 4 random cluster SVM summary.

SVM number	Accuracy	# Training points	# Testing points
1	0.86	554	222
2	0.86	554	222
3	0.89	553	222
4	**0.94**	553	222
Total	0.89	2214	888

6.6   Summary

In all cases the single SVM performed just as well if not better than the cluster-specific classifiers. In experiments 1 and 2 clustering performs just as well as the total accuracy of all SVMs including the single SVM. However, most SVMs classify the testing data into a single class showing that the clustering itself is doing most of the work to classify the data. In some cases these SVMs achieve a very high accuracy. This demonstrates that these regions of the feature space are very good at identifying a given classification. On the other hand, experiments 3 and 4 outperform time series clustering. In both experiment 1 and 3, cluster-specific classification outperformed random cluster classification, while experiments 2 and 4 performed similarly to random clustering. Instantaneous clustering is more adapt at discovering specific clusters that provide high accuracy based on the clustering alone while other SVMs score poorly due to a lack of diversity in the data. On the other hand, time series clustering does provide a more diverse dataset for training, but it does not perform much better overall than the random clustering method. This leads us to conclude that cluster-specific classifiers are not an improvement over a single SVM trained on the entire dataset, in terms of accuracy, although some cluster-based SVMs require significantly less training data to achieve similar results and filtered data does not perform any better than random clustering. In addition, we conclude that, in the case of instantaneous clustering, SVMs trained on the clusters, in general, do not classify data into more than one class, leading us to believe that the clustering itself is achieving the accuracy of the classification.

7   Conclusion

Synchrophasor technology is widely used in modern power systems, resulting in increasing amounts of data being generated on a daily basis. Machine learning methods represent the future directions in processing these data. Although supervised learning methods have been applied for this purpose, in order to prepare the training datasets for those methods, labeling data requires a significant amount of effort.

In this paper, we present our experience in applying unsupervised clustering methods on PMU data collected on a smart grid. We have evaluated multiple clustering methods on two distinct representations of PMU data: time series and instantaneous data points. Specifically, hierarchical clustering method is used to cluster time series data, and both k-means and DBSCAN are used to cluster instantaneous data points. Interestingly, although PMU data are time series data in nature, our results show that clustering on instantaneous data points with carefully selected features performs much better in terms of homogeneity score. Among all the clustering methods we have evaluated, DBSCAN achieves the highest homogeneity score. This work demonstrates potentials of identifying unknown events on a smart grid without substantial training data. In addition, we also present our initial efforts in event classification using cluster-specific SVMs which are trained on individual clusters. For future work, we will apply the clustering methods on a dataset which contains unknown events, namely generator faults, for the purpose of characterizing new events.

Acknowledgments. The authors would like to thank the Department of Energy/ Bonneville Power Administration for their generous support through the Technology Innovation Program (TIP# 319) and for providing the PMU data used in this study.

References

1. Americans for a Clean Energy Grid: Synchrophasors (2014). http:// cleanenergytransmission.org/wp-content/uploads/2014/08/Synchrophasors. pdf. Accessed 08 Sep 2015
2. Antoine, O., Maun, J.C.: Inter-area oscillations: identifying causes of poor damping using phasor measurement units. In: Power and Energy Society General Meeting, pp. 1–6. IEEE (2012)
3. Bailey, K.: Numerical taxonomy and cluster analysis. Typologies Taxonomies **34**, 24 (1994)
4. Chang, G., Chao, J.P., Huang, H.M., Chen, C.I., Chu, S.Y.: On tracking the source location of voltage sags and utility shunt capacitor switching transients. IEEE Trans. Power Delivery **23**(4), 2124–2131 (2008)
5. Cortes, C., Vapnik, V.: Support-vector networks. Mach. Learn. **20**(3), 273–297 (1995)
6. Dahal, O.P., Brahma, S.M., Cao, H.: Comprehensive clustering of disturbance events recorded by phasor measurement units. IEEE Trans. Power Delivery **29**(3), 1390–1397 (2014)
7. Diao, R., Sun, K., Vittal, V., O'Keefe, R., Richardson, M., Bhatt, N., Stradford, D., Sarawgi, S.: Decision tree-based online voltage security assessment using PMU measurements. IEEE Trans. Power Syst. **24**(2), 832–839 (2009)
8. Ester, M., Kriegel, H.P., Sander, J., Xu, X.: A density-based algorithm for discovering clusters in large spatial databases with noise. In: KDD, vol. 96, pp. 226–231 (1996)
9. Gomez, F.R., Rajapakse, A.D., Annakkage, U.D., Fernando, I.T.: Support vector machine-based algorithm for post-fault transient stability status prediction using synchronized measurements. IEEE Trans. Power Syst. **26**(3), 1474–1483 (2011)
10. Jiang, J.A., Yang, J.Z., Lin, Y.H., Liu, C.W., Ma, J.C.: An adaptive PMU based fault detection/location technique for transmission lines–part I: theory and algorithms. IEEE Trans. Power Delivery **15**(2), 486–493 (2000)

11. Keogh, E.J., Pazzani, M.J.: Scaling up dynamic time warping for datamining applications. In: Proceedings of the 6th ACM SIGKDD International Conference on Knowledge Discovery and Data Mining, pp. 285–289. ACM (2000)
12. Liang, X., Wallace, S., Zhao, X.: A technique for detecting wide-area single-line-to-ground faults. In: Proceedings of the 2nd IEEE Conference on Technologies for Sustainability (SusTech 2014), pp. 1–4. IEEE (2014)
13. Liao, T.W.: Clustering of time series data–a survey. Pattern Recogn. **38**(11), 1857–1874 (2005)
14. Liu, G., Venkatasubramanian, V.: Oscillation monitoring from ambient PMU measurements by frequency domain decomposition. In: IEEE International Symposium on Circuits and Systems (ISCAS 2008), pp. 2821–2824, May 2008
15. Nguyen, D., Barella, R., Wallace, S., Zhao, X., Liang, X.: Smart grid line event classification using supervised learning over PMU data streams. In: Proccedings of the 6th IEEE International Green and Sustainable Computing Conference (2015)
16. North American Electric Reliability Corporation: Real-Time Application of Synchrophasors for Improving Reliability (2014). http://www.nerc.com/docs/oc/rapirtf/RAPIR%20final%20101710.pdf. Accessed 08 Sep 2015
17. Ray, P.K., Mohanty, S.R., Kishor, N., Catalão, J.P.: Optimal feature and decision tree-based classification of power quality disturbances in distributed generation systems. IEEE Trans. Sustain. Energy **5**(1), 200–208 (2014)
18. Rokach, L., Maimon, O.: Clustering methods. In: Maimon, O., Rokach, L. (eds.) Data Mining and Knowledge Discovery Handbook, vol. 350, pp. 95–116. Springer, Boston (1989). doi:10.1007/3-540-50871-6_5
19. Rosenberg, A., Hirschberg, J.: V-measure: a conditional entropy-based external cluster evaluation measure. In: EMNLP-CoNLL, vol. 7, pp. 410–420 (2007)
20. Salat, R., Osowski, S.: Accurate fault location in the power transmission line using support vector machine approach. IEEE Trans. Power Syst. **19**(2), 979–986 (2004)
21. Singh, B., Sharma, N., Tiwari, A., Verma, K., Singh, S.: Applications of phasor measurement units (PMUs) in electric power system networks incorporated with facts controllers. Int. J. Eng. Sci. Technol. **3**(3), 64–82 (2011)
22. Tate, J.E., Overbye, T.J.: Line outage detection using phasor angle measurements. IEEE Trans. Power Syst. **23**(4), 1644–1652 (2008)
23. Wagstaff, K., Cardie, C., Rogers, S., Schrödl, S., et al.: Constrained k-means clustering with background knowledge. In: ICML, vol. 1, pp. 577–584 (2001)
24. Zhang, Y.G., Wang, Z.P., Zhang, J.F., Ma, J.: Fault localization in electrical power systems: a pattern recognition approach. Int. J. Electr. Power Energy Syst. **33**(3), 791–798 (2011)

The Structural and Kinematical Analyses of a Wired Robotic Mechanism with Three Degrees of Freedom

Nicolae Bercan[1], Mihaiela Iliescu[2(✉)], and Cristian Matran[1]

[1] Lucian Blaga University, Sibiu, Romania
{nicolae.bercan, cristian.matran}@ulbsibiu.ro
[2] Institute of Solid Mechanics, Romanian Academy, Bucharest, Romania
iliescumihaiela7@gmail.com

Abstract. The spreading presence of the industrial robots in environmental friendly manufacturing systems requires developing of a robots' database. The aim of this material is to present a fundamental model of the mechanism acted with wires. This fact is needed because the literature data from the field of the robotic mechanisms operated through wires is relatively, poor. The paper presents the fundamental model of this type of robots and one of its applications.

Keywords: Robotic mechanism · Coupling · Wires transmission · Pulley

1 Introduction

A documented and thorough analysis evidenced that there are few data in the specific literature on structural, kinematical and dynamic study regarding the wires - pulley mechanisms. This is the reason why specific methodologies for studying these types of mechanisms, from structural, kinematical and static point of views, have to be assessed and implemented. These methodologies can be obtained by "extrapolation" of the study methodologies specific to mechanisms with circular gears.

Mechanisms with pulleys and wires are considered to be analogues, from kinematical and static point of views, to the circular gears mechanisms, gear wheel - rack, or gear wheel – gear wheel type mechanisms.

The mechanism studied in the paper is derived from a robotic mechanism with gears and represents one important component of a (data) base of mechanisms with wires and pulley wheels, used in designing robotic mechanisms.

The solution of replacing the serrated wheels with equivalent mechanisms with pulley wheels and wires is rational and economical – with the assumptions of dealing with small and medium loads.

These mechanisms are used particularly in the nuclear industry, medicine, etc. [1, 2] when low, or non-pollution manufacturing systems are involved.

© Springer International Publishing AG 2017
M. Helfert et al. (Eds.): SMARTGREENS 2016 and VEHITS 2016, CCIS 738, pp. 97–109, 2017.
DOI: 10.1007/978-3-319-63712-9_5

2 Notation and Symbols

The notation and symbols used in this paper are mentioned next

- M - represents the mobility grade of the mechanisms;
- M_I, M_{II}, ... - mobility grade of each of the component mechanisms;
- L_C - number of couplings between the mechanisms;
- ω_a - angular velocity of the "a" element relative to the base;
- C- coupling grade of the motions;
- M_a - the moment of the element "a";
- $\omega_a^{(\alpha)} = \omega_a(\omega_\alpha \neq 0;\ \omega_\beta = 0)$;
- i_{ab}^c - transmission ratio from the element "a" to the element "b", when the angular velocity $\omega_c = 0$;[3].

3 Fundamental Model of Wire Mechanisms; Methods of Kinematical and Static Study for Simple Mechanisms with One Pulley

By mechanisms specific terminology and methodology, there are studied relevant aspects of the structure and kinematics of wire mechanisms, under the assumptions of a set of premises that define the fundamental model of these wires – pulleys mechanisms.

These premises defining the fundamental model are stated below:

- there is neglected the friction loss in bearings;
- there is neglected the mass of wires;
- there is neglected the elongation of wires, considering them not extensible;
- there is neglected the rigidity of wires, considering them of perfect flexibility;
- there is neglected the wire – pulley slip.

Under the assumption of neglecting friction loss, for each of the studied mechanical systems, there is the equation of energetic equilibrium ("power equilibrium"), as follows – according to [4]:

$$\begin{cases} F_0 \cdot \dot{S}_0 + P_n \cdot \dot{S}_n = 0 \\ M_0 \cdot \dot{\theta}_0 + M_n \cdot \theta_n \doteq 0 \end{cases} \tag{1}$$

where: F, P, S, θ, M stand for vector notation of (F, P), linear speeds (S), angular speeds (θ) and, respectively, moment (M).

The indexes are for input coupling (0 index) and for output coupling (n index) in the polinar system.

3.1   Kinematical and Static Model of the Mono-mobile Mechanisms with One Fixed Axis Pulley

For the system with fixed axis (see Fig. 1.a), made of two racks and one double gear wheel, there can be attributed the equivalent mechanism with double pulley with fixed axis and a not extensible wire (see Fig. 1.b).

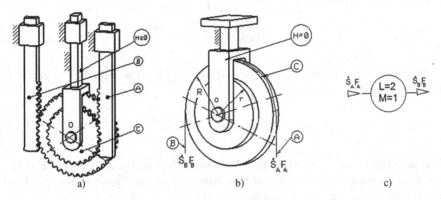

Fig. 1. Mobile mechanism with fixed axis.

Both mechanisms have the same block scheme (see Fig. 1.c) obtained from the structural scheme.

The mechanisms in Fig. 1.a and b are structural characterized by the measures mentioned next:

- L = 2 - inputs and outputs specific for exterior motion and forces: $(\dot{S}_A, F_A)$, $(\dot{S}_B, F_B)$, given by $(S_A, \dot{S}_A, \ddot{S}_A)$ and $(S_B, \dot{S}_B, \ddot{S}_B)$, respectively, F_A and F_B.
- M = 1: - from the kinematical point of view is an independent motion, S_A, and from the static point of view there is a function for force transmission: $F_A = f(\dot{S}_A, F_B)$
- L-M = 1: - function of motion transmission $S_B = f(\dot{S}_A)$ and an exterior independent force: F_B

Due to the fact that L = 2 > M = 1 > 0 => the systems shown in Fig. 1.a and b can structurally function as mechanisms [5].

The motion transmission function can be reduced to that of determining a transmission ratio [4, 6].

$$\dot{S}_B = i_{BA}^H \cdot \dot{S}_A \tag{2}$$

Where:

$$i_{BA}^H = \frac{\dot{S}_B}{\dot{S}_A} = \frac{\dot{S}_{BH}}{\dot{S}_{AH}}$$

is the transmission ratio of speeds from B to A, when H is fixed

In order to determine the transmission ratio "i" there should be used the sign convention proposed in [3, 4, 6], according to Fig. 1.a and b:

$$i_{BA}^{H} = \frac{\dot{S}_B}{\dot{S}_A} = -\frac{\omega \cdot R}{\omega \cdot r} = -\frac{R}{r} \tag{3}$$

By replacing (3) in (2), it results:

$$\dot{S}_B = -\frac{R}{r} \cdot \dot{S}_A \tag{4}$$

The transmission functions for forces are obtained from the equation of energetic equilibrium with no friction:

$$\dot{S}_A \cdot F_A + \dot{S}_B \cdot F_B = 0 = > F_A = \frac{R}{r} \cdot F_B \tag{5}$$

If the mechanism presented in Fig. 1 has equal values for the two gear wheels radii, than there is obtained an equivalent mechanism made of one simple pulley with fixed axis and not extensible wire – see Fig. 2.

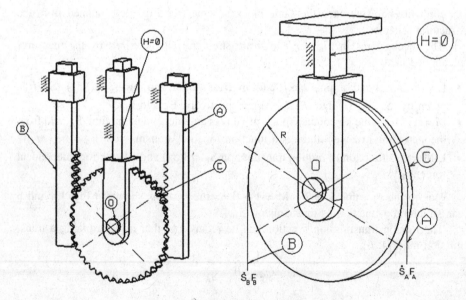

Fig. 2. The equivalent mechanism.

The transmission functions for speeds and forces, obtained from relations (4) and (5) turn into:

$$\dot{S}_B = -\dot{S}_A \tag{6}$$

$$F_A = F_B \tag{7}$$

4 Structure and Kinematical Analyses of the Robotic Mechanism

4.1 Structural Analysis of the Robotic Mechanism

The authors present a version of decoupling the movements by couplings, for a robotic-mechanism whose movement transmission is provided by wires.

There have been done, both, structural and kinematic analyses for the orientation mechanism I and the decoupling movements of mechanism II. Consequently, there were determined the overall functions of transmission gears and moments, as well as the conditions of release movements (see Fig. 3).

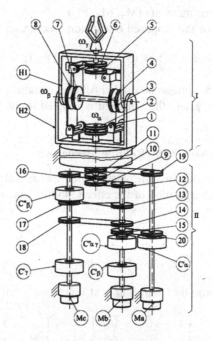

Fig. 3. The robotic mechanism acted by wires.

In terms of kinematic and structural analysis, the proper guidance of mechanism, driven by wires through single or double pulley wheels, it has been extensively analyzed by the analytical method [7].

The robotic-mechanism of orientation I, is formed by combining the cinematic chain bi-mobile open A = (0-H$_1$-H$_2$) with three mono-mobile mechanisms with wires B = (1-3-H$_2$), C = (2-8-H$_2$) and D = (4-5 = 6-7-H$_1$). The mobility grade of the orientation mechanism is given by relation (8):

$$M_I = M_A + \ldots + M_D - L_C = 2 + 1 + 1 + 1 - 2 = 3 \tag{8}$$

Where $L_C = 2$ represents the component between the composing mechanisms (3 = 4) and (8 = 7).

The innovative orientation mechanism I, has $L_I = 6$ external connections, three inputs (0-2-H$_2$) and three outputs (α, β, γ).

Because the mechanism is three-mobile, it results that $M_1 = 3$, as there are independent motions (ω_α, ω_β, ω_γ) and $L_I - M_I = 6 - 3 = 3$, as there are dependent motions (ω_1, ω_2, ω_{H2}).

The mechanism has $L_I - M_I = 3$ independent exterior moments (M_1, M_2, M_{H2}) and $M_I = 3$ dependent exterior moments (M_α, M_β, M_γ)

The coupling grade of the proposed orientation mechanism is:

$$C = C_\alpha + C_\beta + C_\gamma = (3 - 1) + (2 - 1) + (2 - 1) = 4 \tag{9}$$

This means that the α - motion is coupled with the motions β and γ, the β motion is coupled with the motion γ, and the γ motion is coupled to the β motion.

4.2   Kinematical Analysis of the Robotic Mechanism

In order to establish the transmission functions for speeds and moments, the authors apply the principle of superposition of the effects, so that functions (10) are obtained:

$$\begin{cases} \omega_1 = \omega_\alpha - \frac{R_3}{R_1} \cdot \omega_\beta - \frac{R_3 \cdot R_5}{R_1 \cdot R_4} \cdot \omega_\gamma \\ \omega_2 = \omega_\alpha + \frac{R_8}{R_2} \cdot \omega_\beta - \frac{R_6 \cdot R_8}{R_2 \cdot R_7} \cdot \omega_\gamma \\ \omega_{H_2} = \omega_\alpha \end{cases} \tag{10}$$

Written in matrix form, they turn into next functions, given by (11):

$$\begin{bmatrix} \omega_1 \\ \omega_2 \\ \omega_3 \end{bmatrix} = \begin{bmatrix} 1 & -\frac{R_3}{R_1} & -\frac{R_3 R_5}{R_1 R_4} \\ 1 & \frac{R_8}{R_2} & -\frac{R_6 R_8}{R_2 R_7} \\ 1 & 0 & 0 \end{bmatrix} \cdot \begin{bmatrix} \omega_\alpha \\ \omega_\beta \\ \omega_\gamma \end{bmatrix} = A \cdot \begin{bmatrix} \omega_\alpha \\ \omega_\beta \\ \omega_\gamma \end{bmatrix} \tag{11}$$

Where

$$A = \begin{bmatrix} 1 & -\frac{R_3}{R_1} & -\frac{R_3 R_5}{R_1 R_4} \\ 1 & \frac{R_8}{R_2} & -\frac{R_6 R_8}{R_2 R_7} \\ 1 & 0 & 0 \end{bmatrix}$$

With the assumptions of neglecting the abrasion and the inertia forces, the transmission function of the moments can be determined using the principle of the virtual mechanical power, as presented by Eq. (12):

$$\begin{bmatrix} M_\alpha \\ M_\beta \\ M_\gamma \end{bmatrix} = -A^T \cdot \begin{bmatrix} M_1 \\ M_2 \\ M_3 \end{bmatrix} \tag{12}$$

A particular case, with practical application, is that when the radii of the wheels are equal. So, the Eqs. (11) and (12) turn into Eq. (13):

$$\begin{bmatrix} \omega_1 \\ \omega_2 \\ \omega_{H_2} \end{bmatrix} = A_1 \cdot \begin{bmatrix} \omega_\alpha \\ \omega_\beta \\ \omega_\gamma \end{bmatrix} ; \begin{bmatrix} M_a \\ M_b \\ M_c \end{bmatrix} = -A_1^T \cdot \begin{bmatrix} M_1 \\ M_2 \\ M_{H_2} \end{bmatrix} \tag{13}$$

Where

$$A_T = \begin{bmatrix} 1 & -1 & -1 \\ 1 & 1 & -1 \\ 1 & 0 & 0 \end{bmatrix}$$

For the decoupling study, it is most convenient when the transmission functions of the velocity are expressed by relationship (14):

$$\begin{bmatrix} \omega_\alpha \\ \omega_\beta \\ \omega_\gamma \end{bmatrix} = A_1^{-1} \cdot \begin{bmatrix} \omega_1 \\ \omega_2 \\ \omega_{H_2} \end{bmatrix} = \begin{bmatrix} 0 & 0 & 1 \\ -\frac{1}{2} & \frac{1}{2} & 0 \\ -\frac{1}{2} & -\frac{1}{2} & 1 \end{bmatrix} \cdot \begin{bmatrix} \omega_1 \\ \omega_2 \\ \omega_{H_2} \end{bmatrix} \tag{14}$$

Kinematics and structural analysis will be done in particular for the decoupling mechanism II, when for the simplified calculation is being used general analytical method.

The decoupling mechanism II is a tri-mobile mechanism composed from six mono-mobile mechanisms acted by wires E = (11 19), F = (10 16), G = (9 12), H = (13 17), I = (14 18) and J = (15 20) together with five couplings, (C'$_\alpha$, C'$_\beta$, C'$_\gamma$, C''$_{\alpha\gamma}$ and C''$_\beta$). The mechanism is driven by three stepping motors (M$_a$, M$_b$, M$_c$) [8–10].

The coupling degree of the guidance mechanism is calculated as expressed by Eq. (9):

To achieve α movement, the M_a motor in running and will be locked by the stepper motor M_b and M_c (see Fig. 4). Under these conditions, the couplings C'$_α$ and C"$_α$ are coupled and the others are decoupled.

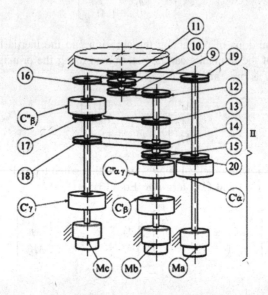

Fig. 4. The α movement conditions.

To achieve the β movement, the M_b motor in running and will be locked by the stepper motor M_a and M_c (see Fig. 5). Under these conditions, the couplings C'$_β$ and C"$_β$ are coupled and the others are decoupled.

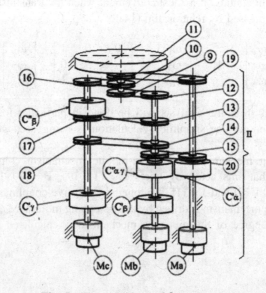

Fig. 5. The conditions of β movement.

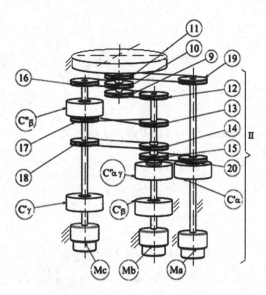

Fig. 6. The γ movement conditions.

To achieve the γ movement, the M_c motor in running and will be locked by the stepper motor M_a and M_b (see Fig. 6). Under these conditions, the couplings C'_γ and C''_γ are coupled and the others are decoupled.

To determine the decoupling conditions of the oriented movements, there areproceeding like in previous cases, so that there are obtained the following transmission ratios equals:

- for decoupling movements γ – β:

$$i_{9-c} = i_{10-c}$$

where

$$i_{9-c} = i_{9-12} \cdot i_{14-18} = \frac{R_{12}R_{18}}{R_9 R_{14}}$$
$$i_{10-c} = \frac{R_{16}}{R_{10}}$$

(15)

- for decoupling movements β – γ:

$$i_{9-b} = -i_{10-b}$$

Where

$$i_{9-b} = i_{9-12} = \frac{R_{12}}{R_9}$$
$$i_{10-b} = i_{10-16} \cdot i_{17-13} = \frac{R_{16}R_{13}}{R_{10}R_{17}}$$

(16)

- for decoupling movements $\alpha - (\beta$ and $\gamma)$ (see Eq. 17)

$$i_{11-a} = i_{10-a} = i_{9-a}$$

Where

$$i_{9-a} = i_{9-12} \cdot i_{15-22} = \frac{R_{12} \cdot R_{20}}{R_9 \cdot R_{15}}$$
$$i_{10-a} = i_{10-16} \cdot i_{18-14} \cdot i_{15-30} = \frac{R_{16} \cdot R_{14} \cdot R_{20}}{R_{10} \cdot R_{18} \cdot R_{15}}$$
$$i_{11-a} = i_{11-19} = \frac{R_{19}}{R_{11}}$$

(17)

From relationships (15), (16) and (17) we obtain the conditions for decoupling, given by Eq. (18).

$$\begin{cases} \frac{R_{16}}{R_{10}} = \frac{R_{12}R_{18}}{R_9R_{14}} \\ \frac{R_{12}}{R_9} = \frac{R_{16}R_{13}}{R_{10}R_{17}} \\ \frac{R_{19}}{R_{11}} = \frac{R_{14}R_{16}R_{20}}{R_{10}R_{18}R_{15}} \end{cases}$$

(18)

These relationships are fulfilled in the particular case of equal radii: $R_9 = \ldots = R_{20}$.

For the robotic mechanism with decoupled movements (see Fig. 3), we obtain the functions of velocity transmission, as follows:

1^0 for $\omega_\beta = 0$ and $\omega_\gamma = 0 \Rightarrow \omega_b = 0$ and $\omega_c = 0$

$$\omega_\alpha = \omega_a \cdot i_{\alpha-a};$$

Where

$$i_{\alpha-a} = i_{11-19} = \frac{R_{19}}{R_{11}} \Rightarrow \omega_\alpha = \omega_a \cdot \frac{R_{19}}{R_{11}}$$

(19)

2^0 for $\omega_\alpha = 0$ and $\omega_\gamma = 0 \Rightarrow \omega_a = 0$ and $\omega_c = 0$

$$\omega_\beta = \omega_b \cdot i_{\beta-b}$$

Where

$$i_{\beta-b} = i_{8-2} \cdot i_{10-16} \cdot i_{17-13} = -\frac{R_2 \cdot R_{16} \cdot R_{13}}{R_8 \cdot R_{10} \cdot R_{17}} \cdot \Rightarrow$$
$$\omega_\beta = -\omega_b \cdot \frac{R_2 \cdot R_{16} \cdot R_{13}}{R_8 \cdot R_{10} \cdot R_{17}} \tag{20}$$

3^0 for $\omega_\alpha = 0$ and $\omega_\beta = 0 \Rightarrow \omega_a = 0$ and $\omega_b = 0$

$$\omega_\gamma = \omega_c \cdot i_{\gamma-c}$$

Where

$$i_{\gamma-c} = i_{6-7} \cdot i_{8-2} \cdot i_{10-16} = -\frac{R_7 \cdot R_2 \cdot R_{16}}{R_6 \cdot R_8 \cdot R_{10}} \Rightarrow \tag{21}$$
$$\omega_\gamma = -\omega_c \cdot \frac{R_2 \cdot R_{16} \cdot R_7}{R_8 \cdot R_{10} \cdot R_6}$$

The velocities functions of overall transmission for the robotic mechanism with decoupled movements are expressed by the matrix form presented in Eq. (22):

$$\begin{bmatrix} \omega_\alpha \\ \omega_\beta \\ \omega_\gamma \end{bmatrix} = \begin{bmatrix} \frac{R_{19}}{R_{11}} & 0 & 0 \\ 0 & -\frac{R_2 R_{13} R_{16}}{R_6 R_{10} R_{17}} & 0 \\ 0 & 0 & -\frac{R_7 R_2 R_{16}}{R_8 R_6 R_{10}} \end{bmatrix} \cdot \begin{bmatrix} \omega_a \\ \omega_b \\ \omega_c \end{bmatrix} \tag{22}$$

In the case of equal values for radii, the relationship (22) turns into (23):

$$\begin{bmatrix} \omega_\alpha \\ \omega_\beta \\ \omega_\gamma \end{bmatrix} = \begin{bmatrix} 1 & 0 & 0 \\ 0 & -1 & 0 \\ 0 & 0 & -1 \end{bmatrix} \cdot \begin{bmatrix} \omega_a \\ \omega_b \\ \omega_c \end{bmatrix} \tag{23}$$

Under the assumptions of neglecting the abrasion and the inertia forces, the transmission function of the moments can be expressed by Eq. (24).

$$\begin{bmatrix} M_a \\ M_b \\ M_c \end{bmatrix} = \begin{bmatrix} -1 & 0 & 0 \\ 0 & 1 & 0 \\ 0 & 0 & 1 \end{bmatrix} \cdot \begin{bmatrix} M_\alpha \\ M_\beta \\ M_\gamma \end{bmatrix} \tag{24}$$

5 Conclusions

There was formulated the concept of fundamental model for wires mechanisms defined by the next set of premises:

- there is neglected bearing's friction loss;
- there is neglected the mass of wires;
- there is neglected the elongation of wires;

- there is neglected the rigidity of wires;
- there is neglected the wire – pulley slip.

The research presented in this paper resulted in specific methodologies for structural, kinematical and static study of wire - pulleys mechanisms, methodologies obtained by "extrapolation" of the study methodologies specific to mechanisms with circular gears.

Mechanisms with pulleys and wires are considered to be analogues, from kinematical and static point of views, to the circular gears mechanisms, gear wheel - rack, or gear wheel – gear wheel type mechanisms.

The presented methods, apart from the already existing ones, enable extension of the study to the mechanisms with high complexity schemes. As example, there is the structural, kinematical and static study for a series of relevant mechanism acted by wires [11].

This solution is also relevant for industrial robots in low and non-pollution manufacturing systems [12].

References

1. Coiffet, Ph.: Robot Sapiens, Robot Habilis. Hermes Publishing House, Paris (1993)
2. Vertut, J.: Teleoperation and Robotics: Applications and Technology. Hermes Publishing House, Paris (2012). ISBN-13: 9789401161053
3. Dudita, Fl., Diaconescu, D.: Curs mecanisme - fascicula 3, Cinematica mecanismelor cu roti dintate. Litografia Universitatii "Transilvania" din Brasov (1984)
4. Dudita, Fl., Diaconescu, D., Gogu, G.: Curs mecanisme, Fascicula 4, Cinematica mecanismelor articulate, Mecanisme clasice, Robotomecanisme, Universitatea din Brsov (1987)
5. Dudita, F.L., Diaconescu, D.: Curs mecanisme, Fascicula 3, Cinematica mecanismelor cu roti dintate, Universitatea din Brasov (1984)
6. Dudita, F.L., Diaconescu, D., Gogu, G.: Mecanisme Articulate. EdituraTehnica, Bucuresti (1989)
7. Bercan, N.: The structural and kinematic analyze for a tri-mobile orienting robotomechanism moved by tendons with decouple motions. In: High Technical Mechanical School - 4th International Conference RaDMI "Research And Development In Mechanical Industry", CD ISBN:86-83803-18-X, vol. 2. Zlatibor, Serbia and Montenegro (2004). ISBN: 86-83803-17-1
8. Bercan, N., Diaconescu D.: Mecanisme cu fire pentru roboti industriali. Editura Universitatii "Lucian Blaga" din Sibiu (1995). ISBN: 973-95604-4-6
9. Bercan, N.: Robotomecanisme cu fire. Baze teoretice. Editura Universitatii "Lucian Blaga" din Sibiu (1999). ISBN: 973-9410-23-0
10. Starețu, I.: Prehensoare antropomorfe cu bare articulate sau cu fire şi role pentru roboți industriali – Sinteză, analiză şi proiectare constructivă. In: Buletinul AGIR nr. 1/2009, Bucuresti (2009)

11. Bercan, N., Iliescu, M., Matran, C.: Design a robotic mechanism - component of low and non-pollution manufacturing systems. Decoupling movement of a robotic mechanism with three degrees of freedom, using couplings and wires transmission. In: Proceedings of the 5th International Conference on Smart Cities and Green ICT Systems, Rome, Italy, 23–25 April 2016, pp. 443–447 (2016). ISBN: 978-989-758-184-7
12. Iliescu, M., Spirleanu, C., Bercan, N., Vladareanu, L.: Flexible robotic cell for optimization of grinding process for 40C130 metallized coating. Acad. J. Manuf. Eng. 13(2), 30–35 (2015). ISSN: 1583-7904

Electric-Motion Infrastructure in Romania - Research on Machining Processes of Mechanical Components of e-Motion Charging Station

Mihaiela Iliescu[1(✉)], Luige Vlădăreanu[1], Nicolae Bercan[2], and Alexandru Rogojinaru[3]

[1] Institute of Solid Mechanics, Romanian Academy, Bucharest, Romania
iliescu.mihaiela7@gmail.com, luigiv2007@yahoo.com.sg
[2] Lucian Blaga University, Sibiu, Romania
nicolae.bercan@ulbsibiu.ro
[3] e-Motion Electric, Ilfov, Romania
alexandru.rogojinaru@e-motionelectric.ro

Abstract. Aspects of electric vehicles specific infrastructure in Romania are evidenced by this paper. The focus is on charging station and fast charging stations designed and installed by the first Romanian company dedicated 100% to e-mobility, E-Motion Electric. Research on machining processes, milling and drilling, of the mechanical components of these stations is also presented. A system for measuring the values of machining forces, data acquisition and processing, as well as real time control scheme does also represent innovation in this paper. The regression models, determined by statistical data processing, should be applied in optimization of machining process.

Keywords: Charging station · Drilling · Milling · Regression model · Control system

1   Introduction

Eco-Technologies include the technologies which does not harm the environment so hard, when compared to traditional similar technologies applied to obtain the products required by the same human need [1].

Energy efficiency is "using less energy to provide the same service" and it is not energy conservation [2]. Most of the times, the energy efficiency can be quantified by comparing the specific energy consumption for obtaining, in the same condition, the product, service or, process required. By reducing these consumptions, without affecting their quality, represents the increase on energy efficiency [3].

The concept of energy efficiency, or optimization of electric energy consumption has become an essential challenge worldwide, nowadays. In fact, saving energy does represent the cheapest energy resource, easy to produce and environmental friendly.

One solution, with highly positive impact on the environment, is represented by the focus on electric vehicles (EV). These vehicles have to be charged and, further, driven, so that to use their required energy in an efficient way, as well as an environmental friendly one.

M. Helfert et al. (Eds.): SMARTGREENS 2016 and VEHITS 2016, CCIS 738, pp. 110–124, 2017.
DOI: 10.1007/978-3-319-63712-9_6

The chargeable electric vehicles, hybrid ones included, have become more and more popular, for person transportation (electric train, electric bus, electric car, electric bike). There are obvious advantages, such as: no CO_2 emission, travel comfort, technology friendly over the environment, low expenses [4].

Based on the aspects mentioned above, it is estimated a, relatively, high need for good charging infrastructure for electric vehicles in Romania.

2   Notation and Symbols

In the past 50 years, Europe has changed a lot - just like the rest of the world. Nowadays, more than ever, in a constantly evolving world, Europe must face new challenges. Economy globalisation, demographic evolution, climate changes, the need for long-lasting energy sources and modern security threats are the main challenges of the XXIst century.

2.1   Context

National and international relationship of Romania, member of European Union and the focus on sustainable development, including friendly environmental technologies, lead to the increasing importance of ecological technologies with high energy efficiency for new generation of vehicles, specially envisaging electric vehicles, more specifically, electric cars.

Environment degradation because of industrial development which has mostly been accomplished in a chaotic way, as well as the consequent hunger of resources, exhaustion

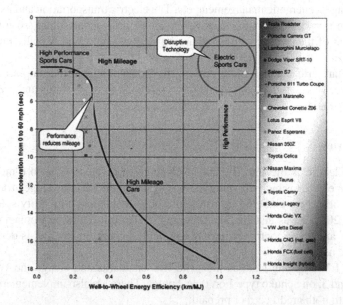

Fig. 1. The highest energy efficiency is that of electric vehicle [6].

of fossil fuels: oil, gas, coal are the reason for efficient use of natural resources and for integrated solution of protection and preservation of the environment [5].

Electric vehicles are sometimes "accused" that they do pollute "somewhere else", because their required energy for battery charging is obtained using industrial procedures that pollute. But, if there were considered all the emissions, from oil extraction, it would result that the electric vehicle is significantly more efficient and pollutes less than any other options – see Fig. 1.

One relevant situation is that where the charging stations (E-Motion Street Box) are situated in isolated areas, with no plugin sources to the electricity distribution network. These stations will be connected to renewable energy sources so that, the electric vehicle charging is 100% green, non-polluting – see Fig. 2.

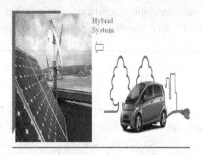

Fig. 2. Eco-technology for charging the electric vehicle [7].

In the context of climate changes and of cities that turn into sustainable smart cities, high attention is given to the systems for monitor, analysis and adjustment to environmental changes, energetic management, etc. The electric transportation and its charging infrastructure represents components of the smart grid of the future, so that further development of the electric vehicles charging stations smart grid is really important – see Fig. 3.

This smart grid enables route optimization depending on the emplacement and performances of existing charging stations, correlated to roads status and traffic situations/ emergencies.

2.2 Overview

e-Motion Electric is the first Romanian company dedicated 100% to e-mobility, as producer for electric vehicle charging stations. It also offers the knowledge in developing the best solutions for charging infrastructure in Romania and e-mobility solutions in, general. In 2011 it was installed the first public charging station in Romania. It has 1 plug 230 V and 16A; controlled access with RFID; energy meter and is designed for semi-public use.

All the EV charging stations meet the IEC standards and charge the vehicles in mode1, 2 and 3, on Schuko type 1 or, type 2 plugs. There are also implemented payment systems with both credit card or prepaid.

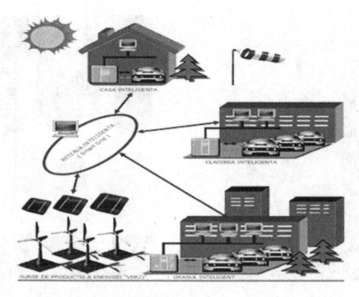

Fig. 3. Urban transportation and its infrastructure – components of the smart city [7].

One of the exterior semi-public charging station designed and installed in Romania is presented in Fig. 4. It is type 1, with 1 plug 230 V and 32 A; controlled access with RFID; energy meter and designed for semi-public use.

Fig. 4. Exterior semi-public charging station [7].

One of the interior private charging stations designed and installed by the company in Romania is shown in Fig. 5. It has 1 plug 230 V and 16 A and energy meter.

The first fast charging station designed and installed in Romania in 2014, for exterior semi-public use, is evidenced in Fig. 6. It has 1 plug 230 V and 16 A, 3,6 kW; Type 2 plug 400 V and 32 A, 22 kW.

In 2013, in Romania, it was installed only 1 (one) public charging station. In 2014, in Bucharest (capital of Romania) there were 9 (nine) public charging stations – see Fig. 7.

Fig. 5. Interior public charging station [7].   **Fig. 6.** Exterior semi-public fast charging station [7].

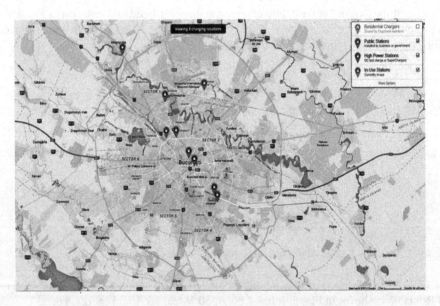

Fig. 7. Public charging stations location in Bucharest district, 2014.

The European Commission announced that soon, there will be rules regarding the development of public charging station infrastructure for electric vehicles. For Romania, the Commission estimated an amount of 10,000 charging stations to be installed by the year 2020.

3   Research on Machining Processes

All the aspects presented above do evidence the importance of developing the infra-structure of charging stations for electric vehicles in Romania. Each of these stations has mechanical components, as for example, the "frame" sustaining all the components for automation.

In Fig. 6, one can notice the support – front case of the fast charging station. It is made of composite material, machined by milling and drilling processes. So, the prescribed geometrical precision parameters: dimensions, tolerances, surface roughness values are be obtained.

In the machining processes, milling and drilling, of the mechanical components, their parameters values required to generate shape and accuracy are estimated not to be optimum ones, as both milling and drilling tools have severe wear and, relatively, low durability. In fact, many times, the milling tool breaks while machining the contour and the drilling tool prove cutting edge severe wear.

That is why, it has been considered of benefit do research on, both, milling and drilling machining process, so that to improve cutting tools durability and, finally, to have an efficient machining process.

3.1   Research Method

The research on studied machining processes, milling and drilling, is done so that to finally obtain a regression models of machining process parameters interdependence, models that enable to determine their optimum values for the process.

There are some specific steps for this research, as mentioned next.

Step 1 – is on the "definition" of material to be machined. In fact, it is a 3 mm thick sheet made of composite polymer, PLEXIGLASS (polymethyl methacrylate, PMMA).

Step 2 – is on the "definition" of the machining equipment. The vertical CNC machining center is an Isel CNC Router [8]. The milling tool is flat end mill, Sandvik Coromant (producer) and the drilling tool is carbide standard spiral, Whiteside (producer).

Step 3 – is on the variables studied, inputs and outputs, as well as to the desired type of mathematical relationship – regression model. The regression analysis is based on design of experiments statistical method and, further, on computer data processing. So, the experiments design is Central Composite Design (CCD) type [9] and the applied software is DOE KISS that enable polynomial regression analysis, optimiza-tion, plotting 2D and 3D, Pareto diagram, Means Plot etc.

Based on preliminary research and previous work [10–12], as well as on the expe-rience and results obtained in practice, the authors have considered fit the choice of the machining processes parameters mentioned next.

Milling process:

- two independent variables (inputs): cutting speed, v (peripheral speed of the cutting tool) and radial depth (of the cut), a_r; speed values were measured in [m/min] and the depth values were measured in [mm].
- one dependent variable considered, due to the interest of this study, the tangential cutting force component, F_y [daN];
- other milling process parameters were set to: 1200 [mm/min] for the feed speed, v_f; 3 [mm] for axial the depth, a_a and cutting fluid (coolant and lubricant).

Drilling process:

- three independent variables (inputs): tool diameter D measured in [mm], feed rate f measured in [mm/rot] and drilling speed v_c measured in [m/min];
- one dependent variable considered, due to the interest of this research, the vertical cutting force component, F_z [N].

3.2   Experiments and Data Processing

Experiments were done at the Production Department of E-Motion Electric Company – see Fig. 8.

Fig. 8. Cylindrical face milling experiments.

In order to measure the machining forces' components, along each of the OX, OY and Oz axes, there was used specific equipment made of:

- dynamometric system with 6 resistive transducers positioned along each axis and connected in a complete Wheatstone electronic bridge;
- 6 channels tension bridge and data acquisition system, with DAQPad-6020E type data acquisition component.

For accurate experimental data, there was used a CCD experimental program (Central Composite Design), each experience repeated 5 times and the processed values being those of average - arithmetic mean, for each set of experiments.

The independent variables are conventionally named z_j. Their coded values, are x_j. while relationship between real and code values is expressed in Eq. (1).

$$x_j = \frac{z_j - \dfrac{z_{min} + z_{max}}{2}}{\dfrac{z_{max} - z_{min}}{2}} \tag{1}$$

where: z_{min} is the minimum value of the variable;

z_{max} - the maximum value of the variable.

For this research, the inputs values are the ones mentioned in relation (2) to relation (6), as mentioned next:

- for the milling process:

$$z_1 = v; v_{min} = 150 \text{ m/min}; v_{max} = 450 \text{ m/min} \tag{2}$$

$$z_2 = a_r; a_{rmin} = 4 \text{ mm}; a_{rmax} = 8 \text{ mm} \tag{3}$$

- for the drilling process:

$$z_1 = D; D_{min} = 3 \text{ mm}; D_{max} = 7 \text{ mm} \tag{4}$$

$$z_2 = f; f_{rmin} = 0.08 \text{ mm/rev}; f_{rmax} = 0.16 \text{ mm/rev} \tag{5}$$

$$z_3 = v_c; v_{cmin} = 14 \text{ m/min}; v_{cmax} = 40 \text{ m/min} \tag{6}$$

Modeling and simulation of the machining process, for one mechanical component of the charging station was done with VisualMILL software. There were considered, both milling and drilling machining procedures and so, the trajectories of cutting tools are to be noticed in Fig. 9.

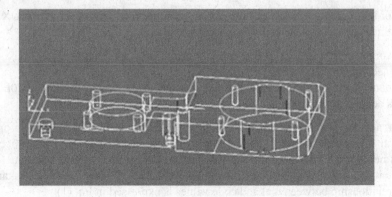

Fig. 9. Simulation of cutting tools trajectories.

More of it, an example of the drilling process simulation, for generating one whole of the front case component is shown in Fig. 10.

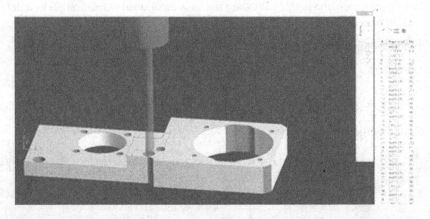

Fig. 10. Simulation of drilling process.

Sequence of the CNC program associated to this drilling process and used with isel CNC Router for machining is shown in Fig. 11.

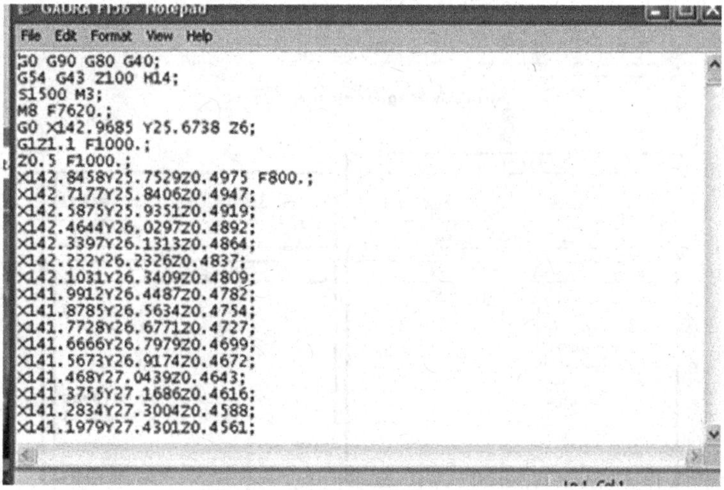

Fig. 11. CNC sequence program.

The obtained results for the tangential cutting force, F_y, are presented in Table 1 and the results for the cutting force's main component, F_z, are presented in Table 2. Each of these results represents the as arithmetic mean values of the 5 experiences repeated in each experiment.

Table 1. Experimental results for milling.

	v [m/min]		a_r [mm]		F_y [daN]
	Real value	Coded value	Real value	Coded value	
1	150	−1	4	−1	26.16
2	150	−1	8	+1	33.85
3	450	+1	4	−1	23.60
4	450	+1	8	+1	28.36
5	300	0	6	0	26.50
6	300	0	6	0	26.42
7	150	−1	6	0	26.58
8	450	+1	6	0	25.82
9	300	0	4	−1	23.28
10	300	0	8	+1	28.80

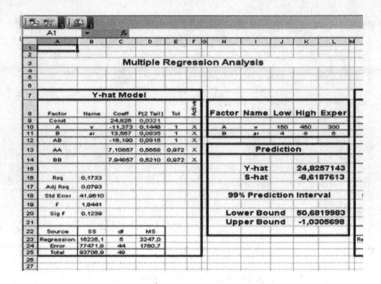

Fig. 12. DOE KISS regression analysis results for milling.

Table 2. Experimental results for drilling.

	D [mm]		f [mm/rot]		v$_c$ [m/min]		F$_y$ [N]
	Real value	Coded value	Real value	Coded value	Real value	Coded value	
1	3	−1	0.08	−1	14	−1	48.8
2	3	−1	0.08	−1	40	+1	47.6
3	3	−1	0.16	+1	14	−1	72.8
4	3	−1	0.16	+1	40	+1	71.1
5	7	+1	0.08	−1	14	−1	92.8
6	7	+1	0.08	−1	40	+1	90.5
7	7	+1	0.16	+1	14	−1	138.6
8	7	+1	0.16	+1	40	+1	135.2

Results of the DOE KISS regression analysis are shown in Figs. 12 and 13 for the milling process and, respectively, the drilling process studied.

Based on regression analysis results, and further processing data – by neglecting the factors that do not have significant influence on the output values, there was obtained the regression model for milling process parameters interaction.

The regression model for coded variables, x_j, is given by Eqs. (7) and (8), for each of the studied machining processes, milling and, respectively drilling:

$$y = 24.826 - 11.373 \cdot x_1 + 13.567 \cdot x_2 - 16.190 \cdot x_1 \cdot x_2 \tag{7}$$

$$y = 86.275 + 26.2 \cdot x_1 + 17.025 \cdot x_2 - 1.975 \cdot x_3 + 5.15 \cdot x_1 \cdot x_2 - 1.25 \cdot x_1 \cdot x_3 \tag{8}$$

Multiple Regression Analysis

Y-hat Model

Factor	Name	Coeff	P(2 Tail)	Tol	Active
Const		86,275	0,0000		
A	D	26,200	0,0000	1	X
B	f	17,025	0,0000	1	X
C	vc	-1,97500	0,0000	1	X
AB		5,15000	0,0000	1	X
AC		-1,25000	0,0000	1	X
BC		-0,42500	0,1068	1	X
ABC		-0,30000	0,2502	1	X

Rsq	0,9979	
Adj Rsq	0,9975	
Std Error	1,6200	
F	2195,9990	
Sig F	0,0000	

Source	SS	df	MS
Regression	40341,9	7	5763,1
Error	84,0	32	2,6
Total	40425,9	39	

Factor	Name	Low	High	Exper
A	D	3	7	5
B	f	0,08	0,16	0,12
C	vc	14	40	27

Prediction

Y-hat	86,275
S-hat	1,54613201

99% Prediction Interval

Lower Bound	81,636604
Upper Bound	90,913396

S-hat Model

Factor	Name	Coeff	P(2 Tail)	Tol	Active
Const		1,54613	Not Avail		
A	D	0,24979	Not Avail	1	X
B	f	0,28506	Not Avail	1	X
C	vc	0,18123	Not Avail	1	X
AB		-0,07737	Not Avail	1	X
AC		0,16738	Not Avail	1	X
BC		0,14630	Not Avail	1	X
ABC		0,04411	Not Avail	1	X

Rsq	1,0000
Adj Rsq	Not Avail
Std Error	Not Avail
F	Not Avail
Sig F	Not Avail

Source	SS	df	MS
Regression	1,9	7	0,3
Error	0,0	0	Not Avail
Total	1,9	7	

Fig. 13. DOE KISS regression analysis results for drilling.

Considering the real variables in this research, relation (1) turns into relation (9), for milling, and relation (10), for drilling.

$$x_1 = \frac{v - 300}{150}; \; x_2 = \frac{a_r - 6}{2} \tag{9}$$

$$x_1 = \frac{D - 5}{2}; \; x_2 = \frac{f - 0.12}{0.04}; \; x_3 = \frac{v_c - 27}{13} \tag{10}$$

Finally, based on all the above, there are obtained the regression models for the studied machining processes, as evidenced by equations below:

– for the milling process:

$$F_y = -90.269 + 0.248 \cdot v + 22.974 \cdot a_r - 0.054 \cdot v \cdot a_r \; [daN] \tag{11}$$

– for the drilling process

$$F_z = 5.936 + 6.673 \cdot D + 103.75 \cdot f + 0.088 \cdot v_c + 64.375 \cdot D \cdot f - 0.048 \cdot D \cdot v_c \tag{12}$$

For validation of the obtained results, has been designed a measuring error real time control scheme – see Fig. 14, thus being possible to compare experimental values to the ones generated by the regression models.

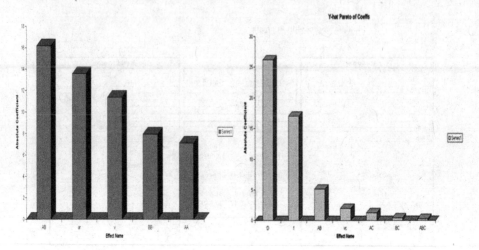

Fig. 14. Pareto chart of coefficients – for milling process

Fig. 15. Pareto chart of coefficients – for drilling process.

DOE KISS software enables the plot of Pareto charts of coefficients – see Figs. 14 and 15. This charts points out how strong the influence of each input, as well as of inputs interactions, is on the output values.

Also, the software enables the use of Expert optimizer, so that to optimize (minimize for this study) the values of the output, in fact the machining force value – see Figs. 16 and 17.

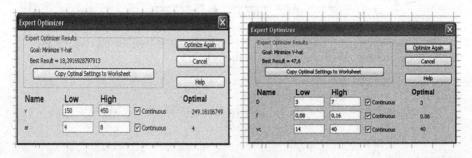

Fig. 16. Expert optimizer – for milling process.

Fig. 17. Expert optimizer – for drilling process.

3.3 Real Time Control System

In order to have real time control of the machining processes, a system for measuring the forces, data acquisition and processing has been designed [13, 14]. Its schematic representation is to be noticed in Fig. 18.

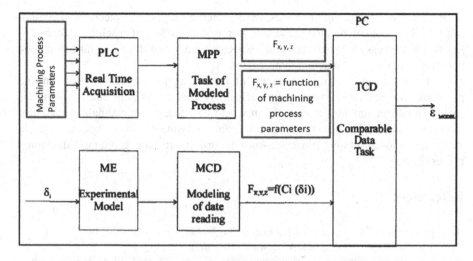

Fig. 18. Measuring error real time control scheme.

One measuring channel is assigned to the classic method, where deformations generated by machining forces are measured, through the experimental module, ME (dynamometric system with 6 resistive transducers). These forces are determined by correction of the deformation values received from the Wheastone electronic bridge, through the reading-modeling module, MCD. So, it is possible to generate, in real time, the values of machining forces along each of the axes, X, Y and Z, meaning F_x, F_y and, respectively, F_z, as Ci (δi).

A second channel is used for signals' acquisition – specific parameters of the machining process, from a PLC system (Programmable Logical Controller) at high sampling rate and processing speed, by rejecting noise signals. The accuracy of measurements is, at least, 11 bits. These signals are numerically processed, according to regression models obtained – see Eqs. (11) and (12), by the machining process modeling module, MPP. This is how machining force's values are real time generated as function of the each machining process parameters values Fx,y,z.

Comparing the two channels generated signals, through data comparing task, TCD, of the PC, results in the modeling errors generated by real time control system.

The measuring errors values less than 1%, obtained by real time data acquisition point out the fact that both experimental results as well as regression models obtained results are correlated. This suggests that there are real possibilities of implementing the described method in order to determine forces values for different machining processes.

4   Conclusions

The research resulted presented in are focused on main aspects of the development of electric vehicles specific infrastructure in Romania, specially the one developed by the first Romanian company dedicated 100% to e-mobility, E-Motion Electric.

Research on machining processes, milling and drilling, of the mechanical components of these stations is also presented. Regression models of machining forces, as function of process input parameters have been obtained and should be further applied in optimization of these machining processes.

A system for measuring the values of machining forces, data acquisition and processing, as well as real time control scheme does also represent innovation in this paper. The development of these system would be adequate for validating analytical models of outputs variables (force, torque, surface roughness, surface hardness, etc.) in different type of machining processes (milling, drilling, turning, grinding). Machining processes type.

References

1. http://www.insee.fr/en/ecotechnologies.htm (2015). Accessed 10 Nov 2015
2. http://eetd.lbl.gov/ee/ee-1.html. Accessed 10 Nov 2015
3. (2015). http://www.utgjiu.ro/revista/ing/pdf/2009-03/35_ALINA_DANIELA_HANDRA.pdf
4. http://birdie-electriccar.eu/ro/transport-de-persoane (2015). Accessed 10 Sept
5. http://e-motionelectric.ro/sites/default/files/cataloage/Catalog%20general%20produse.pdf. Accessed 27 July 2015
6. http://www.evworld.com/library/Tesla_21centuryEV.pdf. Accessed 10 Sept 2015
7. http://e-motionelectric.ro/. Accessed 14 Sept 2015
8. https://www.isel.com/iselcom_en/. Accessed 7 Nov 2015
9. Schmidt, L., et al.: Understanding Industrial Designed Experiments. Academy Press, USA (2005)
10. Iliescu, M., Vlădăreanu, L., Spânu, P.: Modeling and controlling of machining forces when milling polymeric composites. Plast. Mater. **47**(2), 231–235 (2010). ISSN 0025/5289
11. Iliescu, M., Pătraşcu, Al.: Research on regression models of force in drilling mineral composite material 2% glass fiber reinforced. In: The 6th International Conference on Manufacturing Engineering, Quality and Production Systems (MEQAPS 2013), Brasov, Romania, 1–3 June 2013, pp. 141–146 (2013). ISSN: 2227-4588, ISBN: 978-1-61804-193-7
12. Iliescu, M., Bercan, N., Rogojinaru, Al.: Electric-motion in Romania - overview study on machining parameters of EV charging station mechanical components. In: 5th International Conference on Smart Cities and Green ICT Systems, Rome, Italy, 23–25 April 2016
13. Vlădăreanu, L., Şandru, O.I., Velea, M.L., Yu, H.: The actuators control in continuous flux using the winer filters. Proc. Roman. Acad. Ser. A: Math. Phys. Techn. Sci. Inf. Sci. **10**(1), 81 (2009)
14. Vladareanu, V., Schiopu, P., Sandru, O.I., Vladareanu, L.: Advanced intelligent control methods in open architecture systems for cooperative works on 4 Nano-Micro-Manipulators platform. In: Advanced Topics in Optoelectronics, Microelectronics, and Nanotechnologies VII, vol. 9258, ID925804, 21 February 2015. doi:10.1117/12.2070342

Modelling the Diagnosis of Industry Internet of Things

Calin Ciufudean$^{(\boxtimes)}$ and Corneliu Buzduga

Stefan cel Mare University, 13 University, Suceava, Romania
ciufudean.calin@gmail.com, cbuzduga@eed.usv.ro

Abstract. We consider necessary to discuss on a scientific article about the diagnosis of Internet of Things (IoT) for industry applications, e.g. controlled flexible manufacturing systems (FMS). In order to analyse and diagnose the main characteristics of these systems we focus on models realized with Markov chains of FMS with stochastic and not equal throughput rates. Discrete-event models assume that FMS is decomposed, and we study the following events: an Internet server fails, an Internet server is repaired, an Internet server memory buffer fills up, an Internet server memory buffer empties. The IoT diagnosis is performed with by calculating the time to absorption in Markov model of the IoT controlled FMS. Future developments of IoT diagnosis of FMS are also discussed in this work.

Keywords: Discrete event models · Markov chains · Internet of Things · Flexible manufacturing systems · Memory buffers

1 Introduction

EU Projects Research Cluster in the Internet of Things (IERC) defines IoT as follows: "A dynamic global network infrastructure with self-configuring capabilities based on standard and interoperable communication protocols where physical and virtual "things" have identities, physical attributes, and virtual personalities and use intelligent interfaces, and are seamlessly integrated into the information network".

In this work, we assume that a flexible manufacturing system controlled and monitored by Internet of Things (IoT) is similar to a discrete event system (DES) and we model it in a discrete stochastic space. Absorbing states of Markov chain models display a steady-state i.e., the absorbing state attended after time T; therefore, only transient analysis displays the system performance. Our approach deals with an IoT controlled system which displays in time a trajectory modelled with a Markov chain $\{x(t); t \geq 0\}$ with state space $S = \{0, 1, \ldots\}$ and space generator W. Let $i, j \in S$ and, we have [1, 2]:

$$P_{ij}(t) = P\{x(t) = j/x(0) = i\} \tag{1}$$

$$A(t) = [p_{ij}(t)] \tag{2}$$

© Springer International Publishing AG 2017
M. Helfert et al. (Eds.): SMARTGREENS 2016 and VEHITS 2016, CCIS 738, pp. 125–134, 2017.
DOI: 10.1007/978-3-319-63712-9_7

The following equations describe the behavior of the above mentioned Markov chain [1, 3, 5]:

$$\frac{d}{dt}[A(t)] = A(t) \cdot W \tag{3}$$

$$\frac{d}{dt}[A(t)]^* = W \cdot A(t) \tag{4}$$

Where $A(0) = I$. For matrix components we have:

$$\frac{d}{dt}[p_{ij}(t)] = w_{ij} \cdot p_{ij}(t) + \sum_{k=j} w_{kj} \cdot p_{ik}(t) \tag{5}$$

$$\frac{d}{dt}[p_{ij}(t)] = w_{ii} \cdot p_{ij}(t) + \sum_{k=i} w_{ik} \cdot p_{kj}(t) \tag{6}$$

The solution is:

$$A(t) = e^{W \cdot t} \tag{7}$$

$$e^{W \cdot t} = \sum_{k=0}^{\infty} \frac{(W \cdot t)^k}{k!} \tag{8}$$

The state probabilities $Y(t) = [p_0(t), p_1(t), \ldots]$ where $p_j(t) = P\{x(t) = j\}$, $j \in S$, are given by the following equation:

$$\frac{d}{dt}[Y(t)] = Y(t) \cdot W \tag{9}$$

The solution is:

$$Y(t) = Y(0) \cdot e^{W \cdot t} \tag{10}$$

$$p_{ij}(t) = P\{X(t) = j / X(0) = i\} \tag{11}$$

For $t > 0$, and T the time to reach the absorbing state, we obtain:

$$P\{T > t\} = P\{X(t) \notin (m + 1, \ldots, m + n)\} \tag{12}$$

Where $m \geq 0, n > 0$, we have $(m + 1)$ states, and the next states are absorbing ones.

$$P\{T > t\} = 1 - \sum_{j=1}^{n} p_{0,m+j}(t) \tag{13}$$

Then time interval T may be displayed by:

$$F_T(t) = \sum_{j=1}^{n} p_{0,m+j}(t) \tag{14}$$

Where $p_{0,m+j}(t)$ is given by Eq. (3) [5–7].

2 The Model for IoT Diagnosis of FMS

The basic cell of the IoT system diagnosis of a FMS consists of a computer e.g. server connected to Internet, S_i, with memory buffer and its downstream machine from the FMS. In Fig. 1 we depicted the Markov chain model of the one of the n identical cells of our model for IoT control and diagnosis of a FMS, where n represents the number of servers necessary to control the FMS [4, 5].

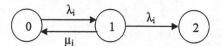

Fig. 1. The basic model of Markov chain for IoT diagnosis.

The meaning of the cell depicted in Fig. 1 is that the server S_i is in state 0 when there is no information to process, and there is the transfer of the information to/from machines of FMS. In state 1, we process information, and a deadlock occurs in state 2. Information bits transfer rate is λ_i and the servers processing rate of information bits is μ_i. The Markov chain model for IoT diagnosis of FMS is depicted in Fig. 2.

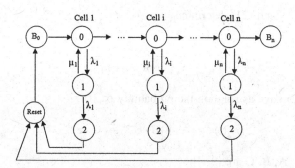

Fig. 2. Markov chain model for IoT diagnosis of FMS.

Here T is the time elapses until deadlock occurs, and deadlock is a probability $Da_T(t) = p_{02}(t)$. In order to determine $p_{02}(t)$ we will use the generator W of the above depicted Markov chain:

$$W = \begin{bmatrix} -\lambda_i & \lambda_i & 0 \\ \mu_i & -(\lambda_i + \mu_i) & \lambda_i \\ 0 & 0 & 0 \end{bmatrix} \tag{15}$$

From Eq. (6) we have the probability $p_{02}(t)$:

$$\frac{d}{dt} p_{02}(t) = w_{00} \cdot p_{02}(t) + w_{01} \cdot p_{12}(t) + w_{02} \cdot p_{22}(t) \tag{16}$$

But we also have $w_{02} = 0$, and therefore:

$$\frac{d}{dt} p_{02}(t) = -\lambda_i \cdot p_{02}(t) + \lambda_i \cdot p_{12}(t) \tag{17}$$

Similar, for $p_{12}(t)$ we have:

$$\frac{d}{dt} p_{12}(t) = w_{10} \cdot p_{02}(t) + w_{11} \cdot p_{12}(t) + w_{12} \cdot p_{22}(t) \tag{18}$$

And $p_{22}(t) = 1$, and therefore:

$$\frac{d}{dt} p_{12}(t) = -\mu_i \cdot p_{02}(t) - (\lambda_i + \mu_i) \cdot p_{12}(t) + \lambda_i \tag{19}$$

Where $p_{ij}(s)$ is the Laplace transform of $p_{ij}(t)$:

$$sp_{02}(s) = -\lambda_i p_{02}(s) + \lambda_i p_{12}(s) \tag{20}$$

$$sp_{12}(s) = \mu_i p_{02}(s) - (\lambda_i + \mu_i) \cdot p_{12}(s) + \frac{\lambda_i}{s} \tag{21}$$

Equations (20) and (21) determine:

$$p_{02}(s) = \frac{\lambda_i^2}{s\left[s^2 + s(2\lambda_i + \mu_i) + \lambda_i^2\right]} \tag{22}$$

And Eq. (22) have as solution the probability $p_{02}(t)$:

$$p_{02}(t) = A + B \cdot e^{-at} + C \cdot e^{-bt} \tag{23}$$

Where, a, b, A, B, C are [2, 3]:

$$a = \frac{2\lambda_i + \mu_i + \sqrt{\mu_i^2 + 4\lambda_i \mu_i}}{2} \tag{24}$$

$$b = \frac{2\lambda_i + \mu_i - \sqrt{\mu_i^2 + 4\lambda_i\mu_i}}{2} \qquad (25)$$

$$A = \frac{\lambda_i}{ab}; \ B = \frac{\lambda_i(b - 2a)}{ab(b - a)}; \ C = \frac{\lambda_i}{b(b - a)} \qquad (26)$$

3   The Events of Memory Buffers

For components manufactured in FMS, the transition from one event to next event depends on current state and on the generator W of the FMS. So, we may say that in a FMS controlled by IoT deadlocks have mainly two possibilities of diagnosis: a blocked server empties its memory or information less (e.g. empty server) commands its downstream machine. Therefore the events dynamic is determined by information which flow both way from S_i to the downstream machine. We consider a FMS controlled by servers S_{i-1}, S_i and S_{i+1}, and the memory buffers B_{i-1} and B_i. We assume that an event occurs at time t and let TA be the estimated time of the next event. We have:

μ_i is the information processing speed (bits-unit/time-unit) of server S_i, i = 1,..., n.

$$S(i,t) = \begin{cases} 1, \text{if server } S_i \text{ is functional} \\ 0, \text{if } S_i \text{ is under repair} \end{cases}$$

$$B(j,t) = \begin{cases} 0, \text{if buffer } B_j \text{ is empty} \\ 2, \text{if buffer } B_j \text{ is full} \\ 1, \text{otherwise state} \end{cases}$$

$$BEj(t) = \begin{cases} 1, \text{if } B_j \text{ empties at time t} \\ 0, \text{otherwise} \end{cases}$$

$T_{1j}(t)$ Time necessary to store information in B_j
$T_{2j}(t)$ Time necessary to deliver information from B_j

We have the following scenarios:
First scenario: server S_{i+1} is faster than S_{i-1}. This is modeled in Fig. 3 and we have [6–8]:

$$(T_{21} > T_{1,i-1} + \frac{1}{\mu_i}) \cap (\mu_{i+1} > \mu_{i-1}) \qquad (27)$$

In Figs. 3 and 4 we depicted with continuous line server data processing and with arrows we depicted data flow [5–7]. Intervals blank mark the idle processing time due to blockage/repair of servers. Memory buffer B_i empties from full memory. The end of processing time of the $(N_i + 1)$ bits on server S_i is greater than the time when memory B_i empties. The dual case is for the first N_i bits. Therefore we have [8]:

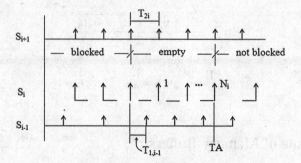

Fig. 3. Dynamic of servers when S_{i+1} is faster than S_{i-1}.

$$t + T_{2i} + \frac{N_i}{\mu_{i+1}} < t + T_{1,i-1} + \frac{N_i}{\mu_{i-1}} + \frac{1}{\mu_i} \tag{28}$$

and

$$TA = t + T_{2i} + \frac{N_i - 1}{\mu_{i+1}} \ge t + T_{1,i-1} + \frac{N_i - 1}{\mu_{i-1}} + \frac{1}{\mu_i} \tag{29}$$

For B_i Eqs. (27) and (28) estimate the bits to next event:

$$N_i = 1 + \text{Int}\left\{ \frac{T_{2i} - T_{1,i-1} - \frac{1}{\mu_i}}{\frac{1}{\mu_{i-1}} - \frac{1}{\mu_{i+1}}} \right\} \tag{30}$$

Another scenario studied here is dual to first discuss: server M_{i-1} process data faster than server S_{i+1} and the empty server S_i fills its memory buffer B_i [9–12]. After that, server S_{i-1} processes N_{i-1} bits, and blockage is modeled in Fig. 4.

$$\left(T_{2i} > T_{1,i-1} + \frac{1}{\mu_i} \right) \cap (\mu_{i-1} > \mu_{i+1}) \tag{31}$$

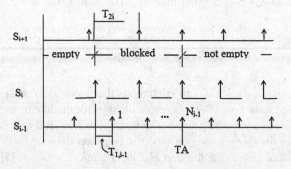

Fig. 4. Dynamic of servers when S_{i-1} is faster than S_{i+1}.

Figure 4 shows that arrival time of $(N_{i-1} + 1)$ bits at buffer B_{i-1} is less than the processing time of server S_i. The dual case holds for the first N_{i-1} bits [13–16]. Therefore we have:

$$t + T_{2i} + \frac{N_{i-1} - 1}{\mu_{i+1}} > t + T_{1,i-1} + \frac{N_{i-1}}{\mu_{i-1}} \tag{32}$$

and

$$TA = t + T_{2i} + \frac{N_{i-1} - 1}{\mu_{i+1}} \leq t + T_{1,i-1} + \frac{N_{i-1} - 1}{\mu_{i-1}} \tag{33}$$

Similar with the first scenario, for B_{i-1} we estimate the next event:

$$N_{i-1} = 1 + \text{Int} \left\{ \frac{T_{1,i-1} - T_{2i} - \frac{1}{\mu_{i+1}}}{\frac{1}{\mu_{i+1}} - \frac{1}{\mu_{i-1}}} \right\} \tag{34}$$

Equations (29) and (33) allow us to avoid the above mentioned scenarios of deadlocks by fairly dimensioning the buffers, and taking into consideration flow rate of bits until next event: $T_{21} = p_{02}$ in relation (29) and, respectively,

$T_{1,i-1} = p_{02}$ in relation (33); where p_{02} is given by relation (23) [16, 17]. As we proved in this paper the failure/blocking of servers can be avoided, if the buffer size is larger than the critical size determined with Eqs. (30), (33) and (34). The necessary and sufficient condition is to have an average time to repair a server smaller than the average time to fill the memory of server.

4   Estimating the Main Characteristics of Industry IoT

For determining the performance of IoT systems, we consider the model described in previous sections and we also consider that our system consists of n servers which receive data according to a Poisson process with rate λ_i, and process workflow data is given by rate μ_i (e.g. each computer receives data with rate λ_i, and processes data with rate μ_i, where i = 1, ..., n; with n the total set of computers in our system). Let W(t) be the number of servers which process data at time t and let Q(t) be the number of servers needed to process data at time t. We will determine the performance parameters for the system described in chapter 2 using the bi-variant system (W(t), Q(t)). As we described earlier our IoT system we can model it as a Markov process with state space S = {1, 2, ..., w} X {1, 2, ..., q}, (where w and q belong to N, the set of natural numbers, and w $\leq$ n; q $\leq$ n), with transitions rates defined as for a classic M/G/1/∞. We discuss two possible cases [18]:

1. The number of servers, w_i, which process data is: $0 \leq w_i \leq n - 1$, and $0 \leq q_i \leq n - 1$, and for this scenario we have an average number of blocked servers given by the following relations:

$$
b_{\left(w_j, q_j\right)} =
\begin{cases}
\lambda, & \left(w_j, q_j\right) = (w_i + 1, q_i) \\
w_i, & \left(w_j, q_j\right) = (w_i - 1, q_i) \\
q_i \mu, & \left(w_j, q_j\right) = (w_i + 1, q_i - 1) \\
-(\lambda + w_i + q_i \mu), & \left(w_j, q_j\right) = (w_i, q_i) \\
0, \text{else}
\end{cases}
\tag{35}
$$

Where $\left(w_j x q_j\right) \in S, w_i \geq w_j; q_i \geq q_j$.

2. The number of servers, w_i, which process data is: $w_i = n - k$, with $k < n, k \in N$, and $0 \leq q_i \leq n - 1$, and for this scenario we have an average number of blocked servers given by the following relations:

$$
b_{(w_j, q_j)} =
\begin{cases}
\lambda, & \left(w_j, q_j\right) = (n, q_i + 1) \\
n, & \left(w_j, q_j\right) = (n - 1, q_i) \\
-(\lambda + n), & \left(w_j, q_j\right) = (n, q_i) \\
0, \text{else}
\end{cases}
\tag{36}
$$

Where $\left(w_j x q_j\right) \in S, w_i \geq w_j; q_i \geq q_j$.

The main characteristics of an industrial IoT are obtained considering the transition probabilities $p_{ij} = P\{W(t) = w_i, Q(t) = q_i\}$ associated to bi-variant system $(W(t), Q(t))$, by solving the Kolmogorov attached Eq.°[19]:

$$
(\lambda + w_i + q_i \mu)p_{ij} = \lambda p_{i-1 j} + (q_i + 1)\mu p_{i-1, j+1} + (w_i + 1)p_{i+1 j}, 0 \leq w_i \leq n - 1
\tag{37}
$$

$$
(\lambda + n)p_{nj} = \lambda p_{n-1 j} + (q_i + 1)\mu p_{n-1 j+1} + \lambda p_{n, j-1}, w_i = n
\tag{38}
$$

Using the system associated to our model, we obtain:
The loss formula [20]:

$$
B(n) = \lim_{t \to \tau} P\{W(t) = n\}
\tag{39}
$$

Where τ is the observation time, e.g. the work flow time, which is a multiple of working shift, or theoretically is ∞.
Relation (39) becomes for our system:

$$
B(n) = \sum_{j=0}^{n} p_{nj}
\tag{40}
$$

The formula for finding the number of servers needed for optimum data processing [21]:

$$D_q = \lim_{t \to \tau} E\{Q(t)\} \tag{41}$$

Where $E\{A(t)\}$ represents the mean value of variable $A(t)$.

Relation (41) becomes for our system:

$$D_q = \frac{(1+\mu)\left\{\lambda + \lambda^2 - E[W(t)]^2\right\}}{\mu(n-\lambda)} \tag{42}$$

The formula for determining the optimum number of servers processing data at time t [21]:

$$S_{PD} = \lim_{t \to \tau} E[W(t)] \tag{43}$$

Relation (43) becomes for our system:

$$S_{PD} = \lambda \tag{44}$$

5 Conclusions

A model for IoT diagnosis of a FMS diagnosis has been proposed in this paper. The model may be obtained with our discrete-event approach or using heuristic models. A discrete-event system formulation and FMS controlled by IoT connected by processing cells and fast determines an accurate diagnosis at an increased speed and costless. We observe that if the deadlock/repair time is known and the duration of diagnosis estimation is less than it, then transient analysis is more appropriate than the steady state analysis. The main characteristics of an IoT were estimated by modelling it with a Markov chain and applying Kolmogorov equations. The results obtained confirm the model we proposed. As far as we know this is a first exercise for its kind and we strongly believe that explosive development of IoT will enrich the literature with more developed models and deepest analysis concerning the future capabilities of Internet. Further development of this approach should focus on intelligent flexible manufacturing systems modelled with Markov chains which have self-recovery algorithms from deadlock situations.

References

1. Viswandham, N., Narahari, J.: Performance Modeling of Automated Manufacturing System. Prentice Hall, Englewood Cliffs, NJ (1992)
2. Kemeny, J., Snell, W.: Finite Markov Chains. Van Nostrand, NJ (1960)

3. Buzacott, J.A., Shantikumar, J.G.: Stochastic Models of Manufacturing System. Prentice Hall, Englewood Cliffs, NJ (1993)
4. Narahari, J., Viswandham, N.: Transient analysis of manufacturing system performance. IEEE Trans. Rob. Autom. **10**(2), 230–234 (1994)
5. Ciufudean, C., Satco, B.: Algebraic formalism for modelling the deadlock in flexible manufacturing systems. J. Appl. Math. **1**(3), 157–165 (2008)
6. Viswandham, N., Ram, R.: Composite performance-dependability analysis of cellular manufacturing systems. IEEE. Rob. Autom. **10**(2), 245–258 (1994)
7. Dallery, J., Gershwin, S.B.: Manufacturing flow line systems: A review of models and analytical results, Technical report 91−002. Laboratory for Manufacturing and Productivity, MIT (1992)
8. Martinelli, F., Shu, C., Perkins, J.R.: On the optimality of Myopic productions controls for single-server continuous-flow manufacturing systems. IEEE Trans. Autom. Contr. **46**(8), 1269–1273 (2001)
9. di Benedetto, M.D., Vintecentelli, A.S., Villa, T.: Model matching for finite state machines. IEEE Trans. Autom. Contr. **46**(11), 1726–1743 (2001)
10. Harrell, C.: The Internet of Things and control system architecture (2014). http://blog.aac.advantech.com/the-internet-of-things-and-control-system-architecture
11. Dolin, R.: Building an IoT for industrial control: Part 1 – What is Industrial IoT? (2015). http://www.embedded.com/design/real-world-applications/4426952/Building
12. Storey, H., Bullotta, R., Drolet, D.: The industrial internet of things (2014). http://www.controleng.com/industry-news/single-article/the-industrial-internet-of-things/c98837a0efec387df9fc14c2de0a3b2f.ht
13. Vermesan, O., Friess, P. (eds.): Internet of Things – From Research and Innovation to Market Deployment. River Publishers, Aalborg, Denmark (2014)
14. Ciufudean, C., Filote, C.: Safety discrete event models for holonic cyclic manufacturing systems. In: Mařík, V., Strasser, T., Zoitl, A. (eds.) HoloMAS 2009. LNCS, vol. 5696, pp. 225–233. Springer, Heidelberg (2009). doi:10.1007/978-3-642-03668-2_22
15. Ciufudean, C., Filote, C., Amarandei, D.: Measuring the performance of distributed systems with discrete event formalisms. In: Proceeding of the 2nd Seminar for Advanced Industrial Control Applications (SAICA), Madrid, Spain (2007)
16. Ciufudean, C., Graur, A., Filote, C., Turcu, C., Popa, V.: Diagnosis of complex systems using ant colony decision petri nets. In: The First International Conference on Availability, Reliability and Security (ARES 2006), Vienna, Austria (2006)
17. Ciufudean, C., Satco, B., Filote, C.: Reliability Markov chains for security data transmitter analysis. In: The Second International Conference on Availability, Reliability and Security (ARES 2007), pp. 886–894 (2007)
18. Taylor, G., McClean, S., Millard, P.: Continuous-time Markov models for Geriatric patient behavior. Appl. Stoch. Models Data Anal. **13**, 315–323 (1998)
19. Kolmogorov, A.N.: Basic Concepts of Probability Theory. ONTI, Moscow (1936)
20. Kendall, D.G.: Some recent works and further problems in the theory of queue. Prob. Th. Appl. **9**(1), 3–15 (1964)
21. Schrijner P.: Quasi-stationarity of discrete time markov chains, Thesis Universiteit Twente Enschede (1995). ISBN:90-9008502-5

Monitoring Data Reduction in Data Centers: A Correlation-Based Approach

Xuesong Peng[✉] and Barbara Pernici

Dipartimento di Elettronica Informazione e Bioingegneria, Politecnico di Milano,
Piazza Leonardo da Vinci, 32, 20133 Milan, Italy
{xuesong.peng,barbara.pernici}@polimi.it

Abstract. Monitoring data are collected and stored in a wide range of domains, especially in data centers, which integrate myriads of services and massive data. To handle the inevitable challenges brought by increasing volume of monitoring data, this paper proposes a correlation-based reduction method for streaming data that derives quantitative formulas between correlated indicators, and reduces the sampling rate of some indicators by replacing them with formulas predictions. This approach also revises formulas through iterations of the reduction process to find an adaptive solution in dynamic environments of data centers. One highlight of this work is the ability to work on upstream side, i.e., it can reduce volume requirements for data collection of monitoring systems. This work also tests the approach with both simulated and real data, showing that our approach is capable of data reduction in complex data centers.

Keywords: Monitoring data · Data reduction · Time-series prediction · Data center

1 Introduction

As data centers need to handle large amounts of service requests, in order to optimize efficiency of resource usage, energy consumption and CO_2 emissions, data centers exploit various monitoring systems currently available in industry and as open-source components to understand the dynamic operating conditions. These monitoring systems provide sensing services both on the physical environment and on computing resources, monitoring variables like CPU usage, memory usage, and power consumption as indicators to measure working conditions of virtual machines and host servers.

Even though monitoring systems aim to improve efficiency, the workload for data collection and data utilization can become a heavy burden because the number of virtual machines and hosts in a data center is always large and values of indicators are continuously changing. Furthermore, in the era of Big Data, the size and energy consumption of data centers are also increasing owing to expansion of the Internet. Future growth of data centers will doubtlessly raise

© Springer International Publishing AG 2017
M. Helfert et al. (Eds.): SMARTGREENS 2016 and VEHITS 2016, CCIS 738, pp. 135–153, 2017.
DOI: 10.1007/978-3-319-63712-9_8

several challenges to the monitoring systems, such as efficiency and cost of data acquisition, data transmission, data storage and so on. In short, the increasing size of data is becoming a key problem.

As a proposal in the direction of reducing this problem, we explore data reduction technologies to reduce data quantity and also keep informative values. This work focuses on monitoring data of data centers, and most data are numerical time-series data, namely, the representation of a collection of values obtained from sequential measurements over time [4]. While other reduction techniques try to bring down costs of data storage or data transmission, this paper looks at the data reduction problem from a different point of view: indicators of data center are not standalone, their correlations reflect characteristics of system behaviors somehow. We consider the common data correlations between indicators as important clues to large amount of data redundancy, which can be reduced at low cost, so reducing only correlated data could avoid much aimless computation and achieve reduction result at a good level. Thus, we introduce a novel approach to exploit correlations between indicators and predict values of some indicators with regression formulas, aiming to decreasing workloads of data collection in monitoring systems. Compared to other reduction techniques, this prediction method could work on the upstream side (namely, data collection) of data streams. Furthermore, for monitoring systems and other information systems driven by massive data, reducing the upstream means reducing workloads, including data acquisition, data transmission, data storage and so on. Extended from its previous conference version [10], which only reports the experimental results in the simulation tool, this book version includes experiment discussion on a real dataset.

The paper is organized as follows. In Sect. 2, we introduce related work of time series data reduction. In Sect. 3, we introduce the concept of correlation model and structure of our framework, and details on the predictor and regression models. We analyze the prediction power of regression formulas in simple controlled conditions in Sect. 4, involving several typical workload patterns. In Sect. 5, we study the predictor performance on simulated data and real data.

2   Related Work

Time series data are collected in various domains, and how to reduce the massive data size has become a main line of research. Dimension reduction techniques have been proposed in past few decades, such as PCA (Principal Component Analysis) [6], PAA (Piecewise Aggregate Approximation) [7], and many projects also used signal transformations like DFT (Discrete Fourier Transform), DWT (Discrete Wavelet Transform), and so on.

Some projects also used common statistical methods. In [3], a clustering method for large-scale time series data called YADING exploits random sampling and PAA to simultaneously reduce multivariate data in both time and dimension directions. The Cypress framework [11] substitutes the single raw data stream with several sub-streams which can support for archival and simple statistical query of massive time series data.

Even though those techniques give solutions to the reduction problem of time series data in information theory, they still have very limited usage in real projects of many domains, because their lack of semantic information cause much aimless computation. Furthermore, in the WSN (Wireless Sensor Network) domain, some projects exploit correlation-based methods to reduce data traffic in networks, the work of [2] improves prediction accuracy of sensing data based on multivariate spatial and temporal correlation, and [16] presents an adaptation scheme using sensors of different types to enhance the system fault tolerance. However, those two methods assume that the correlations between variables are static, while the reality is not.

CloudSense [8] proposes a switch design on the data center network topology, which exploits compressive sensing to lower monitoring data transmission. CloudSense aggregates status information in each switch level and finally provides a general status report of the whole data center, allowing early detection of relative anomalies. However, this work is not able to reduce data collection volume, and only the applications of anomaly detection can use the compressed outputs, ruling out other possibilities.

An initial version of the Correlation-Model Based Data Reduction (CMBDR) framework was proposed in [9], to reduce data by building piecewise regression models for correlated data on the basis of priori knowledge. Based on that proposal, this work elaborates CMBDR further and develops techniques to enable the application of this approach to data centers. Aimed to reduce upcoming data streams, we exploit indicators relation networks of data center to adapt to the specific scenario, and design an online predictor based on CMBDR for dynamic streams.

3   Data Reduction Method

This section illustrates the correlation-based approach of data reduction, which uses regression formulas between correlated indicators, to reduce sampling rate of some indicators, and to reconstruct monitoring data stream with formulas and other indicators. Section 3.1 introduces the data center indicator network proposed in the literature [14], based on which we build our initial correlation model to provide guidance to the reduction process. In Sect. 3.2, the correlation model based data reduction method is presented. Then Sects. 3.3 and 3.4 give details on the stream predictor design and regression techniques respectively.

3.1   Data Center Indicators Relation Network

In [14], an indicator network is proposed to understand the behavior of monitoring variables in data centers. The indicator network model aims to illustrate relations among indicators and provide adaptation actions that lead data center to a better state. The model consists of two layers: goal layer and treatment layer, but this paper only introduces the goal layer as depicted in Fig. 1, because it indicates the knowledge of data correlations. Instead of using a human expertise,

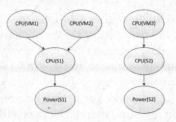

Fig. 1. The indicators relation network [14].

the indicators network automatically learns from historical data. First, possible relations between indicators are learned by putting a threshold over their Pearson correlation coefficients; then a MMHC-like algorithm [12] is applied to orient all network edges; finally a Bayesian Network is derived from monitored data, depicting relations among indicators. Thus, as the starting point of this paper, this Bayesian Network model (a DAG) provides correlations between indicators learned from historical data and it gives an initial input to the data reduction. This paper only takes advantage of the DAG to serve as a model illustrating correlations, called correlation model, and a directed edge from indicator A to indicator B in the model implies that values of B are conditionally dependent on A, thus we could make predictions of B based on the value of A.

3.2 CMBDR Framework

Data centers monitor a variety of variables continuously, so values of each variable are in time-series, among which most are numerical values. In this paper, we refer to those numerical variables as indicators, and we consider the reduction problem of multiple indicators streams. Denoting the set of all indicators as S, this reduction method proposes to use a subset of S, referred as *Regressor Indicators Set* (RS), to predict values of other indicators, denoted as *Dependent Indicators Set* (DS). We try to find a function F to quantify the relation between DS and RS as Eqs. 1 and 2 show, so that data of dependent indicators can be reduced. Namely, on the micro level, each dependent indicator $di_m \in DS$ requires a formula f to reproduce di_m based on values of several regressor indicators $ri_n \in RS$, called *Correlated Regressor Set* (CRS), as Eqs. 3 and 4 show. This work achieves two goals:

- To identify appropriate RS/DS and CRS, derive accurate prediction formulas for dependent indicators;
- To reduce data volume of dependent indicators in data collection.

$$DS = S - RS \tag{1}$$

$$DS = F(RS) \tag{2}$$

$$di_m = f(ri_1, ri_2, \cdots, ri_l) \tag{3}$$

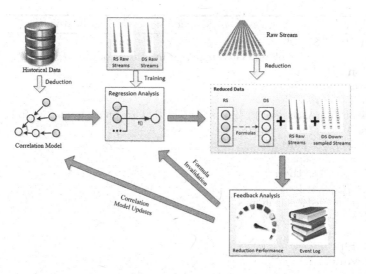

Fig. 2. CMBDR prediction framework.

$$CRS[di_m] = \{ri_1, ri_2, \cdots, ri_l\} \tag{4}$$

With known correlations provided by the correlation model and RS/DS configuration, CMBDR recurses correlations in the DAG to identify CRS, and performs regression analyses on values of correlated indicators in a short period (called training window), to find a formula fitting the quantitative relations of these variables. Thus values of the dependent indicator di_m can be reproduced by the formula and correlated indicators $CRS[di_m]$, achieving data reduction. This framework conducts model-based reduction online, adjusting the CRS and the reduction process based on performance feedback. Depicted in Fig. 2, CMBDR separates the reduction process into several iterations of the following four main steps.

- *correlation model deduction*: It derives the indicators correlation model for the data center as Sect. 3.1 illustrating, assigns RS/DS and selects the correlated regressor indicators $CRS[di_m]$ for each dependent indicator di_m;
- *regression formula learning*: To train a formula for each dependent indicator and quantify their relations with regressor indicators.
- *dependent indicators reduction*: To reduce sampling rate of dependent indicators, and adopt predictions of the formulas to replace lost samples.
- *feedback analysis*: To evaluate the performance of the reduction process, and try to find possible problems and solutions to improve it.

The correlation model deduction is based on the indicator relation network illustrated in Sect. 3.1, which specifies highly-correlated indicators. We generate this indicators network under a variable workload, in order to find workload independent correlations. We consider the correlations as a consequence of interconnections of data center modules, for instance, the CPU usage of a virtual

---

Algorithm 1. Select regressor set for each dependent indicator di_m.

Require: RS, DS, $DAG(V, E)$
Ensure: CRS {the set of correlated regressor indicators of each di_m}
  Function $SelectCRS$
  Stack $stack := \emptyset$
  for ri in RS **do**
    $stack$.push(neighbors(ri)) {find neighbors that are linked by an edge from current
    node v}
    while $stack \neq \emptyset$ **do**
      $v := stack$.pop;
      if v is in DS **then**
        $CRS[v]$.add(ri)
        $stack$.push(neighbors(v))
      else
        continue
      end if
    end while
  end for
  return CRS
  End Function

---

machine is always correlated to the CPU usage of its host. So we extract the DAG of the relation network as correlation model, and with help of this model, we can identify several indicators capable of predicting dependent indicators. Then we assign the nodes of DAG to RS/DS, and select correlated regressor indicators $CRS[di_m]$ of di_m by Algorithm 1. This algorithm selects regressor indicators $ri \in RS$ to predict the dependent indicator $di \in DS$ if ri has a directed path p to di in the DAG, and no other regressor indicators exist on the path p. The selection of RS/DS and CRS has obvious impacts on reduction performance, so in order to minimize the size of RS, we select root nodes of the DAG as regressor indicators of the first loop, and select other nodes as dependent indicators. In case the reduction performance is poor under current RS/DS configuration, we update the RS/DS in the following loops according to feedback analysis results. In addition, the correlation model is not static in the framework, we need to recompute it if some indicators are added or removed in the monitoring system.

In the regression formula learning step, in order to quantify relations between indicators, we exploit regression techniques on correlated indicators. A training window of streaming data is fetched for each group of indicators as selected in the first step, then linear regression analysis is carried out, deriving a prediction formula f that can reproduce values of the dependent indicator.

Then in the dependent indicators reduction step, formulas make predictions to replace raw samples of the dependent indicators partially. As Fig. 2 depicts, sampling rates of dependent indicators are reduced to a lower level, and the lost samples are replaced by the formula predictions, which are derived out of the values of regressor indicators. Furthermore, we compare samples of the dependent indicators to prediction results, providing a glimpse of accuracy performance.

Therefore, the final reduced data is composed of several parts, namely, all raw samples of regressor indicators, training samples and checking samples of dependent indicators, and formulas parameters.

Finally, the framework performs feedback analyses, in which reduction performance and the event log of the data center are analyzed to generate feedbacks, helping to improve the next loop. Reduction performance is evaluated with combined criteria, covering compression ratio, execution time and informative value. By spotting the indicators and formulas with poor performance, we identify problems in each iteration, so we can update the corresponding regression formulas and CRS to improve performance. In addition, events in the log can also guide the reduction process to adapt to the changes of the data center environment. For instance, in the feedback analysis, if we found a virtual machine is added to or removed from a host server in feedback analysis, then we need to recompute the correlation model before running the next loop. Details will be discussed in Sect. 5.

3.3   Indicators Stream Predictor

This section illustrates the design of the indicators stream predictor, which is a first implementation of the CMBDR framework. Based on the correlation model, the predictor tries to figure out formulas of indicators by regression analysis on the training dataset, and reduces their sampling rate to a low level to serve as check items. Its working procedures mainly include two phases: training phase and prediction phase, the predictor always trains the formulas in training phase, and then verifies the formulas in prediction phase. If a prediction result does not match the sample result, then a prediction failure is generated as feedback and the corresponding formula needs to be recomputed in the next training phase. The predictor workflow is depicted in Fig. 3. Before predictor running, the correlation model is initialized and some parameters are configured. After the training phase starts, the predictor carries out regression analysis for each formula which involves a dependent indicator di_m and also correlated regressor indicators $ri \in CRS[di_m]$. Subsequently, we cut down the sampling rate of dependent indicators in the prediction phase. Then we compare each sample with prediction results, and if their difference (residual) exceeds predefined tolerance, the prediction will be considered as a failure and the prediction phase of this formula will be terminated by a new training phase.

In order to control efficiency and accuracy of the reduction process, we introduce three important parameters to the predictor:

- *Length of training data set*: the number of samples required to train a formula, denoted as LT;
- *Prediction tolerance*: the range for prediction errors (or residuals) within which the prediction will not be considered as a failure, denoted as PT;
- *Prediction sampling rate*: sampling rate for dependent indicators in prediction phase, denoted as SR, which should be generally smaller than the original sampling rate.

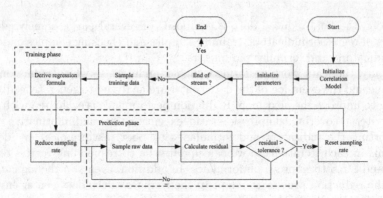

Fig. 3. Predictor workflow.

3.4   Linear Regression Method

To achieve our goal, the adopted reduction methods should have the ability to derive quickly the quantitative relationship between indicators in a time slot, and to predict future values of some indicators. In this approach, we explore methods of regression analysis to discover formulas quantifying the relationships and predicting values of dependent indicators based on regressor indicators. Considering the time to find fitting regression models of streaming indicators, the computation complexity of regression analysis must be limited. Thus, CMBDR should give preference to the regression model with the least time complexity, namely, the linear regression model.

Generally, linear regression is an approach modeling linear formulas between scalar dependent variables and independent variables. While multiple linear regression attempts to model the relationship between two or more independent variables and a response variable by fitting a linear equation to observed data (see Eq. 5), simple linear regression is a special case of multiple linear regression having only one independent variable (see Eq. 6). In the two equations, suppose data consists of n observations $\{y_i, x_{i1}, \cdots, x_{ip}\}_{i=1}^n$, then x_{ij} means the jth independent variable measured for the ith observation, y_i means the response variable measured for the ith observation, α is called intercept, β_j are called slopes or coefficients, ϵ_i are an unobserved random variable that adds noise to the linear relationship.

$$y_i = \alpha + \beta_1 x_{i1} + \cdots + \beta_p x_{ip} + \epsilon_i \tag{5}$$

$$y_i = \alpha + \beta_1 x_i + \epsilon_i \tag{6}$$

If X (the matrix of x_{ij}) is full column rank, CMBDR uses OLS (Ordinary Least Squares) regression method to estimate parameters of the formula minimizing SSR (sum of squared residuals) over all possible values of the intercept and slopes, as shown in Eq. 7. Details of OLS method can be found in [5]. If X is not full column rank, then some column vectors must be linearly dependent, thus CMBDR applies Gaussian Elimination to get the full column rank matrix and then applies the OLS method.

$$SSR = \sum_i (y_i - \alpha - \beta_1 x_{i1} - \cdots - \beta_p x_{ip})^2 \tag{7}$$

4   Prediction Formula Validation

Regression analysis derives the prediction formula that best fits training datasets. Therefore, this formula could maintain a high prediction rate on following testing data until the quantitative relation changes and prediction rate dramatically decreases. So understanding when the relation will change is quite important for predictor performance. In this section, in order to get insights into the behaviors of the predictor, we study prediction failures of the regression formulas under certain controlled conditions, by designing several particular patterns to model typical situations in data centers and validating prediction formulas in each situation.

Experiments are conducted in MATLAB with a data center simulation framework [13]. With proper settings of the simulated data center, we are able to control the framework to generate monitoring data under specific workload, thus we can evaluate performance of the predictor on various conditions.

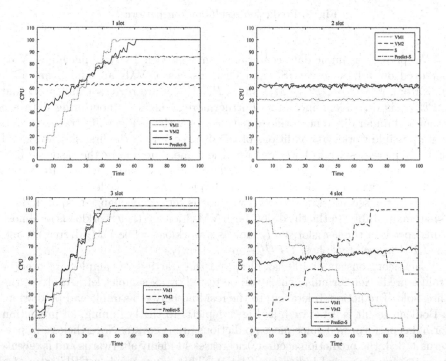

Fig. 4. CPU ratios in four patterns (VM_1 - dotted lines, VM_2 - dashed lines, S - solid lines, Prediction of S - dash-dot lines.)

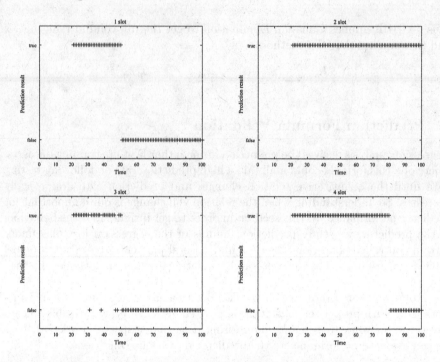

Fig. 5. Prediction results in four patterns.

We prepare a simple data center environment with 2 virtual machines (VM) deployed on 1 host server (S), and CPU usages of VMs are and S are all 3 indicators, in which $CPU(VM_1)$ and $CPU(VM_2)$ are regressor indicators and $CPU(S)$ is dependent indicator. Furthermore, 4 slots of monitoring data are generated under different workload patterns of VMs, as Fig. 4 illustrates, to simulate possible workload conditions of the data center. In the first slot, workload of VM_1 increases while VM_2 remains the same, but due to the resource limits, the indicators $CPU(VM_1)$ and $CPU(S)$ stop increasing when CPU ratios reach 100%, which means the workload requests have exceeded the processing power. In the second slot, two VMs workloads remain unchanged, so all indicators remain stable. In the third slot, both VMs increase their workloads at almost same speed; in the last slot, VM_1 increases workload while VM_2 decreases, and the CPU usage of the host $CPU(S)$ grows slowly.

Each slot consists of 100 samples, and the starting 20 samples are used to train a prediction formula, which will be tested by all samples left. Applying the threshold (Prediction Tolerance) to the residual between sample and prediction, a Boolean result is generated, as Fig. 5 depicts. In the beginning, all prediction formulas perform well since most predictions are accurate. Nevertheless, in patterns 1, 3, 4, the prediction accuracy decreases suddenly afterwards and it reveals a significant change of indicators relation. This happens when CPU ratio of a VM reach 100% so it has to stop the previous trend.

These sudden relation changes can be explained by overload conditions of VMs and the server. In a cloud, when a VM get overloaded, the real CPU consumption of the VM is still increasing even if monitored indicator $CPU(VM)$ remains at 100%, because VM can acquire additional resources from the host server. Thus, the previous prediction formula cannot explain current overload situations, for instance, from the middle part of the first slot, the prediction remains stable since $CPU(VM_1)$ and $CPU(VM_2)$ remain unchanged, but the indicator $CPU(S)$ is still increasing because the real workload request of VM_1 does not stop increasing.

This experiment demonstrates two outcomes. First and most importantly, the regression formula of correlated indicators is capable of making accurate predictions in certain conditions. Secondly, the quantitative relations between indicators are not static, and they evolve with the dynamic data center environment. Considering these two outcomes, in CMBDR framework, we exploit regression formulas to capture temporary quantitative relation between correlated indicators, and with feedback loops we adapt to dynamic changes of formulas and correlations.

5   Experimental Study

In this section, we assess CMBDR performance in data centers based on experimental results. First we conduct experiments in the simulation tool, then we test the framework on a real dataset of a data center.

5.1   Evaluation Criteria

Monitoring data (systems) usually are not targeted to a specific application, therefore, we need to maintain a good quality of monitoring data in general. In order to evaluate the indicator stream predictor comprehensively, this work proposes combined evaluation criteria covering operation speed, reduction volume, and informative values of reduced data. Information value is a general term describing the ability of reduced data for supporting target applications; it could be distinct for wide varieties of applications. Thus, we exploit multiple metrics instead of a single criterion to measure informative values. Details of the combined evaluation metrics are as follows.

- *Execution time*: processing time for the predictor to reduce prepared data stream.
- *Reduction volume*: the difference between raw data size and reduced data size.
- *Hit rate*: Consider the prediction within the error range of raw data as a hit, thus the hit rate is the percentage of accurate predictions, which reflects informative values of reduced data.
- *Relative error*: this metric measures information loss of data reduction process, as shown in Eq. 8, for each indicator, η is relative error, ϵ is absolute error and v is the interval of the values in the test dataset.

$$\eta = \frac{\epsilon}{v} \tag{8}$$

– *Weighted mean of R^2*: R^2 is often used to measure total goodness of fit of linear regression models, as Eq. 9 depicts, y_i is raw value and f_i is prediction value. and $R^2 = 1$ indicates that the regression line perfectly fits raw data. In this work, R^2 is used to measure accuracy in each prediction phase, and length-based weighted average of those R^2 on data stream will be used as a metric to evaluate how well predictions fit raw data.

$$R^2 = 1 - \frac{\sum_{i=1}^{n}(y_i - f_i)^2}{\sum_{i=1}^{n}(y_i - \overline{y})^2} \tag{9}$$

5.2   Experiments in Simulatied Data Center

Experimental Settings. The data center simulation tool [13] creates a virtualized data center environment and allows the collection of monitoring data at different workload. This tool emulates VMs resource allocation on servers and generates monitoring data such as resource usage and power consumption under certain workload rates. It also estimate power consumption of a VM based on the amount of CPU it consumes.

To reveal the performance of CMBDR predictor, we test it in a larger data center. This data center consists of 100 servers with 6 VMs deployed on each server. Monitoring data stream includes 2000 indicators that cover CPU usage, response time and power consumption of both VMs and servers. As Table 1 depicts, in the initial reduction loop of CMBDR framework, we select root nodes (namely, $CPU(VM_{ij})$) of the correlation model as regressor indicators, and take other nodes as dependent indicators. Testing data are generated by the simulation tool under simulated daily workloads, with sampling rate of 1 per minute (1440 samples in one day).

As an important parameter of the predictor, prediction tolerance PT defines the threshold for prediction errors and has a great influence on reduction results. In this work, the value of PT is directly based on the measurement error of raw monitoring data. We first put the data center in a stable workload conditions, and collect values of indicators for a period. Therefore, the multiple samples are repeated measurements on the same state of the data center, they should follow normal distribution around the true value μ and variance is σ^2, as Eq. 10 depicts. Therefore, we exploit the 95% confidence interval (approximately $1.96 \times \sigma$) as a criteria for error behavior of raw samples, and assign it to PT as Eq. 11 shows. We consider the raw sample and the corresponding prediction as two observations on the same indicator, and if the difference between these two observations is within the 95% confidence interval, this prediction could be viewed as an accurate measurement, namely, a true prediction.

$$measurement \sim N(\mu, \sigma^2) \tag{10}$$

$$PT = 1.96 \times \sigma \tag{11}$$

Table 1. Indicators configurations in the first loop.

Indicator	Description	Unit	Indicator set	Regressor Indicators
$CPU(VM_{ij})$	CPU ratio of j_{th} VM deployed on S_i		RS	
$R(VM_{ij})$	Response time of j_{th} VM deployed on S_i	ms	DS	$CPU(VM_{ij})$
$P(VM_{ij})$	Instant power consumption of j_{th} VM deployed on S_i	Watt	DS	$CPU(VM_{ij})$
$CPU(S_i)$	CPU ratio of S_i		DS	$CPU(VM_{i1}) \cdots CPU(VM_{i6})$
$P(S_i)$	Instant power consumption of S_i	Watt	DS	$CPU(VM_{i1}) \cdots CPU(VM_{i6})$

Formulas Revisions. In the experiment, we monitor the reduction process, and measure performance of each formula using the aforementioned criteria. One interesting point we found is that the variability of prediction ability is significant between formulas. Some formulas can make very accurate predictions in a short execution time while some formulas fail frequently and cost more time to train new formulas. The reason for this discrepancy lies in the correlation model. In the reduction process, if a prediction formula does not meet accuracy requirements, then the predictor needs to learn a new regression formula to replace it, thus the formula could be always up-to-date. However, some dependent indicators may be hard to predict by selected regressor indicators, if their correlations are not high enough. Thus, the framework would take much time to update those formulas frequently, even though the general performance increases very little.

Therefore, in order to solve the problem, the predictor need to revise those inefficient formulas in the next reduction loop. We denote dependent indicators of those inefficient formulas as $slowDS$, and we need to expand RS to include a subset of $slowDS$ to enhance prediction ability, since results have proved current RS is not capable of making accurate predictions on those indicators. Among all possible solutions, adding the complete set of $slowDS$ to RS can solve the issue all at once, but obviously it can only achieve minimal data reduction. This work reconsiders correlations between indicators of $slowDS$ in the correlation model, it obtains several disconnected subgraphs of the DAG containing only the $slowDS$ nodes, and add the root nodes of subgraphs to RS. For instance, if any indicators of $slowDS$ are correlated, they must exist in the same subgraph, thus the corresponding root node would serve as the regressor indicator for other nodes in the next loop; otherwise all $slowDS$ will serve as regressor indicators. By this gradual means of expanding RS, appropriate RS/DS could be identified in iterations of reduction loops.

Table 2. Prediction performance of formulas in the same category.

	$R(VM)$	$P(VM)$	$CPU(S)$	$P(S)$	$P(S)revision$
Relative error	3.45E-03	1.97E-03	4.82E-02	4.86E-02	1.19E-04
Average R^2	0.889	0.917	0.220	0.208	1.000
Hit rate	95.96%	98.57%	82.01%	81.85%	100.00%
Reduction volume	1241.46	1304.32	900.37	893.20	1339.25
Execution time sec	0.144 s	0.070 s	0.680 s	0.690 s	0.029 s

In this experiment, CMBDR framework selects the root nodes of correlation model as RS in the first loop. Individual performance of indicators in the first loop are evaluated in the first 4 columns of Table 2, each column representing the average performance of indicators in the same category. Under initial RS/DS configuration, the indicators of $R(VM_{ij})$ and $P(VM_{ij})$ outperform evidently $CPU(S_i)$ and $P(S_i)$, with higher reduction volume, better prediction accuracy and much less execution time. To acquire better performance in the second loop iteration, we need to update RS/DS. By querying in the correlation model, we find $CPU(S_i)$ and $P(S_i)$ are highly correlated. Then we just move one indicator $CPU(S_i)$ from DS to RS, and then call Algorithm 1 to update regressor set CRS for $P(S_i)$, thus $CPU(S_i)$ would be used to predict $P(S_i)$ in the second loop. The performance are also measured, as the fifth column in Table 2 shows, both accuracy and execution speed are improved dramatically and the relative error is at the same level with $P(VM_{ij})$.

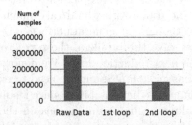

Fig. 6. Data volume before and after reduction.

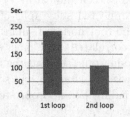

Fig. 7. Execution time of CMBDR loops.

We also measure overall reduction performance of monitoring data in reduction process, to verify the validity of this predictor and to assess the improvement offered by RS/DS updates. As Fig. 6 depicts, in both first and second loops, the predictor reduces the raw monitoring data to slightly above one-third of original volume, and reduction of 2 loops are nearly the same although the predictor involves more regressor indicators in the second loop. However, these new regressor indicators improve processing speed and accuracy performance of the predictor dramatically. As Figs. 7 and 8 show, the second loop doubles processing speed of the first loop, and increases average prediction accuracy by almost an order of magnitude. Results of the second loop in Figs. 7 and 8 also illustrate that, for a data center of 2000 indicators, this predictor is able to reduce daily monitoring data within 100 s, ensuring the average relative error at 10^{-3}.

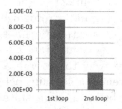

Fig. 8. Average relative error of the predictor.

Above all, this predictor could cut down the volume of data collection in monitoring systems, while still maintaining fast speed and a good quality of informative values.

5.3   Experiments on Real Data

Dataset Descriptions. The dataset is provided by Eco4Cloud in [1, 15], which includes monitoring data of 15 days. All indicators were sampled simultaneously with a sampling interval of 5 min. We select one server with 4 virtual machines as the testing environment, and the 20 indicators for data reduction include:

- $CPU(S)$: CPU ratio of the server.
- $MEM(S)$: Memory usage of the server.
- $P(S)$: Instant power consumption of the server.
- $BW(S)$: Bandwidth of the server.
- $CPU(VM_i)$: CPU ratio of the i_{th} VM.
- $MEM(VM_i)$: Memory usage of the i_{th} VM.
- $BW(VM_i)$: Bandwidth of the i_{th} VM.
- $IO(VM_i)$: I/O of the i_{th} VM.

Experimental Settings. Generally, we should first build a reliable correlation model based on a part of the dataset, and test the predictor with the data left. However, considering the length of this dataset, we do not have enough data to get both reliable correlation model and stable performances. Since the iterative loops can adjust the behavior in the reduction process, therefore we decided to use few data (1 day) to derive correlation matrix, and test the predictor with the data of the following 2 weeks.

To lower the possible impact of the imprecise correlation matrix, we select only one indicator as regressor indicator in the initial loop, and extend RS in the following loops. This indicator should be correlated to most indicators, namely, have high values in the correlation matrix. In this experiment, $CPU(S)$ is selected as the initial regressor indicator, which shares strong correlations ($pearson correlation > 0.5$) with 11 indicators.

As discussed in Sect. 5.2, the value of prediction tolerance PT has a great effect on prediction performances, and a recognized PT can make experiment results convincing. In this experiment, we cannot control VM workloads and measure standard deviation of the same state as in the simulation tool. However, we develop an alternative way to get approximate measurements of the same state. Considering the remarkable daily periodicity of all indicators, we assume that the system would be in the same state at the same time of the day. Furthermore, to avoid IO and bandwidth peaks that occur from time to time, we filter those peaks to get a reliable standard deviation and then set PT as Eq. 11 shows.

Data Reduction on a Typical Server. In the initial loop, all other indicators are predicted by $CPU(S)$ alone, so we expected that the reduction performance would be low. However, the overall result turns out to be very good, as Table 3 demonstrates, 87.9% percents of predictions based on $CPU(S)$ are accurate, with a low level of relative error and a high processing speed. Raw data contains 86880 samples in total, and the predictor achieves a reduction volume of 75872, which is very high because 19 indicators are reduced. On the other hand, the average value of R^2 is low because R^2 of some stable indicators are almost 0, such as $MEM(S)$ and $MEM(VM_4)$. The predictability of $CPU(S)$ can be explained as following:

1. As the existence of resource management in data center, most resources within a server follow similar patterns. For instance, applications always try to balance workloads on every VMs, which makes CPU of VMs share very similar patterns.
2. In this server, some indicators can be nearly invariable for some periods of time, such as memory usage, I/O, and this makes prediction very easy. This stable behavior is generally because the specific application running on the cloud, but we do not have any information of customer applications.
3. There are some peaks from time to time in indicators $BW(VM_i)$ and $IO(VM_i)$, which are hard to predict precisely. Therefore, in the first loop, most inefficient formulas belong to these indicators.

In the first loop, we select 5 inefficient indicators whose hit rate are below 85%, namely, $BW(VM_1)$, $IO(VM_2)$, $IO(VM_3)$, $CPU(VM_4)$, $BW(VM_4)$, $IO(VM_4)$. To improve the performance in the second loop, we need to update RS as in simulation experiments. By querying the correlation matrix, we update prediction formulas of the second loop as following:

– $IO(VM_1)$ serves as the regressor indicator to predict $BW(VM_1)$ and $IO(VM_2)$.
– $IO(VM_4)$ serves as the regressor indicator to predict $BW(VM_4)$.
– $CPU(VM_4)$ serves as a regressor indicator, but do not predict other indicators.
– $CPU(S)$ serves as the regressor indicator to predict all other indicators.

Table 3 shows the performance of the second loop, compared to the first loop, the overall hit rate and processing speed increases a bit, while reduction volume drops obviously. In general, the improvement is not evident, we only trade reduction volume for higher precision. $CPU(S)$ is able to predict most indicators precisely alone, but adding the new regressor indicators have little effect. This interesting result demonstrates a possible ceiling for CMBDR framework in real data centers, where some special properties of data would limit the performance. For instance, the peaks of $BW(VM_i)$ and $IO(VM_i)$ make their hit rates no more than 90% in both iterations.

Even though the predictor has a ceiling problem in the experiments, the performance is still acceptable considering the fast processing speed and the impressive reduction volume. In the future, in order to solve the ceiling problem of prediction, we need to analyze the peaks separately and develop a mechanism to forecast peaks.

Table 3. Prediction performances on real dataset.

	Execution time (sec.)	Hit rate	Reduction volume (of samples)	Average R^2	Relative error
1st loop	19.995	87.9%	75872	0.323	0.030
2nd loop	14.246	89.7%	64248	0.328	0.031

6   Conclusions

This paper presents a design of data reduction framework for data center monitoring systems, which can decrease volume of data collection. This approach exploits regression formulas to quantify the correlations between indicators, and adjusts its behavior in iterative feedback loops, to optimize the reduction performance and adapt to the dynamic environments. Experiments results demonstrate that this approach is capable of reduction in both simulated and real data centers. This approach could provide an extension to other reduction techniques in terms of upstream data reduction, and it could serve as a practical solution for monitoring data streams in which variables are commonly correlated. In our future work, besides more experiments on real datasets, we would investigate peak forecasting, and we may also explore to use this approach to implement fast anomaly detection in data centers.

Acknowledgements. This work has been partially funded by the Italian Project ITS Italy 2020 under the Technological National Clusters program.

References

1. Cappiello, C., Ho, T.T.N., Pernici, B., Plebani, P., Vitali, M.: CO_2-aware adaptation strategies for cloud applications. IEEE Trans. Cloud Comput. **4**(2), 152–165 (2016). doi:10.1109/TCC.2015.2464796
2. Carvalho, C., Gomes, D.G., Agoulmine, N., De Souza, J.N.: Improving prediction accuracy for wsn data reduction by applying multivariate spatio-temporal correlation. Sensors **11**(11), 10010–10037 (2011)
3. Ding, R., Wang, Q., Dang, Y., Fu, Q., Zhang, H., Zhang, D.: Yading: fast clustering of large-scale time series data. Proc. VLDB Endowment **8**(5), 473–484 (2015)
4. Esling, P., Agon, C.: Time-series data mining. ACM Comput. Surv. **45**(1), 12 (2012)
5. Hayashi, F.: Econometrics. Princeton University Press, Princeton (2000). http://gso.gbv.de/DB=2.1/CMD?ACT=SRCHA&SRT=YOP&IKT=1016&TRM=ppn+313736715&sourceid=fbwbibsonomy
6. Jolliffe, I.: Principal component analysis. Wiley Online Library (2002)
7. Keogh, E., Chakrabarti, K., Pazzani, M., Mehrotra, S.: Dimensionality reduction for fast similarity search in large time series databases. Knowl. Inf. Syst. **3**(3), 263–286 (2001)
8. Kung, H., Lin, C.K., Vlah, D.: Cloudsense: Continuous fine-grain cloud monitoring with compressive sensing. In: HotCloud (2011)
9. Peng, X.: Data reduction in monitored data. In: Loucopoulos, P., Nurcan, S., Weigand, H. (eds.) Proceedings of the CAiSE'2015 Doctoral Consortium at the 27th International Conference on Advanced Information Systems Engineering (CAiSE 2015), Stockholm, Sweden. CEUR Workshop Proceedings, vol. 1415, pp. 39–46, 11–12 June 2015. CEUR-WS.org (2015)
10. Peng, X., Pernici, B.: Correlation-model-based reduction of monitoring data in data centers. In: Proceedings of the 5th International Conference on Smart Cities and Green ICT Systems, pp. 395–405 (2016)
11. Reeves, G., Liu, J., Nath, S., Zhao, F.: Managing massive time series streams with multi-scale compressed trickles. Proc. VLDB Endowment **2**(1), 97–108 (2009)
12. Tsamardinos, I., Brown, L.E., Aliferis, C.F.: The max-min hill-climbing bayesian network structure learning algorithm. Mach. Learn. **65**(1), 31–78 (2006)
13. Vitali, M., O'Reilly, U.M., Veeramachaneni, K.: Modeling service execution on data centers for energy efficiency and quality of service monitoring. In: 2013 IEEE International Conference on Systems, Man, and Cybernetics (SMC), pp. 103–108. IEEE (2013)
14. Vitali, M., Pernici, B., OReilly, U.M.: Learning a goal-oriented model for energy efficient adaptive applications in data centers. Inf. Sci. **319**, 152–170 (2015)

15. Wajid, U., Cappiello, C., Plebani, P., Pernici, B., Mehandjiev, N., Vitali, M., Gienger, M., Kavoussanakis, K., Margery, D., García-Pérez, D., Sampaio, P.: On achieving energy efficiency and reducing CO_2 footprint in cloud computing. IEEE Trans. Cloud Comput. **4**(2), 138–151 (2016). doi:10.1109/TCC.2015.2453988

16. Zhou, S., Lin, K.J., Na, J., Chuang, C.C., Shih, C.S.: Supporting service adaptation in fault tolerant internet of things. In: 2015 IEEE 8th International Conference on Service-Oriented Computing and Applications (SOCA), pp. 65–72 (2015)

Adopting DDS to Smart Grids: Towards Reliable Data Communication

Alaa Alaerjan[✉] and Dae-Kyoo Kim

Department of Computer Science and Engineering, Oakland University,
2200 N Squirrel Rd, Rochester, MI 48309, USA
{asalaerjan,kim2}@oakland.edu

Abstract. The rapid growth of technologies in smart grid (SG) enables reliable data communication. SG involves many sub-domains each of which involves various types of components and devices which require significant data communication in an efficient manner. Thus, a key success factor for SG lies in reliable data exchange between components and domains. Data Distribution Service (DDS) is a standard for data-centric communication based on a publish-subscribe protocol for distributed applications. DDS enables reliable data communication supported by various features such as quality-of-service (QoS). In this paper, we describe the potential of DDS for SG for reliable and efficient data communication. We first give an overview of DDS and discuss its benefits for SG. We then describe communication requirements and constraints in SG. Finally, we discuss how DDS can be tailored to SG with respect to the requirements and constraints.

Keywords: Communication · DDS · Discovery mechanism · Publish/Subscribe · QoS · Smart grids · System reliability

1 Introduction

The traditional power grid uses the simple power generation and consumption paradigm which involves little management for efficiency, and thus has significant power loss. According to the report by The World Bank [22], the U.S loses 6% from its total power in transmission and distribution process, the U.K loses 8%, China loses 12%, some other countries even lose a significant amount, such as Iraq which loses about 35% of its produced power. Furthermore, traditional power generation systems create a large amount of carbon dioxide (CO_2) contaminating the environment.

Smart grid (SG) has emerged as the next generation for improved efficiency of power production and consumption based on data communication. Unlike the traditional power grid which is not designed for data communication, SG aims at facilitating data communication between various equipment and devices across the power domain. It enables bidirectional data exchanges between power suppliers and consumers for improved power management [8]. As an example,

© Springer International Publishing AG 2017
M. Helfert et al. (Eds.): SMARTGREENS 2016 and VEHITS 2016, CCIS 738, pp. 154–169, 2017.
DOI: 10.1007/978-3-319-63712-9_9

smart meters in SG, which measure power consumption at the household level, sends energy consumption information to utilities which in turn send real-time pricing back to smart meters.

SG involves significant data exchanges between various types of devices and components each having different requirements and time constraints, which makes communication management challenging. Devices and components belong to different domains of SG such as power transmission and consumption each having a different nature of communication, which aggravates the difficulty of communication management. Thus, the communication protocol used in SG should be scalable and capable of supporting such a variety of devices. Some protocols such as the Distributed Network Protocol (DNP3) [13] and Modbus [12] have been tried to address the challenges in SG. However, they introduce significant overheads and latency which make them unsuitable for SG (which is discussed in details in Sect. 2).

DDS has emerged as a potential model to address the communication concerns in SG. Based on a simple publish/subscribe protocol and QoS policies, it is designed to support high-performance, scalable, dependable, and real-time data exchange between components with little overheads. In this paper, we describe how DDS can be tailored to SG. We first identify communication requirements for different types of devices and components in SG and discuss how DDS should be tailored to satisfy those requirements in terms of QoS attributes and discovery mechanisms. In this work, we focus on the *Reliability, Deadline, Latency Budget, Transport Priority*, and *Time Based-Filter* QoS attributes which are more relevant to SG. For each attribute, we discuss how it should be tailored, where it can be tailored in communication layers, and how the tailored attribute can be designed for implementation. We also discuss tailoring the discovery services of DDS with respect to the available resources and capabilities of SG devices.

The remainder of the paper is organized as follows. Section 2 gives an overview of DDS and describes the advantages of applying it to SG. Section 3 outlines related research on communication protocol for SG and discuss how this work is different from the existing work. Section 4 describes communication requirements for different types of devices and component in SG. Section 5 describes how DDS should be tailored to SG based on the requirements. Finally, Sect. 6 concludes the paper with a discussion on the future work.

2   Overview of DDS

Data Distribution Service (DDS) [15] is a data-centric middleware standard for communication by the Object Management Group (OMG). It was introduced in 2004 as a Publish/Subscribe protocol to address the data sharing needs for a wide variety of computing environments, ranging from small networks to large systems. DDS provides a scalable platform and location-independent infrastructure to connect publishers and subscribers. DDS also supports a wide variety of quality-of-service (QoS) properties such as time sensitivity and reliability [3].

The DDS specification is described in terms of two layers – Data Local Reconstruction Layer (DLRL) and Data-Centric Publish-Subscribe (DCPS). DLRL is the upper layer, defining how DDS-enabled applications should interface with DCPS. Below DLRL, DCPS is defined to allow heterogeneous components to communicate each other through reading and writing data from/to the global data space. Components interact by declaring their intent to publish or subscribe to the data. From an implementation perspective, DCPS is required and the core of DDS, while DLRL is optional. Figure 1 shows the architecture of DDS. DDS involves different types of entities as described below:

- *Domain.* This represents a global data space shared by components (e.g., publishers, subscribers) for publishing and subscribing data. There can be several domains within SG each providing a different type of data (e.g., command/control, status). Only the components in the same domain can communicate each other. This allows data isolation and optimized communication.
- *Domain Participant.* This represents an entity (e.g., publishers, subscribers) that participates in the domain of the application where the entity is being used. Each process (e.g., reading process, writing process) has one unique domain participant in the data domain.
- *Data Writer (DW).* This entity writes data and is an access point to its publisher which can be associated with multiple DWs.
- *Data Reader (DR).* This entity reads received data. It is also used as the access point to its subscriber handling multiple DRs.
- *Publisher.* This entity is responsible for data issuance to the domain. It can be used by an application to group multiple DWs.
- *Subscriber.* This entity represents a subscriber of data. Similar to Publishers, a Subscriber can be used as a container to group multiple DRs.
- *Topic.* This represents a basic data object to be published/received. A given topic must match in order to establish a connection between a Publisher and a Subscriber. A topic is defined in terms of name, data type, and QoS.

DW, Publisher, DR, and Subscribers are used in an application which allows them to participate in the domain of the application. In this paper, we use the term component interchangeably with device.

DDS has many advantages over other communication protocols (e.g., DNPs, Modbus) that are used in the power domain. First, DDS is simple and flexible, yet supports complex messaging scenarios as opposed to Modbus [12]. Second, unlike DNP3 which induces 50%–80% of processing delay in embedded power devices [10], DDS does not introduce any overhead to the system because it takes to account the available resources in the system in behavior. DDS also enables high-performance data exchange and various QoS attributes on a component base. In addition, it supports different types of communication such as one-to-one, one-to-many, many-to-many, and many-to-one [15]. These features allows DDS as a potential solution to address the communication challenges in the future grid.

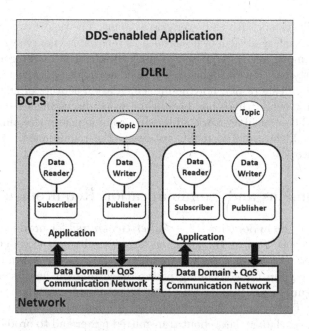

Fig. 1. DDS architecture.

3 Related Work

Smart grid is still in its infancy stage. Organizations and researchers have been trying to use and integrate different protocols to improve the communication system in SG. Some works in the literature [1,2,20] have considered use of middleware solutions such as DDS or message-oriented middleware to address the communication needs in SG.

The work by Bakken *et al.* [2] advocates the use of middleware solutions to address interoperability and data exchange issues in SG. They justify the advantages of middleware standards over other protocols on achieving reliable end-to-end communication. Our work is along the line of their work and we focus on tailoring DDS to SG to address the communication needs in SG.

In the same light as Bakken *et al.*'s work, Alkhawaja and Ferreira [1] also considered integrating DDS with SG. They discuss use of existing middleware solutions for supporting QoS requirements of large-scale distributed applications and emphasize the benefits of applying DDS to SG. They show that the light-weight architecture of DDS ensures high performance and predictability by its capabilities of reserving resources and enforcing QoS attributes. However, the scope of their work does not considers the communication requirements of SG which are perquisite for any communication protocol to be adopted. In our work, we focus on SG communication requirements for DDS tailoring.

The report by Twin Oak Computing [20] describes the capabilities of DDS in general. It describes how the DDS infrastructure can improve communication in a large-scale system such as power grid systems. The report argues that DDS can be used for safety critical systems such as renewable energy systems. It also describes the importance of DDS in achieving communication interoperability in large-scale systems. However, this report does not address neither the communication requirements of SG, nor the implementation aspects of DDS in SG.

In summary, while there has been some work discussing the potentials of DDS in SG. There is little work addressing communication requirements and how DDS should be tailored to SG to satisfy the requirements, which is the focus of this work.

4   SG Domains and Communication Requirements

SG involves four main domains [13] – *Power Generation* for producing power on high voltage levels, *Power Transmission* for transmitting the generated power to substations, *Power Distribution* for distributing power to end users, and *Power Consumption* for consuming power. Each domain has its own components and requirements. Figure 2 depicts the communication between different domains [13]. The power generation domain communicates with the transmission domain to exchange data about transmitted power and to protect the power transmission process for safety. The transmission domain communicates with the distribution domain is for advanced protection (e.g., data about circuit breakers) and automation to improve the reliability of the power grid. On the other hand, the communication between the power consumption domain and the distribution domain is to report on the power demand at the end users (e.g., homes, businesses) and to optimize the process of power distribution.

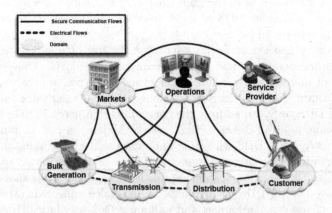

Fig. 2. Domains and communication in Smart Grid.

A prerequisite to adopting DDS to SG is a clear understanding of communication requirements in SG, which forms the basis for implementing DDS. In this work, we study different types of devices involved in SG communication. We discuss the communication in the above four domains and identify communication requirements and constraints imposed by SG devices. In the rest of this section, we discuss the four domains in terms of devices and related requirements on latency, reliability, and dynamism.

4.1 Devices in Power Generation

Power generation consists of large generation plants such as nuclear plants, fossil fuel plants, and hydroelectric power generators which are capable of generating high voltage power. Those plants work as systems that involve many devices such as generators, transformers, compressors, and turbines, which are critical in power generation and should be continuously monitored and reported on their status. Beside those physical devices, there are also software components that are used for remote control such as Remote Management System (RMS). RMS controls a power grid with time constraints on data communication with monitored devices. For example, data from Breaker shall arrive no later than 2 s after the event has occurred [7]. In order to secure the power system from critical consequences, the communication system of the power grid must satisfy such a requirement. Another important component in power generation is wireless sensors which are used to monitor the health of generation-related devices. They communicate with each other to detect a fault in the generation process. Therefore, reliable communication of wireless sensors is critical for safe power generation. However, They are vulnerable to harsh environmental conditions such as wind and rain [21], which increases communication dynamism, an important attribute to be considered in the design of SG communication.

4.2 Devices in Power Transmission

Supervisory control and data acquisition (SCADA) systems are widely used in power transmission for remote monitoring and control. A SCADA system consists of various types of devices such as the Intelligent Electronic Devices (IEDs) which control and monitor different areas of the power grid. An IED interacts with other IEDs and the control center for exchanging data. Certain types of IEDs have time constraints on communication. For example, IEDs that are responsible for substation protection and control are required to transmit data within 12–20 ms [7]. This requires a reliable communication protocol to satisfy the requirement.

Phasor Measurement Unit (PMU) is a device that measures the health of the grid, which is important in monitoring the status of power transmission. PMU is capable of processing and communicating data with other devices and the control center [5]. In communicating with the control center, PUM is required to send data at the rate of 6–60 samples/second [17] which is critical for safety and control.

Protection relay is a device for detecting and overcoming a failure in power transmission. In general, a protection relay is required to respond within 3 ms to avoid a failure which may lead to blackout [9,18]. In a power grid, a substation is managed by Human Machine Interface (HMI) which is a software system supervising the devices in the substation and displaying their state to the human operator. HMI may communicate with the SCADA system supervising the substation to send the status of the devices in the substation. The SCADA system may also communicate directly with IEDs within the substation through the gateway. In general, multiple substations are supervised by one SCADA system and in turn multiple SCADA systems are supervised by Energy Management System (EMS) which monitor, controls, and optimizes the performance of the power gird [6]. EMS also uses visualization tools to aid the human operator for monitoring the status of the grid.

Figure 3 shows an example of communication for data acquisition and analysis in power transmission. In the example, a SCADA system collects data from IEDs and PMUs and the collected data is sent to the EMS for monitoring and control. Circuit breakers and protection IEDs (which are responsible for protection) are required to respond to a fault within 100 ms. Similarly, data delivery from IEDs to the SCADA system is constrained within 12–20 ms [7] which is critical especially for protection IEDs. PMU typically measures the waveforms of voltage and currents at a sampling rate up to 1200 samples per second [6] which is demanding. The communication protocol in SG should be able to support the above requirements for the safety of the grid.

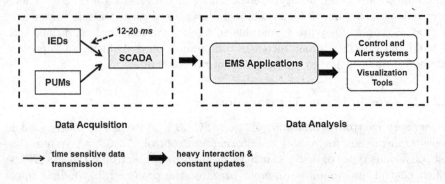

Fig. 3. Data communication in power transmission.

4.3 Devices in Power Distribution

Power distribution includes Distributed Energy Resources (DER) (e.g., solar panels, wind turbines) which are smaller power resources together producing power for energy demands. They contain components to generate power and communicate with other devices (e.g., sensors, actuators). Communication between DER and other devices is challenging due to unreliable environments. A large number of DER are envisioned to communicate via wireless connection which is vulnerable to interference and harsh weather conditions [23].

DER has a set of communication constraints to be satisfied for the reliability of the grid. For example, the reading interval of meters measuring generated power has to be 5–15 min [4]. This requires a DER device to issue its data within the specified interval and a violation of the constraint might result in unreliable data.

4.4   Devices in Power Consumption

Power is consumed through various kinds of devices such as smart meters and wireless energy monitors. Smart meters communicate with power utilities to send and receive data such as the total cost of electric power and pricing information in real-time [4]. They can also communicate with each other to optimize the overall energy consumption via load balancing. Sensors are also widely deployed in power consumption [13] for collecting and reporting data on events (e.g., power outage, generator overheating). There are various types of sensors such as light sensors, motion sensors, and temperature sensors which communicate with each other and other devices such as IEDs to produce desired results. Sensor data is sporadic and volatile, which requires reliable communication to ensure delivery.

Advanced Metering Infrastructure (AMI) is responsible for monitoring and optimizing the power consumption of the entire power grid. AMI can be hierarchical, involving a structure of different types of metering networks. Figure 4 shows an example. In the example, AMI is structured in terms of neighborhood area networks (NANs), building area networks (BANs), and home area networks (HANs) top to bottom. A NAN monitors the energy consumption for a larger area such as a neighborhood. It covers several BANs which are responsible for monitoring and optimizing the energy consumption for smaller areas such as buildings. Similar to BANs, but smaller in size, HANs are responsible for managing the energy use of individual homes. HANs send data on power consumption and appliance control to their respective BAN which collects the received data and manages the energy consumption of the HANs under its supervision and forwards the collected data to its supervising NAN for global energy management. AMI consists of intelligent networks of electronics instruments such as sensors and actuators to facilitate energy management. Significant data communications are involved between levels [19] where a lower level reports to the upper level for its energy consumption and usage and the upper level sends back pricing information to the lower level and forwards the report to the next upper level, the utility, or the control center for monitoring and controlling energy consumption. Such interactions require a reliable and efficient communication protocol.

Data communication also occurs between domains in SG. Many decisions such as power generation, power reconnection after outages, and connecting/ disconnecting a microgrid are made based on data communication between domains. The future grid is also projected to include non-traditional communication such as satellite connection [8], which necessitates a flexible communication protocol that can accommodate various types (e.g., wired and wireless communication) of communication.

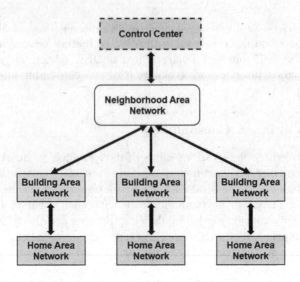

Fig. 4. Hierarchical Advanced Metering Infrastructure (AMI).

5   Tailoring DDS

In this section, we describe how the DDS framework can be tailored to satisfy the communication requirements identified in Sect. 4. We explain how the reliability and time constraints can be addressed by the QoS attributes in DDS. We also discuss tailoring the discovery services in DDS to address the dynamism requirements in SG communication. We categorize the devices discussed in Sect. 4 based on their functionalities into publisher-related, subscriber-related, and system-related. Figure 5 shows the categorized devices. In the figure, the rectangle shape represents the components that can work as a system (with multiple components inside) in the domain. The oval shape represents publishers and the dashed rectangle represents the components that can work as both publishers and subscribers. Sensors are categorized as publishers as their major role is sensing and reporting. Smart meters in power consumption are also categorized as both publishers and subscribers as they are used to send (publish) usage readings to utilities and receive (subscribe) the total cost of the readings from utilities. On the other hand, SCADA systems in power transmission are categorized as systems because they consist of multiple devices with data sending and receiving functionalities.

DDS requires its implementation to be capable of scaling to a large number of subscribers [14]. It also requires the implementation to have a built-in discovery service that allows publishers to dynamically discover the existence of subscribers and subscribers to identify topic of interest. The DDS specification also prescribes publishers and subscribers to be able to set up QoS contracts at the time when their intent to publish/subscribe data is declared [14]. Given that, we focus on two aspects in tailoring DDS to SG – (1) tailoring QoS attributes

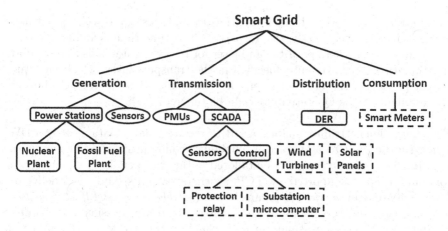

Fig. 5. Devices in Smart Grid.

to satisfy reliability and time constraints and (2) tailoring discovery services to improve the dynamism in SG.

5.1 Tailoring QoS Attributes

A significant feature of DDS is the provision of QoS on a per-entity base. That is important especially in systems whose involved devices have different require- ments for the same quality concern (e.g., latency). DDS does not only offer a set of QoS attributes, but also allows system developers to configure them for different entities (e.g., Topics, DRs, DWs) within the same framework. To sat- isfy the time constraints and reliability requirements for SG communication, the QoS attributes in the DDS framework need to be tailored. Different components (e.g., publishers, subscribers) should be able to set different contracts on QoS attributes and only those that have an agreement can communicate each other. We consider the following QoS attributes to be tailored – *Reliability, Deadline, Latency Budget, Transport Priority, and Time Based-Filter* which are relevant to time constraints and reliability requirements discussed in Sect. 4. We describe how these attributes can be tailored with respect to the communication stack of DDS.

Figure 6 shows the QoS attributes mapped to the layers of the DDS stack. The *Reliability* attribute can be tailored either at the DCPS layer if it is implemented over UDP since UDP does not guarantee data delivery or at the transport layer if it is implemented over TCP which ensures reliable data transmission. The *Deadline (Latency)* attribute is required to be fully controlled by the concerned entity which resides in the DCPS layer where all DDS entities are defined. Thus, the *Deadline* attribute should be tailored and implemented in the DCPS layer. Also, this attribute is required to work with listener objects which are responsible for keeping track of latency contracts between agreed entities defined in the DCPS layer. The *Latency Budget* attribute can be tailored and utilized in the transport layer because it depends on priorities of data streams which are defined in the transport layer. Lastly, the *Transport Priority* attribute can be tailored in the network layer where priority can be set for received data. This also supports the *Latency Budget* attribute specified in the transport layer, which facilitates the integration of the network layer with the transport layer. In the following, we describe how the QoS attributes can be tailored.

Reliability: This attribute enables a DR to receive reliably data sent by a DW, which can be used to address the reliability requirements of SG communication. In DDS, this attribute can be tailored in the transport layer where reliable communication is supported by TCP which retransmits data until delivered. The attribute defines two sub-parameters – *Reliable* and *Best Effort*. The *Reliable* parameter enforces persistent data delivery by retransmission. For example, for the components (e.g., smart meters) that can tolerate a certain latency of data receiving, it can be set for retransmitting data until its receipt. On the other hand, the *Best Effort* parameter enables delivery of up-to-date data. For instance, it can be set for the components (e.g., data sensors) that periodically publish data samples where only the latest one matters. Depending on reliability requirements, these parameters can be configured appropriately. This attribute can be tailored either in the transport layer or the DCPS layer depending on the underlying transport protocol as discussed in Fig. 6.

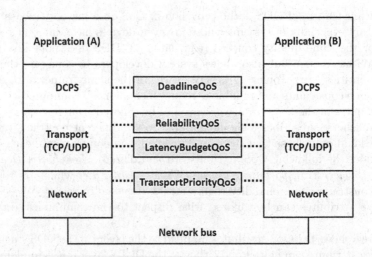

Fig. 6. QoS attributes on DDS communication stack.

Latency (Deadline): This attribute is used to set a deadline in data communication, which can be used to address the time constraints in SG communication. For example, publishers and subscribers in SG may have a deadline set for publishing and receiving data [15]. The maximum time for sending and receiving data samples of a topic can be specified. Tailoring this attribute depends on the time constraints of individual components. For instance, for protection relays which are mission-critical, it can be tailored to set a rigid deadline for data transmission. This quality attribute can be tailored in the DCPS layer as discussed in Fig. 6.

From an implementation perspective, tailoring this attribute requires a listener object for maintaining the deadline contract between entities. Figure 7 shows a design for implementation of the *Latency* attribute. In the figure, the *Entity* class represents DDS entities such as DW, DR, Publishers, and Subscribers. It defines getter and setter operations for accessing associated QoS policies and listener implementation. The *QosPolicy* class defines the policies for deadline in receiving data. A getter and setter are defined for accessing deadline policies. The *ListenerImpl* class maintains and keeps track of deadline contracts between entities which establish a communication between agreed entities. When the contact is violated, the class informs the entity about the violation, for example the DR about missing the requested deadline through the *on_requested_deadline_missed*() method and the DW in contract about missing the offered deadline through the *on_offered_deadline_missed*() method. The informed entities then take a proper action (e.g., retransmitting) to fix the violation. The *ListenerImpl* class also allows the system to be aware of changes in communication status. Each *Entity* object has a dedicated *ListenerImpl* object. A similar design can be envisioned for other QoS attributes.

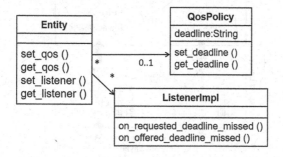

Fig. 7. Implementation design for tailoring QoS attributes.

Latency Budget: This attribute is used for setting the maximum acceptable latency on subscribers from the time of data written by publishers to the time of being inserted into the cache of subscribers, which helps to address the time constraints in SG communication. The use of *Latency Budget* depends on the priority of data streams which is set by the *Transport Priority* attribute. Therefore, it can be tailored in the transport layer where the priority of data streams can be set. This attribute can be tailored to address the time constraints of SG communication by defining communication rules. One approach is to use it in conjunction with a priority-based transport protocol to set up higher priority for data with low *Latency Budget*. For example, if an application sends two data samples every given time, *Latency Budget* can be used to specify that one sample has higher priority over the other.

Transport Priority: This attribute is used to set priority on data streams, which can be used to address the reliability requirements of SG communication. This allows data streams for a particular Topic or DW to have higher priority over other types of data. This attribute relies on the underlying transport to set priorities on data streams, which justifies its tailoring to be conducted in the network layer. It also enables a smooth integration of the network layer with the transport layer through mapping the values of of *Transport Priority* to the values of *Latency Budget* in the transport layer during the configuration of the transport from the transport layer to the network layer.

Priority-based transmission has been proposed in the literature (e.g., [11]). Maslekar *et al.* discuss how to specify priority for data transmission on the publisher side by dividing data samples into data streams to be prioritized. Figure 8 shows the data flow in the DDS communication stack where data is divided into streams in the transport layer. A data stream is prioritized based on the priority of the data samples within the stream. On the publisher side, the stream with the highest priority is sent first to accommodate the latency on the subscriber side. A similar process is taken on the subscriber side to prioritize data streams of received data samples and read them by priority.

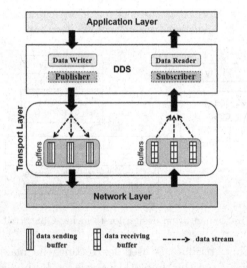

Fig. 8. Data flow in DDS communication stack.

Time-Based Filter: This attribute is used for setting a minimum separation period of data delivery, which can be used to address the time constraints in SG communication. This attribute enables to improve system efficiency by limiting data delivery, which is important particularly for the components that have limited resources (e.g., memory, bandwidth) and computing power (e.g., IEDs). For example, an IED playing the DR role may use this parameter to specify the time interval of data samples to be received [16]. It can be tailored in the DCPS layer where DR resides because DR is the one that can decide how fast data can be received. A similar approach to the *Latency* attribute can be used for tailoring *Time-Based Filter* using the *ListenerImpl* class in Fig. 7 for keeping track of the specified time. The *ListenerImpl* object is also responsible for informing involved entities for any violation of the specified time and the entities take an appropriate action in response to the violation.

5.2   Tailoring Discovery Mechanism

A key for establishing communication between publishers and subscribers is discovering the existence of participants. In the DDS context, this requires DDS entities to be informed of each other's existence for communication. Not only this, the discovery feature should also provide communication guides between entities. For example, communication guides can be provided as IP multicasting by devices where the DDS infrastructure manages the group membership. The DDS specification defines a Real-Time Publish Subscribe (RTPS) protocol [14] which provides a discovery functionality. The main purpose of RTPS is to support the interoperability of applications that are built upon different implementation platforms of vendors. RTPS defines two discovery protocols – Participant Discovery Protocol (PDP) and Endpoint Discovery Protocol (EDP). PDP is used for discovering different domain participants, while EDP is used for matching data readers and data writers. However, these protocols are defined in a generic way which may cause some drawbacks with respect to system dynamism. For example, they require a large amount of periodic data exchanges, which is intolerable for the components that have limited computing power. In the following, we describe features to be supported by tailoring DDS discovery services to support the dynamism of SG communication.

Dynamic Accommodation of Various Types of Components. SG requires a dynamic communication system to cope with frequent addition and removal of components as discussed in Sect. 4. Thus, DDS discovery services should be tailored to support the dynamism of SG communication. For example, when a new component (e.g., publishers, subscribers) is added to the system, the component can be reached efficiently by the use of discovery hints such as the group membership provided by DDS.

Diverse Discovery Strategies for Different Types of Components. The DDS specification allows the separation of its implementation from the discovery service [14]. However, a DDS implementation for SG should have a built-in discovery service to support the flexible and dynamic discovery of components. However, this involves a significant amount of interactions which can be overwhelming for the components with limited resources to handle such heavy interactions. To address this, an alternative discovery mechanism should be provided by DDS. For example, Simple Service Discovery Protocol (SSDP) can be used for IEDs and sensors in SG. On the other hand, static discovery or file-based or server-based discovery mechanisms can be provided for those components that are capable of managing heavy interactions.

Integration of the DDS Discovery Service with the Underlying DDS Infrastructure. As discussed above, the discovery service of DDS can be separate from the implementation of the DDS infrastructure. However, this makes it difficult to manage the communication of components in SG due to its dynamic nature. This can be effectively addressed by requiring the discovery service to be integrated with the implementation of the DDS infrastructure, which enables dynamic reconfiguration of components. Integration can be established by allowing components to use a common discovery service in addition to the discovery mechanism in individual components. For example, components that use SSDP as their discovery protocol can be configured to locate the common discovery service to discover other components.

6   Conclusion

In this work we have identified communication requirements in SG based on the devices that are involved in four different domains of SG. Given the requirements, we described how DDS can be tailored to SG in terms of QoS attributes and discovery mechanisms. The *Reliability, Deadline, Latency Budget, Transport Priority,* and *Time Based-Filter* attributes have been considered. For each attribute, we discussed tailoring in terms of communication layers and implementation design. We also discussed how the discovery features of DDS should be tailored to support the dynamic nature of SG communication.

For the future work, we plan to investigate other QoS attributes such as data availability and resource limits in the context of SG. We also plan to further study how the tailoring points identified in this work can be applied to the design specification of DDS. In particular, we will look into how the two layers of DLRL and DCPS in DDS can be used to improve data communication in SG. Based on the design specification of DDS, we also plan to study the data model that fits both DDS and SG to facilitate interoperability of involved systems.

References

1. Alkhawaja, M.A.A., Ferreira, L.: Message oriented middleware with QoS support for smart grids. In: Conference on Embedded Systems and Real Time, Caparica, Portugal, pp. 1–13 (2012)
2. Bakken, D., Schantz, R., Tucker, R.: Smart grid communications: QoS stovepipes or QoS interoperability. Technical report TR-GS-013, Washington State University, November 2009
3. Corsaro, A.: The data distribution service tutorial. Technical report 4.0, PrismTech, May 2014. http://creativecommons.org/licenses/by-sa/4.0
4. DNV.GL: A review of distributed energy resources. Technical report 6.1, DNV GL, September 2014. https://www.dnvgl.com/energy/
5. Ek, E.B.: Utilization of phasor measurement unit measurements as basis for power system state estimation interface. Ph.D. thesis, Norwegian University of Science and Technology, Norway, June 2014

6. Ekanayake, J., Liyanage, K., Wu, J., Yokoyama, A., Jenkins, N.: Smart Grid Technology and Application. Wiley, Chichester (2012)
7. Ericsson, G.N.: Cyber security and power system communication-essential parts of a smart grid infrastructure. IEEE Trans. Power Deliv. **25**(3), 1501–1507 (2010)
8. Fang, X., Misra, S., Xue, G., Yang, D.: Smart grid-the new and improved power grid: a survey. IEEE Commun. Surv. Tutor. **14**(4), 944–980 (2012)
9. IEEE-Power-Engineering-Society: IEEE standard communication delivery time performance requirements for electric power substation automation. Technical report 1646 (2004)
10. Lu, X., Lu, Z., Wang, W., Ma, J.: On network performance evaluation toward the smart grid: a case study of DNP3 over TCP/IP. In: Global Telecommunications Conference, Houston, TX, pp. 1–6. IEEE (2011)
11. Maslekar, N., Boussedjra, M., Mouzna, J., Pai, M.: QoS in mobile networks by assigning priorities to SCTP streams. In: The 8th International Conference on ITS Telecommunications (2008)
12. Modbus-IDA: Modbus protocol specification. Technical report, December 2006. http://www.mod-bus.org/docs/Modbus_Application_P/-rotocol_V1_1b.pdf. Accessed 12 Feb 2015
13. NIST: NIST framework and roadmap for smart grid interoperability standards. Release 1.0, National Institute of Standards and Technology, January 2010
14. Object-Management-Group: The real-time publish-subscribe protocol (RTPS) DDS interoperability wire protocol specification. Version 2.2 formal/2014-09-01, September 2014
15. Object-Management-Group: Data Distribution Service (DDS). Version 1.4 formal/2015-04-10, April 2015
16. Pardo-Castellote, G., Farabaugh, B., Warren, R.: An introduction to DDS and data-centric communications. Technical report 2, Real-Time Innovations, August 2005
17. Rihan, M., Ahmad, M., Beg, M.: Phasor measurement units in the Indian smart grid. In: Conference of Innovative Smart Grid Technologies, Kollam, Kerala, pp. 261–267 (2011)
18. Schwarz, K.: IEC61850 communication networks and systems in substations. Technical report 2004–03-22, International Electrotechnical Commission (2004). http://www.iec.ch/smartgrid/standards/
19. Sharma, K., Saini, L.: Performance analysis of smart metering for smart grid: an overview. Renew. Sustain. Energy Rev. **49**, 720–735 (2015). Elsevier
20. Twin Oaks Computing, Inc.: What can DDS do for you. Technical report 6, December 2011. www.twinoakscomputing.com
21. US.DOE: Assessment study on sensors and automation in the industries of the future. Technical report, Department of Energy Efficiency and Renewable Energy (2004)
22. World-Bank: Electric power transmission and distribution losses. Technical report, The World Bank (2015)
23. Yu, F., Zhang, P., Xiao, W., Choudhury, P.: Communication systems for grid integration of renewable energy resources. IEEE Netw. **25**, 22–29 (2011)

The Surveillance Society: Which Factors Form Public Acceptance of Surveillance Technologies?

Julia van Heek[✉], Katrin Arning, and Martina Ziefle

Human-Computer Interaction Center, RWTH Aachen University,
Campus-Boulevard 57, 52074 Aachen, Germany
{vanheek,arning,ziefle}@comm.rwth-aachen.de

Abstract. Currently, surveillance technologies are increasingly used to give people a sense of safety in medical as well as crime surveillance contexts. On the one hand, perceived safety can be supported by adequate surveillance technologies (e.g., cameras), however, the systematic use of surveillance technologies undermines individual privacy needs on the other hand. In this empirical study, we explore users' perceptions on safety and privacy in the context of surveillance systems. In order to understand if the acceptance of surveillance depends on usage contexts, surveillance technologies in the urban were compared to the medical context. Using an online survey, 119 users were requested to indicate their acceptance regarding different types of surveillance contexts and technologies, differentiating perceived benefits and barriers as well as safety and privacy needs. We investigate acceptance differences towards surveillance technologies at various locations (private and public) as well. In this paper, we especially explore the impact of different surveillance contexts, locations and individual perceived crime threat on the acceptance of surveillance technologies and on the needs for privacy and safety.

Keywords: Technology acceptance · Surveillance technologies · Privacy · Safety · Fear of crime · Medical vs. Crime surveillance · Public vs. Private environments

1 Introduction

One of the major challenges of modern societies is to meet the complex demands of urbanization processes, in particular the impact of an aging society and the need to maintain liveable, sustainable, safe and smart cities. Up to 2030, more people will live in cities than in other regions and this development is forecasted to increase further. In line with these fundamental urbanization processes, consecutive challenges arise. Beyond issues of economy, health care, transportation or governance, nowadays' major keystones of urban planning are the broadly accepted implementation of technical infrastructures and (smart) city concepts [1]. All over the world, an increasing number of surveillance technologies (especially surveillance cameras) is used to prevent or time-critically detect crime in order to improve safety in cities and especially at high frequented public locations [2]. Perceived safety represents an essential prerequisite for

© Springer International Publishing AG 2017
M. Helfert et al. (Eds.): SMARTGREENS 2016 and VEHITS 2016, CCIS 738, pp. 170–191, 2017.
DOI: 10.1007/978-3-319-63712-9_10

the participation in social and economic life and is a valuable good for cities. However, the main drawback of surveillance technologies is the perceived privacy violation by the public through the recordings and processing of data [3]. Therefore, smart city concepts must meet a wide range of residents' needs, including high comfort regarding safety, sustainability, but also consider different levels of perceived crime threat, and protection of privacy [4]. Facing the demographic change, smart city concepts should also address the diversity of urban residents. Although they are essential for all dwellers, especially different ages of residents should be taken into account. If individual needs and wishes of both younger and older people are considered, the fundament for liveable and safe future cities is granted [5]. Thus, surveillance represents a conflict between two archaic motives: the wish to be safe in urban environments and the wish to stay private. This conflict is difficult to address for city planners without understanding the individual tolerance of citizens for surveillance technologies. Therefore, in this paper, the acceptance of surveillance technologies in urban contexts is focused. Though, surveillance technologies are not only used in the context of city security, but are also quite popular in the context of chronic illness and medical monitoring [6–8]. Even if the medical case is quite different, still, the trade-off between safety and privacy protection is also crucial here. In the following this critical trade-off is empirically assessed with a main focus on surveillance in urban environments. It is scrutinized to what extent users' evaluation of the trade-off between security and privacy changes depending on the context and the city location in which surveillance is applied. Also, the individual responsiveness of persons towards crime threat and their tolerance towards surveillance technology is analyzed.

2 Acceptance of Surveillance Technologies

For a free, unrestricted and unworried life in urban areas, people need to feel safe. In this context, crime threat in cities is a central challenge [9, 10]. The consequences of crime for urban safety and individual risk perception are well described and represent a serious barrier for many residents [e.g., 11, 12]. While it is undisputed that safety and crime prevention are major goals for urban development, the realization of effective safety measures is controversially evaluated [13–15].

Technically, surveillance technologies are at hand and are already widely used in urban environments to increase safety [16, 17]. Most of all city centers use close-circuit television in public spaces and in public transport systems. However, the acceptance of these systems in general and, more specific, the individual perception of safety does not necessarily rise, when surveillance systems are installed [18]. Instead, perceived fear of crime in urban environments is rather shaped by physical features, such as visibility or lighting, prospect such as open spaces, opportunities to escape [19]. But not only physical characteristics of urban spaces, but also perceived incivilities in surrounding areas strongly affect fear of crime [18]. Therefore, the installation of technical safety measure needs to carefully address individual perceptions of safety at different locations to support safe living in smart cities.

Apart from the goal of enhanced safety, surveillance systems also pose ethical concerns. In terms of privacy, protection is one of the key human rights. Technical monitoring of people in urban environments for safety reasons conflict with individual rights for privacy [20], which – beyond legal concerns – might lead to a public rejection of monitoring technologies in city locations [21]. Accordingly, the relationship between individual needs for safety from crime and the individual need for protecting one's own privacy is complex and does not follow a simple arithmetic, but rather varies with usage context, individual characteristics and city needs [22]. The safety-privacy-relationship for crime surveillance technologies can only be understood if the trade-off between both basic motives is empirically addressed.

3 Individual Factors for Crime Surveillance Acceptance

The population in cities is characterized by a high heterogeneity. Residents' needs and wishes towards quality of city life as well as related experiences and attitudes are affected by a multitude of individual factors. Though there are individual key characteristics, which allow defining groups with specific needs regarding safety and privacy. One important factor is age, which becomes even more relevant with the on-going demographic change. For instance, age-related changes in health conditions and changed leisure time activities after retirement lead to specific mobility and accessibility needs [23]. Especially for older people, perceived safety in their living environment is essential for maintaining social contacts [24]. Gender is another factor, which strongly affects needs for safety and privacy. Elderly women, for example, have higher needs for safety than men, reducing their willingness to use public transportation or carpooling [22]. Beyond age and gender, but strongly interrelated, the perceived level of crime fear is another important factor for the acceptance of surveillance technologies in smart cities. Fear of crime, defined as the emotional response to possible violent crime and physical harm [25], has been intensively re-searched in the last decades by various scientific disciplines in the context of urban development. Two central findings are specifically noteworthy: (a) crime fear is an individual perception not necessarily associated with objectively measurable crime statistics. Thus, even when persons live in a comparably safe residence, they might perceive higher levels of crime fear. (b) individual factors (age, gender, experience with crime) further affect fear of crime. A well-replicated finding is the inverse relationship of victimization rate and crime fear: the most fearful individuals (elderly women) have the lowest victimization rate, the least fearful (young men) have the highest victimization rate [26]. The strong interrelations of age, gender and crime fear suggest, that age and gender serve as "carrier variables" for different levels of perceived crime fear. Accordingly, the present study focuses on the inter-individually different effects of crime fear on surveillance technology acceptance. The usage of crime surveillance technologies in urban environments is one (technical) approach to enhance perceived safety and to reduce crime rates. Yet, only sparse knowledge is available about acceptance patterns of residents towards benefits and barriers of crime surveillance technologies, which are assumed to increase safety perceptions in the context of smart cities.

The goal of the present study is to understand peoples' acceptance of crime surveillance technologies in urban environments, taking needs of safety and privacy into account. The paper is an extension to previous work [27], in which general findings on crime surveillance had been reported.

4 Methodology

In the following section, the implemented research model and associated research questions, the questionnaire, and the sample are detailed.

4.1 Research Model and Research Questions

We applied an online questionnaire to understand which factors form public acceptance of surveillance technologies. The research approach is outlined in Fig. 1 and was following three main research questions.

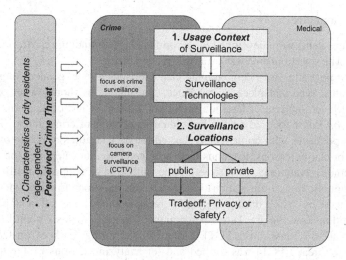

Fig. 1. Research approach.

- *Is surveillance acceptance context-sensitive?*
  Results of single case studies hypothesize context-sensitive differences in surveillance acceptance [6–8]. Therefore, we directly compare two important usage contexts in this study: crime surveillance and medical surveillance. For each usage context, different technologies, different locations, perceived benefits and barriers, and the trade-off between privacy and safety are addressed to answer this research question.
- *Which role do the types of supervised locations play for surveillance acceptance?*
  In a second step, we focus on crime surveillance acceptance because previous studies already focused on acceptance of medical surveillance technologies (e.g., [21, 29]). A lot of different locations of surveillance are under study in order to be able to get an exact picture of desired and rejected areas of surveillance. In a third step, we focus on surveillance cameras as surveillance technology because it is the most used technology in urban areas [2]. As mentioned in chapter 3, the population in cities is characterized by a high heterogeneity. Hence, different characteristics of

city residents have to be considered and the residents themselves have to be focused, because especially their perceived crime threat (-as important user diversity factor for crime surveillance focused in this study-) could be an influential factor on the acceptance of surveillance technologies.

- *Does the perception of crime threat influence the acceptance of surveillance?*

Previous experience with crime threat could considerably impact the acceptance for surveillance (technologies), especially at specific city locations. On the base of perceived crime threat rating, the sample was cut into a group with lower and higher perceived crime threat, and a comparison of acceptance levels for surveillance was carried out.

4.2 Questionnaire

Questionnaire items were developed based on focus group findings carried out prior to this study. The questionnaire was arranged in six sections.

The *first part* addressed demographic characteristics as age, gender, family status, children status, type and place of residence, housing status (homeowner or tenant), educational level, (current or last) job sector and current or last occupation.

The *second part* focused on the individual perception of crime threat (PCT) and potential experiences with crime. (1) We asked for PCT at different places by day and by night. For clarity reasons, locations were arranged into four categories (private (e.g., garden), rather private (e.g., own street), rather public (e.g., shopping mall), and high frequented public (e.g., train station) locations). The question "to what extent do you feel threatened by crime during the day?" were evaluated for different public and private locations (see Fig. 1). Threat perceptions were rated on a six-point Likert scale (1 = not at all; 6 = very strong PCT). Based on PCT ratings an between-factor "perceived crime threat" (PCT) was formed and for analyzing reasons PCT ratings were summed up (max = 156), transformed to a value of 100 and a median split was conducted (cut-off = 34.62), which separated two groups with low PCT and high PCT. (2) We asked for individual crime threat concerning different crime offenses, which had to be evaluated on a six-point Likert scale. (3) The final aspect focused on experiences with crime: respondents indicated whether they, their family, friends, relatives or acquaintances had become victims of offenses themselves (e.g., theft or bodily injury).

The *third part* assessed technologies and traditional measures enhancing perceived safety in private and public environments. Thus, different technologies (e.g., camera surveillance, ambient lighting, microphones) but also non-technical measures (e.g., police presence) had to be rated on a six-point Likert scale (1 = strongly disagree; 6 = strongly agree) for a private as well as a public context of use.

The *fourth part* of the questionnaire asked about the acceptance of crime surveillance technologies at different locations. (1) Participants were asked to evaluate to what extent they would accept technologies like standard cameras, microphones, cameras with face recognition and location determination in their private living environment. (2) Participants had to do the same in the case of a public environment. (3) Further, we asked for acceptance of surveillance cameras at different private and public locations (be evaluated on a six-point Likert scale (1 = strongly disagree; 6 = strongly agree). (4) Then, we asked about perceived benefits and barriers of crime surveillance (6-point Likert scale, see above). Benefits of crime surveillance were examined in seven items, which referred to safety aspects (e.g., prevention of crime, sense of safety or the felt deterrent effect for potential criminals). Barriers referred to eight items relating to privacy aspects (e.g., protection of civil rights and personal freedom, storage of recorded data or inference of being under general suspicion).

The *fifth part* focused on the trade-off between the need for safety vs. the need for individual privacy. Respondents had to trade-off between individual needs for safety and privacy when considering the employment of crime surveillance technologies at different locations (10-point scale; 1 = increase of safety; 10 = protection of privacy).

To compare different usage contexts of surveillance, a medical scenario for health status surveillance and detection of emergencies (e.g., stroke, heart attack) was introduced in the *sixth part*. Different types of surveillance technologies, acceptance at different locations as well as perceived benefits and barriers of surveillance had to be evaluated. Finally, participants had also to indicate their individual needs for safety and privacy when considering the employment of medical surveillance technologies at different locations on a 10-point scale (see above).

Completing the online questionnaire took about 20 min. Overall, the questionnaire was made available for about 8 weeks in the beginning of 2013 in Germany. In that time, there was no high impact society events (e.g., terrorist attacks). Participation was voluntary and was not gratified.

4.3 Sample

Overall, 99 fully completed data sets were analyzed. The mean age of the participants was 37.8 (SD = 15.5) with 58.6% females and 41.4% males. Asked for having children, the majority of 65.7% answered to have no children. Demanded for the number of persons living in their household, 38.4% reported to live in pairs, 31.3% live alone, 15.2% live in a threesome, 9.1% live with four persons, 3.0% live with five persons and also 3.0% live with more than five persons in their household. Asked for their residence, 23.2% reported to live in a detached, 13.1% in a semi-detached and also 13.1% in a townhouse. The majority of 50.5% reported to live in an apartment building. 45.5% of the sample reported to be the house owner (54.5% live for rent). Regarding their area of residence, 35.4% live in a city centre, 29.3% in outskirts, 21.2% in suburban areas and 14.1% live in rural areas.

5 Results

First, to understand whether the surveillance context affects the acceptance of surveillance technologies, the results of crime and medical surveillance are compared. In a second step, the influence of different locations on surveillance acceptance is presented. Finally, the results of the user diversity factor *perceived crime threat* on crime surveillance acceptance are shown. Data was analyzed descriptively and, with respect to the effects of usage contexts, locations and user diversity, by (one-way repeated measure) (M)ANOVA procedures (significance level at 5%).

5.1 Usage Context

Following the hypothesis that the acceptance of surveillance is context dependent, we analyzed two different usage contexts of surveillance. As it is shown in Fig. 2, diverse types of surveillance technologies are evaluated differently for crime and medical surveillance contexts. In general, rather low evaluations of all surveillance technologies are apparent for the medical usage context. While *face recognition* (M_{Crim} = 4.2; SD_{Crim} = 1.8; M_{Med} = 3.8; SD_{Med} = 1.6) and *location determination* (M_{Crim} = 3.6; SD_{Crim} = 2.0; M_{Med} = 3.1; SD_{Med} = 1.5) are slightly more accepted for crime surveillance, the use of *microphone* technologies (M_{Crim} = 3.3; SD_{Crim} = 1.7; M_{Med} = 3.8; SD_{Med} = 1.6) is rather favoured in the context of medical surveillance. The use of cameras shows the most striking differences: for crime surveillance it is clearly accepted, however, it is rather rejected for medical surveillance (M_{Crim} = 4.8; SD_{Crim} = 1.4; M_{Med} = 3.0; SD_{Med} = 1.5; $F(1,95)$ = 45.5; $p < 0.01$).

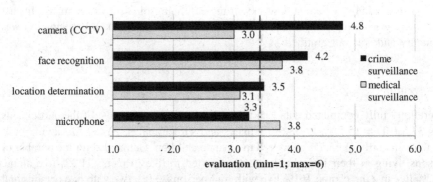

Fig. 2. Evaluation of diverse surveillance technologies for medical and crime surveillance.

The influence of different surveillance contexts revealed even more clearly in the evaluation of supervised locations (see Fig. 3). For the crime surveillance scenario, a distinct pattern emerged: the use of surveillance technologies was strongly rejected at private locations, e.g., *living room* (M_{Crim} = 1.6; SD_{Crim} = 1.1), while it was rather accepted at more public locations, e.g., *museums* (M_{Crim} = 3.9; SD_{Crim} = 1.7) or *schools* (M_{Crim} = 3.9; SD_{Crim} = 1.6). Crime surveillance at highly frequented public locations - where a lot of people passing by, e.g., *public transport* (M_{Crim} = 4.5; SD_{Crim} = 1.5) and *train stations* (M_{Crim} = 4.8; SD_{Crim} = 1.4) received the highest evaluations and were clearly accepted. In contrast, there is no distinct pattern for the medical usage scenario: unlike the crime surveillance scenario, private locations, e.g., *living room* (M_{Med} = 4.4; SD_{Med} = 1.6; $F(1,93)$ = 131.7; $p < 0.01$) and *bedroom* (M_{Med} = 4.6; SD_{Med} = 1.5; $F(1,94)$ = 316.2; $p < 0.01$), received the highest evaluations and surveillance at these locations was clearly accepted for medical surveillance.

Surveillance at more public locations, e.g., museums, schools, was not evaluated differently for both usage contexts. For medical usage, surveillance was clearly more accepted at locations in a relatively private setting, e.g., *church* (M_{Crim} = 2.5; SD_{Crim} = 1.6; M_{Med} = 4.2; SD_{Med} = 1.7; $F(1,92)$ = 28.7; $p < 0.01$) and *pub* (M_{Crim} = 2.7; SD_{Crim} = 1.5; M_{Med} = 4.3; SD_{Med} = 1.5; $F(1,93)$ = 32.6; $p < 0.01$). Finally, surveillance at highly frequented public locations, e.g., *train stations* (M_{Med} = 3.3; SD_{Med} = 1.7; $F(1,92)$ = 28.9; $p < 0.01$), was slightly rejected for medical usage, while it was the most favored location for the crime surveillance context.

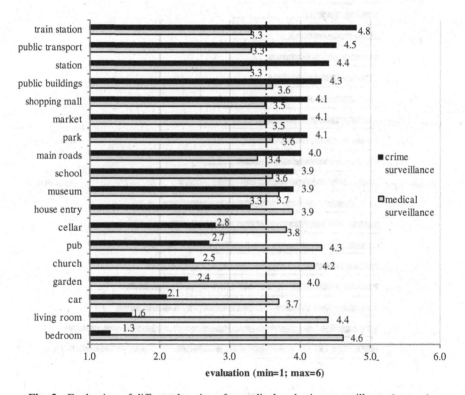

Fig. 3. Evaluation of different locations for medical and crime surveillance (camera).

Regarding the question if needs for safety or privacy depend on different locations and usage contexts (see Fig. 4), the results show a clearly more desperate decision pattern for crime surveillance (range: min = 2.7; max = 9.6) than for medical usage (range: min = 4.7; max = 7.7). For both contexts, privacy was favored over safety at private locations, whereas this was expressed even more strongly for crime surveillance, e.g., *living room* (M_{Crim} = 9.0; SD_{Crim} = 1.9; M_{Med} = 7.3; SD_{Med} = 3.0; $F(1,86)$ = 39.1; $p < 0.01$) or *bedroom* (M_{Crim} = 9.6; SD_{Crim} = 1.3; M_{Med} = 7.7; SD_{Med} = 2.9; $F(1,86)$ = 38.2; $p < 0.01$). Safety was clearly preferred for crime surveillance at public locations. For medical surveillance rather neutral evaluations and no explicit decision between safety and privacy were found, e.g., *market* (M_{Crim} = 3.8; SD_{Crim} = 2.6; M_{Med} = 5.0; SD_{Med} = 3.2; $F(1,86)$ = 18.7; $p < 0.01$) or *train station* (M_{Crim} = 2.7; SD_{Crim} = 2.4; M_{Med} = 4.7; SD_{Med} = 3.2; $F(1,86)$ = 48.9; $p < 0.01$). Overall, the results showed that the acceptance of surveillance technologies depends strongly on the context of surveillance. Hence, it is important to analyze the different surveillance contexts in detail and in this paper we focus on crime surveillance.

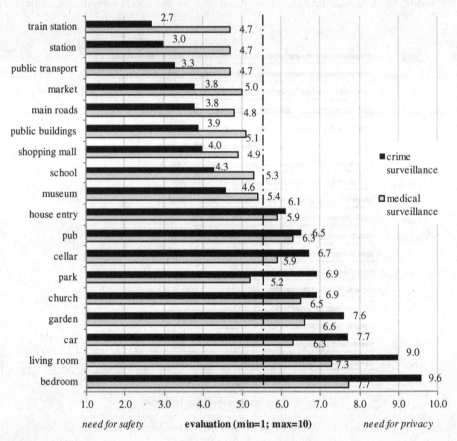

Fig. 4. Trade-off between safety and privacy at different locations for crime and medical surveillance.

5.2 Locations of Surveillance

First, we analyzed whether the acceptance of different crime surveillance technologies depends on different types of areas. First, it was roughly distinguished between a private and public area of surveillance. As it is shown in Fig. 5, all technologies were evaluated higher for usage at public areas. Especially *camera surveillance* (M_{pub} = 4.8; SD_{pub} = 1.5; M_{priv} = 3.2; SD_{priv} = 1.7; $F(1,97)$ = 107.3; $p < 0.01$) and *face recognition* ($M_{pub} = 4.2$; $SD_{pub} = 1.5$; $M_{priv} = 2.8$; $SD_{priv} = 1.6$; $F(1,97) = 87.0$; $p < 0.01$) were accepted at public areas, while they were rejected at private areas. *Location determination* ($M_{pub} = 3.5$; $SD_{pub} = 2.0$; $M_{priv} = 2.6$; $SD_{priv} = 1.5$; $F(1,95) = 47.3$; $p < 0.01$) and usage of *microphone technologies* ($M_{pub} = 3.2$; $SD_{pub} = 1.7$; $M_{priv} = 2.1$; $SD_{priv} = 1.3$; $F(1,96) = 64.9$; $p < 0.01$) were rather rejected at public areas and even more declined at private areas.

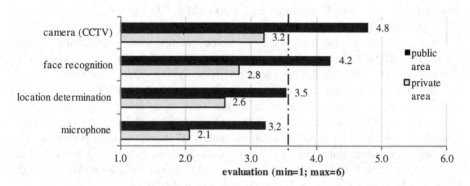

Fig. 5. Evaluation of different technologies for crime surveillance at public and private areas.

In a second step, we analyzed the influence of locations in detail for crime surveillance purposes (Fig. 6). Surveillance acceptance considerably depended on the type of supervised location and was accepted at highly frequented public locations and rejected at rather private locations (e.g., *living room* ($M = 1.6$; $SD = 1.1$) or *cellar* ($M = 2.8$; $SD = 1.2$)).

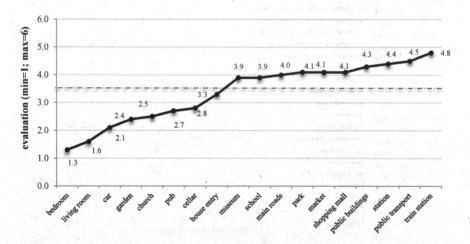

Fig. 6. Acceptance of crime surveillance technologies depending on different locations.

We assumed that one reason for this could be the individual and location-dependent perception of crime threat. Therefore, we asked for perceived crime threat at various locations during day- and nighttime (Fig. 7).

During *daytime:* In total, i.e. summed up for all locations, the PCT during daytime was rather low (M = 36.3 on a scale with max = 100; SD = 12.9). The majority of private locations was perceived as only lightly threatening, e.g., *own garden* (M = 1.3; SD = 0.6) or *own home* (M = 1.4; SD = 0.8), while high frequented public locations were perceived as more threatening, e.g., *parks* (M = 2.8; SD = 1.3), *train stations* (M = 3.0; SD = 1.4) or *underground car park*s (M = 3.3; SD = 1.6).

During *nighttime*: In total, PCT nighttime ratings were significantly higher (M = 43.4; SD = 15.5) compared to daytime ratings (F(1,97) = 15.4; p < 0.01). However, the PCT at night did not vary strongly across the different locations. Private and rather private locations were not perceived very differently by day or by night. Concerning rather public locations a higher PCT was found, e.g., for *market* (M_{Night} = 2.9; SD = 1.4; M_{Day} = 2.4; SD = 1.2; F(1,98) = 35.7; p < 0.01) by night. Regarding high frequented public locations, nearly all locations were perceived significantly more threatening by night, e.g., *train stations* (M_{Night} = 3.9; SD = 1.8; M_{Day} = 3.0; SD = 1.4; F(1,98) = 102.1; p < 0.01) as well as *parks* (M_{Night} = 4.0; SD = 1.5; M_{Day} = 2.8; SD = 1.2; F(1,98) = 175.6; p < 0.01).

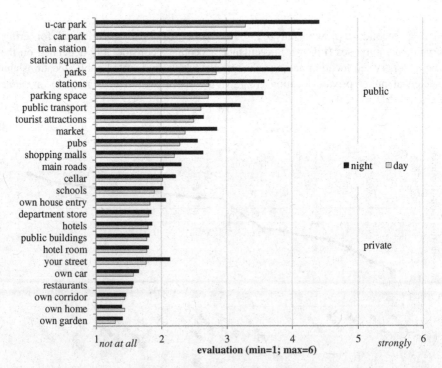

Fig. 7. Overview of perceived crime threat ratings at various locations.

Overall, results show that crime surveillance acceptance depends on locations of surveillance and on the location-dependent perception of crime threat. Hence, it is of great importance to analyze individual levels of perceived crime threat.

5.3 Individual Factors: Perceived Crime Threat as User Splitting Variable

Since we assumed that the perceived necessity and acceptance of crime surveillance technologies is affected by individual levels of crime fear, we systematically included "perceived crime threat" as group splitting variable [37].

Segmentation of User Groups. Based on respondents' ratings of crime threat at different locations two groups with high and low levels of perceived crime threat (high and low PCT, cut-off = 34.6 on scale with max = 100) were formed by median split. Below, groups are described by socio-demographic factors. The group with high PCT consisted of a higher proportion of women than in the low PCT group (though not significant). Concerning age there was a similar distribution in groups 1 and 2 without significant differences. Both groups differed in terms of family status and children status significantly ($p < 0.05$). Group 1 (low PCT) consists mainly of singles (60%), while group 2 (high PCT) mainly consisted of married people or people living with a partner. Regarding children status there was a higher percentage of people with children (44,9%) in the high PCT group than in the low PCT group (24%). In terms of type and place of residence there were in parts slightly different distributions, which failed to meet significance level (Table 1).

Table 1. Segmentation of PCT groups.

	Group 1 (n = 50) "low PCT"	Group 2 (n = 49) "high PCT"	p
Gender	52% female	65.3% female	n.s.
	48% male	34.7% male	
Age	M = 36.7	M = 38.9	n.s.
	SD = 14.4	SD = 16.5	
Familiy status	Single 60%	Single 36.7%	<.05
	Partner/Married 38%	Partner/Married 59.2%	
	Divorced 2%	Divorced 4.1%	
Children status	Yes 24%; No 76%	Yes 44.9%; No 55.1%	<.05
Type of residence	Detached house 16%	Detached house 30.6%	n.s.
	Semi-detached house 14%	Semi-detached house 12.2%	
	Townhouse 10%	Townhouse 16.3%	
	Apartment building 60%	Apartment building 40.8%	
Place of residence	City centre 46%	City centre 24.5%	n.s.
	Outskirts 22%	Outskirts 36.7%	
	Suburban area 16%	Suburban area 26.5%	
	Rural area 16%	Rural area 12.2%	

We also asked for "experience" with crime: participants had to indicate whether they in person or their close family circle have ever fallen victim to different crime offenses. The results (Fig. 8) show that both groups differed significantly concerning their experiences with three crime offenses and each time the high PCT group was "more experienced": With regard to *theft of the own vehicle* a higher proportion of the high PCT group have been affected ($_{high}$PCT: 22.4%; n = 11; $_{low}$PCT: 6%; n = 3; p < 0.05). Nearly half of the high PCT group have been fallen victim to *fraud*, while this was true for almost a quarter of the low PCT group ($_{high}$PCT: 49%; n = 24; $_{low}$PCT: 24%; n = 12; p < 0.01). The same pattern appeared for *material damage*: the high PCT group has significantly more frequently been affected by it compared with the low PCT group ($_{high}$PCT: 69.4%; n = 34; $_{low}$PCT: 42%; n = 21; p < 0.01).

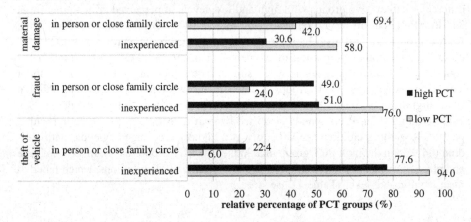

Fig. 8. Significant differences of PCT groups regarding experiences with crime offenses.

All in all, these results showed that both PCT groups differ with regard to their experience with crime and hence, crime experience could be an explanatory factor for higher levels of crime fear.

Fear of Crime Offenses. In a first step, we analyzed to what extent people with high and low PCT differ with regard to fear of several crime offenses (see Fig. 9). People with high PCT reported to feel significantly more threatened than those with low PCT (F(1,97) = 48.1; p < 0.01), except for the item "bicycle theft".

This result pattern applied for "light" offenses, e.g. material damage (M_{Low} = 3.0; SD = 1.3; M_{High} = 4.2; SD = 1.2; F(1,97) = 22.9; p < 0.01) or theft (in/from house) (M_{Low} = 2.6; SD = 1.4; M_{High} = 3.9; SD = 1.3; F(1,97) = 20.9; p < 0.01) as well as for "serious" offenses, for example sexual crimes (M_{Low} = 1.7; SD = 1.2; M_{High} = 3.4; SD = 1.5; F(1,97) = 40.1; p < 0.01), offenses against life (M_{Low} = 1.5; SD = 1.0; M_{High} = 3.2; SD = 1.5; F(1,97) = 44.4; p < 0.01) and terrorism (M_{Low} = 1.3; SD = 0.8; M_{High} = 3.0; SD = 1.4; F(1,97) = 54.5; p < 0.01). All PCT group differences were highly significant. However, for serious offenses (e.g. offenses against life) the differences between fear of crime ratings for people with low and high PCT were stronger pronounced.

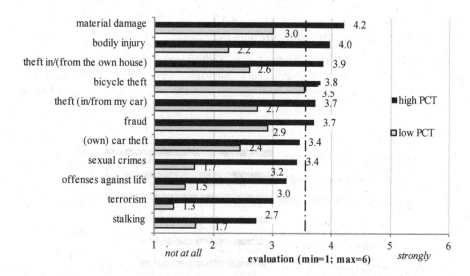

Fig. 9. Fear of crime offenses for low and high PCT groups.

Perceived Benefits of Crime Surveillance Technologies. In a next step we analyzed to what extent perceived benefits of crime surveillance were influenced by PCT (see Fig. 10). Nearly all benefits were significantly more accepted by the high PCT group, except *investigation of crimes,* which was most accepted, but not evaluated differently by the two PCT groups. *Deterrent effect* (M_{Low} = 4.2; SD = 1.6; M_{High} = 4.8; SD = 1.1; F (1,98) = 4.5; p < 0.05), *safer feeling in darkness* (M_{Low} = 3.6; SD = 1.7; M_{High} = 4.8; SD = 1.3; F(1,98) = 14.7; p < 0.01), *sense of safety* (M_{Low} = 3.5; SD = 1.5; M_{High} = 4.8; SD = 1.2; F(1,98) = 20.0; p < 0.01), *safer feeling when traveling alone* (M_{Low} = 3.5; SD = 1.6; M_{High} = 4.7; SD = 1.3; F(1,98) = 18.8; p < 0.01), and *measure against*

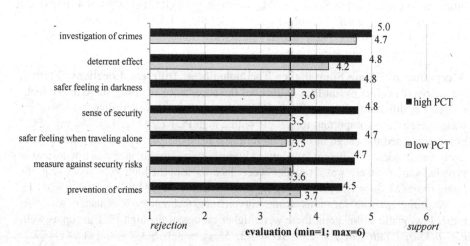

Fig. 10. Perceived benefits of crime surveillance technologies for high and low PCT groups.

safety risks (M_{Low} = 3.6; SD = 1.6; M_{High} = 4.7; SD = 1.3; F(1,98) = 15.2; p < 0.01) were also accepted and favoured by the high PCT group.

Perceived Barriers of Crime Surveillance Technologies. We also examined, how perceived barriers of crime surveillance technologies were influenced by PCT (see Fig. 11). The highest concern for both groups was the *protection of personal infor-*

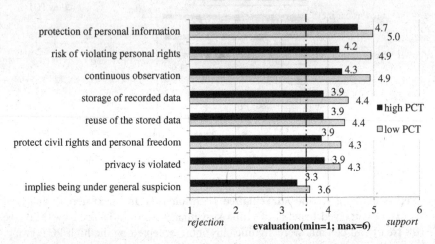

Fig. 11. Perceived barriers of crime surveillance technologies for high and low PCT groups.

mation. Interestingly, both PCT groups did not differ significantly in this concern. This also applied to the barriers *reuse of the stored data, implies being under general suspicion, violation of personal data* and *protecting civil rights and personal freedom*.

In contrast, group differences were found for *risk of violating personal rights* (M_{Low} = 4.9; SD = 1.3; M_{High} = 4.2; SD = 1.3; F(1,98) = 6.9; p < 0.01), *continuous observation* (M_{Low} = 4.9; SD = 1.4; M_{High} = 4.3; SD = 1.5; F(1,98) = 4.4; p < 0.05) and *storage of recorded data* (M_{Low} = 4.4; SD = 1.4; M_{High} = 3.9; SD = 1.3; F(1,98) = 4.2; p < 0.05). These barriers were rated higher by the low PCT group than by the high PCT group.

Acceptance of Crime Surveillance Technologies at Different Locations. Further, we analyzed to what extent PCT influences the acceptance of crime surveillance technologies at different locations. First of all, the usage of crime surveillance technology was generally more important for people with a high PCT (see Fig. 12). The high PCT group evaluated the usage of crime surveillance technologies significantly more positively independent of different locations. Although crime surveillance was not desired at *private* locations, there was a broader acceptance for it in the high PCT group, e.g. for *living room* (M_{Low} = 1.3; SD = 0.6; M_{High} = 1.9; SD = 1.3; F(1,98) = 10.0; p < 0.01).

At *rather private* locations crime surveillance technology acceptance was also rather low, while at this point there were higher ratings of the high PCT group as well, e.g. *favourite pub* (M_{Low} = 2.0; SD = 1.2; M_{High} = 3.3; SD = 1.4; F(1,98) = 22.1;

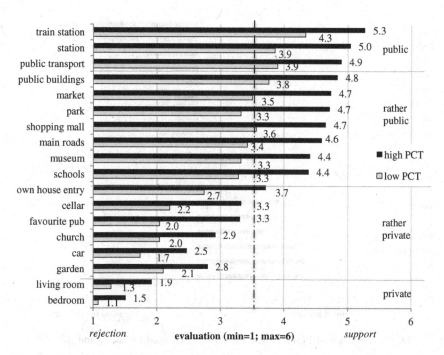

Fig. 12. Influence of PCT on the acceptance of crime surveillance at different locations.

$p < 0.01$) or *own house entry* ($M_{Low} = 2.7$; SD = 1.8; $M_{High} = 3.7$; SD = 1.6; $F(1,98) = 7.9$; $p < 0.01$).

At *rather public* locations the low PCT group rather rejected crime surveillance, while it was accepted by the high PCT group, e.g. *schools* ($M_{Low} = 3.3$; SD = 1.7; $M_{High} = 4.4$; SD = 1.5; $F(1,98) = 12.2$; $p < 0.01$) or *parks* ($M_{Low} = 3.3$; SD = 1.7; $M_{High} = 4.7$; SD = 1.2; $F(1,98) = 22.3$; $p < 0.01$). Finally, at highly frequented *public* locations crime surveillance technologies were rather accepted by the low PCT group, while it was strongly desired by the high PCT group, e.g. *public transport* ($M_{Low} = 3.9$; SD = 1.7; $M_{High} = 4.9$; SD = 1.2; $F(1,98) = 11.4$; $p < 0.01$) or *train station* ($M_{Low} = 4.3$; SD = 1.6; $M_{High} = 5.3$; SD = 1.0; $F(1,98) = 11.4$; $p < 0.01$).

Trade-off between Safety and Privacy. In a last step, we examined the effects of PCT on the trade-off between looking for safety and protecting one's own privacy (see Fig. 13). All in all, there were significant differences in the assessment of the relationship between safety and privacy concerning both PCT groups.

Concerning *private* locations there were no differences between both PCT groups, because both groups desired to protect their own privacy at those locations. Regarding *rather private* locations, the low PCT group had a significantly greater need for protecting own privacy than the high PCT group for nearly all *rather private* locations, e.g. *cellar* ($M_{Low} = 7.8$; SD = 2.5; $M_{High} = 5.9$; SD = 3.1; $F(1,98) = 10.7$; $p < 0.01$), *garden*

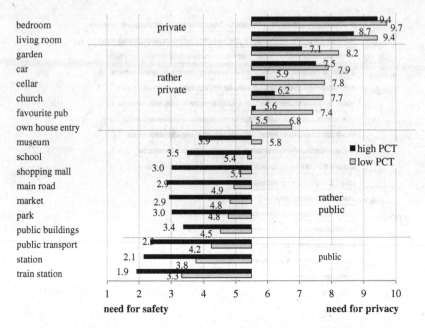

Fig. 13. Influence of PCT on the trade-off between need for safety and privacy.

(M_{Low} = 8.2; SD = 2.3; M_{High} = 7.1; SD = 2.9; $F(1,98)$ = 4.7; $p < 0.05$) *or favourite* pub (M_{Low} = 7.4; SD = 2.4; M_{High} = 5.6; SD = 2.8; $F(1,98)$ = 11.8; $p < 0.01$).

At *rather public locations* there were significant differences for all locations: for the low PCT group privacy was more important, while the high PCT group preferred safety, e.g. *schools* (M_{Low} = 5.4; SD = 3.2; M_{High} = 3.5; SD = 2.6; $F(1,98)$ = 10.2; $p < 0.01$), main roads (M_{Low} = 4.9; SD = 3.0; M_{High} = 2.9; SD = 2.1; $F(1,98)$ = 15.9; $p < 0.01$). Concerning *public locations*, the low PCT group had a significantly stronger need for privacy, while the high PCT group strongly favoured safety, e.g. *train station* (M_{Low} = 3.3; SD = 2.7; M_{High} = 1.9; SD = 1.5; $F(1,98)$ = 10.3; $p < 0.01$) or *public transport* (M_{Low} = 4.2; SD = 3.1; M_{High} = 2.3; SD = 1.9; $F(1,98)$ = 13.3; $p < 0.01$).

6   Discussion

This study revealed insights into acceptance patterns regarding the use of surveillance technologies in urban environments. In order to understand the specific needs of a diverse resident population, we examined the tolerance towards such technologies at various public and private urban locations differentiating between two usage contexts. The results provide valuable insights for city planners regarding an acceptable employment of (crime) surveillance technologies at different locations in urban environments, which consider individual needs for privacy and safety.

6.1 Usage Context and Locations as Determinants of Surveillance Acceptance

Focusing on crime surveillance, surveillance technologies are accepted in those locations in which crime threat is present. Crime threat reports were higher in public spaces such as train stations or parks, especially during night time. Accordingly, conventional crime surveillance technologies (i.e., CCTV systems), but also conventional measures such as lighting are well accepted - as long as they are visible and installed in public spaces. Especially in urban transportation hubs such as train stations, stations or main roads, where a high number of people passes by, surveillance technologies are strongly accepted. Accordingly, a map or cartography of acceptable locations for the acceptable installation of surveillance technologies in urban environments can be derived from our findings. A completely different acceptance picture can be drawn for the acceptance of surveillance technologies in private spaces. Here, perceived crime threat is comparably low, and the use of cameras or microphones for the surveillance of private spaces is distinctly rejected. Instead, lighting and motion detectors are the only accepted measures.

However, this finding does not allow jumping to the conclusion that surveillance technologies in private space are rejected in general. Combined with different functionalities than crime-stopping functions, surveillance technologies already have entered private spaces, e.g. webcams for medical monitoring or "nanny- or mummy-cams" [28]. Moreover, the context-specificity of technology-acceptance was already shown for wireless technologies either used for ICT- or for medical monitoring purposes [29]. This study's direct comparison of crime and medical surveillance shows that surveillance acceptance is greatly context-sensitive and is perceived differently accordingly by city residents. In contrast to crime surveillance, medical surveillance acceptance is generally lower and private as well as rather private locations (e.g., own home environment, church, pub) are preferred. However, medical surveillance at public locations is rather rejected or merely tolerated. A possible explanation for this might be that the usage context "medical surveillance" is often associated with monitoring of older people to prevent or detect falls that mainly happen at private home environments [30, 31]. Furthermore, feedback of our participants showed that public locations are judged to be inappropriate for medical surveillance because a large number of people has to be monitored simultaneously. Hence, participants have doubts as to whether an adequate health care of individual persons can be provided in emergency situations.

The type of accepted surveillance technologies also differed with respect to surveillance contexts. While the use of cameras is desired for crime surveillance, it is rejected for medical surveillance. However, for medical surveillance purposes other technologies, e.g., microphones and face recognition, are more accepted. This may be due to the fact that a lot of people associate camera surveillance with a feeling of being watched [32]. For perceived benefits of crime surveillance the participants hazard these consequences, while they do not accept it for medical surveillance. Future studies will have to investigate the effects of usage context on the acceptance of surveillance technologies and their perceived benefits and barriers in more detail and by means of different methodical approaches (see Sect. 6.4).

6.2   Privacy and Safety as Determinants of Crime Surveillance Acceptance

The assessment of individual privacy and safety needs provides an explanation for the identified acceptance patterns regarding different types of locations. In public spaces, people have a higher need for safety, i.e. they "sacrifice" their privacy rights for a higher safety from potential crime assaults. In turn, in private spaces, where perceived safety is higher, the need for privacy is dominating. However, in the present study, surveillance technology was operationalized as "presence of a camera", without giving information about further processing or usage purposes of recorded data. We assume, that this operationalization is ecologically valid, since people usually do not know, which of their actions are monitored and how or for what purpose surveillance data is further processed and used [33]. Accordingly, we doubt that people are fully aware of potential privacy violations, which might occur during the following data processing stages. A next step of our research agenda is, to investigate the effects of information about potential privacy violations of subsequent processing stages on privacy perceptions and behavior. Research on privacy issues and user behavior in social networks showed, that people – although claiming to be aware of their privacy rights – show a completely different behavior pattern, i.e. exposing huge amounts of personal information [34]. Looking at perceived barriers and benefits of crime surveillance technologies, which might serve as explanatory variables for acceptance, we were rather surprised by the result pattern. Almost all benefit items received comparable levels of affirmation, which might be explained by a biased response behavior or by an insufficient item design. For barrier-items we found a slightly more differentiated result pattern. The barrier "being under general suspicion" received the lowest affirmation in our study. This is especially noteworthy, since the issue of "general suspicion" is a widely used counter-argument in research literature ethical implications of surveillance technologies (e.g., [35]), but is apparently not reflected in individual perceptions. This result further indicates, that the ethical-normative approach of technology acceptance research needs to be complemented by a "user-focused" perspective to derive implications and design guidelines which meet public acceptance.

6.3   Perception of Crime Threat as Influential User Diversity Factor

Besides usage contexts and location of surveillance, user diversity in terms of different crime threat levels is a crucial factor in the context of crime surveillance acceptance. The contrast of people with high and low crime fears shows – not surprisingly – that crime surveillance measures and their related benefits are more accepted by people with higher fear levels. The question if these different fear groups can be further profiled alongside of other demographic variables revealed that the two groups with high and low crime fears did not differ in their age or gender but in family status and experiences with crime. In this study's sample, there is not a hypothetically typical and assumed distribution with mainly women and older people who feel more threatened by crime than men and younger people [36]. The distribution of segmented PCT groups indicated that nearly each city dweller could be part of the group with a high PCT and that perceived PCT should be the starting point for the development of urban surveillance concepts. Overall, the predominantly technology-centered planning of infrastructural city concepts, without integrating citizens into the decision-making processes, seems not sufficient to cover persons' attitudes regarding safety and privacy concerns in the context of smart cities.

6.4   Limitations and Future Research

Our empirical research approach was provided valuable insights into the acceptance of crime surveillance technologies. Some methodological issues should be taken into account, though. First, some aspects have to be criticized in terms of content. The very similar evaluation of perceived benefits of crime surveillance showed that the item content might have been too similar. For further studies it would be desirable to use more specific and tangible items concerning perceived safety aspects, e.g. a quantifiable potential decrease in criminality rates. The same applies for perceived barriers of crime surveillance: participant's feedback showed that the queried items could be more differentiated. In further studies more specifications regarding privacy aspects will be examined (different handling of recorded data, storage issues or even face recognition). Concerning crime surveillance technologies this study focuses on the distinction between visible and invisible technologies. Future studies should differentiate between specific visible and invisible technology types. Another note refers to the classification of locations. Here, we assumed the classifications that were made by the participants of previous focus groups. The distinction between public and private locations is comprehensive and uncontroversial, whereas the difference between rather public and rather private locations is rather small. Therefore, in further studies a more precise definition of location categories is necessary.

Besides terms of content, for further studies other methodological approaches than the assessment of single questions that are independently of each other could be useful. In a real world scenario, we do not evaluate single factors, acceptance for or against a technology usage is formed by the concurrent evaluation of a complex scenario. Since four relevant attributes (location types, safety aspects, privacy aspects and technology type) were identified in this study, the implementation of a conjoint analysis could be useful to gain a deeper insight into the acceptance of crime surveillance. This way, the relative importance of different attributes could be determined and the trade-off between safety and privacy could be characterized precisely. This kind of analysis could also be used to compare crime and medical surveillance acceptance in detail and to analyze whether the importance of locations, technologies, and privacy-safety-trade-off is context-sensitive.

Further, the sample size of this study was rather small, so the findings should be replicated in larger and more representative. To involve place of residence as a hypothetically influencing variable, further samples have to contain a higher number of people living in rural areas. Finally, as this study only focuses German city dwellers, our approach and findings could be replicated in other countries to compare crime surveillance needs and desires of city dwellers of different countries and cultures.

References

1. Ziefle, M., Schneider, C., Valeé, D., Schnettler, A., Krempels K.-H., Jarke, M.: Urban Future Outline (UFO): a roadmap on research for livable cities. ERCIM News **98** (2014). http://ercim-news.ercim.eu/en98/keynote-smart-cities
2. La Vigne, N.G., Lowry, S.S., Markman, J.A., Dwyer, A.M.: Evaluating the Use of Public Surveillance Cameras for Crime Control and Prevention. Final Technical Report. The Urban Institute, Washington, DC (2011)
3. Whitaker, R.: The End of Privacy: How Total Surveillance is Becoming a Reality. The New Press, New York (1999)
4. Ziefle, M., Wilkowska, W.: What makes people change their preferences in public transportation – opinions in different user groups. In: Giaffreda, R., Cagáňová, D., Li, Y., Riggio, R., Voisard, A. (eds.) IoT360 2014. LNICST, vol. 151, pp. 137–143. Springer, Cham (2015). doi:10.1007/978-3-319-19743-2_21
5. Plouffe, L., Kalache, A.: Towards global age- friendly cities: determining urban features that promote active aging. J. Urban Health **87**(5), 733–739 (2010)
6. Leonhardt, S.: Personal healthcare devices. In: Mekherjee, S., et al. (eds.) AmIware: Hardware Technology Drivers of Ambient Intelligence, pp. 349–370. Springer Netherlands, Dordrecht (2006)
7. Klack, L., Möllering, C., Ziefle, M., Schmitz-Rode, T.: Future care floor: a sensitive floor for movement monitoring and fall detection in home environments. In: Lin, J.C., Nikita, K.S. (eds.) MobiHealth 2010. LNICST, vol. 55, pp. 211–218. Springer, Heidelberg (2011). doi:10.1007/978-3-642-20865-2_27
8. Klack, L., Schmitz-Rode, T., Wilkowska, W., Kasugai, K., Heidrich, F., Ziefle, M.: Integrated home monitoring and compliance optimization for patients with mechanical circulatory support devices (MCSDs). Ann. Biomed. Eng. **39**(12), 2911–2921 (2011)
9. Smith, M.J., Clarke, R.V.: Crime and public transport. Crime Justice **27**, 169–233 (2000)
10. Marshall, R.D., Bryant, R.A., Amsel, L., Suh, E.J., Cook, J.M., Neria, Y.: The psychology of ongoing threat: relative risk appraisal, the September 11 attacks, and terrorism-related fears. Am. Psychol. **62**(4), 304 (2007)
11. Baumer, T.L.: Research on fear of crime in the US. Victimology **3**, 254–264 (1978)
12. Loewen, L.J., Steel, G.D., Suedfeld, P.: Perceived safety from crime in the urban environment. J. Environ. Psychol. **13**(4), 323–331 (1993)
13. Isnard, A.: Can surveillance cameras be successful in preventing crime and controlling anti-social behaviours? In: Proceedings of the Character, Impact and Prevention of Crime in Regional Australia Conference, Townsville, Australia, 2–3 August 2001
14. Wiecek, C., Saetnan, A.R.: Restrictive? Permissive? The Contradictory Framing of Video Surveillance in Norway and Denmark. Norwegian University of Science and Technology, Working Paper 4 (2002)
15. Sheldon, B.: Camera surveillance within the UK: enhancing public safety or a social threat? Int. Rev. Law Comput. Tech. **25**(3), 193–203 (2011)
16. Chattopadhyayr, D., Dasgupta, R., Banerjee, E.R., Chakraborty, A.: Event driven video surveillance system using city cloud. In: Proceedings of the first International Conference on Intelligent Infrastructure at the 47th Annual National Convention Computer Society of India (2013)
17. Song, M., Tao, D., Maybank, S.J.: Sparse Camera Network for Visual Surveillance – A Comprehensive Survey. Cornell University (2013)
18. Lewis, D.A., Maxfield, M.G.: Fear in the neighborhoods: an investigation of the impact of crime. J. Res. Crime Delinq. **17**(2), 160–189 (1980)

19. Blöbaum, A., Hunecke, M.: Perceived danger in urban public space: the impacts of physical features and personal factors. Environ. Behav. **37**(4), 465–486 (2005)
20. Gumpert, G., Drucker, S.J.: Public boundaries: Privacy and surveillance in a technological world. Commun. Q. **49**(2), 115–129 (2001)
21. Arning, K., Kowalewski, S., Ziefle, M.: Modelling user acceptance of wireless medical technologies. Wirel. Mobile Commun. Healthcare **61**, 146–153 (2013)
22. Arning, K., Ziefle, M., Muehlhans, H.: Join the ride! user requirements and interface design guidelines for a commuter carpooling platform. In: Marcus, A. (ed.) DUXU 2013. LNCS, vol. 8014, pp. 10–19. Springer, Heidelberg (2013). doi:10.1007/978-3-642-39238-2_2
23. Alsnih, R., Hensher, D.A.: The mobility and accessibility expectations of seniors in an aging population. Transp. Res. Part A. Policy Pract. **37**(10), 903–916 (2003)
24. Dickerson, A.E., Molnar, L.J., Eby, D.W., Adler, G., Bédard, M., Berg-Weger, M., Trujillo, L.: Transportation and aging: a research agenda for advancing safe mobility. Gerontologist **47**(5), 578–590 (2007)
25. Covington, J., Taylor, R.B.: Fear of crime in urban residential neighborhoods. Sociol. Q. **32**(2), 231–249 (1991)
26. Scarborough, B.K., Like-Haislip, T.Z., Novak, K.J., Lucas, W.L., Alarid, L.F.: Assessing the relationship between individual characteristics, neighborhood context, and fear of crime. J. Crim. Justice **38**(4), 819–826 (2010)
27. Heek, J., Arning, K., Ziefle, M.: Safety and privacy perceptions in public spaces: an empirical study on user requirements for city mobility. In: Giaffreda, R., Cagáňová, D., Li, Y., Riggio, R., Voisard, A. (eds.) IoT360 2014. LNICST, vol. 151, pp. 97–103. Springer, Cham (2015). doi:10.1007/978-3-319-19743-2_15
28. Kientz, J.A., Arriaga, R.I., Chetty, M., Hayes, G.R., Richardson, J., Patel, S.N., Abowd, G.D.: Grow and know: understanding record-keeping needs for tracking the development of young children. In: Conference on Human Factors in Computing Systems, pp. 1351–1360. ACM, NY (2007)
29. Himmel, S., Ziefle, M., Arning, K.: From living space to urban quarter: acceptance of ICT monitoring solutions in an ageing society. In: Kurosu, M. (ed.) HCI 2013. LNCS, vol. 8006, pp. 49–58. Springer, Heidelberg (2013). doi:10.1007/978-3-642-39265-8_6
30. World Health Organization. Ageing & Life Course Unit: WHO global report on falls prevention in older age. World Health Organization (2008)
31. Lord, S.R., Menz, H.B., Sherrington, C.: Home environment risk factors for falls in older people and the efficacy of home modifications. Age Ageing **35**(2), 55–59 (2006)
32. Koskela, H.: 'The gaze without eyes': video-surveillance and the changing nature of urban space. Prog. Hum. Geogr. **24**(2), 243–265 (2000)
33. Patton, J.W.: Protecting privacy in public? Surveillance technologies and the value of public places. Ethics Inf. Technol. **2**(3), 181–187 (2000)
34. Debatin, B., Lovejoy, J.P., Horn, A.-K., Hughes, B.N.: Facebook and online privacy: attitudes, behaviours, and unintended consequences. J. Comput. Mediat. Comm. **15**(1), 83–108 (2009)
35. Marx, G.T.: Ethics for the new surveillance. Inform. Soc. **14**(3), 171–185 (1998)
36. Mark, W.: Fear of victimization: why are women and the elderly more afraid? Soc. Sci. Q. **65**(3), 681–702 (1984)
37. van Heek, J., Arning, K., Ziefle, M.: How fear of crime affects needs for privacy safety - Acceptance of Surveillance Technologies in Smart Cities. In: Proceedings of the 5th International Conference on Smart Cities and Green ICT Systems (SMARTGREENS 2016), pp. 32–43 (2016)

A Smarter Sidewalk-Based Route Planner for Wheelchair Users: An Approach with Open Data

Nádia P. Kozievitch$^{(\boxtimes)}$, Leonelo D.A. Almeida, Ricardo Dutra da Silva, and Rodrigo Minetto

Federal University of Technology, Curitiba, PR 80230-901, Brazil
{nadiap,leoneloalmeida,rdutra,rminetto}@utfpr.edu.br

Abstract. In this chapter we describe an approach to integrate GIS maps (endorsed by discrete features, such as points, lines, polygons), in order to develop a route planner for wheelchair users. We integrate public available data and an approach with free software with a novel model for route planning, based on sidewalks, crosswalks and curb ramps, as opposed to traditional street-based approaches. We show that our sidewalk-based model is more suitable than available route planning services under mobility constraints, using a case study in Curitiba, Brazil.

Keywords: Route planner · Wheelchair users · GIS · Open data

1 Introduction

In the constructing of a sustainable city, issues like urban mobility must be featured during the entire urban planning process. The effective interaction with traffic participants is an open challenge, in order to consider vulnerable road users like pedestrians.

Increased use of wheelchairs is expected, along with the aging of the populace within the recent years. In particular, several efforts have been made to develop route planning services for people with disabilities [9,11,14]. This is a challenging problem that involves the processing of a huge amount of data, such as maps, images, detailed public transport information and collaborative user feedback, to properly define wheelchair accessible paths. Nevertheless, there is a lack of route planning services (such as the route planner of Google maps[1]) that take into consideration wheelchair users needs and preferences, as shown in Fig. 1.

If we consider route planners, the current available solutions for wheelchair users are street-based. Nevertheless, a myriad of complex spatial factors could be considered in order to locate the best routes, such as sidewalks, crosswalks and curb ramps. In many applications, such as geographic information systems (GIS), data can set the stage by displaying individual maps of decision criteria, in order to provide the detailed information needed to locate the best route.

---

[1] https://maps.google.com Last visited on 01/07/2015.

© Springer International Publishing AG 2017
M. Helfert et al. (Eds.): SMARTGREENS 2016 and VEHITS 2016, CCIS 738, pp. 192–206, 2017.
DOI: 10.1007/978-3-319-63712-9_11

Fig. 1. The standard Google maps engine does not have an option for wheelchair users.

In this chapter we are concerned with the routing problem for wheelchair users. The input data for this problem is a set of base map layers (streets, sidewalks and city blocks). The output data is a cost weighted map, which we also present as a graph. The novelty is, taking advantage of open data, to include additional factors (such as distinct sidewalks in a street or missing curb ramps), in order to propose a best route to a wheelchair user. Finally, we present some preliminary tests, using open data and GIS. The main goal is to discover what the data and method can tell us about the observed mobility plan with the help of visualization and display techniques of GIS.

We explore our method using data from Curitiba, a city located in the south of Brazil, housing 1.8 million people in a total area of 430,9 km^2, according to the Brazilian Institute of Geography and Statistics (IBGE)[2]. The city belongs to the *C40 cities*[3], a group which set ambitious targets to improve urban life quality and protect their environment.

The remainder of this chapter is organized as follows. Section 2 contains a description of related work. Section 3 presents an overview of our method. Section 4 presents the experiments and, finally, Sect. 5 state the conclusions and future work.

2   Related Work

Several online libraries and services are already available for route planning (such as Google Directions API[4], the JavaScript API Yandex.Map[5], or other online services [6]). In particular, fewer of them are toward specific functionality, such

---

[2] http://www.ibge.gov.br – Last visited on 14/05/2015.

[3] http://www.c40.org Last visited on 30/05/2015.

[4] https://developers.google.com/maps/documentation/directions/ Last visited on 23/06/2015.

[5] https://tech.yandex.ru/maps/ Last visited on 23/06/2015.

[6] http://wiki.openstreetmap.org/wiki/Routing/online_routers Last visited on 23/06/2015.

as wheelchairs (as OpenRouteService[7], Routino[8], Guia de Rodas (portuguese acronym for Wheel Guide[9] and OpenTripPlanner[10]). Nevertheless, some of the online libraries also present accessibility problems [10].

There are norms for urban environments that define accessibility specifications as DIN 18024-1 [7] from Germany and ABNT NBR 9050:2004 [1] from Brazil. Other studies as Kasemsuppakorn and Karimi [8] investigated the most relevant aspects regarding wheelchair accessibility, for each segment of the route network (i.e. length, width, slope, sidewalk surface, steps, sidewalk conditions and sidewalk traffic). Moreover, some studies consider not only barriers but also provide information about relevant locations (called Points of Interest - POI) as restaurants, bus stops, accessible toilets, and police departments (e.g. Menkens et al. [11], and Wheelmap[11]).

Sumida et al. [14] argue that barriers information should be collected through actual measurement data. They adapted an electric wheelchair for collecting data as the force necessary to move the wheelchair and the passage width. Other studies use data provided by the routing service users (e.g. OpenRouteService, and Menkens et al. [11]), volunteers (e.g. OpenRouteService; Menkens et al. [11]; Kulakov et al. [9]), authorities (e.g. Kulakov et al. [9]). Consequently, the collected data is usually limited to a city or a district. An exception is the Wheelmap project that provides resources for crowd sourcing information based on OpenStreetMap data. The project already have more than 470.000 data inputs and an average of 35 thousand users per month.

The lack of public available information regarding accessibility of urban spaces (e.g., streets, sidewalks, curbs, and type of surface) contribute to the fact that most of studies on accessible routing are constrained to cities or districts. Some initiatives as Wheelmap explore the aspects of crowds for collecting relevant information regarding POI. Currently, to our knowledge, none of such initiatives are widely adopted in Curitiba (e.g. there are only about 10 POI registered in Wheelmap, most of them are accessible bus stops). Antonio et al. [2] proposed a crowd-based system for collaboratively filtering bus routes in Curitiba. The focus of that study was on accessibility for visually impaired people and the estimation considered the similarity of the current user to those who generated the accessibility information.

Routing estimation is another challenging task. In order to improve the results of routing estimation, some services provide additional parameters (e.g., maximum inclination, type of surface, maximum curb height, personalized estimation according to the users' profile (e.g. Menkens et al. [11]). As already noted by A. M. Bishop within the Routino application, routing planning can use graph algorithms (e.g. Dijkstra and A*) for calculating the shortest/least-cost path. Some of those studies adapt these algorithms aiming at improving performance

---

[7] http://www.rollstuhlrouting.de/ Last visited on 23/06/2015.

[8] http://www.routino.org/ Last visited on 23/06/2015.

[9] http://www.guiaderodas.com/ Last visited on 23/06/2015.

[10] http://www.opentripplanner.org/ Last visited on 23/06/2015.

[11] http://wheelmap.org/en. Last Visited 24/08/2015.

in terms of execution time (e.g. the concepts of super-segments and super-nodes from A. M. Bishop).

From the database perspective, spatial analytical queries might be used to perform hundreds to several millions of shortest distance computations, processing tasks such as region, KNN, distance matrix and trajectory queries [12]. The challenge is how to embed the row representation in a database, such as pgRouting[12] extension within PostGIS database, using original graph representation. PgRouting provides libraries for the shortest path (including turn restriction, driving distance, among others) through various algorithms such as Bi-directional Dijkstra and All Pairs Short Path. PgRouting can also be effectively used for implementing the real world scenarios [13].

Others claim that there is no clear answer as to shortest path algorithm which runs fastest on real road networks (due to real time computation, the large network size, and the resulting intensive computing) [16]. Among other critical factors for route planning we can mention: (1) types of barriers considered for collecting and estimating routes, (2) data sources for maps information and barriers, and (3) approaches for route planning.

The art of the science is in the identification, calibration and weighting of appropriate routing criteria. That identification is rarely based on only one factor, such as visual, sufficient to identify an overall preferred route [5].

3 Our Method

Problem Formulation. For GIS applications, the shortest path based on a road is a basic operation. In practice, however, users are always interested in several constraints (such as the combination of spatial and textual information [15]). From GIS and map analysis perspective, the routing problem can be described as a three steps process: the calculation of discrete cost, accumulated cost and steepest path [4]. The idea is, using base maps (such as roads), create other derived maps (to calculate information that is too difficult to collect, such as curb ramps) in order to finally create cost/avoidance maps which translate this information into decision criteria. Within this perspective, map layers are thematic representations of geographic information, as shown in Fig. 2. In particular, base maps can be represented by streets, street blocks (Fig. 9) and sidewalks, among others.

The derived maps, composed by large polygon subdivisions, are often simplified in order to reduce the total number of vertices which defines it (known as the map simplification problem [6]). The calibration of the individual cost maps is an important and sensitive step in the siting process. Usually, this step requires human judgment due to the complexity and subjectivity of such decision. As an example, you might be interested in identifying the most preferred route for a wheelchair user that minimizes its visual exposure to huge avenues, and maximizes the visual exposure to bus stops.

---

[12] http://pgrouting.org/ Last visited on 23/09/2015.

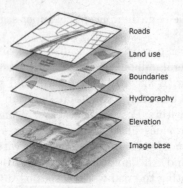

Fig. 2. Map layers (http://webhelp.esri.com/ Last access on 17/09/2015).

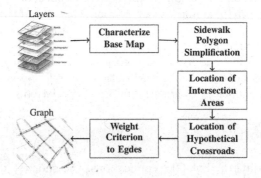

Fig. 3. Overview of the proposed system.

From the geometry perspective, streets are one or more single lines (which can also be represented by one ore more edges in a graph), which thereby are composed by points (which can also be represented by a vertice in a graph). Sidewalks can be decomposed by the respective lines, and lines can be decomposed by respective points (Fig. 7).

Formally, a GIS database contains a set of geometries which can be resumed as a set P of points on a network $G = (V, E)$, where V represents vertices and E represents edges. The network is a directed connected graph. A point $p \in P$ locates on an edge $e \in E$. The distance between any two points (or vertices) can be denoted as $d(p_i, p_j)$, as the length of the shortest path connecting them.

Our Approach. Our method comprised the following steps (shown in Fig. 3) toward a sidewalk-based model: (1) the base map (streets, sidewalks, blocks, etc.) characterization; (2) the creation of derived map for sidewalk polygon simplification; (3) the creation of derived map for location of intersection areas; (4) the creation of derived map for hypothetical crossroads; (5) the establishment of a weighting criterion to edges (in particular, considering wheelchair users); and (6) the generation of the graph.

For the characterization of the base maps (identified by Figs. 6 and 7), external open data were integrated with data from Open Street Map with a spatial database. The complete data set initially included streets (39.948 rows), sidewalks (9.614 rows) and blocks (13.459 rows) from Curitiba. The complete data set was inserted in a PostGIS[13] database. Later, specific tablespaces and indexes were created in order to optimize the access. Nevertheless, several semantic errors were present (such as different street geometries and names - more details in [3]). The data was visualized with QGIS[14].

The second step started with the simplification of sidewalk polygons and their derived points (performed with a spatial database function named *st_simplify*).

The next derived map comprised the road intersection areas, basically discovering the average distance among streets and sidewalks. Circles in Fig. 8 represent this phase, performed with spatial functions, such as *st_buffer*.

The last derived map comprised the hypothetical crossroads, identified by lines, triangles and rectangles inside the road intersection area (circles). Basically this map was derived using spatial database functions such as *st_convexhull* (shown in Fig. 4).

The weighting criterion (step 5) was initially set as the distance between points if the "edge" has no barriers, or infinite if it does. Lately these weights could be modified to register temporal issues, such as constructions which might impact the normal flow of pedestrians. In practice, these distances can be obtained with spatial functions, such as *st_distance*.

```
create table batel_cruzamentos201509 as
select B.gid, st_convexhull(st_collect(K.points))
from (select B.gid, pointsfrompolygon points from batel_simp A,
          batel_raioteste B
      where st_contains(raiogeom, pointsfrompolygon)) K,
          batel_raioteste B
where K.gid=B.gid
group by B.gid
```

Fig. 4. Example of SQL query to compute crosswalks.

From the GIS perspective, the shortest path would not be based on the street map, but on the composition of the sidewalk map and on the derived map for the crossroads. Note that: (i) the same sidewalks could have temporally distinct costs (if for example, one sidewalk is next to a construction during the beginning of an year) and (ii) the distinct crossroads geometries could help the identification of most dangerous locations for pedestrians.

4 Experiments

We concentrated our efforts in preliminary experimental results, using an ordinary linux server, and exploring spatial database functions. In order to simplify our tests, we explored the shortest path as a graph (step 6), but indeed, there

---

[13] http://www.postgis.net Last visited on 15/05/2014.
[14] http://www.qgis.org Last visited on 15/05/2015.

```
CREATE TABLE arruamento.arruamento_quadras
(
    gid serial NOT NULL,
    tipo character varying(50),
    shape_area numeric,
    shape_len numeric,
    geom geometry(MultiPolygon,4326),
    CONSTRAINT arruamento_quadras_pkey PRIMARY KEY (gid)
)
WITH (
    OIDS=FALSE
)
```

Fig. 5. Example of SQL for street block creation.

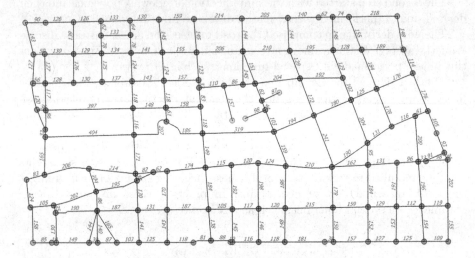

Fig. 6. The streets and respective lengths.

are already ongoing projects (such as pgRouting) which could be used within the spatial database.

Datasets. In particular, we are exploring a case study in Curitiba. Curitiba has 1.8 million people inside a total area of $430{,}9\,\mathrm{km}^2$, IDH of 0,823, according to the Brazilian Institute of Geography and Statistics (IBGE)[15]. This area encompasses 75 neighborhood districts. According to the same census, Curitiba had in the urban region approximately 95 thousand people with some degree of motor disability. Among them, more than 31 thousand informed to experience, at least, great difficulty for locomotion. Despite of not providing more detailed information regarding barriers for motor impaired people, the Census revealed that only 12.6% of the urban area of Curitiba presented lowered curbs. Thus, currently, providing effective and efficient route plannings for people with motor disabilities, especially wheelchair users, is potentially relevant for removing barriers to people's daily lives.

---

[15] http://www.ibge.gov.br. Last visited on 14/05/2015.

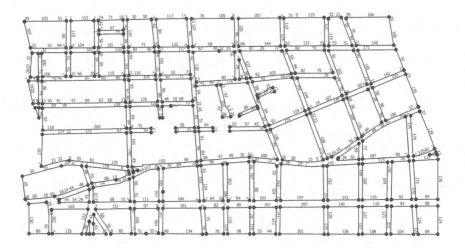

Fig. 7. Example of sidewalks and respective points and lengths.

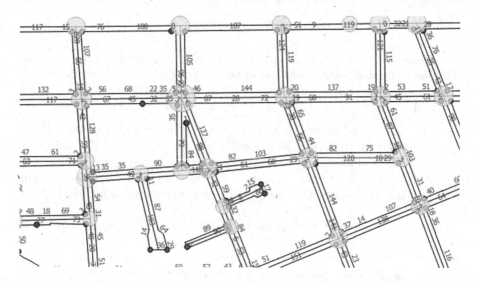

Fig. 8. Example of sidewalks, streets and road intersection areas.

We used for the acquisition/characterization of the base maps, the dataset from the Institute of Research and Urban Planning of Curitiba (IPPUC[16]), along with data from Open Street Map[17]. Figure 5 shows the DDL example for the creation of street block table. The complete data set initially included streets (39,948 rows), sidewalks (9,614 rows) and blocks (13,459 rows) from Curitiba.

---

[16] http://www.ippuc.com.br. Last visited on 14/05/2015.
[17] http://www.openstreetmap.org Last visited on 14/05/2015.

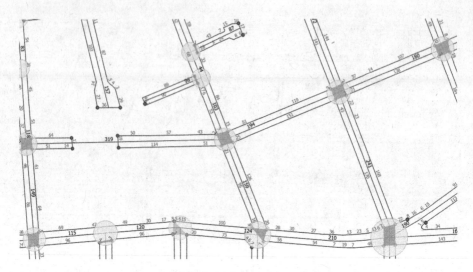

Fig. 9. Hypothetical crossroads, with street lengths (in black) and sidewalk lengths (gray).

The complete data set was inserted in a PostGIS[18] database. Later, specific tablespaces and indexes were created in order to optimize the access. Nevertheless, several semantic errors were present (such as different street geometries and names - more details in [3]). The data was visualized with QGIS[19].

Tests. For our tests, the three base maps toward the selected area of the Batel district resulted in 51 streets, 94 sidewalks and 71 blocks. The derived maps resulted in 309 road intersection areas (within a zoom in Fig. 8) and 185 number of possible crossroads (within a zoom in Fig. 9). Note that crossroads within Fig. 9 can belong to geometric groups: lines and polygons (with three or four edges).

Consider the shortest walking path (highlighted in Fig. 10) from point A on Benjamin Lins Street to point B on Vicente Machado Avenue. The path is computed by considering the possible combination of streets that can be followed in order to get from one point to another. A subset of the combinations can be modeled by a graph as the one in Fig. 10. The vertices are a set of intersections and the edges are segments of streets defined by two intersections.

The graph reflects the input data used for computing shortest paths on common route planning. This is a street-based graph which takes into account a weight factor for each edge according to known properties of street segments, such as the distance between two intersections, the slope of a street segment and the condition of a sidewalk. The graph in Fig. 10 considers distances between intersections.

---

[18] http://www.postgis.net Last visited on 15/05/2014.
[19] http://www.qgis.org Last visited on 15/05/2015.

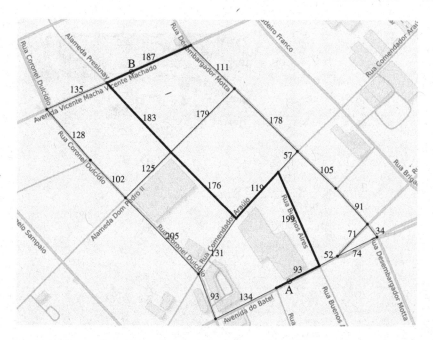

Fig. 10. Shortest walking path between points A and B computed using a street-based graph.

People with disabilities, such as wheelchair users, may face some problems due to conditions not captured in route planners considering such a model. As highlighted in Fig. 11, there is a crossing without curb ramps that would make it difficult to proceed along the route. The model must be able to encode that kind of constraints perhaps by using a weight on the vertices of the graph or by making it reflect on the weight of the streets. Anyway, those can also be flawed solutions: it is possible one street has sidewalks on both sides and one side has problems while the second one is in perfect conditions to go along.

The sidewalk-based model proposed in this chapter allows to make all of these conditions explicitly available for a route planner, making it more suitable for searching paths that meet the needs of people with disabilities. The model for the same region of the previous discussion is summarized by the graph in Fig. 12. The hypothetical curb ramps are vertices of the graph and its edges are sidewalks or adjoining curb ramps on streets. Thereafter, every sidewalk can have its own weight and the lack of curb ramps between adjoining streets also be encoded on the edges connecting them. It is possible, therefore, to avoid streets without curb ramps and sidewalks on poor conditions. The shortest path in our model is highlighted in Fig. 12, depicting not only which sidewalk to follow along a street but also which curb ramps to use.

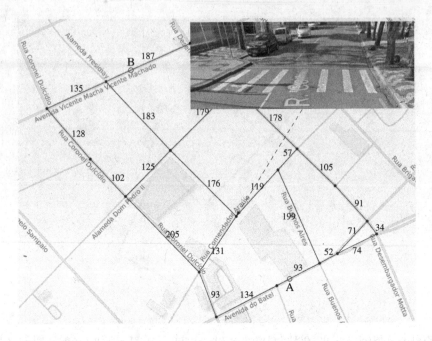

Fig. 11. Ordinary route planners do not consider accessibility constraints.

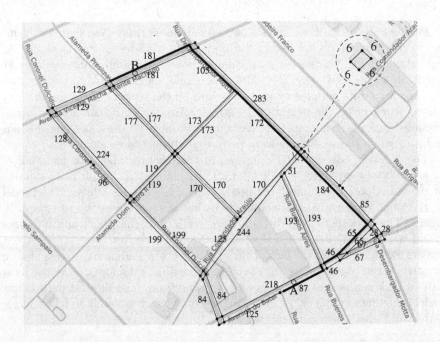

Fig. 12. A sidewalk-based model and a route considering accessibility.

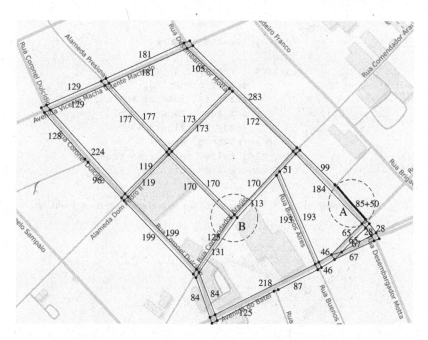

Fig. 13. Modified sidewalk-based model: a sidewalk was given a bigger weight (see region A) and a curb ramp, along with a crosswalk, was added (see region B).

The model may have its attributes modified by users: (i) an edge (segment of a sidewalk) of the graph could have its weigh increased if the condition of the sidewalk is degraded due to holes in the pavement, narrow width, obstruction, among others; and (ii) previously nonexistent curb ramps and their related crosswalks could be added to improve the route planning. The two types of modifications are illustrated in Fig. 13. The weight of one edge was modified due to a possible poor condition of the sidewalk. In the second modification a vertex and an edge were added to the model to illustrate that a new curb ramp has been built.

PgRouting Preliminar Tests. For the preliminary tests with pgRouting, the streets table with used along with Dijkstra algorithm, as indicated in Fig. 14. Basically, the algorithm uses an identification of a source, a destiny, and the edges cost (within the table, the street length) to calculate the shortest path between two points. Considering the same origin and destination from Fig. 10, the Dijkstra algorithm returned a slight different street-based path, as indicated in Fig. 15.

Since sidewalks and crossroads were already listed in Fig. 9, the Dijkstra computation on a sidewalk-based path could be applied, after a correct calibration of path costs, along with the algorithm. Note also that Fig. 9 uses the city open data, while Fig. 13 is using an online search service, and some street names (along with street lengths) might present differences.

```
select *
        from arruamento.network
        join
        (select * from pgr_dijkstra('
                select gid as id,
                start_id::int4 as source,
                end_id::int4 as target,
                shape_len:float8 as cost
        from arruamento.network',
        16, 114, false, false)) as route
        on network.gid=route.id2;
```

Fig. 14. Example of query for running Dijkstra algorithm in pgRouting.

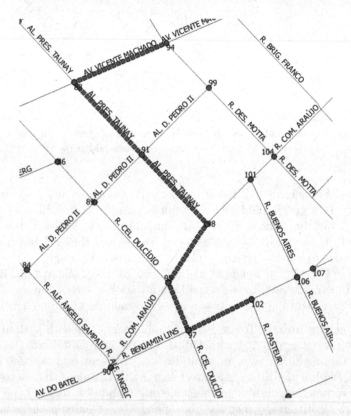

Fig. 15. Visualization of Dijkstra algorithm from pgRouting.

Discussion. Among the parameters which impact the planning of a route for wheelchair users, we can mention: **Database issues:** lack of standard within the data sources (the different data semantics, geometries, etc.), the domain understanding of how GIS geometries might be mapped and how they can be explored in other domains (such as graphs), the theoretic abstraction of how different layers of points, lines, geometries can be mapped to multigraphs, among others; **Domain issues:** how to manage different areas (such as databases, human computer interaction, theory of computation, urbanism, etc.) toward working in an unified solution, regarding terms and technologies; **Theory:** how to theoretically add temporal events which might change in a graph (such as edge weights which change along the interactions); how to develop a mathematical approach and elaborate algorithms of route building on the graph on condition of various types of obstacles; how to better calculate the edge weight estimation. Although being preliminary, the tests state that the implementation of the method is suitable for wheelchair users. In summary, we understand that better approaches to the routing problem depends on a sinergic combination of data, knowledge domain, and user feedback.

5   Conclusions

Research in urban mobility, and in particular, accessibility and GIS is not recent, but the exploration through different domains is still an ongoing effort.

We described in this chapter an alternative wheelchair route planning model, along with the concepts, application, and their challenges. Later the definitions were explored in a case study, within the Curitiba region, Brazil. Finally, we presented preliminary tests using open data, Postgis and pgRouting.

Future work includes the inclusion of topography, public transportation maps, along with the bus accessibility routes. We also pretend to test KNN and distance matrix under pgRouting.

Acknowledgments. We would like to thank the Curitiba City Municipality, IPPUC, and EU-BR EUBra-BigSea project (MCTI/RNP 3rd Coordinated Call).

References

1. ABNT (Brazilian Association of Technical Standards): Abnt nbr 9050:2004: Accessibility to buildings, equipment and the urban environment (2004). http://www.abntcatalogo.com.br/norma.aspx?ID=1000
2. Antonio, M.F., Côgo, F.R., Steinmacher, I., Chaves, A.P.: Filtragem colaborativa de rotas de ônibus usando dados sobre a acessibilidade das vias urbanas. In: Society, B.C. (ed.) Proceeding of the 11th Brazilian Symposium on Collaborative Systems, pp. 126–133 (2014)
3. Barczyszyn, G.L.: Integration of geographic data for the urban planning of the city of Curitiba. Universidade Tecnológica Federal do Paraná, 7 October 2015. (in Portuguese)
4. Berry, J.K.: Beyound Mapping - Concepts, Algorithms and Issues in GIS, vol. 1. John Wiley Publishers, London (1993)
5. Berry, J.K.: Map Analysis - Understanding Spatial Patterns and Relationships, vol. 1. GeoTecMedia (2007). http://www.innovativegis.com/basis/Books/MapAnalysis/

6. Estkowski, R., Mitchell, J.S.B.: Simplifying a polygonal subdivision while keeping it simple. In: SCG 2001, pp. 40–49. ACM (2001). http://doi.acm.org/10.1145/378583.378612

7. German Institute for Standardization: Barrier-free design - part 1: Streets, places, roads and recreational areas; planning basics. Standard Specification 18024–1, German Institute for Standardization, Berlin (1998)

8. Kasemsuppakorn, P., Karimi, H.A.: Personalised routing for wheel-chair navigation. J. Locat. Based Serv. **3**(1), 24–54 (2009). http://dx.doi.org/10.1080/17489720902837936

9. Kulakov, K., Shabaev, A., Shabalina, I.: The route planning services approach for people with disability. In: FRUCT 2015, pp. 89–95, April 2015

10. Medina, J.L., Cagnin, M.I., Paiva, D.M.B.: Evaluation of web accessibility on the maps domain, SAC 2015, pp. 157–162. ACM, New York (2015). http://doi.acm.org/10.1145/2695664.2695771

11. Menkens, C., Sussmann, J., Al-Ali, M., Breitsameter, E., Frtunik, J., Nendel, T., Schneiderbauer, T.: Easywheel - a mobile social navigation and support system for wheelchair users. In: ITNG 2011, pp. 859–866, April 2011

12. Peng, S., Samet, H.: Analytical queries on road networks: an experimental evaluation of two system architectures. In: Proceedings of the 23rd SIGSPATIAL International Conference on Advances in Geographic Information Systems, GIS 2015, pp. 1:1–1:10. ACM, NewYork (2015). http://doi.acm.org/10.1145/2820783.2820806

13. Singh, P.S., Lyngdoh, R.B., Chutia, D., Saikhom, V., Kashyap, B., Sudhakar, S.: Dynamic shortest route finder using pgrouting for emergency management. Appl. Geomatics **7**(4), 255–262 (2015). http://dx.doi.org/10.1007/s12518-015-0161-4

14. Sumida, Y., Hayashi, M., Goshi, K., Matsunaga, K.: Development of a route finding system for manual wheelchair users based on actual measurement data. In: UIC/ATC 2012, pp. 17–23, September 2012

15. Yao, B., Tang, M., Li, F.: Multi-approximate-keyword routing in GIS data, GIS 2011, pp. 201–210. ACM, New York (2011). http://doi.acm.org/10.1145/2093973.2094001

16. Zhan, F.B.: Three fastest shortest path algorithms on real road networks: data structures and procedures. J. Geogr. Inf. Decis. Anal. **1**(1), 69–82 (1997)

A Simplified Methodological Approach Towards the Net Zero Energy District

Sesil Koutra[1(✉)], Vincent Becue[2], and Christos S. Ioakimidis[1]

[1] 'Net-Zero Energy Efficiency Unit on City Districts', Research Institute for Energy, University of Mons, Mons, Belgium
{sesil.koutra,christos.ioakeimidis}@umons.ac.be
[2] Faculty of Architecture and Urban Planning, University of Mons, Mons, Belgium
vincent.becue@umons.ac.be

Abstract. Zero energy conceptual framework is attracting increasing interest in European target policies aiming at more sustainable and liveable urban and built environments. Despite its compelling context in scientific literature and practical applications, the commonly used approach is principally adopted on the aspect of an individual building. Cases with zero energy concept are few in literature. The aim of this paper is the development of a methodological approach to extend the 'zero energy building' to the 'zero energy district' by taking into account two challenges: (1) the impact of urban structure (typo-morphology) on the actual energy needs and (2) the location. It proposes a simplified methodology within three strategic axes through the systemic approach of the district and thereby opens and addresses future research perspective to be widely investigated to develop 'smart' districts with operational and long-term context by introducing the notion of 'smart ground'.

Keywords: Case-study · Energy · Morphology · Smart · Typology

1 Introduction

The future of the majority of citizens' is undeniably urban. Contemporary cities aim at upgrading and enhancing their attractiveness [1]. In this current context of urbanisation and the overall growth phenomenon (projected to reach 60% of the global population by 2030), managing to strategic planning with 'sustainable' terms appears as a policy target. Controversial aspects of the cities' future debate exist in the literature and the term 'smart' ('intelligent') but actually, there is no agreed definition of its context [2]. What is certain, though, is that it represents a multi-disciplinary rising field of the 21st century.

Cities are undoubtedly the core of economic activities, the sustainable development and the key for the 'smart growth' [3] and are by definition a focal point of energy

---

S. Koutra—ERA Chair.
C.S. Ioakimidis—ERA Chair (*Holder).

© Springer International Publishing AG 2017
M. Helfert et al. (Eds.): SMARTGREENS 2016 and VEHITS 2016, CCIS 738, pp. 207–224, 2017.
DOI: 10.1007/978-3-319-63712-9_12

consumption and production, while buildings are a major consumer of energy worldwide – considered to be responsible for more than 20% of the greenhouse emissions in Europe [4, 5]. To respond to these phenomena, energy-oriented techniques, incentives, and regulative instruments are held towards the achievement of low carbon (or energy) districts, such as the European and National Directive on Energy Performance of Buildings (EPBD) on nearly Zero Energy Buildings[1] proposing that by 31.12.2020 all newly constructed buildings shall produce as much energy as they consume on-site [5]. Today, the problematic of '**zero energy**' concept is arising an increasing interest as shown in a scientific literature review [4] to alleviate issues regarding the depletion of energy resources and the requirement to minimise the energy needs and use alternative sources along with the track of environmental protection [6].

The purpose of this paper is, therefore, to identify the 'Net-Zero Energy' conception in a district scale and, by doing so, it introduces a simplified methodological framework by identifying the drivers of this discourse and reaching to preliminary conclusions regarding its future strategic urban planning. The paper is structured accordingly. Section 2 presents the description of the methodological framework recommended for NZED, Sect. 3 identifies the correlation between the urban structure, the building sector, and the transport with energy consumption, Sect. 4 illustrates the state-of-the-art of ten case-studies under a multi-thematic approach, the evaluation and the preliminary results, Sect. 5 discusses the results emerged from the research, while Sect. 6 highlights the future research work.

2   A Net-Zero Energy District (NZED) Framework: Method and Assumptions

2.1   Net-Zero Energy Concept

The concept of '**Zero Energy Buildings**' (ZEB) is proved to act as a key factor in the development of the 'smart city' with the perspective (and at the same time the challenge) to contribute significantly on the energy aspect. It is considered as a progressive evolution of low-energy and passive building designs including - apart from minimising the required energy demand (heating, cooling, etc.) by adopting well-balanced operations between consumption and production coupled with successful grid integration [7].

Many developed and developing countries have already introduced their own building energy standards and guidelines specifically to suit, among other things, the local climates as well as the prevailing architectural designs and construction practices (i.e. Energy Performance of Building Directive - EPBD, etc.) ([5, 8]). The EPBD recast clarified the concept of ZEB, the framework, and boundaries that have been set to proceed along this track. Art. 2 defines a 'nearly Zero Energy Building' (nZEB) as "*a building that has a very high energy performance and the very low amount of energy required should be covered to a very significant extent by energy from renewable*

---

[1] Directive 2010/31/EU of the European Parliament and the Council of 19th May 2010 on the energy performance of buildings: http://eur-lex.europa.eu/LexUriServ/LexUriServ.do? uri=OJ:L:2010:153:0013:0035:EN:PDF.

alternative sources, including energy from renewable sources produced on-site or nearby", while Art. 9 requires that [9]:

(a) By 31st December 2020, all new buildings to be of zero (or nearly) energy
(b) After 31st December 2018, new buildings occupied and owned by public authorities to be of nearly zero energy

The timeline for the implementation of ZEBs according to the EPBD recast is schematised in Fig. 1 [6]:

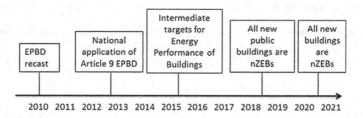

Fig. 1. Timeline for NZEBs' implementation according to EPBD recast (Source: European Commission, 2009).

2.2 The Role of the District

In literature, the zero energy objective is often related and considered on a building scale. However, despite its particular interest, the research of the concept on the individual scale of the building as an autonomous entity ignores the significance of other phenomena linked to larger territorial scales concerning the efficiency and performance of renewable energies, the impact of the transportation system, etc. [10]. Besides, the achievement of a low (or even zero) energy district (Net-Zero Energy District, NZED) depends not only on the energy balance of the building stock but as well on its holistic urban metabolism including the human factor.

'District' level appears interesting in an operational and multi-thematic context for modelling and exemplifying the realisation of a 'smart city' within the introduction and the application of modern technological techniques and practices. The 'district', as a micrograph and a constructive element of the city [11] identifies the patterns of energy consumption and concrete solutions towards 'sustainability'. Well-situated to experiment within specific practices to improve the sustainability of the urban and built environment but also the application of the net-zero energy concept in real life. From the authors' point of view, as a result of previous analysis of ten European case-studies, challenges are important to consider the net-zero energy conceptual framework in a district:

1. The district scale is particularly interesting within its interconnections and interfaces among the diverse components at a larger scale than a building.
2. The challenge of both developing innovative and energetically performative urban structure and concurrently retrofitting the existing building stock.

3. The significant increase in actual energy needs to the phenomenon of demographic growth in a horizon up to 2050.
4. The impacts of parameters linked to the urban structure on the energy performance of buildings and the energetic hybridisation within the use of renewable energy resources.
5. The impact of location, typology and morphology of the district related to the energy consumption and production to attain the (annual) balance in the district.

2.3 Systemic Approach

For this study, the district is understood as an 'urban block' and a complicated system with diverse key parameters and interconnections (Fig. 2) [12]:

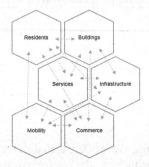

Fig. 2. District components and interconnections.

The 'Net-Zero Energy District' idea is conceptualised and described by analogy with the NZEB as a territory in which the balance of the energy consumption and production for buildings (Fig. 3) [13]:

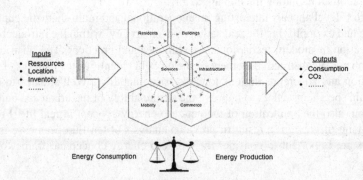

Fig. 3. Systemic approach of a NZED.

Generally, the methodological steps are described in Fig. 4 briefly:

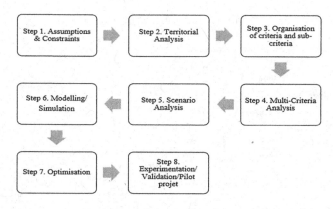

Fig. 4. Description of methodological steps.

2.4 Assumptions

The *main assumptions* for the achievement of a NZED are the following ones:

1. The (annual) balance between the energy production and energy consumption (including buildings, production of on-site renewable energy)
2. The 'smart location' emphasised on 'smart geographical site' of a district (regarding its distance to the city centre, the interdependencies with the adjacent districts, etc.)
3. The mixed-use character of the district (social and functional mixing)
4. The maximisation of use of alternative renewable sources and solar gain
5. …..

The processes of optimisation, evaluation and monitoring of urban projects require a defined framework and methodology. A typical compilation of qualitative and quantitative criteria as shown in Fig. 5 [12]:

1. *Optimisation of actual occupants' needs:* key indicators that frame the district's 'anatomy' (profile)
2. *Use of energetic hybridisation*: reflects the successful incorporation and combination of energetic systems' and technologies' variety combining with local production of renewable energy sources
3. *Organisation of storage*: energy performance of technologies, systems, and techniques installed to reduce energy consumption.

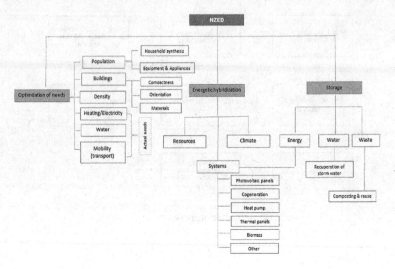

Fig. 5. Analysis of the three pillars of a NZED.

2.5 Territorial Analysis

The next step includes the territorial analysis and the characteristics of the district's profile ('anatomy') among two strategic research questions:

1. Where to locate the NZED (i.e. geographical site, etc.) and what urban characteristics of the district exist presently? (i.e. population, buildings' typology/morphology/ construction age, materials, land uses, transportation system, natural resources, weather data, etc., definition of residents'/users' energy needs, average number of buildings, etc.)
2. What is the 'optimised' (or appropriate) urban structure (typology and morphology) to give to the NZED? (so that to minimise the energy/heat losses and optimise key parameters, such as solar gain, less car dependency, etc.).

2.6 Organisation of Criteria and Sub-criteria

The organisation of the criteria is performed in accordance with the three pillars of evaluation (Fig. 5) and within the axis of (1) typology and (2) morphology of the districts. The analytical approach of the diverse criteria is briefly presented subsequently below.

Typology.

(a) Location/Geographical site/Topography/Natural resources
The potential of natural resources along with the reduction of energy consumption are probably the major aspect of characterising a district as 'net-zero energy'. Girardet [14] proposes the concept of the 'urban metabolism' to explain the use of the natural resources in a city (or a district). The energy needs (heating, cooling, etc.) are minimised from the beginning (conception) of the urban project. The focus

on renewable energies (used for heating and electricity) enables the reduction of the environmental impacts and the independence from fossil and gas emissions.

(b) Buildings/Physical composition/Land uses

Anon [15] defines the building typology regarding their physical composition and are basically categorised into the following divisions:

1. *Free-standing (or detached or single-family) dwellings.*
2. *Attached or multi-user or multi-family dwellings*: classification of built environment, where multiple separate units are contained within one building.
3. A building comprising two units' *side by side* is typically considered as 'semi-detached' on separate properties sharing a common wall with separate entrances and without common inside areas.
4. *'Duplex house'*: dwelling comprising two units on two different floors. Accordingly, the triplex, four-plex dwelling, etc.
5. *'Apartments'*: building with multiple floors containing multiple apartments on each floor. In contrast with a low-rise and single-family houses, apartment blocks accommodate more inhabitants per unit of area of land.

(c) Users/Residents/Occupants

In this category, there is a series of criteria of the 'district typology' that affect the net-zero energy concept:

1. *Household Synthesis*: number of persons per household
2. *Equipment/Appliances*: type and quantity that affect the energy consumption in a household and as a consequence in a district as totality in an annual basis
3. *Population/Residential Density*: choice of housing type is strongly related to the urban form; the odds that a household of a multi-family housing is seven times greater for compact cities than for sprawling counties [16]. The criterion of 'density' is described in two different ways: **compactness** – (architectural viewpoint)– and **population or dwelling unit density** (number of inhabitants or units per ha) (planning perspective).

(d) Mobility

The compilation of the criteria focuses mainly on the district's location in relation to the city centre, the distances from the other districts, etc.

Morphology. Key parameters that influence the district morphology of the buildings are:

(a) Compactness

The shape of buildings is an aspect strictly related to energy consumption. Two core parameters are (1) **surface-to-volume ratio or compactness** and (2) the **ratio of passive-to-non-passive zones**. Compactness is relevant to the energy consumption of building since and represents the amount of surfaces exposed to the outside environment, responsible for heat losses. It also refers to urban contiguity (and connectivity).

(b) Geometry

One of the most important key factors to determine the building's energy use. The 'geometry', or 'urban geometry', influences the energy performance and affects the energy performance in two main ways: mutual shading and microclimate [17].

(c) Orientation

The orientation of an urban pattern is a spatial parameter to analyse the accessibility of solar energy and daylight in an urban area and the natural lighting. An overall reflection integrating the benefits of the solar energy are conducted during the planning and architectural composition of the NZED. Briefly, the criteria and sub-criteria defined for a NZED are presented in Tables 1 and 2:

Table 1. Qualitative and quantitative criteria for district typology.

District typology				
	Criterion	Qualitative	Quantitative	Units
Location	Geographical site	x		
	Climate/Weather		x	Temperature (°C)
	Natural resources		x	Distance (m or km) from district
Buildings	Land uses (Residential, Non-residential, …)	x		
	Physical composition	x		
	Floors		x	Number of floors
	Rooms		x	Number of rooms
	Dwellings		x	Number of dwellings
	Household synthesis		x	Number of persons per household
	Equipment/Appliances		x	Energy consumption per appliance
Occupants/ Residents	Population density		x	Number of people per ha
	Residential density		x	Number of dwellings per ha
Mobility	Transport services		x	Distances (km from the city centre, etc.)

Table 2. Qualitative and quantitative criteria for district morphology.

District morphology				
	Criterion	Qualitative	Quantitative	Units
Compactness	Form	x		
	Size	x		
	Volume	x		
Geometry	Building shape	x		
	Building height		x	Number of m per building structure
Orientation	Angle		x	° of the angle to maximize solar gain and natural lighting
	Dwellings		x	° of the angle to maximize solar gain and natural lighting

2.7 Multi-criteria Analysis (MCA)

The combination of the multi-criteria analysis method and the procedure of weighting the key factors as defined at Tables 1 and 2.

2.8 Scenario Analysis

This methodological stage includes the formalisation and structure of scenarios design following the referential district typo-morphologies of the case-studies' selected and the previous analysis.

2.9 Modelling/Simulation Results

After the preliminary scenario analysis (definition of various and possible typo-morphologies), this step models the most interesting urban structures to follow as a NZED (or to exclude).

Typical example of the modelling procedure:

Type A: Scenario 0. Mono-functional residential district, 4 façades and single-family, no compactness (energy losses, etc.)

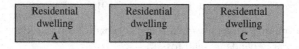

NZED mono-functional residential building model of 4 façades: to be excluded!

2.10 Optimisation

Before the final methodological step of the experimentation and validation through a pilot project of the procedure is described. At this phase, the model optimises the previous steps according to the prerequisites and assumptions for the NZED context.

Emphasis is given to the attainment of:

1. Mixed-use and compact character of the district
2. Minimisation of the energy needs of residents and district users
3. Maximisation of solar gain and natural lighting (orientation)
4. Maximisation of combined use of natural resources.

2.11 Experimentation/Validation/Pilot Project

As a final step, the experimentation and the validation of the previous methodological steps through a pilot project (possibly district of Epinlieu, Mons) are proposed.

3   District Typo-morphology and Energy

3.1   Urban Typo-morphology and Energy

The urban tissue of a district is organised within a particular philosophy in a certain period of the city history. The common assumption is the recognition of a systemic organisation of the tissue between the urban morphology and the building typology. However, this relation is absent is contemporary cities characterised by an absence of structure. The objective of a typo-morphological frame is the analysis of the physical and spatial structures and their transformation as well. However, the analysis is a critical evaluation of the urban 'organisms' to preserve the patrimony and cultural landscape [18].

On the other hand, energy consumption in a territory is considered as the total consumption required for the construction, the planning, the use and the maintenance of the buildings (residential, commercial, etc.) in function with the public spaces, the transport or even the production chain and the mobility. A policy for the strategic territorial planning for buildings' energy performance but also the qualification of the urban structure and the maximisation of the production of local renewable resources. The 'intelligent' choice of district location (geographical site, topography, etc.), the renewable sources and the urban structures have a significant impact on energy losses.

For a Net-Zero Energy District, it is proposed [19]:

1. A functional mixing (diversity) and a dense urbanisation to reduce transportation actual needs, car dependency and fossil
2. A compact urban form (multi-family housing, terraced or apartment blocks) to improve the thermal building performances
3. A preservation of vegetation and green spaces

3.2   Buildings and Energy

Since the energy crisis of the 1970s, the scientific review extended from the building design to the impact of urban structure and the building energy use. Thus, the determination of the urban typo-morphology in a district is elusive. Simulation studies focus on the impacts of key variables (i.e. dwelling size, typology, layout, design, etc.), on urban microclimate (i.e. solar access, ventilation, temperature, etc.), comfort or building energy use (Fig. 6). On the other side, as the emergent need for policies regarding the energy management and the reduction of greenhouse gas emissions increases, literature focus on strategic urban planning to discuss whether (or not) there is a considerable impact on individual buildings (or districts') energy use [20].

Generally, the impact of building typology on energy use is significant among different types [20]. Building typology affects the surface area to volume ratio, which is the most relevant key parameter to heat transfer. Given the same building volume, a single-family detached dwelling has a higher ratio and it is more likely to lose or gain heat, thus consuming more energy than a multi-family dwelling. In general, housing type is correlated with housing size and density [20]. It focuses on the connections between the urban morphology and the energy consumption (principally of the

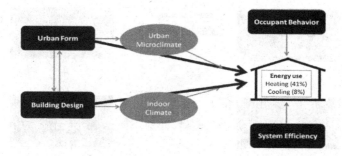

Fig. 6. Building energy use as a function of urban form, building design, energy system efficiency & occupant behaviour (Source: Kang, 2012, p. 7).

residential buildings) in a twofold aspect: (1) the intersection between the morphological criteria and key parameters and the energy consumption as well as (2) the weighting of the factors that influence the energy consumption (i.e. users' behaviour, etc.).

Studies related to residential building energy consumption remain at the scale of the individual building. Various technical models have been developed and validated to study and simulate the buildings' attitude in order to improve the energetic and environmental performance. Notwithstanding, models adopt, in general, the building perspective by considering it as an autonomous entity but ignoring the importance of a larger territorial scale. Ratti et al. [21] propose that the building energy performance depends on *(1) urban geometry (context) related to the availability of the sunlight and natural lighting on building façades, (2) building design, (3) efficiency of energy systems used* and mainly on *(4) the occupants' (users') behaviour* (Fig. 7). However, despite the undoubted liaison between the urban geometry and the energy consumption, this link is usually neglected by the simulation models (mainly concentrated on more technical or architectural characteristics), possibly because of its complexity (Fig. 8).

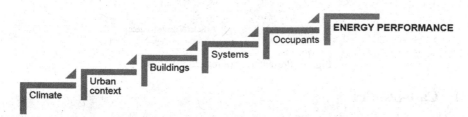

Fig. 7. Factors that affect the energy consumption of the buildings (Source: Baker et al., 2000, p. 7).

Ewing and Rong [16] propose the urban structure is a conceptual frame appropriate for the energy efficiency that should be concentrated in a *'housing (dwelling) level'* (Fig. 8).

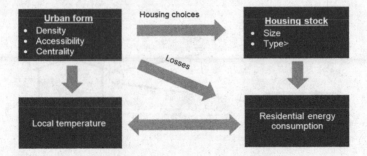

Fig. 8. Conceptual frame: urban structure and energy consumption (Source: Rong, 2008, p. 7).

Fig. 9. Presentation of ten case studies.

4   Case-Studies

4.1   State-of-the-Art Analysis: Description of Ten European Case-Studies

The analysis describes the conceptual frame of the district typo-morphology and the energy consumption as a key parameter for the interpretation of the NZED [4]. The state-of-the-art analysis includes a number of districts with an 'ecological' character developed since the 90's in the North Europe supporting the idea of the urban metabolism into more 'sustainable' towards the sensitivity for the environment and the quality of life. Despite the general context of the sustainable development in urban projects, innovative realisations of the 'eco-districts' adopt an approach more sectorial and less global with specific and particular objectives (i.e. zero carbon, case of Bed ZED, etc.). A brief review of ten representative case-studies (Fig. 9) at a European level is performed in this study as a first reflection of the understanding of the sustainable context in a district scale for three principle reasons:

- More than 50% have been implemented
- The availability of the information
- The European geographical scale

The cases studies selected are:

4.2   Evaluation/Comparative Analysis

The evaluation of the case-studies is realised in accordance with the criteria described in two phases:

1. A general comparative analysis of the results that describes the districts' profiles (parameters of the urban context, etc.) focusing also on the issues of energetic hybridisation and the organisation of energy storage.
2. A particular comparative analysis in accordance with the three pillars that consist the systemic approach of the NZED.

Evaluation axis 1. Optimisation of actual energy needs
The main findings of this criterion are presented in this section related to the districts' profiles (i.e. period of launch and implementation as well as data including surface, density, etc.):

Evaluation axis 2. Energetic Hybridisation
Concerning the energy field and the systems used by the different cases, almost all of them use photovoltaic and solar panels. Despite the use of complicated energy systems, their energy consumption does not often achieve their initial objectives. The tendency of their hybridization is obvious for the majority of the cases. The use of gas and biomass seem to be reduced.

Evaluation axis 3. Organisation of Energy Storage
The organisation of energy storage remains a challenge and it is unexplored both in the literature review and in real life. The analysis of ten European 'eco-cases' reveals efforts towards mainly the recuperation of storm water.

4.3   Preliminary Results

The state-of-the-art and the comparative analysis and the evaluation procedure of the ten cases reveal the potential of four of them (BO01 - Malmo, Kronsberg - Hanover, Eva-Lanxmeer - Culemborg and Pic-Au-Vent - Tournai) to be transformed into the 'net-zero energy' context. Preliminary results regarding their typo-morphological attributes are presented. The results of the comparative analysis of the four evaluated cases are presented in the following diagrams. The analysis conducts a preliminary vision of the NZED typo-morphology.

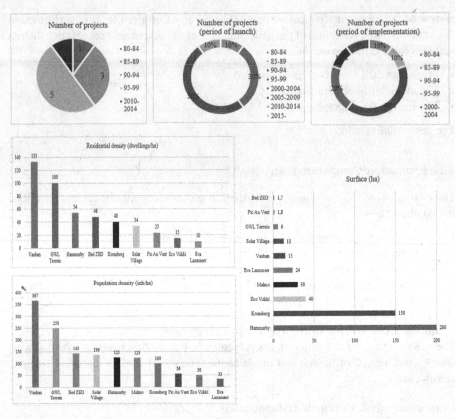

Diagram 1. Identification of districts' profiles – Optimisation of actual energy needs.

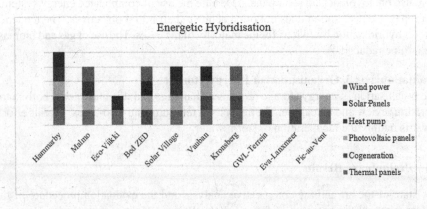

Diagram 2. Energetic hybridisation of ten case studies.

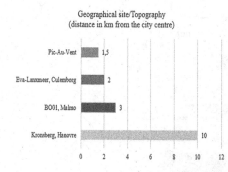 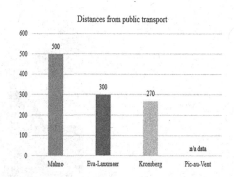

Diagram 3. Preliminary results of the 4 case studies.

From the previous preliminary state-of-the-art analysis and evaluation among ten European representative case-studies, the most interesting conclusions about the NZED type are:

  I. Well-situated districts close to city centres (≤10 km) and potential of natural resources (energetic hybridisation) and well-served by the public transport (distances between the diverse stops: 200 – 500 m)

  II. Diversity on key parameters: i.e. surface (ha), number of dwellings and population

  III. Number of floors: 2 – 5

  IV. Mixed-use districts with diverse land uses and building typology (mainly apartments)

  V. Organisation of energy storage with focus on the recuperation and reuse of storm water.

Further, detailed analysis is expected on the modelling of NZED typo-morphology within the Step of Experimentation/Validation of a pilot project/real case.

5 Discussion

In the previous section, the preliminary typo-morphological analysis presents the results of four proposed typo-morphologies for a NZED concept. Further analysis is required to frame the district with the net-zero energy concept. The study concludes with the introduction of the **'smart ground'**. The innovative notion of 'smart ground' is defined in accordance with the development of effectively performed districts towards the 'smart city' and symbolises the hybridisation of technologies, multi-energy systems, and renewable energy produced on-site introducing the urban reflection and importance at its planning and design. A compilation of qualitative and quantitative criteria (and sub-criteria) is acquainted with the authors in accordance with two strategic axes: 'smart location' and 'smart morphology' (Fig. 10) [12]:

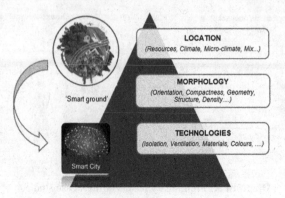

Fig. 10. From the 'smart ground' to the 'smart grid'.

5.1 The Smart 'Location'

Four essential criteria synthesise this axis (in a non-exhaustive way):

1. *Climate (and micro-climate)*: weather conditions (i.e. temperature, daylight, the wind, etc.) that influence the occupants' actual requirements in energy and policies pursued (i.e. impediments for mild modes of transport-in cold climates, etc.).
2. *Potential of natural resources*: constitutive key factor for the 'smart location'.
3. *Proximity*: the proximity of services and facilities for the site (i.e. the presence of an existing transportation network enables savings and ensures the connections to the city and encouragement of 'green' mobility, less dependency on car use, etc.).
4. *Mixing*: 'functional autonomy' of the district within its economic centre and diversified services and social mixing of its population.

5.2 The Smart 'Morphology'

The 'smart morphology' is associated with the reflection of the district's urban structure:

1. *Density (residential and population):* central to the urban planning of a district: (a) limit displacements and car dependency and (b) the economy of land use.
2. *Orientation:* spatial district's urban pattern that reflects the integration of benefits of solar gain within its architectural and urban composition. Marique and Teller [13] consider an angle of 25° measured horizontally at a central point of each façade of the NZED to maximise the solar gain.
3. *Compactness:* crucial to reducing energy consumption. Maignant [22] underlines the optimum compactness with spherical geometrical shape, while simultaneously public transport is more cost-effective, accessible and effective in a denser urban tissue.

6 Conclusions

This paper explores the path from the 'smart ground' to the 'smart city' as a result of the rising interest in the urban metabolism of the contemporary districts and proposes a simplified methodological framework within three interrelated pillars in a multi-criterion concept. The goal of this paper is to contribute to the existing scientific review regarding the 'zero-energy' objective by investigating its feasibility in terms of a district. This work highlights the opportunities for the interest to extend the boundaries of the individual building to a larger territorial unit (i.e. district).

This work opens numerous future research perspectives to be investigated widely to develop NZEDs with a concrete and operational context in real life. The proposed methodological framework (systemic approach of the district, multi-criteria approach related to three levers of evaluation, etc.) will be extended and completed as a further step in the scope of defining and transforming modern districts into sustainable, and energetically performed, validated and completed as a further step of this study within a real case-study (i.e. Epinlieu, Mons, Belgium).

Acknowledgements. This research was funded by the EC under the FP7 RE-SIZED 621408 (Research Excellence for Solutions and Implementation of Net-Zero Energy City Districts) project.

References

1. De Jong, M., Joss, S., Schraven, D., Zhan, C., Weijnen, M.: Sustainable–smart–resilient–low carbon–eco–knowledge cities; making sense of a multitude of concepts promoting sustainable urbanization. J. Clean. Prod. **109**, 25–38 (2015)
2. Angelidou, M.: Smart cities: a conjuncture of four forces. Cities **47**, 95–106 (2015)
3. Vollaro, R., Evangelisti, L., Carnielo, E., Gori, P., Guattari, C., Fanchiotti, A.: An integrated approach for an historical buildings energy analysis in a smart cities perspective. In: 68th Conference of the Italian Thermal Machines Engineering Association, ATI 2013, Bologna, pp. 372–378 (2014)
4. Marique, A.F., Reiter, S.: A simplified framework to assess the feasibility of zero-energy at the neighbourhood/community scale. Energy Build. **82**, 114–122 (2014)
5. European Parliament and the Council of the European Union: Directive 2010/31/EU of 19 May 2010 on the energy performance of buildings (recast). In: Official Journal of the European Union, pp. 13–35 (2010)
6. Li, D., Yang, L., Lam, J.: Zero energy buildings and sustainable development implications - a review. Energy **54**, 1–10 (2013)
7. Carlisle, N., Geet, O., Pless, S.: Definition of a 'Zero Net Energy' Community. National Renewable Energy Laboratory, Colorado (2009)
8. Concentrated action: Energy Performance of Buildings (EPBD). http://www.epbd-ca.eu/
9. Mcallister, G., Pellegrino, A.: Inclusion of Energy Generation in Building Energy Efficiency Standards. Technical report, Australian Government, Department of Climate Change and Energy Efficiency (2012)

10. Marique, A.F., Penders, M., Reiter, S.: From zero energy building to zero energy neighbourhood: urban form and mobility matter. In: 29th PLEA Conference on Sustainable Architecture for a Renewable Future, Munich, pp. 1–6 (2013)

11. Pérez, G.R., Rey, E.: A multi-criteria approach to compare urban renewal scenarios for an existing neighborhood. Case study in Lausanne (Switzerland). Build. Environ. **65**, 58–70 (2013)

12. Koutra, S., Becue, V., Ioakimidis, C.: From the 'smart ground' to the 'smart city' an analysis of ten European case-studies. In: 5th International Conference on Smart Cities and Green ICT Systems, pp. 179–188 (2016)

13. Teller, J., Marique, A.: Réferentiel Quartiers Durables. Technical report, SPW Editions, Guides Méthodologiques (2014)

14. Girardet, H.: Creating Sustainable Cities. The Schuma, Totnes (2007)

15. Anon, R.: Housing Typology. Technical report, Metropolitan Design Center, College of Architecture and Landscape Architecture, University of Minnesota (2005)

16. Ewing, F., Rong, R.: The Impact of Urban Form on U.S. Residential Energy Use. Housing Policy Debate **19**, 1–30 (2008). Virginia

17. Sattrup, P.: Building typologies in Northern European cities: daylight, solar access and building energy use. J. Architectural Plann. **30**, 1–21 (2013)

18. Amar, B., Boukedjar, Y., El Sharkawi, A., Oubadji, M., Terkia, S.: Méthode d'analyse: typomorphologie. Technical report (2006)

19. Astier, M., Contamine, S., Tropini, N., Deboaisne, D., Avril, S.: Urbanisme et énergie: les enjeux énergie-climat dans les documents d'urbanisme. Technical report (2009)

20. Kang, Y.: The Energy Impact of Urban Form: an approach to morphologically evaluating the energy performance of neighborhoods. University of California, Berkeley (2012)

21. Ratti, C., Baker, N., Steemers, K.: Energy consumption and urban texture. Energy Build. **37**, 762–776 (2005)

22. Maignant, G.: Compacité et forme urbaine, une analyse environnementale dans la perspective d'un développement urbain durable. In: Développement urbain durable, gestion des ressources et gouvernance, Lausanne, pp. 1–17 (2005)

Vehicle Technology and Intelligent Transport Systems

Optimal Strategies for Adaptive Cruise Control

Clement U. Mba[1]([⊠]) and Carlo Novara[2]

[1] Department of Mechanical and Aerospace Engineering, Politecnico di Torino,
Corso Duca Degli Abruzzi, 24, Turin, Italy
clement.mba@polito.com
[2] Department of Control and Computer Engineering, Politecnico di Torino,
Corso Duca Degli Abruzzi, 24, Turin, Italy
carlo.novara@polito.com

Abstract. In addition to providing good tracking capability and reducing fuel consumption, an Adaptive Cruise Control (ACC) system is required to be very comfortable. Although several appealing ACC policies have been introduced so far, a few of which are currently in use, it is still difficult in general to find an ACC policy that is able to optimally combine requirements such as high safety, low fuel consumption and satisfactory comfort level. Additionally, no systematic methods are available for the optimization of a control policy performance. This chapter addresses these problems by comparing different ACC policies and developing an optimization method based on a multi-objective Pareto criterion, finalized at designing policies with an all-around performance. Furthermore, the designed optimal policy is tested in view of its application on real vehicles via simulations.

Keywords: Adaptive Cruise Control · Test simulation · Performance optimization

1 Introduction

Driving can be defined as a set of operations aimed at controlling a motor vehicle, where control is typically performed by a human driver. However, the human driver behavior may tend sometimes to cause undesirable vehicle behaviors. In modern vehicles, to avoid or prevent these kinds of behaviors, control is usually done by the human driver with the help of some Driver Assistance Systems, one of the most important of which is the Cruise Control.

Cruise Control (CC) has the task of maintaining the vehicle speed at a desired value. However, a drawback of CC is that it cannot vary the speed of the vehicle: whenever a vehicle in front of the vehicle equipped with CC is traveling slower than the latter, the driver has to step on the brakes in order to deactivate the Cruise Control and step on the accelerator when the preceding vehicle speeds up [2]. As a result, Cruise Control has to be reset from time to time. This drawback is overcome by the more advanced Adaptive Cruise Control (ACC), which is able to adjust the speed of the vehicle, depending on various factors influencing it

© Springer International Publishing AG 2017
M. Helfert et al. (Eds.): SMARTGREENS 2016 and VEHITS 2016, CCIS 738, pp. 227–241, 2017.
DOI: 10.1007/978-3-319-63712-9_13

without manual intervention from the driver [2–4]. Some of them, like the "stop and go", can bring the vehicle to a stop and start it moving [3,4].

In general, the design of an ACC begins with an ACC policy. Different ACC policies have been proposed: Constant Time Gap (CTG), Constant Distance, Constant acceptance, Constant Stability and Constant safety factor [1]. ACC policies specify the desired steady state distance between two vehicles in succession. Note that ACC policies can be either autonomous [5], cooperative [6,7] or a combination of both [8]. Introducing and maintaining continuous inter-vehicular communication, which is the main feature of cooperative policies causes network effects that can undermine the performance of the ACC [7]. Moreover, maintaining continuous inter-vehicular communication is costly [9–11]. Thus, the autonomous operation seems like the most preferred choice at present, and it is the area of focus in this paper.

The performance of an ACC system is based on the particular control policy that it employs. The basic control policies are the Constant Spacing Policy (CSP), Constant Time Gap (CTG) and Variable Time Gap (VTG). All the other policies are usually variants of these basic policies. However, even though all these policies are appealing from a methodological point of view, it is difficult in general to understand which is the actual performance that can be guaranteed on a real vehicle. Another relevant issue is that, to the best of our knowledge, no systematic methods can be found for the optimization of the control policy performance.

In this perspective, the main contributions of the paper are two. First, the control policies employed by the "standard" ACC systems are compared by means of extensive simulations, considering different realistic road scenarios. This kind of study is important to understand which control policies and, more in general, which control approaches can be more effective in view of their implementation on real vehicles. Second, an optimization strategy based on a multi-objective Pareto criterion is proposed, finalized at designing high-performance control policies. The strategy is tested by means of extensive simulations, involving different realistic road scenarios. These simulations show that the method allows the design of control policies able to perform significantly better with respect to the "standard" policies, in terms of safety, fuel consumption and comfort.

2   Vehicle Model and Control Policies

In this section, we introduce the vehicle and control models that will be used in the simulations, first to compare the "standard" ACC systems, then to test our optimal control policy design method.

The following assumptions were made:

- All vehicles are identical and move in a straight line.
- Before the maneuver of the lead vehicle, all the vehicles were moving at the same steady state speed.

– The lead vehicle takes a finite amount of time to perform a maneuver prior to reaching steady state speed.

The longitudinal dynamics of each vehicle (plant) can be approximated by the following model (see [5,12,13]):

$$\tau \dddot{p} + \ddot{p} = u \tag{1}$$

where p is the vehicle longitudinal position, u represents a "desired" longitudinal acceleration and τ is the vehicle time constant.

The desired acceleration u is the control input, which can be used to improve the vehicle performance in terms of safety, comfort and fuel consumption. This task can be accomplished by a proper control policy, as shown schematically in Fig. 1, where the block "Vehicle" is a dynamic system described by (1) and ϵ is the spacing error to be defined subsequently.

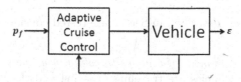

Fig. 1. Adaptive Cruise Control structure.

Usually, the control policies should satisfy string stability requirements in order to give a good performance. String stability is defined as stability with respect to the spacing between vehicles. It ensures that the spacing error, defined as the difference between the actual and desired spacing, do not get larger as it propagates upstream in a string of Adaptive Cruise Control vehicles using the same control law [5,8,11–14]. The CSP policy requires inter-vehicular communication if string stability is to be guaranteed [11,15], while the CTG and VTG policies overcome this limitation [9–11,13]. Since we are only considering the autonomous operation, our tests are conducted only on the CTG and VTG policies.

The CTG policy is defined by the control law

$$u = -\frac{(\dot{p} - \dot{p}_f + \lambda \varepsilon)}{h} \tag{2}$$
$$\varepsilon = p - p_f + L_{des}$$

where p and p_f are the positions of a vehicle and the preceding vehicle respectively, and ε is the deviation from the desired spacing, otherwise known as the spacing error, [5,12,13,17].

λ, L_{des} and h are design parameters, to be chosen in order to obtain the desired longitudinal dynamics performance. λ is a control gain, L_{des} is the desired spacing between the vehicles and h is called the time gap (it represents the time distance between the two vehicles).

Combining the vehicle Eq. (1) with the control Eq. (2), we obtain an Linear Time Invariant (LTI) system, with input p_f and output $y = \varepsilon$. Note that, on a vehicle equipped with an ACC systems, p_f is typically measured by a radar.

The VTG has several variants [9, 12, 16–20], which are similar to each other. The Nonlinear Range Policy (NRP) [16, 20] is considered here because of its simple structure. This policy is defined by the control law

$$u = (1 - \frac{\tau k}{h} - \frac{\tau \lambda k}{h^2} \frac{h^2}{k})\ddot{p} + (\frac{\tau k}{h^2})\dot{p}_f - \dot{p} \tag{3}$$

where k is a design parameter, called the scaling factor [16, 20].

As for the VTG policy, combining the vehicle Eq. (1) with the control Eq. (3), we obtain an LTI system, with input p_f and output $y = \varepsilon$.

3   ACC Policies Comparison

The two ACC policies described in Sect. 2 are tested considering three different scenarios:

Scenario 1. Constant number of vehicles traveling in a line
In this scenario, 10 vehicles are traveling in a line and the lead vehicle makes some critical manoeuvre. Three kinds of critical manoeuvres are simulated - Manoeuvre 1: The lead vehicle suddenly increases its speed; this manoeuvre was obtained simulating u_1 (the input of the leading vehicle) as a filtered positive step. Manoeuvre 2: The lead vehicle suddenly increases its speed and then goes back to the original speed; this manoeuvre was obtained simulating u_1 as a filtered positive impulse. Manoeuvre 3: The lead vehicle decelerates continuously; this manoeuvre was obtained simulating u_1 as a filtered negative ramp.

Scenario 2. Vehicles joining and leaving the line
In this scenario, 10 vehicles are traveling in a line and one or more vehicles join or leave the line at different times; this manoeuvre was simulated just by suddenly increasing or decreasing the number of vehicles in the line with the gap between the vehicles taken into consideration to prevent collision. Note that this simulation is more challenging than a real situation, where the process of joining or leaving the line is "more continuous". We considered up to 5 vehicles joining or leaving the line.

Scenario 3. Traffic flow
In this scenario, 10 vehicles are traveling in a line and one or more vehicles join or leave the line at different times. We considered up to 5 vehicles joining or leaving the line. As an additional complication, the line may stop at different times due to the presence of traffic lights; The stop at the light was obtained simulating u_1 as a filtered negative ramp that, after a certain time, becomes constant.

We considered different combinations of the values of the parameters characterising the vehicle model and the control policies. In particular, the following parameter ranges were assumed:

$$\tau \in [0.5, 0.95]\,\text{s}$$
$$\lambda \in [0.4, 2]$$
$$h \in [0.1, 2]\,\text{s}$$
$$k \in [2, 15]$$
$$L_{des} = 40\,\text{m}.$$

For each manoeuvre of scenario 1 and for each parameter combination, we performed one simulation. This simulation was long enough to reach steady-state conditions. For each of scenarios 2 and 3 and for each parameter combination, we performed a sufficiently long simulation, in order to capture all relevant situations that can occur in a real road scenario. In particular, the duration of the simulated road scenarios was about 107 h, corresponding to about 4 h of Matlab run time. The simulations were done using Matlab R2014a and its simulink environment.

To evaluate the performance of an ACC control policy, we considered the following indexes:

- *Recovery time*: The recovery time of a vehicle is defined

$$T_R = T_{ss} - T_c$$

where T_c is the time at which a critical event occurs (e.g., a critical manoeuvre, a vehicle joining or leaving the line, or a stop at the light) and T_{ss} is the 2% settling time (that is, the time after which the system output is always within an interval with center at the steady-state value of the output and amplitude 2% of this value).
- *Input signal Root Mean Square value*:

$$RMS_u = ||\tilde{u}||_2/\sqrt{N} \tag{4}$$

where $\tilde{u}$ is the (discrete-time) command input signal of a vehicle acquired from the simulation, $||.||_2$ is the vector 2-norm and N is the length of $\tilde{u}$.
- *Output signal Root Mean Square value*:

$$RMS_y = ||\tilde{y}||_2/\sqrt{N} \tag{5}$$

where $\tilde{y}$ is the acquired (discrete-time) output signal of a vehicle.
- *Peak input signal*:

$$MAX_u = ||\tilde{u}||_\infty \tag{6}$$

where $||.||_\infty$ is the vector ∞-norm.
- *Peak output signal*:

$$MAX_y = ||\tilde{y}||_\infty. \tag{7}$$

The recovery time measures the capability of the control policy to promptly bring the vehicle back to its "normal" operation conditions. RMS_y and MAX_y essentially measures the mean deviation of the output from the desired value (hence, it is also an indirect measure of the recovery time). RMS_u and MAX_u are related to the energy spent by the control policy in order to obtain the desired performance while RMS_J is related to passenger comfort in a vehicle.

Table 1. Scenario 1, Manoeuvre 1. Average performance indexes.

Strategy	$\bar{T}_R$ [s]	$R\bar{M}S_u$	$R\bar{M}S_y$
CTG	33.14	12.508	1.1199
NRP	4.5	14.7154	0.1833

Tables 1, 2, 3, 4, 5 and 6 show the performance indexes obtained in the simulations, averaged over all the vehicles composing the line, all the critical events (i.e., vehicles joining and leaving the line and stops at the lights) and all the parameter combinations. The averages are indicated with a bar. In Figs. 2 3, 4, 5 and 6, we can observe the performance indexes obtained in the simulations, averaged over all the vehicles composing the line and all the critical events.

Tables 1, 2 and 3 show that the NRP generally recovers faster when subjected to critical conditions, involving also lower values of $R\bar{M}S_y$. However, the required command activity, measured by $R\bar{M}S_u$, is higher. Similar results are shown by Tables 4, 5 and 6.

Table 2. Scenario 1, Manoeuvre 2. Average performance indexes.

Strategy	$\bar{T}_R$ [s]	$R\bar{M}S_u$	$R\bar{M}S_y$
CTG	36.7	0.0228	0.0286
NRP	5.14	0.0820	0.0237

Table 3. Scenario 1, Manoeuvre 3. Average performance indexes.

Strategy	$\bar{T}_R$ [s]	$R\bar{M}S_u$	$R\bar{M}S_y$
CTG	6.7	35.3265	1.5331
NRP	0.55	45.1805	0.0996

Table 4. Scenario 2, Vehicles joining. Average performance indexes.

Strategy	$R\bar{M}S_u$	$R\bar{M}S_y$
CTG	111.7	6.9109
NRP	115.3	5.8677

Table 5. Scenario 2, Vehicles leaving. Average performance indexes.

Strategy	$R\bar{M}S_u$	$R\bar{M}S_y$
CTG	109.6	7.1459
NRP	114	6.0608

Table 6. Scenario 3. Average performance indexes.

Strategy	$R\bar{M}S_u$	$R\bar{M}S_y$
CTG	436	5.608
NRP	441.7	4.191

Given that $\tau \geq 0.5$ and $\lambda = 0.4$, the NRP is more flexible than the CTG, in the sense that h can be varied from 0.1 to more than 1.8 without the spacing errors getting larger as they propagate upstream in vehicles using NRP. When $h = 0.1$, for the NRP the recovery time as well as the $R\bar{M}S_y$ value is "small", with a high value of $R\bar{M}S_u$ on the command input activity.

The average recovery time increases a little for vehicles using the NRP as τ gets higher. In the case of the CTG, the average recovery time increases considerably as τ gets higher. Accordingly, it can be said that higher values of τ for each of the vehicles do not have as much influence on vehicles using the NRP as they do on vehicles that use the CTG. This is most likely to be a result of the high value of h that is required in the CTG when $\tau > 0.5$, to prevent the spacing errors from getting larger as they propagate upstream.

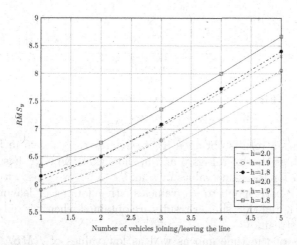

Fig. 2. Scenario 2 (CTG with $\tau = 0.5\,\text{s}$, $\lambda = 0.4$).

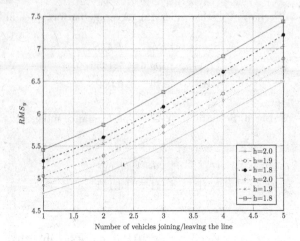

Fig. 3. Scenario 2 (NRP with $\tau = 0.5\,\mathrm{s}$, $\lambda = 0.4$, $k = 4$).

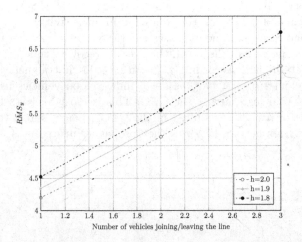

Fig. 4. Scenario 3 (CTG with $\tau = 0.5$, $\lambda = 0.4$).

The simulation results obtained from scenario 2, as shown in Figs. 2 and 3, and scenario 3, as shown in Figs. 4 and 5, show that the NRP has lower $R\bar{M}S_y$ than the CTG for the same values of h and τ. The two lines with the same h in Figs. 2 and 3 correspond to the vehicles either joining or leaving the line. It should also be noted that similar results are obtained when τ is different for each vehicle in the stream.

Low values of the time gap as well as low values of $R\bar{M}S_u$ are desirable but these act in contrast to each other. As stated earlier, lower values of the time gap require higher command input activity. Indeed, $R\bar{M}S_u$ and $R\bar{M}S_y$ are two contrasting criteria. This is important for the NRP, since it can sustain

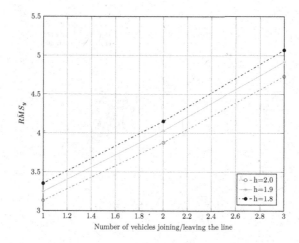

Fig. 5. Scenario 3 (NRP with $\tau = 0.5$, $\lambda = 0.4$, $k = 4$).

$h \in [0.1, 2]$. It is our deduction that if h remains in a "low value zone" for instance $h \in [0.1, 0.3]$ for a long time during driving, a lot of energy due to control activity might be expended. A possible way to mitigate this could be to design the control algorithm in such a way that the time gap does not exceed a certain amount of time when it is in the "low value zone". It is important to determine the right amount of time. This amount of time could depend on whether there are vehicles joining or leaving the stream as well as on their number, or on what the design objective of the car manufacturer is (i.e., energy reduction or inter-vehicular space reduction to increase traffic output).

4   Optimization Strategy

As discussed in the previous section, in the design of an ACC system there is a trade-off between two contrasting requirements. On the one hand, the ACC system must provide a satisfactory performance in terms of safety and prompt answer to external disturbances. On the other hand, the ACC system must not require a too large command activity, which may lead to a high consumption of fuel and/or electrical power.

To quantify the ACC performance we hereby consider the RMS_y index defined in (5). To quantify the command activity we consider the RMS_u index defined in (4). We would like to minimise both these coefficients but clearly this cannot be done, since these indexes are in contrast with each other. In other words, we are dealing with a multi-objective optimization problem.

This kind of problems can be efficiently solved considering a Pareto optimality criterion, [21]. Let $RMS_y(C)$ and $RMS_u(C)$ be respectively the performance and

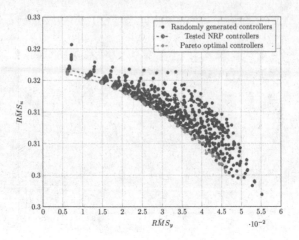

Fig. 6. Pareto optimization. (Color figure online)

command activity indexes of a given ACC controller C. A controller C^1 is said to *dominate* another controller C^2 if

$$RMS_y(C^1) \leq RMS_y(C^2) \text{ and } RMS_u(C^1) < RMS_u(C^2)$$

or

$$RMS_y(C^1) < RMS_y(C^2) \text{ and } RMS_u(C^1) \leq RMS_u(C^2). \tag{8}$$

A controller C^* is said *Pareto optimal* if it is not dominated by any other one. In other words, no other controller exists that can be overall better than an optimal controller. If a controller is better than an optimal one with regard to a single objective (e.g., $RMS_u(C)$), it is certainly worse with respect to the other (e.g., $RMS_y(C)$). The set of Pareto optimal controllers define a curve in the performance index space called *Pareto front* (see the green line in Fig. 6).

Based on these concepts, the optimization strategy that we propose is as follows:

– Perform a Monte Carlo simulation, consisting of N_T trials.
– In each trial:
  • Choose random values of the parameters h, k and λ (clearly, these values must be reasonable from a physical point of view). Each parameter 3-tuple defines a controller C^i, with $i = 1, ..., N_T$.
  • For the chosen parameter 3-tuple, perform N_S simulations considering realistic road scenarios.
  • compute the averages $R\bar{M}S(C^i)_y$ and $R\bar{M}S(C^i)_u$ of the N_S values of $RMS(C^i)_y$ and $RMS(C^i)_u$.

– Considering that the pairs $(R\bar{M}S(C^i)_y, R\bar{M}S(C^i)_u)$, with $i = 1, ..., N_T$, define points in the two-dimensional performance index space, construct the Pareto optimality front, using (8) to individuate those controllers that are not dominated.

Note that τ and L_{des} are assumed fixed but they can be included in the optimization process without significant modifications.

Following this strategy, a Monte Carlo simulation was performed, with $N_T = 4760$. In each trial, random values of h, k and λ were taken from the intervals [0.1,2], [2,15] and [0.4,2], respectively (a uniform distribution was considered for all the three parameters). The values $\tau = 0.5\,\mathrm{s}$ and $L_{des} = 40\,\mathrm{m}$ were also assumed. For each random 3-tuple (corresponding to a randomly generated controller), $N_S = 10$ simulations were performed considering Scenario 3 (traffic flow with 10 vehicles in a line and 5 vehicles randomly joining or leaving the line). Then, the performance averages $R\bar{M}S(C^i)_y$ and $R\bar{M}S(C^i)_u$ were computed. Finally, the Pareto optimality front was constructed.

The results of this procedure are shown in Fig. 6. We can distinguish a number of randomly generated controllers (blue dots) and the Pareto optimal controllers (green line). These are compared with the tested NRP controllers (red dots). The performance in terms of spacing errors of a set of "standard" vehicles and a set of Pareto optimal vehicles is plotted in Figs. 7 and 8, respectively. These results show that an improvement of about 30% can be obtained using a Pareto optimal controller with respect to using a "standard" controller, indicating that the proposed optimization strategy can lead to high-performance ACC systems.

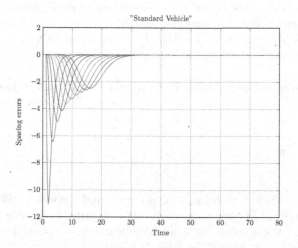

Fig. 7. Performance of the NRP controllers ($\tau = 0.5\,\mathrm{s}$, $L_{des} = 40\,\mathrm{m}$, $h = 1.3\,\mathrm{s}$, $k = 4$, $\lambda = 0.4$). The different lines correspond to the spacing errors of each NRP controlled vehicle in the stream.

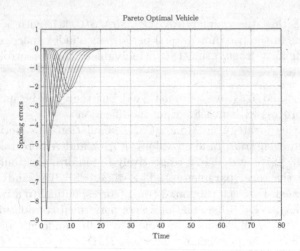

Fig. 8. Performance of the Pareto optimal controllers ($\tau = 0.5\,\text{s}$, $L_{des} = 40\,\text{m}$, $h = 0.9\,\text{s}$, $k = 10$, $\lambda = 1.6$). The different lines correspond to the spacing errors of each Pareto optimal vehicle in the stream.

5   Comfort Analysis

While reduced spacing errors and command inputs can help to improve the safety and to lower the fuel consumption, the aspect of comfort is also very important. Indeed, comfort is commonly considered a very important and vital part of vehicle design and ergonomics. According to some studies, comfort is a crucial requirement that passengers consider when evaluating a vehicle. Most passengers cite discomfort as the reason for not using ACC [22]. Thus, ACCs with a suitable amount of comfort could lead to a higher acceptance of ACCs by the society.

Generally, the comfort of passengers in ground transport systems is deduced from motion changes in all directions and other environmental issues [23]. An efficient and simple way of estimating the comfort level of a vehicle is to calculate the rate of change of acceleration of the vehicle, that is, the jerk of the vehicle [22,23], defined as

$$J = \frac{d\ddot{p}}{dt} \tag{9}$$

where $\ddot{p}$ is the vehicle longitudinal acceleration and t refers to time. Note that comfort and jerk act in contrast to each other. In order to achieve a satisfactory level of comfort, the absolute value of the jerk should be as small as possible. To measure this quantity, we use the following index:

– *Jerk signal Root Mean Square value:*

$$RMS_J = ||\tilde{J}||/\sqrt{N} \tag{10}$$

where $\tilde{J}$ is the acquired (discrete-time) jerk of a vehicle.

– *Peak jerk signal*:

$$MAX_J = ||\tilde{J}||_\infty. \tag{11}$$

Figures 9 and 10 show the relationship between the averages of the root mean square values and the peak values of the jerk and spacing errors for both the Pareto optimal vehicles and "standard" vehicles. It can be seen that the same amount of jerk matches a lower spacing error for the Pareto optimal vehicle and a higher spacing error for the "standard" vehicle. When the spacing errors in Fig. 9 are traced to Fig. 6, the required command input for the Pareto optimal vehicle is always lower than that of the "standard" vehicle. This demonstrates further that a Pareto optimal controller could give a better all around performance in terms of safety, comfort and fuel consumption.

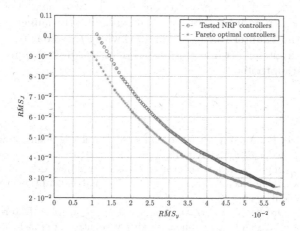

Fig. 9. Plot of average spacing errors and jerk.

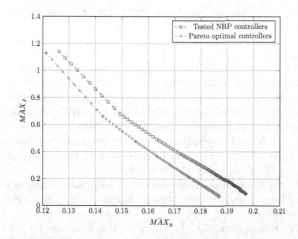

Fig. 10. Plot of peak values of spacing errors and jerk.

6   Conclusions

In spite of the benefits that passengers stand to gain from the use of ACCs, most passengers would rather not use ACCs due to reliability and comfort concerns. Indeed, autonomous ACC policies that take all the necessary factors into account needed for the overall satisfaction of a customer are almost non-existent. This chapter addresses this issue in two steps. In the first step, a systematic simulation procedure is developed for comparing different Adaptive Cruise Control (ACC) policies. This is needed to develop a proper understanding of how different ACC policies would react to different situations. In the second step, a multi-objective optimization technique, based on a Pareto efficiency criterion is proposed and tested. The optimal controller designed by means of this technique shows better results when compared with the "standard" ACC policies in terms of safety, fuel consumption and comfort. As a part of ongoing efforts to make ACCs more effective, future research activities will focus on extending the numerical simulations considered in this chapter to curve situations where the radar is unable to sense the vehicle in front for a while and on developing a user-friendly performance ACC optimization toolbox.

References

1. Xiao, L., Gao, F.: A comprehensive review of the development of adaptive cruise control systems. Veh. Syst. Dyn. **48**, 1167–1192 (2010)
2. Howard, B.: What is adaptive cruise control, and how does it work? (2013). http://www.extremetech.com/extreme/157172-what-is-adaptive-cruise-control-and-how-does-it-work
3. Shakouri, P., Ordys, A., Askari, M.: Adaptive cruise control with stop & go function using the state-dependent nonlinear predictive control approach. ISA Trans. **51**, 622–631 (2012). Elsevier
4. Shakouri, P., Ordys, A.: Nonlinear model predictive control approach in design of adaptive cruise control with automated switching to cruise control. Control Eng. Pract. **26**, 160–177 (2014)
5. Ziefle, M., Beul-Leusmann, S., Kasugai, K., Schwalm, M.: Public perception and acceptance of electric vehicles: exploring users' perceived benefits and drawbacks. In: Marcus, A. (ed.) DUXU 2014. LNCS, vol. 8519, pp. 628–639. Springer, Cham (2014). doi:10.1007/978-3-319-07635-5_60
6. Schakel, W., Arem, B., Netten, B.: Effects of cooperative adaptive cruise control on traffic flow stability. In: Proceedings of the 13th IEEE Annual Conference on Intelligent Transportation Systems, pp. 759–764 (2010)
7. Oncu, S., Wouw, N., Nijmeijer, H.: Tradeoffs between control and network specifications. In: Proceedings of the 14th International IEEE Conference on Intelligent Transportation Systems, pp. 2051–2056 (2011)
8. Swaroop, D.: An Application to platooning in automated highway systems. Ph.D. dissertation, Department of Mechanical Engineering, University of California Berkeley (1995)
9. Yanakiev, D., Kanellakopoulos, I.: Variable time headway for string stability of automated heavy-duty vehicles. In: Proceedings of the 34th IEEE Conference on Decision and Control, pp. 4077–4081 (1995)

10. Yanakiev, D., Kanellakopoulos, I.: Variable longitudinal control of heavy-duty vehicles for automated highway systems. In: Proceedings of the American Control Conference, pp. 3096–3100 (1995)
11. Yanakiev, D., Kanellakopoulos, I.: Nonlinear spacing policies for automated heavy-duty vehicles. IEEE Trans. Veh. Technol. **47**, 1365–1377 (1998)
12. Santhanakrishnan, K., Rajamani, R.: On spacing policies for highway vehicle automation. IEEE Trans. Intell. Transp. Syst. **4**, 198–204 (2003)
13. Swaroop, D., Hedrick, J., Chien, C., Ioannou, P.: A comparison of spacing and headway control laws for automatically controlled vehicles. Veh. Syst. Dyn. Int. J. Veh. Mech. Mobil. **23**, 597–625 (1994)
14. Chi-Ying, L., Huei, P.: Optimal adaptive cruise control with guaranteed string stability. Veh. Syst. Dyn. **31**, 313–330 (1999)
15. Swaroop, D., Hundra, R.: Intelligent cruise control system design based on a traffic flow specification. Veh. Syst. Dyn. **30**, 319–344 (1998)
16. Zhou, J., Peng, H.: Range policy of adaptive cruise control vehicles for improved flow and string stability. In: Proceedings of the IEEE International Conference on Networking, Sensing and Control, pp. 595–600 (2004)
17. Zhao, J., Oya, M., Kamel, A.: A safety spacing policy and its impact on highway traffic flow. In: Intelligent Vehicles Symposium, pp. 960–965 (2009)
18. Wang, J., Rajamani, R.: Should adaptive cruise-control systems be designed to maintain a constant time gap between vehicles? IEEE Trans. Veh. Technol. **53**, 1480–1490 (2004)
19. Wang, J., Rajamani, R.: Adaptive cruise control system design and its impact on highway traffic flow. In: Proceedings of American Control Conference, pp. 3690–3695 (2002)
20. Zhou, J., Peng, H.: Range policy of adaptive cruise control vehicles for improved flow and string stability. IEEE Trans. Intell. Transp. Syst. **6**, 229–237 (2005)
21. Brownstein, B.: Pareto optimality, external benefits and public goods: a subjectivist approach. J. Libert. Stud. **4**, 93–106 (1980)
22. Luo, L., Li, H., Li, P., Wang, H.: Model predictive control for adaptive cruise control with multi-objectives: comfort, fuel-economy, safety and car-following. J. Zhejiang Univ. Sci. **11**, 191–201 (2010)
23. Martinez, J.J., Canudas-de-Wit, C.: A safe longitudinal control for adaptive cruise control and stop-and-go scenarios. IEEE Trans. Control Syst. Technol. **15**, 246–258 (2007)

An Automatic Traffic Congestion Identification Algorithm Based on Mixture of Linear Regressions

Mohammed Elhenawy, Hesham Rakha$^{(\boxtimes)}$, and Hao Chen

Virginia Tech Transportation Institute,
3500 Transportation Research Plaza, Blacksburg, VA 24061, USA
{elhenawy,hrakha,hchen}@vt.edu

Abstract. One innovative solution to traffic congestion is to use real-time data and Intelligent Transportation Systems (ITSs) to optimize the existing transportation system. To address this need, we propose an algorithm for real-time automatic congestion identification that uses speed probe data and the corresponding weather and visibility to build a unified model. Based on traffic flow theory, the algorithm assumes three traffic states: congestion, speed-at-capacity, and free-flow. Our algorithm assumes that speed is drawn from a mixture of three components, whose means are functions of weather and visibility and defined using a linear regression of their predictors. The parameters of the model were estimated using three empirical datasets from Virginia, California, and Texas. The fitted model was used to calculate the speed cut-off between congestion and speed-at-capacity by minimizing either the Bayesian classification error or the false positive (congestion) rate. The test results showed promising congestion identification performance.

Keywords: Transportation planning and traffic operation · Real-time automatic congestion identification · Mixture of linear regression · ITS

1 Introduction

Traffic congestion has become one of the problems of modern life in many metropolitan areas. This growing problem has environmental effects. During congestion, cars cannot run efficiently, so air pollution, carbon dioxide (CO_2) emissions, and fuel use increase. In 2007, Americans lost \$87.2 billion in wasted fuel and lost productivity from congestion. This waste reached \$115 billion in 2009 [1]. Congestion also increases travel time; for example, in 1993 driving under congested conditions caused a delay of about 0.6 min per km of travel on expressways and 1.2 min of delay per km of travel in arterials [2]. The congestion problem has only grown since then. The Texas Transportation Institute has reported that the number of hours Americans wasted in traffic congestion increased fivefold between 1982 and 2005. Moreover, congestion has an economic effect. Studies show that congestion slows metropolitan growth, inhibits agglomeration economies, and shapes economic geographies [3]. Traffic congestion can be caused by an obstruction or lack of road capacity, which is an inefficient use of the roads. This problem can be reduced by increasing budgets for the

© Springer International Publishing AG 2017
M. Helfert et al. (Eds.): SMARTGREENS 2016 and VEHITS 2016, CCIS 738, pp. 242–256, 2017.
DOI: 10.1007/978-3-319-63712-9_14

construction of roads and infrastructure. But adding more road capacity is costly, budgets are limited, and the construction itself takes a long time.

With the continuous increase in traffic volumes, managing traffic, particularly at times of peak demand, is a good and inexpensive solution to congestion. Advanced traffic management systems (ATMS) use various applications of intelligent transportation systems (ITS) to manage traffic and reduce congestion problems. Recently, advancements in communication and computers have greatly improved ITS and made it more capable of identifying and reducing congestion. ITS is an effective solution to traffic problems because it improves the dynamic capacity of the road system without building extra expensive infrastructure [4]. Accurate and real-time traffic information is the foundation of ITS.

Congestion usually starts from a road bottleneck, then spills over to neighboring road segments. It takes time until this congestion disappears. Depending on the frequency of occurrence, traffic congestion can be divided into two categories [5]. The first is recurrent traffic congestion, and the second is accidental (non-recurring) traffic congestion. Recurrent traffic congestion, which usually results from exceeding the road capacity, is easier to identify and predict. Accidental traffic congestion usually results from traffic incidents or severe weather conditions. Traffic congestion is different for different locations, time periods, and weather conditions.

The impact of weather on freeway traffic operations is a major concern of roadway management agencies; however, little research has been done to link weather and congestion in a quantitative sense. Two groups at the University of Washington correlated weather and traffic phenomena using the Traffic Data Acquisition and Distribution (TDAD) data mine and the Doppler radar data mine [6]. Their basic idea was that if moving weather cells could be tracked and predicted using weather radar then a correlation between the properties of the weather cell and observed traffic states could be found. Nookala studied the traffic congestion caused by weather conditions and their effect on traffic volume and travel time [7]. He observed an increase in the traffic congestion during inclement weather conditions resulting from a drop in freeway capacity without a corresponding significant drop in traffic demand. Chung et al. used traffic data collected over a 2-year period from July 1, 2002, to June 30, 2004, at the Tokyo Metropolitan Expressway (MEX) and showed a decrease in free-flow speed and in capacity with increasing amount of rainfall [8]. Brilon and Ponzlet used 3 years of historical data for 15 freeway sites in Germany to investigate the impacts of several factors, including weather, on speed-flow relationships [9]. They found that wet roadway conditions cause different reductions in speed on highways with different numbers of lanes. Agarwal et al. emphasized that the results obtained from studies outside the United States cannot be applied within the United States due to different roadway and driver characteristics. Moreover, the results obtained from rural freeway segments within the United States may be different from urban freeways [10]. Ibrahim and Hall used a limited historical dataset and multiple regression analysis to study the impact of rain and snow on speed [1]. Their results showed that light rain and snow cause similar reductions in speeds (3%–5%), while 14%–15% and 30%–40% reductions in speed are caused by heavy rain and heavy snow respectively. Rakha et al. used weather data (precipitation and visibility) and loop detector data (speed, flow, and occupancy) obtained from Baltimore, Maryland, Minneapolis/St. Paul, Minnesota, and Seattle, Washington, in the United States to quantify the impact of inclement weather on traffic stream behavior and key traffic stream parameters, including free-flow speed, speed-at-capacity, capacity, and jam density [11].

During the last few years, many automatic congestion identification algorithms have been proposed. ASBIA is an algorithm that uses speed measurements over short temporal intervals and spatial segments to identify the status of a segment using the t-test [12]. The outputs of the algorithm are the status of the roadway segment (free-flow or congested) and the confidence level of the test (p-value). Another algorithm uses vehicle trajectories in an intelligent vehicle infrastructure co-operation system (IVICS) [4]. The spatial-temporal trajectories are considered as an image to extract the propagation speed of a congestion wave and construct a congestion template. The correlation is evaluated between the template and the spatial-temporal velocity image to identify the congestion. A parallel support vector machine (SVM) is used in [13] to identify traffic congestion. The authors proposed parallel SVM instead of SVM because the training computation cost of SVM is expensive and congestion identification is a real-time task.

Floating car data are used in [14] to find meaningful congestion patterns. The analysis of the floating car data is done using a method based on a data cube and the spatial-temporal related relationship of the slow-speed road segment to identify the traffic congestion. The research team at the Center for Sustainable Mobility (CSM) at the Virginia Tech Transportation Institute (VTTI) developed an algorithm to identify congested segments using a spatiotemporal speed matrix [15]. The proposed algorithm fits two log-normal (or normal) distributions to the training dataset.

To the best of our knowledge, no research addresses the impacts of both visibility and weather conditions on congestion identification. In this paper, the impacts of weather conditions and visibility levels on the congestion identification algorithm are investigated by modeling the speed distribution as a mixture of three log-normal components whose means are linear functions of weather condition and visibility level. So that based on weather condition and visibility level the three log-normal components may get close or apart and the cut-off speed is changed. The proposed algorithm was built using three different datasets from three different states (Virginia, Texas, and California). The results of our proposed model are promising and reasonable; for example, the cut-off speed increases as the visibility level increases.

The remainder of this paper is organized as follows. First, a brief background of the method used is given. After that, the proposed algorithm is introduced. The datasets used in the case study are described. Subsequently, the result of the experimental work is explained and an illustrative example is given to show how to implement the proposed model. Finally, conclusions are presented.

2   Mixture of Linear Regressions

Finite mixture models are powerful tools for analyzing a wide variety of random phenomena. They are used to model random phenomena in many fields, including agriculture, biology, economics, medicine, and genetics. A mixture of linear regressions is one of the mixture families that has been studied carefully in the literature [16, 17]. It can be used to model the speed for different traffic regimes at different weather condition and visibility levels.

The mixture of linear regression can be written as:

$$p(y|X) = \sum_{j=1}^{m} \frac{\lambda_j}{\sigma_j \sqrt{2\pi}} e^{-\frac{\left(y - x^T \beta_j\right)^2}{2\sigma_j^2}} \tag{1}$$

Or as

$$y_i = \begin{cases} x_i^T \beta_1 + \epsilon_{i1} \text{ with probability } \lambda_1 \\ x_i^T \beta_2 + \epsilon_{i2} \text{ with probability } \lambda_2 \\ \vdots \\ x_i^T \beta_m + \epsilon_{im} \text{ with probability } 1 - \sum_{q=1}^{m-1} \lambda_q \end{cases} \tag{2}$$

where y_i is a response corresponding to a predictors vector x_i^T, β_j is a vector of regression coefficients for the jth mixture component, λ_j is a mixing probability of the jth mixture component, ϵ_{ij} are normal random errors, and m is the number of components in the mixture model. Model parameters $\psi = \{\beta_1, \beta_2, \ldots, \beta_m, \sigma_1^2, \sigma_2^2, \ldots, \sigma_m^2, \lambda_1, \lambda_2, \ldots, \lambda_m\}$ can be estimated by maximizing the log-likelihood of Eq. (1) given a set of response predictor pairs, $(y_1, x_1), (y_2, x_2), \ldots, (y_n, x_n)$, and using the Expectation-Maximization algorithm (EM).

2.1 EM Algorithm

The EM algorithm iteratively finds maximum likelihood estimates by alternating the E-step and M-step. Let $\psi^{(k)}$ be parameter estimates after the kth iteration. On the E-step, the posterior probability of the ith observation comes from component j and is computed as shown in Eq. (3).

$$w_{ij}^{(k+1)} = \frac{\lambda_j^{(k)} \phi_j\left(y_i | x_i, \psi^{(k)}\right)}{\sum_{j=1}^{m} \lambda_j^{(k)} \phi_j\left(y_i | x_i, \psi^{(k)}\right)} \tag{3}$$

where $\phi_j\left(y_i | x_i, \psi^{(k)}\right)$ is the probability density function of the jth component.

On the M-step, new parameter estimates $\psi^{(k+1)}$ maximizing the log-likelihood function in Eq. (1) are calculated, as shown in Eqs. (4) and (5).

$$\lambda_j^{(k+1)} = \frac{\sum_{i=1}^{n} w_{ij}^{(k+1)}}{n} \tag{4}$$

$$\widehat{\beta}_j^{(k+1)} = (X^T W_j X)^{-1} X^T W_j Y \tag{5}$$

where $X_{nx(p+1)}$ is the predictors matrix, Y_{nx1} is the corresponding response vector, and W_{nxn} is an diagonal matrix having $w_{ij}^{(k+1)}$ along its diagonal.

$$\widehat{\sigma}_j^{2(k+1)} = \frac{\sum_{i=1}^n w_{ij}^{(k+1)}(y_i - x_i^T \widehat{\beta}_j^{(k+1)})^2}{\sum_{i=1}^n w_{ij}^{(k+1)}} \tag{6}$$

The E-step and M-step are alternated repeatedly until the incomplete log-likelihood change is arbitrarily small, as shown in Eq. (7).

$$\left| \prod_{i=1}^n \sum_{j=1}^m \lambda_j^{(k+1)} \phi_j\left(y_i | x_i, \psi^{(k+1)}\right) - \prod_{i=1}^n \sum_{j=1}^m \lambda_j^{(k)} \phi_j\left(y_i | x_i, \psi^{(k)}\right) \right| < \xi \tag{7}$$

where ξ is a small number.

3 The Proposed Algorithm

The proposed algorithm is the result of a research effort that extended over a couple of years. Our research efforts resulted in the development of three algorithms. The first algorithm is based on the one-sample t-test [12]. This algorithm uses speed measurements over short temporal intervals and spatial segments to identify the status of the center point as being in a free-flow or congested state using a t-test. The drawbacks of this algorithm are its need of future speed readings, a normality assumption, and multiple testing corrections. In order to overcome the drawbacks of this algorithm, we proposed a second algorithm.

The second algorithm fits a mixture of two components using a historical dataset [15]. The fitted mixture model is used to calculate a threshold to distinguish between free-flow and congested traffic. If the speed of a segment is greater than this threshold, the segment is considered to be in a free-flow state; otherwise the segment is considered congested. The second algorithm overcomes the model deficiencies of the t-test-based algorithm, and it overcomes the normality problem by using the log-normal distribution to model skewed data. It is also suitable for online (real-time) application because it does not require knowledge of future speed readings. However, the drawback of this algorithm is that it does not consider any weather conditions or visibility levels.

The third algorithm uses a mixture of two linear regressions to model the speed distributions for different traffic conditions, including free-flow and congested traffic [18]. The speed of each regime is modeled as a distribution whose mean is function of weather condition and visibility level. The threshold that separates free-flow and congested traffic becomes a function of weather and visibility level as well. The proposed model overcomes the problem of limited data for some weather conditions and visibility levels by pooling the data during model fitting. However, this algorithm has a serious problem in that it overestimates the thresholds separating the free-flow and congested regimes. To overcome this problem, we used the traffic flow theory fundamental diagram, which assumes that there are three traffic states: free-flow, speed-at-capacity, and congested.

As shown in the fundamental diagrams in Fig. 1, we divide the traffic states of a road segment into three traffic regimes where the speed of each regime can be modeled by a log-normal distribution. Consequently, the overall speed distribution can be represented as a mixture of three log-normal components. The first regime is free-flow, which has the speed distribution with the highest mean. At free-flow, traffic density lies below the capacity density. The second regime is congested flow, which has the speed distribution with the lowest mean. Congested flow is characterized by traffic density between the capacity density and the jam density. The third regime is capacity flow, which separates free-flow from congested flow. Its speed distribution has a mean between the means of the other two regimes.

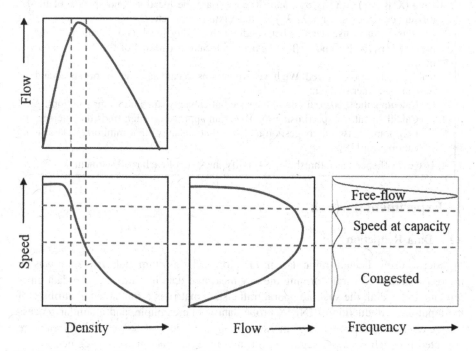

Fig. 1. Illustration of link between the fundamental diagrams and the three components mixture.

As has been shown in several studies, the flow fundamental diagram is affected by weather conditions [11, 19, 20]. Thus, we expect the mean of the speed distribution corresponding to each regime to change with weather and visibility. The proposed algorithm uses a mixture of three linear regressions and real datasets to learn the means of the distribution as a function of weather and visibility and find the boundary between the three regimes. The proposed algorithm is shown below in Table 1.

All segments with speeds greater than the threshold are classified as free-flow segments, and other segments are classified as congested segments. The output of the above algorithm is a spatiotemporal binary matrix with dimensions identical to the spatiotemporal speed matrix. A "1" in the binary matrix identifies a segment as congested, and a "0" represents free-flow conditions.

Table 1. The proposed algorithm.

1. Use the EM algorithm described earlier to fit three component distributions to locally collected data, as demonstrated in Equation (8).

$$(\log{(y)}|\ \lambda_1,\lambda_2,\beta_1,\beta_2,\beta_3,\sigma_1,\sigma_2,\sigma_3) = \lambda_1 \frac{1}{\sqrt{2\pi}\sigma_1} e^{\frac{\left(\log{(y)}-X^T\beta_1\right)^2}{2\sigma_1^2}} + \tag{1}$$

$$\lambda_2 \frac{1}{\sqrt{2\pi}\sigma_2} e^{\frac{\left(\log{(y)}-X^T\beta_2\right)^2}{2\sigma_2^2}} + (1 - \lambda_2 - \lambda_1)\frac{1}{\sqrt{2\pi}\sigma_3} e^{\frac{\left(\log{(y)}-X^T\beta_3\right)^2}{2\sigma_3^2}}$$

   where vector X is a vector of weather conditions and visibility predictors.
   Here $(X^T\beta_1, \sigma_1)$, $(X^T\beta_2, \sigma_2)$, and $(X^T\beta_3, \sigma_3)$ are the locations and spreads of the mixture components, and (λ_1, λ_2) are the mixture parameters.
2. For unseen data, use the weather condition, visibility level, and equations of the means $(X^T\beta_1, X^T\beta_2,$ and $X^T\beta_3)$ to calculate locations (means) of the three components.
3. Calculate the cut-off speed. We have two options to calculate the cut-off speed and we can use either of them:
   (a) Calculate the 0.001 quintile of the speed-at-capacity (the middle distribution).
   (b) Calculate cut-off speed using the Bayesian approach, which finds the intersection point (between congestion and speed-at-capacity) that minimizes classification error [18].
4. Use cut-off speed as a threshold to classify the state of each road segment.

4   Experimental Work

4.1   Data Reduction

In order to use collected traffic data in the proposed algorithm, data reduction was an important process for transforming the raw measured data into the required data input formats. In general, the spatiotemporal traffic state matrix is a fundamental attribute of the input data. Reduction of INRIX probe data is one example, and a similar process can be applied to other types of measured data (e.g., loop detector). INRIX data are collected for each roadway segment and time interval. Each roadway segment represents a traffic management center (TMC) station. Geographic TMC station information is also provided. The average speed for each TMC station can be used to derive a spatiotemporal traffic state matrix. However, raw INRIX data includes geographically inconsistent sections, irregular data collection time intervals, and missing data. Considering these problems, the data reduction process is illustrated in Fig. 2.

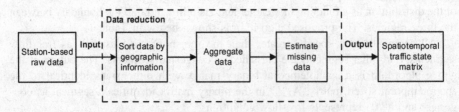

Fig. 2. Data reduction of INRIX probe data.

Based on the geographic information of each TMC station, raw data are sorted by roadway direction (e.g., eastbound or westbound). As part of this step, the data should be checked for any overlapping or inconsistent stations along the direction. Afterwards, speed data should be aggregated by time intervals (e.g., 5 min), according to the algorithm's resolution requirement. In this way, raw data can be aggregated into a daily matrix format along spatial and temporal intervals, It should be noted that missing data usually exist in the developed data matrix. Therefore, data imputation methods should be conducted to estimate the missing data based on neighboring cell values. Consequently, the daily spatiotemporal traffic state matrix can be generated for congestion and bottleneck identification.

4.2   Study Sites

INRIX traffic data from three states (Virginia, Texas, and California) were used to develop the proposed automatic congestion identification algorithm. Specifically, the study included 2011~2013 data along I-66 eastbound, 2012 data along US-75 northbound, and 2012 data along I-15 southbound. The selected freeway corridor on I-66 is presented in Fig. 3, which includes 36 freeway segments along 30.7 miles. Average speeds (or travel times) for each roadway segment are provided in the raw data, which were collected every minute. In order to reduce the stochastic noise and measurement error, raw speed data were aggregated by 5-minute intervals. Therefore, the traffic speed matrix over spatial (upstream to downstream) and temporal (from 0:00 to 23:55) domains could be obtained for each day. For the other two locations, daily speed matrices were obtained using the same procedure. Selected freeway corridors on US-75 and I-15, which include 81 segments across 38 miles and 30 segments across 15.6 miles, respectively, are presented in Figs. 4 and 5.

Fig. 3. Layout of the selected freeway stretch on I-66 (Source: Google Maps).

Fig. 4. Layout of the selected freeway stretch on US-75 (Source: Google Maps).

Fig. 5. Layout of the selected freeway stretch on I-15 (Source: Google Maps).

4.3 Effect of Visibility and Weather Conditions

This subsection describes the investigation of weather and visibility impacts on the cut-off speed (threshold) that is used to define the congested condition. The investigation was limited by the fact that data could not be divided into bins containing each weather condition and visibility level. Moreover, many bins had small amounts of data or no data at all. With this in mind, a mixture of linear regressions was used to pool data and estimate cut-off speeds, without sorting the data into clusters. In this subsection, we describe a speed model featuring a mix of three linear regressions. Each linear equation describes a relationship between independent variables (visibility and weather) and the dependent variable, which is speed. In other words, instead of mixing three components with unchanged means, the speed model mixes three components whose means are a function of weather and visibility.

4.4   Unified Model

In order to get a unified model that is independent of the location or the speed limit, we did the following:

1. Weather conditions for the three datasets were consolidated based on precipitation, as shown in Appendix A. Weather conditions from all three datasets were then mapped onto these weather groups.
2. We put all three datasets in one pool and did not include indicator variables that would identify the dataset.
3. The speed was normalized by dividing the speed at each road segment by the posted maximum speed at this segment.

The unified model has a response which is the normalized speed coming from the three datasets. The predictors are the indicator variables for the weather groups and the visibility level.

Before applying the mixture of three linear regression models was applied, speed and visibility data were grouped by weather. Because the dataset was huge and we could not estimate the model parameters using the whole dataset at once due to memory issues, a total of 7,000 random samples were drawn randomly from each weather group to construct a realization (dataset). Each random sample included the speed and visibility level, together with indicator variables for the weather. Because speed distributions are skewed, the log-normal distribution is preferred to the normal distribution. Log speed was used as the response variable. Weather code and visibility were the explanatory variables (predictors). Coefficients of the predictors $(\beta_1, \beta_2, \beta_3)$, the variance of each component $(\sigma_1^2, \sigma_2^2, \sigma_3^2)$, and the proportions $(\lambda_1, \lambda_2, \lambda_3)$ of each component were estimated using the iterative EM algorithm (Eqs. 3–6). This procedure was repeated 300 times by bootstrapping the sample construction without replacement. Final model parameters were the mean or median of all model coefficients. Once the final model was derived, we could observe the shift of the distribution mean with the weather condition and visibility level in the three regimes (free-flow, speed-at-capacity, and congested). Given any combination of weather and visibility, the final model computes mean speeds for the three regimes. Furthermore, using the estimated model's parameters, the model computes Bayesian and 0.001 quantile cut-off speeds.

The estimated general model's parameters are shown in Table 2. As shown in Fig. 6, the results are sensible because all weather groups have cut-off speeds lower than or equal to the clear group. Moreover, the cut-off speed increases as visibility increases. We should mention that the cut-off speeds for clear and light rain are very close, so we can apply the cut-off speed of the clear condition to light rain as well. Appendix B shows the speed matrix and the corresponding binary matrix after applying the proposed algorithm.

Table 2. Unified model's parameters.

	Congestion	Speed-at-capacity	Free-flow
"Clear" (Intercept)	−0.9025	−0.1947	0.0335
"Visibility"	0.0260	0.0229	0.0026
"Medium Rain"	−0.0722	−0.0024	−0.0238
"Heavy Rain"	−0.0398	−0.0465	−0.0308
"Freezing Rain"	0.2809	−0.1134	−0.0018
"Snow"	0.1754	−0.0740	−0.0149
σ	0.4881	0.1027	0.0680
λ_j	0.0846	0.1123	0.8028

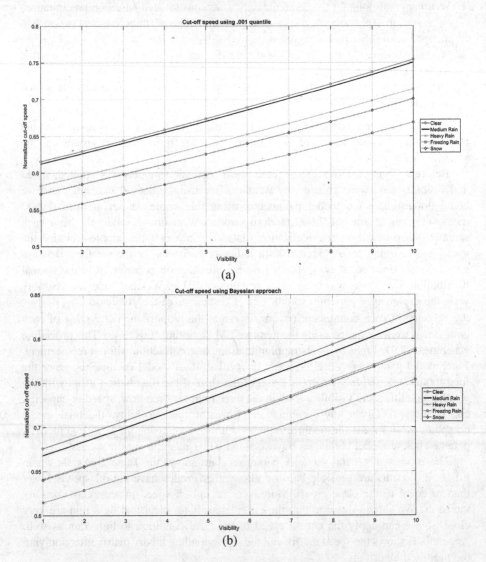

Fig. 6. Unified model's cut-off speeds (a) quantile, (b) Bayesian.

4.5   Example Illustration

The model that explains the variation in normalized speed using weather and visibility is shown in Eq. (9):

$$(\log(y)|\lambda_1, \lambda_2, \beta_1, \beta_2, \beta_3, \sigma_1, \sigma_2, \sigma_3) = \lambda_1 \frac{1}{\sqrt{2\pi}\sigma_1} e^{\frac{(\log(y)-X^T\beta_1)^2}{2\sigma_1^2}} +$$
$$\lambda_2 \frac{1}{\sqrt{2\pi}\sigma_2} e^{\frac{(\log(y)-X^T\beta_2)^2}{2\sigma_2^2}} + (1-\lambda_2-\lambda_1) \frac{1}{\sqrt{2\pi}\sigma_3} e^{\frac{(\log(y)-X^T\beta_3)^2}{2\sigma_3^2}} , \quad (9)$$

where vector X is the vector of weather conditions and visibility predictors, and y is the normalized speed. Here $(X^T\beta_1, \sigma_1)$, $(X^T\beta_2, \sigma_2)$, and $(X^T\beta_3, \sigma_3)$ are the locations and spreads of the mixture components and (λ_1, λ_2) are the mixture parameter.

Table 2 shows that the equations that govern the locations of the three components are

$$\mu_{Congestion} = -0.9025 + 0.0260 * \text{Visibility} - 0.0722 * \text{Medium Rain} - 0.0398 *$$
$$\text{Heavy Rain} + 0.2809 * \text{Freezing Rain} + 0.1754 * \text{Snow} \quad (10)$$

$$\mu_{Speed-at-capacity} = -0.1947 + 0.0229 * \text{Visibility} - 0.0024 * \text{Medium Rain} -$$
$$0.0465 * \text{Heavy Rain} - 0.1134 * \text{Freezing Rain} - 0.0740 * \text{Snow} \quad (11)$$

$$\mu_{Free-flow} = 0.0335 + 0.0026 * \text{Visibility} - 0.0238 * \text{Medium Rain} - 0.0308 *$$
$$\text{Heavy Rain} - 0.0018 * \text{Freezing Rain} - 0.0149 * \text{Snow} \quad (12)$$

We provide an example to show how to come up with the Q-quantile cut-off speed for a given weather group and visibility level. Based on the model, the predictors' vector is as shown in Eq. (13):

$$X^T = [\text{Visibility Medium Rain Heavy Rain Freezing Rain Snow}]. \quad (13)$$

Assume the weather is *"FreezingRain"* and the visibility is "2"; what is the Q-quantile cut-off speed? Given the previous information, the predictors vector is shown in Eq. (14):

$$X^T = [12 \quad 0\ 0\ 1\ 0]. \quad (14)$$

Then the mean of speed-at-capacity component is calculated as shown in Eq. (15):

$$\mu_{Speed-at-capacity} = -0.1947 + 0.0229 * 2 - 0.0024 * 0 - 0.0465 * 0 - 0.1134 *$$
$$1 - 0.0740 * 0. \quad (15)$$

Manipulating the above equation, we get -0.2623 as the mean of the speed-at-capacity component. Using the Matlab command "norminv(Q, -0.2623, 0.1123)" we get the Q-quantile cut-off speed where 0.1123 is the standard deviation for the speed-at-capacity component. Note that the standard deviation and the proportion parameters are constant and do not depend on the weather group or visibility.

Assume we are interested in the 0.001 quantile for "*FreezingRain*" and visibility is "2." Using the Matlab command "norminv(0.001, -0.2623, 0.1123)" we get the 0.001 quantile cut-off speed, which is -0.6093. -0.6093 is the cut-off speed on the log scale, and thus the cut-off speed used to compute the binary matrix is $\exp(-0.6093) = 0.5437$, which means the 0.001 quantile cut-off speed is 0.5437 of the posted speed. In other words, the cut-off speed is $0.5437 \times 65 = 35.34$ mph if the posted speed is 65 mph.

5 Conclusions

In this paper we propose an algorithm for real-time automatic congestion identification. The proposed algorithm models the speed distributions in free-flow, speed-at-capacity, and congested traffic states using a mixture of linear regressions. To the best of our knowledge, our proposed algorithm is the first methodology that considers the impact of weather and visibility in automated congestion identification. The parameters of the speed distributions were estimated using three different datasets covering three diverse regions, thus making this methodology more portable and transferable to any stretch of road in North America and potentially worldwide. The proposed algorithm is expected to be the state of practice and one of the routines used daily at many Departments of Transportation because of its simplicity, promising results, and suitability for running real-time scenarios. Because the proposed algorithm accurately identifies traffic congestion, both spatially and temporally, it is expected to be the state of practice pre-processing step toward identifying and ranking bottlenecks.

Acknowledgements. This effort was funded by the Federal Highway Administration and the Mid-Atlantic University Transportation Center (MAUTC).

Appendix A

See Table 3

Table 3. Six weather groups.

Groups	#
Clear	1
Light Rain	2
Rain	3
Heavy Rain	4
Freezing Rain	5
Snow	6

Appendix B

Figure 7 shows the speed matrix and the corresponding binary matrix after applying the proposed algorithm. The binary matrix will be further filtered to fill gaps and remove noise using image-processing techniques.

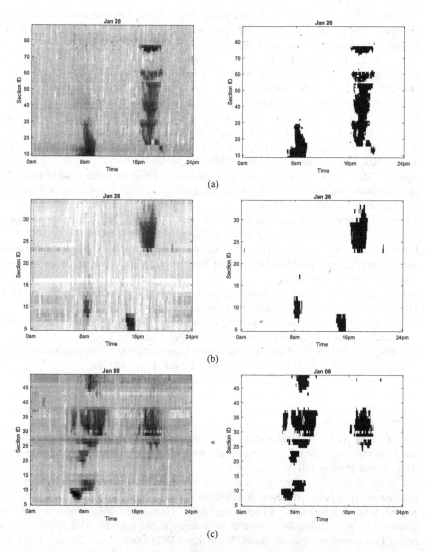

Fig. 7. Speed (left) and binary matrix after applying algorithm (right); (a) Texas, (b) California, (c) Virginia.

References

1. Ibrahim, A.T., Hall, F.L.: Effect of adverse weather conditions on speed-flow-occupancy relationships. Transportation Research Record 1457 (1994)
2. Arnott, R., Small, K.: The economics of traffic congestion. Am. Sci. **82**(5), 446–455 (1994)
3. Sweet, M.: Does traffic congestion slow the economy? J. Plan. Lit. **26**(4), 391–404 (2011)
4. Jianming, H., et al.: Traffic congestion identification based on image processing. Intell. Transp. Syst. IET **6**(2), 153–160 (2012)
5. Guiyan, J., et al.: The method of traffic congestion identification and spatial and temporal dispersion range estimation. In: 2nd International Asia Conference on Informatics in Control, Automation and Robotics (2010)
6. Dailey, D.J., Trepanier, T.: The use of weather data to predict non-recurring traffic congestion. No. WA-RD 655.1. Washington Department of Transportation (2006)
7. Nookala, L.S.: Weather Impact on Traffic Conditions and Travel Time Prediction. University of Minnesota Duluth, Duluth (2006)
8. Chung, E., et al.: Does weather affect highway capacity. In: 5th International Symposium on Highway Capacity and Quality of Service. Yokohama, Japan (2006)
9. Brilon, W., Ponzlet, M.: Variability of speed-flow relationships on German autobahns. Transp. Res. Rec. J. Transp. Res. Board **1555**(1), 91–98 (1996)
10. Agarwal, M., Maze, T.H., Souleyrette, R.: Impacts of weather on urban freeway traffic flow characteristics and facility capacity. In: Proceedings of the 2005 mid-Continent Transportation Research Symposium (2005)
11. Hranac, R., Sterzin, E., Krechmer, D., Rakha, H.A., Farzaneh, M., Arafeh, M.: Empirical studies on traffic flow in inclement weather. Report No. FHWA-HOP-07-073 (2006)
12. Elhenawy, M., Rakha, H.A., Hao, C.: An automated statistically-principled bottleneck identification algorithm (ASBIA). In: 16th International IEEE Conference on Intelligent Transportation Systems (2013)
13. Sun, Z.-Q., et al.: Traffic congestion identification based on parallel SVM. In: Eighth International Conference on Natural Computation (2012)
14. Xu, L., Yue, Y., Li, Q.: Identifying urban traffic congestion pattern from historical floating car data. Procedia – Soc. Behav. Sci. **96**, 2084–2095 (2013)
15. Elhenawy, M., Rakha, H.: Automatic congestion identification with two-component mixture models. Transp. Res. Rec. J Transp. Res. Board **2489**, 11–19 (2015)
16. De Veaux, R.D.: Mixtures of linear regressions. Comput. Stat. Data Anal. **8**(3), 227–245 (1989)
17. Faria, S., Soromenho, G.: Fitting mixtures of linear regressions. J. Stat. Comput. Simul. **80**(2), 201–225 (2009)
18. Elhenawy, M., Chen, H., Rakha, H.A.: Traffic congestion identification considering weather and visibility conditions using mixture linear regression. In: Transportation Research Board 94th Annual Meeting (2015)
19. Saberi, M., Bertini, R.L.: Empirical analysis of the effects of rain on measured freeway traffic parameters. Transportation Research Board 89th Annual Meeting. No. 10-2331 (2010)
20. Smith, B.L., Byrne, K.G., Copperman, R.B., Hennessy, S.M., Goodall, N.J.: An investigation into the impact of rainfall on freeway traffic flow. In: 83rd Annual meeting of the Transportation Research Board, Washington DC (2004)

Dos and Don'ts of Datasharing in V2X-Technology

User Diverse Perspectives in Different Traffic Scenarios

Teresa Schmidt[(✉)], Ralf Philipsen, and Martina Ziefle

Human-Computer Interaction Center,
RWTH Aachen University, Aachen, Germany
{schmidt,philipsen,ziefle}@comm.rwth-aachen.de

Abstract. Currently, the trust in V2X-technology is naturally expected. To share private data with novel technologies is not a new phenomenon today, but data security and privacy are worldwide topics, which are constantly gaining importance. Therefore, the present paper will show influential user factors for technology acceptance and the willingness to share data like prior experience with driver assistance systems. Also technical affinity and frequency of car usage are investigated user requirements. By focusing different traffic scenarios, results show also an undeniable reluctance towards sharing private data with other traffic participants or companies. Traffic management such as police or the infrastructure itself are however entrusted with various personal information and data. Further, it was possible to identify different user profiles in data sharing behavior.

Keywords: Mobility · V2X-communication · User diversity · Privacy · Intelligent transportation system

1 Research Perspective and State of the Art

Integrating smart mobility in metropolitan areas and urban city parts is also an important step for a sustainable supply of all residents, no matter age, health status or distance to a city center. With intelligent transportation systems, not only the quality of life could enhance, but also the feeling of care which is taken to support and optimize the current situation of urbanization. A large part of lived mobility takes place on the street, more precisely in motorized personal transport (MIV). On the MIV accounts for just over 80% of passenger kilometers (PKM) measured in motorized passenger transport performance (BMVI 2014). In 2012 were the 914.6 billion passenger kilometers. In the future, this type of transport should continue to rise: Despite the stagnating population development predicts the BMVI, among others due to increasing travel distances, an increase in performance of the MIV from 8.44% to 2030 compared to 2012. Further, the number of traffic accident fatalities (in Germany) increased – reportedly 335 people died in road accidents in August 2015 (Destatis 2015) which shows an increase of 18.4% compared to August 2014. A main goal is therefore to offer people a safe and intelligent technology, which helps to lower the number of traffic crashes by using it. By implementing new, smart technologies like the electronic

© Springer International Publishing AG 2017
M. Helfert et al. (Eds.): SMARTGREENS 2016 and VEHITS 2016, CCIS 738, pp. 257–274, 2017.
DOI: 10.1007/978-3-319-63712-9_15

stability control could be confirmed, that this technology can be used to decrease car crashes (Farmer 2004, Breuer et al. 2007). In addition, the integration of intelligent communication systems into vehicles has the potential to further increase traffic safety by exchanging sensor data between road users and road infrastructure to broaden the information base for decision making of drivers and autonomous vehicles in safety critical situations (Picone et al. 2015, Endsley and Garland 2000). Moreover, the so called V2X-technology that make collaborative road environments possible could lead to a more efficient and more comfortable individual mobility. While current research mainly focusses on technical issues, for example the development of specialized network technology (Ma et al. 2009, Trivisonno et al. 2015, Wedel et al. 2009), there is still little known about users' demands on V2X-technology. Most studies that take the user into account concentrate on usability issues, e.g., data visualization or transfer of control (simTD 2013, Rakotonirainy et al. 2014), but neglect the users' requirements on the information exchange in traffic conditions in general. The acceptance or willingness to actively use V2X-technology or cooperate by sharing (personal) data within transport systems is incompletely explored so far. Previous studies (Schmidt et al. 2015b) could identify general concerns and drawbacks such as a steadily growing distrust to share data. The more personal data gets; the less willing are users to share it with an intelligent traffic network.

However, the influence of user diversity on the acceptance of V2X-technology in general and the information exchange in particular is still insufficiently explored. The effect of user factors like age or gender on technology acceptance in different mobility contexts has been shown in previous studies (Ziefle et al. 2014) and is expected to influence the requirements for V2X-technology as well. In addition, there might be context dependent acceptance patterns, which should be taken into account during technology development to increase users' acceptance. In particular, the prior experience with technology in general, but also the experience with driver assistance systems as well as the driving experience could be influential factors that modulate users' willingness to share data in V2X-technology contexts (Schmidt et al. 2016).

2   Research Model and Questions Addressed

Identifying acceptance patterns is an important consideration to achieve a more user-focused design in V2X-technology. Consequently, it is necessary to integrate the user into the research approach. For an understanding which major topics regarding an accepted V2X-technology deployment are in the focus of users, we followed a two-step procedure. First, qualitative focus group discussions with possible technology users of a western European area were run prior to a quantitative acceptance study which is reported here. The collected insights enabled future research in order to understand benefits and barriers of driver assistance technology from average traffic behavior, which is comparable across Germany and characterized as connected to public transport. Also possible user scenarios with V2X-technology and argumentation lines for and against the usage of the technology could be collected. The participants were not preselected, but randomly invited to the discussions.

The results were utilized into quantitative online-studies in order to analyze which user factors are most influential. The present work focuses mainly on effects of different individual user factors like age and gender on technology acceptance in two different mobility contexts. Also, an analysis of further possible influences like technical affinity, frequency of car usage and prior experience with driver assistance systems was carried out.

As can be seen from Fig. 1, the methodological concept shows that criterions like duration of data storage, storage location and type of data receiver were also examined further. The question, whether they play a more important role for willingness to share (personal) data is a second focus of this work.

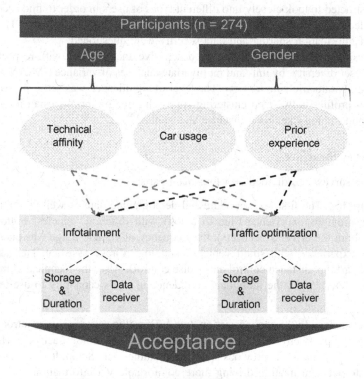

Fig. 1. Methodological concept of research model.

The main research questions addressed are:

1. Are there situational influences on the willingness to share (a specific type of) data?
2. Who may receive the data and how long may it be stored?
3. Which user factor has influence on the willingness to share data?

3 Methodological Approach

In order to follow the research model, a three-tiered approach was conducted. First, we identified possible user scenarios to test the appreciation of technical support in form V2X-technology supported driving through structured focus group discussions with different user characteristics (e.g. age, gender or technical affinity). The focus groups lasted between 25 and 70 min. The audio recordings were fully transcribed and analyzed, using qualitative content analysis. The thereby identified traffic scenarios were classified and used to derive different insights of using V2X-technology.

The further empirical approach reported here is the outcome of two surveys, which were constructed to look closely into different types of users in order to find acceptance patterns dependent on the beforehand mentioned specific traffic situations. Therefore, aspects of information sharing and data security were questioned.

The resulting data were analyzed by descriptive analysis and, with respect to the effects of user diversity, by uni- and multivariate analyses of variance ((M)ANOVA) as well as non-parametric counterparts. The level of significance was set to $p = 0.05$. To create user profiles, a two-step clustering approach utilizing the Bayesian information criterion and the log-likelihood distance was applied.

3.1 Survey Structure

The online survey was divided into four main parts.

Demographics. The first section addressed demographic data as well as information about the previous experience (due to a job) with different vehicles. Following a question about the driver's licence(s), the frequency of vehicle usage was questioned. Then, the experience with smart vehicle technology (brake assistant, lane assistant, automatic parking, distance control and cruise control). Also, the technical affinity was measured (Beier 1999), the individual confidence in one's capability to use technical devices.

Traffic Scenarios. In the second section, two V2X traffic scenarios were introduced to help the participants envision the possibilities of V2X-technology actively. Here, we were able to fall back on previous qualitative studies (cf. Schmidt et al. 2015a) to differentiate between making driving more comfortable via information visualization and make driving more efficient by optimizing routes (e.g. smart traffic light, re-arranging of order).

V2X-technology. A set of seven items (6-point Likert scale, 5 = full agreement) questioned the usage of V2X-technology in form of which data would be shared (see Table 1).

Table 1. Item example of approval of data collection.

What information about you or your vehicle may be collected/would be shared?
• Current motion data (e.g. position)
• Intention to move (e.g. planned route in navigation system)
• Information of past trips (e.g. average speed, preferred routes)
• Type of road user (e.g. bus, pedestrian)
• Vehicle specifications (e.g. safety equipment)
• Demographic data of driver (e.g. age, gender)
• Physiological data of driver (e.g. reaction rate, emotional state)
• Other personal data (e.g. driving experience)

And a set of four items which questioned from whom and how long the data may be stored (see Table 2).

Table 2. Item example of data handling and storage.

Who may collect information about you (and your vehicle) and how long may the collected information be used / stored?	
Local road users Local road infrastructure (e.g. traffic light system) Central servers of traffic management and public authorities Central servers of companies (e.g. car manufacturer / insurance companies)	Capture and process Short-term storage Long-term storage

Ranking. The last part of the survey conveyed a ranking of six different factors. Participants were asked to rank the following criteria due to their own perception of importance: *control, cost, comfort, safety, privacy and time (saving)*.

3.2 Traffic Scenarios

Infotainment. The first scenario invited the participants to envision a situation in which they are the driver of a car in an unknown city (see Fig. 2). In need of information about a place to eat or where the next ATM is positioned. This scenario includes the integration of all, most of personalized value-added services that increase the comfort, entertain or inform. The spectrum of possible applications is very versatile

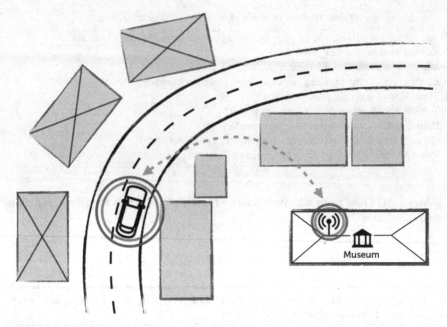

Fig. 2. Infotainment. A car drives through an unknown city and gets information via V2X-technology.

and ranges from automated payment systems, the integration of games and multimedia, information on local attractions to personalized advertising. Manufacturing and maintenance-oriented applications, such as automatic software updates or the transmission of data on vehicle condition to the favored workshop, are in the literature partly its own category (Dressler et al. 2014).

Traffic Optimization. Participants had to envision the scenario in which they are again the driver of a car. In this situation, they are driving on a highway with a building site. Here, they need to rearrange to another line with the zipper method. Here, the smart vehicles or infrastructure use applications that improve the flow of traffic. This prevents traffic jams and environmental pollution can be reduced by a reduced fuel consumption. Through local networking of vehicles and infrastructure an optimal, environmentally friendly driving behavior can be recommended to the driver or warning signals and traffic lights are switched according to the current volume of traffic. The central processing of traffic data allows an intelligent traffic and redirect management (see Fig. 3).

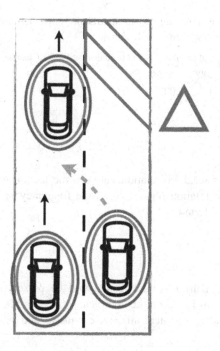

Fig. 3. Traffic Optimization. A car drives on a highway and rearranges to another line with assistance of V2X-technology.

3.3   Sample

In total 274 participants took part with an **age** range of 17 to 70 years (Mean = 33.02; Standard Deviation = 12.51). The **gender** distribution is symmetrical with 137 men (50%) and 137 women (50%). The sample contains 45.4% with a university degree (n = 124), followed by 34.1% with a technical college degree (n = 93) and 12.1% did vocational training (n = 33) plus 4.4% stated another level of education (n = 12). All participants reported a rather high **technical affinity** with 3.70/5 (SD = 1.16).

All participants hold a driving license (age 17 holds a driving license class B17, which corresponds accompanied driving). Overall, 72.2% (n = 195) use their private or company car at least once a week, 122 of them every day. In contrast, 39 participants (14.4%) stated that they drive never or less than monthly (in terms of **car usage** frequency). For further research, users had to classify if they used driver assistance systems (brake assistant, lane assistant, automatic parking, distance control and cruise control) in vehicles before. Here, the overall sample has rather little **prior experience** M = 1.82 (scale form 0 = no experience to 5).

As can be seen in Table 3, there were several significant interrelationships between age, gender on the one hand and the different facets of expertise on the other. First, older people showed higher frequencies of driving. Second, there were several differences between gender regarding the expertise: Men are slightly more technical affine (M = 4.12; SD = 0.98) than women (M = 3.29; SD = 1.18) and have slightly more prior experience with driver assistance (M = 2.25; SD = 1.61) than women (M = 1.39; SD = 1.50).

Table 3. Correlation coefficients for linear interrelationships between explored user factors. (* = p < .001; coding of gender: male = 1, female = 2).

	Age	Gender	Technical affinity	Car usage	Prior experience
Age	1.000	−.155*		.289*	
Gender		1.000	−.316*		−.255*
Technical affinity			1.000		.233*
Car usage				1.000	
Prior experience					1.000

Finally, there was a weak correlation between the technical affinity and the prior experience, whereas no relationships between the frequency of driving and the other facets of expertise were found.

4 Results

In the following section the obtained results will be presented in detail. First, the findings for both scenarios based on the complete sample will be reported. Afterwards, the effects of age, gender, technical affinity, car usage and prior experience will be introduced extensively.

4.1 Overall Findings

In a first step, we report a general evaluation about which information of the user may be collected or in other words which information the user is willing to share with regard to the two scenarios introduced above.

Infotainment. Among the more uncritical data, which participants would mostly agree on sharing in the context of gaining information while driving, is type of road user (M = 2.89, SD = 2,10), current motion data (M = 2.76, SD = 2.04) and intention to move (M = 2.50, SD = 2.05). There is overall a lower propensity to share information about past trips (M = 1.33, SD = 1.75) and vehicle specifications (M = 1.16, SD = 1.69). Most critical are demographic data (M = 0.86, SD = 1.35), other personal data (M = 0.48, SD = 1.05) or the physiological state of the user (M = 0.45, SD = 1.01).

Traffic Optimization. In the second scenario are similar findings identified. Here, current motion data (M = 3.49, SD = 1.70) and type of road user (M = 3.44, SD = 1.87) would be shared immediately, but the intention to move is not perceived as uncritical data (M = 2.25, SD = 2.01). Further, information about past trips (M = 1.50, SD = 1.83) and vehicle specifications (M = 1.47, SD = 1.85) would not be shared without hesitation. The most critical data is again demographic data (M = 0.59, SD = 1.21), but also physiological data (M = 0.58, SD = 1.22) and other personal information (M = 0.54, SD = 1.15) like driving experience.

Storage and Duration. All participants had to identify the tolerated duration of data storage and the recipients, which should be allowed to store it. Table 4 shows the findings of the Infotainment scenario.

As can be seen from Table 4, the most tolerated time span is capture and process the data in the very moment of the traffic situation (in all cases above 62.0% agreement of all participants). The agreement scores lower tremendously when asking about a short-term storage (max. storage of one week), with scores from 16.1% to 25.0%. Generally disliked is the long term/permanent storage of the data, here, the scores are in all cases the lowest of the storage duration possibilities.

Table 4. Overall agreement of storage (who may keep the data) and duration time (how long may it be stored) of Infotainment scenario in %.

	Infotainment			
	Capture & process	Short-term storage	Long-term storage	n
Road user	78.9	16.1	4.9	223
Infrastructure	70.0	22.9	7.0	227
Traffic management	62.5	25.0	12.5	208
Companies	77.9	16.1	6.0	199

The very same results for the Traffic Optimization scenario can be found in Table 5. Here, the most tolerated time span is also capture and process the data in the very moment of the traffic situation (in all cases above 59.0% agreement of all participants).

Short-term storage had scores from 17.1% to 26.6% - thus slightly higher as in the Infotainment scenario (see Table 5). Also generally disliked is the long-term storage of data (from 4.4% up to 14.4%). Other road users and companies have the lowest scores in both short-term and long-term storage time spans, but they are the most liked data receivers when the data is just captured and processed.

Table 5. Overall agreement of storage (who may keep the data) and duration time (how long may it be stored) of Traffic Optimization scenario in %.

	Traffic optimization			
	Capture & process	Short-term storage	Long-term storage	n
Road user	76.9	18.7	4.4	251
Infrastructure	59.7	26.2	14.1	248
Traffic management	59.0	26.6	14.4	229
Companies	77.1	17.1	5.9	205

Ranking. Finally, the importance rankings are reported, in which participants were asked to prioritize six criterions according to perceived importance. The results show that *safety* is the most important factor (M = 1.87, SD = 1.10), followed by *privacy* (M = 2.93, SD = 1.71) and *control* (M = 3.10, SD = 1.65). *Saving time* (M = 4.28, SD = 1.41), *cost* (M = 4.30, SD = 1.22) and *comfort* (M = 4.49, SD = 1.35) are evaluated with less importance.

4.2   Effects of Age

In the following section age will be considered in detail as the first of the examined user factors.

First, age had effects on the willingness to share information in both scenarios: There was a significant correlation between age and the agreement on revealing demographic data in Infotainment use cases (p = .002, r = −.145). The older the participants were, the more consent to limit the exchange of demographic information could be observed. With regard to Traffic Optimization scenarios, age influenced the willingness to disclosure both the intention to move (p = .006, r = .126) and the vehicle specifications (p = .000, r = −167). Older participants tended to state slightly higher agreement levels concerning the sharing of intended movements than younger participants and vice versa in regard to technical information of the vehicle. Second, age influenced the consent to long-term data storage by infrastructure. This effect was significant for traffic optimization scenarios with F(2.243) = 4.183, p = .016. The older the participants were, the more willingness to accept longer storage periods could be determined.

Finally, several effects of age on the ranking of V2X-evaluation criteria could were revealed: Age correlated with the items *control* (p = .001, r = .123), *comfort* (p = .001, r = −.150) and *saving time* (p = .000, r = −.183). Hence, comfort and the economy of time were more important for older participants, while younger people tended to attach higher importance to control aspects.

4.3   Effects of Gender

In contrast to age, gender appeared to be less decisive for the willingness to share data. With regard to gender, only a few significant effects were found. The willingness to disclosure which type of road user someone is was higher in women (M = 3.23, SD = 1.97) than in men (M = 2.56, SD = 2.19). This effect was significant but small with t(274) = −2.640, p = .009, d = .319 and limited to the Infotainment scenario. Moreover, there was no influence of gender on both the willingness to share any other type of data and the question who is allowed to store the information.

In view of the evaluation criteria a quite uniform picture emerged. Both men and women rated safety, privacy and control as the most important criteria for evaluating V2X-technology. However, the ranking of safety was more important for women (Mdn = 1) than for men (Mdn = 2) with U = 7664.5, Z = −2.831, p = .005, r = −.174. A complete overview of gender-based rankings can be found in Table 6.

Table 6. Median ranks of V2X-evaluation criteria based on gender (1 = most important criteria, 6 = least important criteria).

	Women		Men	
Order of importance	Evaluation criteria	Median	Evaluation criteria	Median
1	Safety	1	Safety	2
2	Privacy	3	Privacy	3
3	Control	3	Control	3
4	Cost	4	Comfort	4
5	Saving time	4	Cost	4
6	Comfort	5	Saving time	5

4.4 Effects of Technical Affinity

Infotainment. With regard to the influence of participants' technical affinity, two significant effects were found for the Infotainment scenario. The willingness to share technical data decreases with a lower level of technical affinity ($r = .-105$, $p < .028$). Also other personal data about the driver decreases with a lower technical affinity ($r = .158$, $p < .001$). Thus, persons with a lower technical affinity are quite hesitant to disclose technical and personal data with V2X-technology.

Traffic Optimization. A close evaluation of the results of the second scenario showed critical significant differences in willingness to share data. A lower level of technical affinity indicates on the one hand a smaller propensity to share the current motion data ($r = .105$, $p < .024$) and type of road user ($r = .093$, $p < .047$). On the other hand, this group is more willing to share physiological data about the driver ($r = -.118$, $p < .016$) and other personal data (e.g. driving experience) ($r = -.128$, $p < .010$).

Storage and Ranking. There were no significant differences in the storage and duration of data with regard to technical affinity. There were also no significant differences in the ranking of the important criteria between participants with a low or high technical affinity.

4.5 Effects of Driving Experience (Car Usage Frequency)

Infotainment and Traffic Optimization. No effects of car usage frequency were found with regard to the Infotainment scenario. In contrast, car usage was significantly correlated with the approval rate for sharing information of both past trips ($r = .126$, $p = .014$) and the intention to move ($r = .110$, $p = .029$) for the purposes of traffic optimization. Thus, a higher frequency of driving was accompanied with a higher willingness to share these types of data.

Storage and Ranking. Car usage had no effect on the preferred storage location and duration of data, whereas the ranking of evaluation criteria varied depending on the frequency of driving. *Comfort* ($r = -.156$, $p = .002$) and *saving time* ($r = -.147$, $p = .004$) were more important for frequent drivers, while *privacy* was ranked significantly less important in comparison to infrequent drivers ($r = .102$, $p = .042$).

4.6 Effects of Prior Experience with Driver Assistance Systems

Infotainment. In this scenario, the group without any prior experience denies to share any kind of data except the information about what type of road user they are ($M = 2.73$, $SD = 2.11$). The group with prior experience however would share the type of road user ($M = 3.09$, $SD = 2.10$), current motion data ($M = 3.04$, $SD = 2.05$) and the intention to move ($M = 2.84$, $SD = 2.11$). Sharing other types of data are denied by both groups, which individually answered below an arithmetic mean of 1.60 (below $2.50 =$ rejection). Further, the unexperienced group showed significantly lower scores in the following data types: current motion data ($t(265) = -2.208$; $p < .028$), intention to move (M = 2.19, SD = 1.99) (t(265) = −2.579; p < .010) and information of past trips (M = 1.09, SD = 1.54) (t(264) = −2.062; p < .040).

Traffic Optimization. Participants without and with prior experience with driver assistance systems would both be willing to share what type of road user they are (M = 3.15, SD = 1.97; M = 3.86, SD = 1.63) and the current motion data (M = 3.26, SD = 1.79; M = 3.83, SD = 1.48). The experienced group would also share their intention to move (M = 2.52, SD = 2.12). From Fig. 4 is apparent that the experienced group has higher agreement scores overall. The only exception is the vehicle specification (M = 1.45, SD = 1.88), which data both groups do not want to share, but the unexperienced slightly more (M = 1.48, SD = 1.84).

Here again, the assent of participants without prior experience was significantly lower in four different types of data, namely type of road user (t(264) = −3.177; p < .002), current motion data (t(265) = −2.832; p < .005), intention to move (M = 2.03, SD = 1.91) (t(264) = −1.982; p < .049) and information of past trips (M = 1.21, SD = 1.62) (t(265) = −2.767; p < .006).

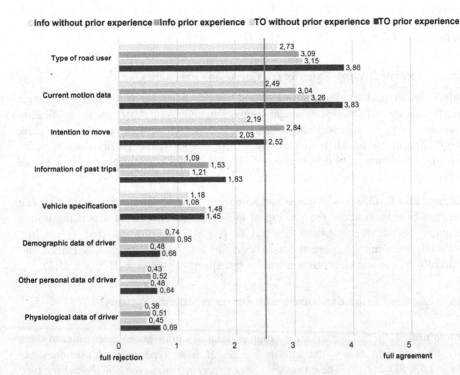

Fig. 4. Arithmetic means of data sharing agreement differentiated by traffic scenario and prior experience (min = 0, max = 5; scores < 2,50 = rejection).

Storage and Ranking. The critical issue of storing data did not show any significant differences between the experience groups. There were no significant differences in the ranking of the important criteria with regard to prior experience.

4.7   User Profiles in Data Sharing Behavior

Two-step clustering revealed three user groups which show a distinct response behavior regarding the willingness to share data (see Fig. 5). The first and smallest group included 39 participants (14.5%) and can be characterized as the *willing* one: the group members showed a high willingness to share most of the queried data types. A neutral position can only be found regarding the sharing of physiological and other personal data of the driver, whereas no data type is clearly rated as not shareable.

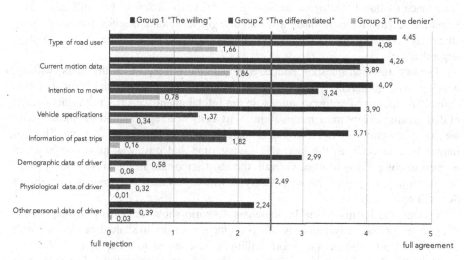

Fig. 5. Average willingness to share data regardless of usage scenario differentiated by user groups (min = 0, max = 5; scores < 2,50 = rejection).

The second group (n = 122, 45.4%) showed a *differentiated* answer behavior. The participants agreed to share information about the current and planned movement as well as what type of road user they are. The sharing of all other types of data is refused. While the rejection of disclosing vehicle specifications and information of past trips is rather negligible, there is nearly a full rejection with regard to all person-related data.

108 participants (40.1%) could be assigned to the last user group, which are characterized by a reluctant attitude towards data sharing in general regardless of the specific information. The average willingness for most data types was close to the scale minimum. Therefore, this type of user can be denoted as *deniers*.

Although the user profiles can be clearly distinguished on the basis of their response behavior, the profiles cannot be described alongside the individual variables (age, gender, technical affinity or the prior experience with driver assistance systems). However, the frequency of driving is significantly higher in the *willing* group. 65.9% of group members used a car on a daily basis, while the share of daily drivers in the other two groups was about 40% (χ^2 = 6.394, p = .041).

5 Discussion and Conclusion

In order to get a first impression on what information would be shared with this novel technology, we used a well-educated, but diverse sample. With a wide age range and a symmetrical gender distribution, it was possible to take a closer look on both user specifications. Further, the participants were questioned about general and traffic addressing information about themselves in order to characterize the sample into diverse user types such as prior experienced with driver assistance systems, frequently car users or highly technical affine - which could be important corner stones for the acceptance of novel intelligent technologies. An introduction to two different traffic scenarios set the focus towards a distinguishing level of efficiency for daily traffic situations, allowing us to understand, if the willingness to share data is context dependent.

The first research question addressed situational influences on the users' willingness to share (different types) of data. Therefore, we analyzed the results of two beforehand identified traffic situations. In the Infotainment scenario, no further benefit of data-sharing except more information about a city or a region could be gained. Here, we saw that women are more willing to share what type of road user they are. This can maybe be connected to the fact, that saving time and cost was more important to women in comparison to men. Overall, the most important factor of V2X-technology or all participants was increasing safety – which validates past research results of Schmidt et al. (2015a).

Further, the results of the Infotainment scenario show that also prior experience with driver assistance systems has effects on the propensity to share data. Persons with experience tend to share data more willingly, in contrast to inexperienced persons, which mostly deny data sharing. Thus, experience shapes the threshold of sharing, even though the nature of this threshold effect is not clear. The effect could be mediated by a higher understanding for the benefit of data sharing or by a lower concern that the data could be misused or merely by a higher mindlessness due to a higher familiarity with using such systems. Comparing the amount of shared data of non experienced drivers to the data a simple navigation system uses – which is at least the direction in which the driver is moving, speed and route – this finding is rather surprising. For a situation without further benefit as information support, they are not willing to share information with the infrastructure. This leads to the question, if traffic participants are basically aware of current privacy situations (e.g. privacy settings of a navigation system or application) and if they are aware of how detailed the information is, which is already shared with that kind of technology. The second scenario showed the ability of V2X-technology to increase the driving efficiency by optimizing the behavior of all traffic participants. Here could be identified that younger people tend to be more curious about the disclosure of technical information about their vehicle, whilst older people have less concerns about their intention to move (direction or destination). Regarding an overall look at the data, the intention to move would not be shared by the overall sample. This finding is extremely confusing, because the optimization of traffic cannot work without knowledge of the theoretical next position of all traffic participants. Not sharing that information would immediately interfere with the given scenario. Further, even common technologies like navigation systems need and receive the drivers' intention to move via destination input and these are frequently used support systems (Yamashita 2004). In comparison can be seen that physiological data, demographic data and other person data would not be shared by either one of the prior experience groups. This is interesting, because people are not willing to give too many information about themselves as drivers to the infrastructure – not even for more efficiency in the overall traffic behavior. Here we can see that privacy is very critical, which can be seen in the ranking of the V2X-evaluation criteria. Nevertheless, we can see, that experience seems to be a crucible factor of willingness to share data – even more if there is a benefit in traffic behavior and not only more information.

A very different outcome could be identified for the second question how long data may be stored and which authority may be allowed to store it. Basically, data should be only captured and processes, if at all, however the storage is seen highly critical. Neither gender, nor prior experience or technical affinity have any influence here. Only older people were willing to accept longer periods of storage in the Traffic Optimization scenario, which is the only effect detected so far. This result leads to the conclusion that duration (short-term storage is preferred in all scenarios and groups) and storage are kinds of universal factors. In the cases of long-term storage, there is an undeniable reluctance towards sharing private data with companies or other traffic participants on the one hand. One the other hand, traffic management, such as police or the infrastructure itself are however increasingly entrusted with private information. Also surprising is the result that companies are entrusted with information in the shortest duration possibility (capturing and processing). We cannot explain these response patterns on the basis of the present results. Here, future work has to address the complex conglomerate out of the wish to control and protect data and the perceived characteristics of the authority, which is allowed or not allowed to keep or process personal information and data. Apparently, distrust in authorities and a generic uncertainty in terms of what could happen with the data is of impact here as well as the bad feeling of being controlled is a serious concern for participants (Ziefle et al. 2016).

Addressing the third and last research question, which user factor has influence on the willingness to share data, it can be stated that several findings can be highlighted. Whereas age had an overall effect on the willingness to share different types of data, it could also be shown that younger users tend to perceive control as more important than older users. Further, the willingness to share data decreases with less technical affinity. Also for frequent car users, comfort and saving time seem to be more important than to users, who do not frequently use a private vehicle.

Although it was possible to identify three different user profiles – the willing persons, the deniers and a group with a more differentiated perspective on data sharing in V2X-technologies – we were not able to characterize the persons alongside the typical demographics (age, gender, or education). This leads to the conclusion, that there are crucial factors, which influence data sharing in general or in special cases, but no universal factors could be identified so far. Strictly speaking we can only say that the three profiles exist without being able to refer the different openness to personal characteristics or habits. Possibly, persons might differ in their general sensibility to external control or in individual extent of trust and risks when using novel technologies. This is a timely research duty, which will be pursued in future work.

6 Limitations and Future Work

Even though the findings of the study revealed interesting insights into effects of user diversity and the willingness to share data in V2X-technologies, the findings here still represent only a small glimpse of the diversity of user types and was able to identify key factors which influence the willingness to cooperate with future technology systems. Overall, the testing should be replicated with a larger and more diverse sample. An important limitation was also the online-based study method, here, a more realistic approach (e.g. simulation environment or real site testing) should be conducted to validate current findings. In addition, the willingness of persons to share data is indeed cultured (Krasnova and Veltri 2010) as the socioeconomic situations and the historic handling of personal rights and freedom is cultured, too. We only have a german-centric point of view in our sample and it would be interesting to validate those findings with insights of other countries and cultures, likewise.

Also, the understanding of privacy and data sharing in general should be questioned as well as possible trade-offs and drawbacks. This would lead to a deeper understanding about the already shared data in persons daily lives out of the user's perspective. Further future research should also compare more fatal roadside scenarios in order to see, if traffic participants are willing to share personal data to protect themselves and others.

V2X-technology is focused by an increasing research community, often regarding technical issues (Ardelt 2012, Lefevre 2013). Bringing V2X step by step to the user or even integrating users in the development of the technology is therefore an inevitable step for further research. Another fruitful research topic could relate to the different cultural attitudes with respect to safety and data privacy – as different countries show different legal and societal etiquette to handle this trade-off.

Acknowledgments. We owe gratitude to the reviewers for their profound input in an earlier version of this study. Many thanks go to Jonas Hemsen for research assistance. This project was supported by the Center of European Research on Mobility (CERM) – funded by both strategy funds at RWTH Aachen University, Germany and the Excellence Initiative of German State and Federal Government. Further, thanks go to the project I2EASE, funded by the German Federal ministry of Research and Education [under the reference number 16EMO012K].

References

Ardelt, M., Coester, C., Kaempchen, N.: Highly automated driving on freeways in real traffic using a probabilistic framework. IEEE Trans. Intell. Transp. Syst. **13**(4), 1576–1585 (2012)
Beier, G.: Kontrollüberzeugungen im Umgang mit Technik [Locus of control when interacting with technology]. Rep. Psychol. **24**(9), 684–693 (1999)

Breuer, J.J., Faulhaber, A., Frank, P. and Gleissner, S.: Real world safety benefits of brake assistance systems. In: 20th International Technical Conference on the Enhanced Safety of Vehicles (ESV) (2007)

BMVI (Bundesministerium für Verkehr und digitale Infrastruktur): Verkehr in Zahlen 2014/2015. Hamburg: DVV Media Group GmbH (2014). http://www.bmvi.de/SharedDocs/ DE/Artikel/K/verkehr-in-zahlen.html. Accessed 09 Nov 2015

Destatis: Zahl der Verkehrstoten im August 2015 stark gestiegen (2015). https://www.destatis.de/ DE/PresseService/Presse/Pressemitteilungen/2015/10/PD15_392_46241.html. Accessed 09 Nov 2015

Dressler, F., Hartenstein, H., Altintas, O., Tonguz, O.: Inter-vehicle communication: quo vadis. IEEE Commun. Mag. **52**(6), 170–177 (2014)

Endsley, M.R., Garland, D.J. (eds.): Situation Awareness Analysis and Measurement. CRC Press, Boca Raton (2000)

Farmer, C.M.: Effect of electronic stability control on automobile crash risk. Traffic Inj. Prev. **5** (4), 317–325 (2004)

Krasnova, H., Veltri, N.F.: Privacy Calculus on social networking sites: explorative evidence from Germany and USA. In: 43rd Hawaii International Conference on System Sciences (HICSS), Hawaii, USA, pp. 1–10 (2010)

Lefevre, S., Petit, J., Bajcsy, R., Laugier, C., Kargl, F.: Impact of V2X privacy strategies on intersection collision avoidance systems. In: Proceedings of IEEE Vehicular Networking Conference, Boston, United States (2013)

Ma, Z., Kargl, F., Weber, M.: A location privacy metric for V2X communication systems. In: Sarnoff Symposium, SARNOFF 2009, pp. 1–6. IEEE (2009)

Picone, M., Busanelli, S., Amoretti, M., Zanichelli, F., Ferrari, G.: Advanced Technologies for Intelligent Transportation Systems. Intelligent Systems Reference Library, vol. 139. Springer International Publishing, Cham (2015)

Rakotonirainy, A., Schroeter, R., Soro, A.: Three social car visions to improve driver behaviour. Pervasive Mob. Comput. **14**, 147–160 (2014)

Schmidt, T., Philipsen, R., Ziefle, M.: Safety first? V2X – perceived benefits, barriers and trade-offs of automated driving. In: Proceedings of the 1st International Conference on Vehicle Technology and Intelligent Transport Systems (Vehits 2015), pp. 39–46. SCITEPRESS (2015a)

Schmidt, T., Philipsen, R., Ziefle, M.: From V2X to Control2Trust. In: Tryfonas, T., Askoxylakis, I. (eds.) HAS 2015. LNCS, vol. 9190, pp. 570–581. Springer, Cham (2015b). doi:10.1007/978-3-319-20376-8_51

Schmidt, T., Philipsen, R., Themann, P., Ziefle, M.: Public perception of V2X-Technology– evaluation of general advantages, disadvantages and reasons for data sharing with connected vehicles. In: IEEE Intelligent Vehicles Symposium (IV), pp. 1344–1349 (2016)

simTD: TP5-Abschlussbericht – Teil B-2 Nutzerakzeptanz, IT-Sicherheit, Datenschutz und Schutz der Privatsphäre (2013). http://www.simtd.de/index.dhtml/object.media/deDE/8127/ CS/-/backuppublications/Projektergebnisse/simTD-TP5-Abschlussbericht_Teil_B-2_ Nutzerakzeptanz_V10.pdf. Accessed 09 Nov 2015

Trivisonno, R., Guerzoni, R., Vaishnavi, I., Soldani, D.: SDN based 5G mobile networks: architecture, functions, procedures and backward compatibility. Trans. Emerg. Telecommun. Technol. **26**(1), 82–92 (2015)

Wedel, J.W., Schuenemann, B., Radusch, I.: V2X-based traffic congestion recognition and avoidance. In: 10th International Symposium on Pervasive Systems, Algorithms Parallel Architectures, Algorithms, and Networks (ISPAN), pp. 637–641. IEEE Computer Society (2009)

Yamashita, T., Izumi, K., Kurumatani, K.: Car navigation with route information sharing for improvement of traffic efficiency. In: The 7th International IEEE Conference on Intelligent Transportation Systems, Proceedings, pp. 465–470 (2004)

Ziefle, M., Beul-Leusmann, S., Kasugai, K., Schwalm, M.: Public perception and acceptance of electric vehicles: exploring users' perceived benefits and drawbacks. In: Marcus, A. (ed.) DUXU 2014. LNCS, vol. 8519, pp. 628–639. Springer, Cham (2014). doi:10.1007/978-3-319-07635-5_60

Ziefle, M., Halbey, J., Kowalewski, S.: Users' willingness to share data in the Internet: Perceived benefits and caveats. In: Proceedings of the International Conference on Internet of Things and Big Data (IoTBD 2016), pp. 255–265. SCITEPRESS – Science and Technology Publications (2016). ISBN: 978-989-758-183-0

ICT for Urban Area Logistics with Electric Vehicles Compared Within Simulated and Real Environments

Volkmar Schau, Sebastian Apel$^{(\boxtimes)}$, Kai Gebhardt, Johannes Kretzschmar,
Christian Stolcis, Marianne Mauch, and Johan Buchholz

Department of Computer Science, Friedrich Schiller University Jena,
Ernst Abbe Platz 2, Jena, Germany
{volkmar.schau,sebastian.apel,kai.gebhardt,johannes.kretzschmar,
christian.stolcis,marianne.mauch,johan.buchholz}@uni-jena.de

Abstract. ICT-systems for electric vehicles (EVs), e.g. planing, monitoring and analysing for urban area logistics, can become complex and difficult to use. Evaluating them within acceptance tests requires a lot of experimentees as well as a lot of equipment. Unfortunately, mostly more than available within the project. The following approach within the research project Smart City Logistik (SCL), funded by the German Federal Ministry for Economic Affairs and Energy (BMWi), tries to use the ICT-system as it is and connects those system through a dynamicly and proceduraly generated simulation environment, based on real road and terrain data. Finally, the results will be compared to real environments by using EVs.

1 Introduction

The launch of the German national development plan for electric mobility [1] has spawned some activities and projects, ranging from research to industrial development, and sporting goals with short-term as well as long-term lifelines. In most cases the obvious shortcomings of currently available, fully electric vehicle (EVs) are addressed and tackled with a particular mix of various technologies.

The main problem identified was, of course, the limited range of available cars. Long-term projects focus, in this context, to a large extend on the development of innovative battery technologies. However, most researchers agree that until 2020, and well beyond, batteries will not be able to guarantee driving ranges close to what can be achieved today with traditional gasoline-driven engines, as least if a viable weight to power ratio must be the goal. Thus, a number of alternative projects have taken as a premise that we will have to cope with limited ranges for at least the next decade. Based on this assumption the challenge is to support available EVs by other technologies to reach maximum usability. One of these alternatives, and maybe the most important one, is information and communication technology (ICT).

© Springer International Publishing AG 2017
M. Helfert et al. (Eds.): SMARTGREENS 2016 and VEHITS 2016, CCIS 738, pp. 275–295, 2017.
DOI: 10.1007/978-3-319-63712-9_16

The special federal research program Information and Communication Technologies for Electric Mobility II (ICT EM II) has, thus, been established in Germany to leverage the capabilities of ICT-based research by adapting available and new concepts to the individual needs of electric mobility [2]. The projects funded by this program strive mostly for short and medium-term solutions with a clear focus on immediate applicability and an early market entry. The coordinator and manager of this research program is the German Federal Ministry for Economic Affairs and Energy (BMWi).

Achieving these goals, is done by bundling research institutions with industrial partners within related service domains. Thus, each research project combines EV suppliers, end-users (application partners, companies, and individual drivers), and other domain-specific players (in this case a provider for logistics and fleet management software). The so formed consortium will not only strive to reach some well-structured research goals they will work towards a prototype solution industrial strength. Thus, besides research and development objectives the project will also address questions regarding marketing and sales. Deliverables include not only papers and concepts but also readily available tools and a viable evaluation of the integrated solution in a practical setting (major field test). In most cases this leads to a consortium that has a well-established track record in a particular application domain. Also, a real life test-bed has to be located to enable the physical field test.

The Smart City Logistik (SCL) project [3] targets the application domain of inner-city merchandise traffic. The concept is to unload cargo from heavy trucks on the city's perimeter and to run the last miles with small and medium sized EVs. In most cases the logistics partners also utilize storage facilities outside the city to provide additional buffer capabilities and to decouple long-range from short-range traffic in this way. The city of Erfurt, in Thuringia, Germany, has been chosen as test-bed because it has passed stringent laws regarding inner-city transport that will, most likely, favor EVs as the main transport medium of the future.

The challenge is to support this fleet of transport-EVs with an ICT-system that provides for an integrated interface to existing logistics systems, as well as to estimate and manage each individual vehicles range, itinerary, and routes with a highly adaptive solution. Based on limited battery capacity, always changing environmental conditions, the usual short-term necessary adaptations in the planned itinerary, and stringent legal requirements SCL expects a steady rate of exceptions that have to be handled by the system in real-time. Besides, there will be no guarantee that all EVs in the fleet will be online all the time, simply due to possible problems with the cell-phone network in more remote areas, during inclement weather, or because of overload and technical defects.

From a technological point of view (see Fig. 1) the SCL system is a distributed, mobile ICT-system with a central server unit and fat DAC that have the capability to run independently from the main server while computing, at least, all essential services in the case of a disconnect. The central server itself can be used as a standalone service as well as a system in addition to existing system

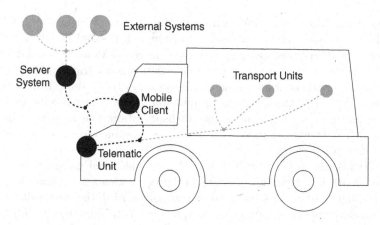

Fig. 1. SCL platform overview: in-car elements like DAC, transportation units and telematic unit communicates over the air with a centralized server which is used as a planing, monitoring and data system and can be used as a bridge through external systems.

landscapes within logistical companies. Runtime consumption and vital data from EVs in this setup have to be collected and transmitted by using telematic units as interfaces for EVs controller area network (CAN) busses. Furthermore, it is important to know about the acceptance of drivers by using the DAC. By performing multiple acceptance tests within SCL, not only by testing the DAC, it is possible to ensure the usability of the resulting systems. As a federally funded project, SCL also strives for a solution that is not proprietary to a company, open for changes and additions in the future, and based on a widely published and standardized ICT-architecture [4].

The paper starts with an overview on ICT and EV related projects. After that, the paper outlines the main problems within the domain of urban logistic, followed by the ICT-system which would help to solve these problems. After that the acceptance study design, about how to evaluate this ICT-system, is presented as well as the simulation environment which can be used in addition to field tests. Finally current evaluation results, concerning the applicableness of this solution, are presented.

2   Related Work

The German BMWi funds multiple projects which investigates into the key subjects of ICT EM II. The focus of ICT EM II is on new concepts for intelligent technology in EVs (Smart Car) combined with power supply (Smart Grid) and concepts for mobility (Smart Traffic) [2].

The ICT EM II funded collaborative research project sMobility tried to link existing components of the infrastructure using an open ICT-platform. Special focus was on price controlled and decentralised charging of EVs and on navigation, which is optimized for journey time using actual traffic and car data, as well as on intelligent flow regulation technology. In the city of Erfurt, an intelligent and linked transport infrastructure was constructed. Related live data was provided within a distributed cloud system [5]. Like SCL sMobility created a range prediction model to optimize the route considering local traffic information. A unique characteristic of sMobility is the collection of traffic data using detectors along the road. The sMobility range prediction model is less specific than SCL and focusing on intermodal and private transportation. On the other hand, the high-detailed data can be used within SCL as possible data sources for more precise range predictions.

iZEUS was also funded by ICT EM II and considered more complex standards for controlled charging of EVs. The project idea was about the examination of huge fluctuations in the power supply during the whole day caused by regenerative energy like photovoltaics and wind turbines and attempting to regulate the charging intensity in a way of drivers needs with less restrictions. Thus, decentral storage in EVs with an energetic recovery system was one of their primary project goals. An onboard charging system and an efficient energy management with an infrastructure for communication between two actors of a B2B car fleet was conceptualized. A service detected the next electric charging station and municipality. Private and business customer tested the technology [6] and evaluated the usability within an acceptance survey. In contrast, to SCL the focus is on the calculation of efficient routes and visualization of remaining ranges to specific destinations. Unfortunately, the management and range prediction isn't working together as required in SCL to support an installation within most logistic scenarios.

Adaptive City Mobility (ACM), funded by ICT EM II, developed an electric micro car with a portable system to change rechargeable batteries for urban traffic and logistic - used as eTaxi fleet [7]. As mentioned in other projects before ACM linked several components like the ICT of the EV, mobile units, central cloud services and - unique for this project - charging stations. Concerning of self-designed electric micro car and their telematic unit ACM can provide information about the state of the rechargeable battery, the remaining range and the next charging station within their mobile client.

eTelematik was a second collaborative research project in cooperation with Friedrich-Schiller-University Jena [8] and was funded by Zentrales Innovationsprogramm Mittelstand (ZIM). The project focused on a solution for municipality using a special prototype of Multicar as a EV. That EV can be utilized (e.g.) as a road sweeper or a snow plow through different extensions. The Multicar was equipped with an individual telematic unit, to collect data, and with a driver assistance system. The realized system platform focused on task management, and the enclosed range estimation model is based on neuronal networks. This kind of model leads to machine learnable results but is expensive in calculation [9].

E-Wald, funded by a Bavarian research program, is a collaborative research project in Bavarian Forest that aims at rural areas. Using newly developed and intelligent charging devices and communication concepts E-Wald wants to proof that electric mobility works in that rural areas as well. The project is developing a new generation of a fast charging station for all charging systems. Focus is on a wire- and plugless charging concept. Just as SCL it uses a range estimation model. The range estimation model uses geographical information, the state of the rechargeable battery, outdoor temperature, driveability, as well as information about topography and road system based on a statistical model. The range estimation, used by a mobile client, is shown like a blue sky on the map and is calculated car dependent [10]. Step by step E-Wald optimized their range estimation model by adding one parameter at the time. In contrast SCL examines the parameter which influences the range of an EV in the first step and designes the range estimation model in the second step.

3 Problem Analysis

The shift from conventional gasoline to electric driven vehicles in the automotive industry has been a widely discussed topic for years. Despite promising impacts on quality of life (reduced noise emission), ecological (carbon dioxide and fine dust pollution) and economic aspects (exploit alternative energy resources), there usually is a reserved acceptance of such technology. In case of inner-city logistics the application field can be clearly determined to the general reduced operation range and charging behaviour of EVs. There are several solutions imaginable to shatter these concerns. Providing a close network of charging infrastructure, better energy storages or systems for battery-change could partially solve the flaws of present EV-technologies. All of these approaches require immense investments (regarding the extension of infrastructure) and inherit long-term development due standardisation processes. Thus, our approach tends to use state of the art technology to build up an information and communication technology, which provides an assistance tool for the most possible effective and efficient using present EVs in inner-city logistics.

Regarding this, we have identified six areas of concern, we want to approach:

P1. The ICT-system is build as an reference architecture and should be adaptable to all major inner-city logistic scenarios.

P2. Current transport management software is not capable of responding to the needs of applying EVs in logistical scenarios, like the restricted operation range or low coverage of charging infrastructure.

P3. The application domain calls for a lot of different heterogeneous data sources like different types of application partner software, traffic- and weather information retrieval services. There has to be an easy configurable interface and data model to adapt the reference based ICT-system to a specific application environment.

P4. Dispatching, scheduling and planning in logistics are quite sophisticated challenges, which can only be fulfilled with an appropriate domain knowledge. The ICT-system should be able to assist in these tasks by infer implicit knowledge provided by different data sources from P3 or even identify critical flaws early.

P5. There has to be an adequate range prediction model to simulate and monitor dispatched tours. This helps to overcome the operation range restriction from P2 by enabling the ability to intervene.

P6. The ICT-system is used by various actors within the inner-city logistic domain. There should be an acceptance study to verify and confirm the applicability, functionality and correctness of the basic SCL approach.

The problem P1 of building a reference architecture for logistic ICT-systems calls for a wide variety of solutions regarding the adaptability of the overall system. Main focus points are hereby configurable interface descriptions P3, a comprehensive generic data model with semantic annotations P4 and a self-learning range prediction to minimize modelling costs (P5).

Especially P3 and P4 bring up the need of a logic based description of data with formal semantics. Therefore we try to attach and combine a formal description logic to the expected relational structural data of application partners and integrated services. Such an ontology can help in two essential ways. The ontological description of data concepts and relations allows to integrate and migrate outside data models semi-automatically. Interchangeable data classes can be located and class relations inferred. On the other hand, such a technology enables to deduce implicit knowledge. By this it would be possible to determine flaws in dispatched tours. Formal ontologies are well known and researched for logistics scenarios. But by now, they are only used in a descriptive manner to standardize a set of logistics terminology. We need and want to bring these concepts into application, fill an ontology from existing structural data and use these to assist and speed up dispatching processes.

By now, there is no ontology specialized on logistics with EVs. So, there is the need to expand given standards by the aspects for electric driven automotion. This includes the description of prediction range models to determine the operation range of a EVs. Thus, we need to analyse the influence factors on electric driving and combined these in a comprehensive model (P5). Some of these aspects are shown in Fig. 2. Unfortunately, these aspects vary in a wide range and are strongly influenced by vehicle- and driver-specific features, which are unknown at time of modelling and building up the ICT components. Because of this, we focus on a self-learning adaptive model which configures itself to a specific EVs-fleet on runtime.

An important step in the development process of such an ICT-system is an acceptance study (P6), which guarantees that the system is appropriate for the multiple envisaged use cases. Such a study should cover all types of stakeholders existent in logistics scenarios, like drivers, distribution, dispatchers and customers. There is a strong focus on the user experience and usability of the developed user interfaces and functionalities in combination with the special requirements of EVs.

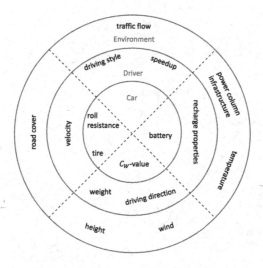

Fig. 2. Influence factors on range of EVs [11].

4 ICT-System

Logistic companies mostly use specialized supply chain management (SCM) systems like transport management system (TMSs) or warehouse management system (WMSs) to manage their orders. Unfortunately, these systems don't care about special range restriction of EVs and their requirements for transportation tours, regarding P3, P4 and P5. To get in these existing system landscapes two analyses has to be done: (1) what's about their processes and which software is involved, and more specifically (2) which interfaces can be used to get related data. For (1) processes could be analysed and generalized by using previously done interviews [12] and validation in literature about SCM [13] and logistic processes [14]. The second analysis about interfaces leads to a difficult challenge within this domain. Taking a closer look at available systems shows a heterogen interface landscape [15–18]. There are several process standardizations like RosettaNet[1] and United Nations Electronic Data Interchange for Administration, Commerce and Transport (UN/EDIFACT)[2] influencing the way these systems works, as well as what terminology to use within this domain. Unfortunately, the data exchange itself is not standardized. Adding known interface use cases in addition to required interfaces from the driver assistence client DACs and the telematic units would lead to a wide range as shown in Fig. 3.

---

[1] RosettaNet is globally organized between nearly 600 companies and managed by the GSI US, defines logistical processes and terminology.

[2] Known as X12 from USA and EDIFACT from Europe and combined to the global standard UN/EDIFACT can be used as exchange standards for logistic related data.

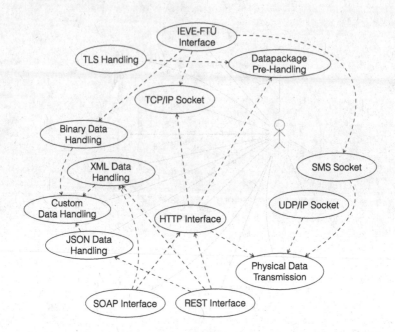

Fig. 3. Use cases for interfaces within the SCL system landscape.

To achieve these goals several required components has to be orchestrated within an architecture as shown in Fig. 4 for planing, monitoring and analyzation. All components has to communicate by using a internal communication bus. This part is based on a observer pattern [19], furthermore those observers would not be registered for special observables, they will be registered in a global contex. External systems can be embedded within this architecture by adding a specific interface component. This architecture draft adapts the Model-View-Controller (MVC) [20] pattern to minimize coupling and maximize cohesion.

Challenging the problems with this wide range of possible external systems is done by splitting up each part of a communication between two participants. Thus, the SCL platform uses the pipeline strategy to get configurable interfaces for wide ranges of existing systems. The system described above and realized within SCL is used as a basic infrastructure within the SCL platform and as a solution for P2 and P3 mentioned in section Problem Analysis.

Regarding P4 for a software architecture to support EVs in logistics, a comprehensive conceptual data model has to be developed. This model should be able to support the delegation and monitoring of transport chains and tasks in all kind of versatile logistic scenarios. Due to the requirements analysis, there were several problems:

– The data model should be easily and potentially semi-automatically adoptable to all kinds of different logistic scenarios.

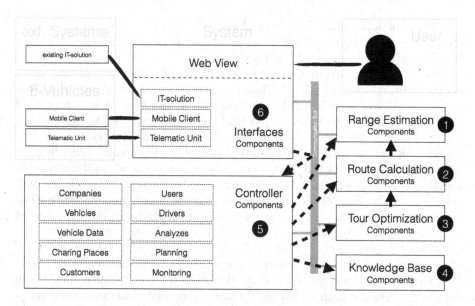

Fig. 4. Overview of the SCL architecture. Each model, controller and view component interacts within this system by using a communication bus for private and broadcast messages.

- Data aggregation and management is supposed to be directly supported by the data model itself. This point is especially targeted to the fact, that the data model should include some kind of semantic data layer. By this, it would be possible to combine and integrate databases of different application partners.
- It should enable gaining extensive implicit information and data, which support the disposition of tours, staff and ressources actively.
- Finally, the data model should cover especially the electric specific aspects of logistic domains.

The generic requirement and the extraction of implicit information suggest the use of a descriptive, logic based specification for the data model. There are far reaching works in this field of research in context of logistic applications like [21] or [22]. The SCL approach is based on existing formal ontologies like GenCLOn [23], which provide an essential vocabulary to describe logistic concepts and relationships. The use of quasi standards also enables the subsequent implementation and application of the SCL system by referencing to top domain models.

Unfortunately, none of these existing ontologies and models covered all necessary aspects of the underlying SCL application area. Therefore, the conceptual model has to be extended due to the primarily use of EVs at first. These enhancements were made especially regarding the influence parameters for the range of EVs. The limited range and charging behaviours are a critical factor for the acceptance of application of EVs and should be therefore supported by the data model. The goal is hereby to assist the dispatcher and the DAC to identify early flaws of a given tour or execution state.

The SCL system is supposed to be a comprehensibly assisting system, which is able to recognize legally invalid tours by checking the consistency of a given rule base. Although such a rule base provides a very elegant way to extend and adopt to future use cases or potentially changes according to law without the need of changing data processing algorithms based on a specific underlying model. This approach is described on the basis of driving licences according the EU norms in [24] in detail. Here, the implementation of the rule base occurred in a Prolog program and information was retrieved by reasoning. By this the SCL system is able to support the dispatching of logistic tours as systematic queries restricted given options and to give a solution for the challenge P4. Errors could be prevented by early consistency checks and even corrected automatically.

The ontology, respectively the rule base, represents the formal semantic layer of a given data model, which is given by an external application partner. There-fore, there has to be a specific import algorithm for every data model, which realizes the inflation of the ontology. By this, the ontology only serves as a infer-ential data base. Database changes are made in the common data model and are imported back to the semantic layer. Due to the complexity of logic descrip-tions and inferential data it is not feasible to transfer data from the semantic description to conventional relational data bases.

As mentioned before in P5 the use of EVs is challenging in the logistic area due to the relative low range of available small and medium sized transport vehi-cles. Thus, there is an urgent need for precise range estimation method, which can calculate the energy consumption of a tour as accurately as possible. Impor-tant influence factors are shown in Fig. 2 [11]. A weakness of existing solutions is a very high dependency on the regarded car type. Rogge et al. tries to model a Mitsubishi i-MiEV in Matlab and uses as influence factors the cars weight, average energy consumption of an i-MiEV, ramp of road, air resistance and fric-tions [25]. Most of this parameters are vehicle specific. Ondruska and Posner use a similar approach with a combination of stochastic methods and physical considerations [26] which bases on technical aspects of a Nissan Leaf.

Therefore, an algorithm without physical considerations can avoid these dis-advantages. The energy consumption of a new tour is predicted by comparing the tour with known tracks. First, a model is developed to describe a tour by dividing it in segments. Figure 5 shows an example. A tour is analyzed from start to end and a new segment begins at each point where at least one parameter changes the value. The example uses the road parameters velocity and ramp. It follows that a segment can described by constant values in each influence factor. As presented in Fig. 6, groups are formed by using the cross product of segments for each influence factor. Each group is visualized with one cuboid. For example, velocity is divided in three intervals with the limits zero to ten, ten to twenty and twenty to thirty.

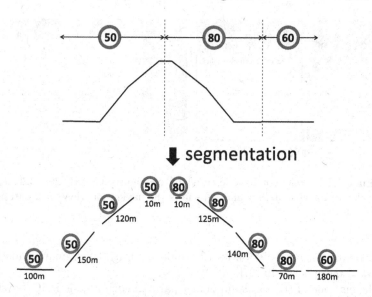

Fig. 5. Segmentation of a tour.

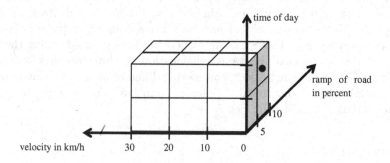

Fig. 6. Visualization of groups.

The estimation method is based on a learning data set. Measured values per segment as learning data set can update the range estimation model without additional development efforts. The learning data segments are sorted into groups depending on there values for the influence factors. Then for each group the average energy consumption of segments in this group is calculated. On this way a lookup table is generated with the energy consumption of each group. To estimate the consumption of a new segment, the known factors of influence of this segment has to be used to get the related group. The average energy consumption of this group is used as approximation for the energy consumption of the new segment. The approach was tested on a real data set, which was generating with a Mitsubishi i-MiEV. The prediction result only has a relative error about eight percent, which is a good standing similar to the approach of Ondruska and Posner. But the benefit of this approach is the run-time as well

(a)   (b)

Fig. 7. Final GUI-version of DAC created by Navimatix GmbH [29]. (a) shows an overview about the current tour and (b) shows the navigation view with current consumption indicators.

as an adequate range prediction for the challenge P5. The estimation method is described in more detail in [27].

At the end one of the most important parts in such a holistic ICT-system is the assistance for the driver. In a complex socio-technical system where EVs are used for inner-city logistic, the driver needs to cope with additional information (such as range, battery status etc.) in order to fulfill the main task of delivering goods. To reduce stress and uncertainty resulting from these important additional parameters, a DACs was developed and implemented during the SCL project. Basically the DAC works as a navigation system, providing optimized routes for EVs used in the project, considering different range-affecting parameters of the EV while focussing on the planned tour [28]. The final graphical user interface (GUI) is provided by Fig. 7.

5   Acceptance

Since the DAC should assist the driver while driving and reduce the added complexity, it needs to be easy-to-use in a vehicle. To find an optimal way to support the driver two different horizontal prototypes, as shown in Fig. 8(a) and (b), were developed at an early stage of the project.

The main challenge was to meet with the participants in selected companies for restrictions caused by standardized workflows and internal procedures. During the week there was almost no time to interview more than a few drivers per day, that made personal interviews or a supervised experimental setting inefficiently and costly. The alternative, an unsupervised setting for testing the DAC and filling out the questionnaire raises methodological challenges (e.g. how to guarantee a similar experimental set-up for each participant). To address this problem, a contact person from the participating companies was provided with detailed instructions about the experimental setting and a short 20-minute online survey was elaborated. Several methods like access codes, randomization and the analysis of metadata (e.g. time-stamps and IP-addresses) that was stored in our

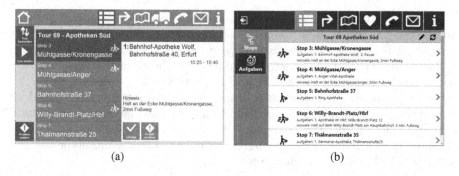

(a)   (b)

Fig. 8. GUI horizontal prototype 1 (a) and 2 (b).

online-questionnaire, helped to address methodological concerns regarding the unsupervised setting.

In the beginning, each participant received an impersonalized envelope with information about the procedure and a unique access code from the contact person in their company. Each participant had a personal computer with the online survey and a tablet showing the prototypes in front of him. The access code was needed to start the survey on the PC and the first prototype (which was displayed in randomized order) on the tablet. After answering some questions concerning general and specific attitudes towards EV and technological solutions in general, the participant was asked to perform basic tasks using the prototype. Based on this tasks, the participant had to answer some questions regarding the functionality and the design of the prototype of the DAC. Finally, the participant had to perform exactly the same steps also for the second prototype, answering the same questions as for the first one.

Except for general attitudes to EV and technology at the beginning and demographic attributes at the end, the questionnaire itself was created based on an operationalization of the ISONORM 9241-110 standard [30,31] for software evaluation, which has been adapted to the specific research context. For each prototype, the participants were asked to evaluate the adequateness, handling and intuitiveness. The questions itself could be rated on an ordinal scale with seven possible values between "$- - -$" and "$+ + +$".

While analysing the dataset, the access code was used to assign the answers to the specifically evaluated prototype and to compare the answers on a company-level without revealing the participants identity. This procedure prevents a bias resulting from the order of prototype evaluation. Each access code could be used only one time. Additional security was added through an encrypted connection to the servers. Furthermore, the use of the online survey system allows to exclude incomplete or corrupted answers based on the time of completion of each segment and the participants IP-addresses.

Overall participating companies 43 participants filled out the survey evaluating the two prototypes, from which five could not be used because they were not completed. Regarding the two prototypes, it turned out, that none of them was evaluated better than the other. Prototype 1, as shown in Fig. 8(a), obtained better results regarding the usability while prototype 2, as shown in Fig. 8(b), achieved better results in clearness of the design and intuitiveness. Based on this results a set of adaptation recommendations was elaborated which basically combined the positive characteristics of both prototypes. Finally, this set of adaptations has been used, to build the fully functional prototype as used within the ICT-system and shown in Fig. 7.

6   Simulated Environment

Many efforts, e.g. in projects like iZEUS, eTelematik, sMobility and E-Wald, are done to evaluate ICT-system support for EVs in context of smart future cities. Furthermore, each innovative ICT-system solution itself has to be tested by particular end-users. Unfortunately, there are mostly not enough end-users directly involved into these projects. At least, involved end-users do not have enough resources, e.g. man power or EVs, in large-scaled test scenarios to serve the required number of experimentees and driven km. In case of SCL, four companies are available to evaluate the described solution. Four partners with multiple users, in numbers nearly 50 possible experimentees. However, to get a large-scaled insight about how the solution performs, much more is required.

In case of evaluating DACs for EVs in inner-city logistic scenarios each SCL proband require access to the whole system setup as described in Sect. 4. This means the DAC installation into mobile hardware (e.g. a smartphone), access to the centralized server, the telematic unit attached to the CAN-Bus and for sure the EV itself. This setup is too bulky. Mostly external companies, asked for participate in evaluation processes, dropped their interest at this point.

SCL starts to address this by using a procedural generated simulation environment in combination with specific simulator hardware as evaluation platform. This setup would held every described component as used in usual real scenarios and will simulate the related environment. The environment itself is based on real map data and generated through procedural mechanism. This simulates specific scenarios like transportation from hub into town with multiple stops. The simulation environment is able to fully generate terrain with height profiles, different types of roads, houses and road signs based on different kind of input data like ASTER GDEM V2 for height profiles and map data like OSM for road and house information.

Getting this into practice requires functional components as shown in Fig. 9. Primarily, some kind of virtual simulation environment is required (1). This is because of using simulated environments in combination with real components, e.g. the DAC (2) and server (3), realistic simulation behaviours and position mapping is inalienable. The next step is to attach the simulation through the telematic unit by using some kind of CAN-Bus. This would be possible, but not

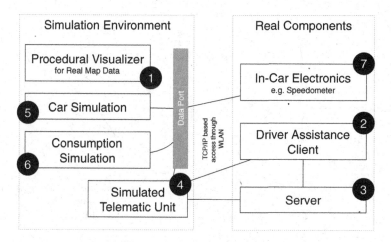

Fig. 9. Components within the simulation environment.

necessary. Much more applicable is to extract the communication components from the embedded runtime environment of this unit and reuse them directly attached to the simulated data source. This one is called the simulated telematic unit (4). Finally this setup needs the car simulation (5) itself, some kind of consumption simulation (6) which produces consumption based on user input when interaction with the simulated car and in-car electronics (7), e.g. speedometer and switches for hardware elements like light and air condition.

SCL composes the components shown in Fig. 9 into a simulator called Eltrilo [32]. This one uses common available hardware like TV screens, steering wheel, throttle and brake control, as well as touch displays for in-car electronics. Setups like this cabin can be transported to each experimentee and practice a homogenous scenario for studies about the DAC within this cabin. In context of SCL this cabin will configurated onto a scenario in Erfurt starting at a local hub, followed by freight transportation through two stops and finalized with the way back to the hub. Another setup is for a public purpose which considers a test drive about an express order from a suburb to the city center delivering goods. Time for the order is around 5 min. In the beginning, there is an area to be familiar with the EV. All the time a virtual assistant driver is helping per voice. In the test drive, there is an average working day and no rush hour. On midway, the weather pattern is changing. At the end of the trip, the driver gets a report how to improve their next tour.

7 Evaluation

What's about measured data from simulated and real environments? Furthermore, what's about using simulated environments as a suitable alternative in combination with SCL related elements like DAC or server? In fact, the whole

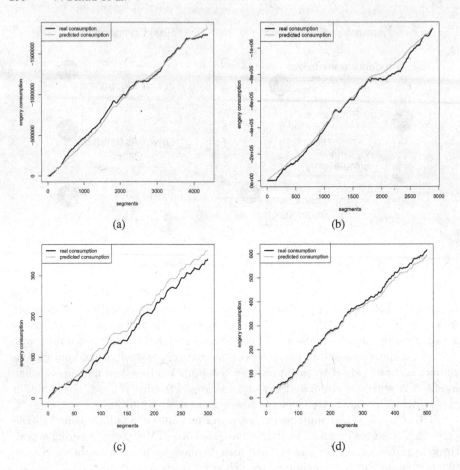

Fig. 10. Calculate forecast stability with recorded i-MiEV (a and b) and simulation (c and d) data.

system and related services are based on the range prediction model to help plan, optimize and analyse the usage of EVs. Measure the correctness of this model can be used to demonstrate how this simulation environment and embedded consumptions behaves.

First of all, results generated by using real EV data are required and have to be analysed as reference. These results can be used as a reference about correctness of range prediciton and can be compared to results created with data within the simulated environment. In this case the real data is collected manually by driving with an i-MiEV on uniform routes. Overall there are 40 trips with something around 7500 km. Figure 10(a) and (b) shows real and predicted consumption from two of those routes. Furthermore, Fig. 10 (a)-(d) shows comparable, nearly the identical consumption between real and predicted values. The prediction is done by using range prediction model with all routes, excluding the current one, and calculate the accumulated consumption from start to current position. For example, an already driven segment has a consumption about two watt-hour (Wh) and the forecast might be 1.8 Wh, than the relative error would be $err = |2\,\mathrm{Wh} - 1.8\,\mathrm{Wh}|/2\,\mathrm{Wh} * 100\% = 10\%$. Consider all driven routes lead to an average relative error of 11.9 % when forecasting the consumption of this i-MiEV routes.

Apart from relative errors calculated from real EV data, SCL wants to look onto relative errors calculated by using data from the simulated environment. SCL constructs and uses the presented cabin within science lab tests where experimentees has to drive a predefined route. The surrounding landscape is much bigger, which results in driving errors and differing driven routes. Each experimentee has to manage the simple logistical task as described in Sect. 6. Every 500 ms the cabin data logger writes a record about velocity, acceleration, temperature and height, as well as addition information about acitvated consumers and driving behaviour. Finally more than 10,000 trips with about 500 trip segments are driven and can be analysed as shown above. So the entire data set contains more than five million segments. Compared to reality these 10,000 tours would be something around 45,000 km and more than 110 full working days with constantly driven 50 km/h or more than 450 full working days when adopt 100 km per day[3].

Processing the data set all segments with velocity zero are removed, and trip segment's energy consumption is normalized by distance. Thus, the distance parameter could be eliminated in the range estimation model. Therefore, it is necessary to remove all items with a distance less than 0.001. Otherwise, energy consumption scores absurd high. As a result, 5,097,588 segments remain.

By using the same strategy in data analysation as used for real EV data, accumulated consumption e.g. as shown in Fig. 10(c) and (d) for simulated environments can be received. Again small differences between consumption and prediction can be observed. Consider all driven routes within the simulated environment lead to an average relative error of 11.3 %.

Figure 11 visualizes all analysed tours and their overall relative errors. The Fig. 11(a) and (b) shows the already mentioned relative errors in compair to all analysed tours. Finally, an additional data source, as shown in Fig. 11(c), was analysed to calculated forecasts and compair them with the real consumption. This one is measured by analysing daily tours driven by one of our logistical partners within the SCL project. This additional case visualizes a small data set, where the overall relative errors seems to be very height. This can be reasoned with the small amount of tours.

---

[3] Inner-city logistical tours analysed within SCL have 80 to 100 km per full working day.

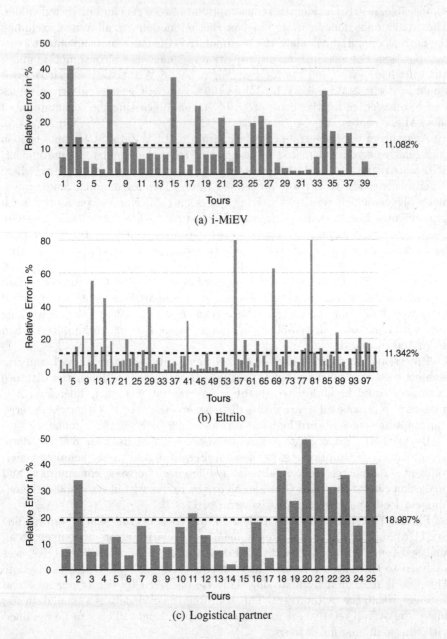

Fig. 11. Analysing relative errors among the available tours to get overall relative error with i-MiEV (a) and simulation data (b), as well as an additional data source from our logistical partner (c). Concerning the amount of routes in case of the simulated environment, only a smaller part is shown in (b).

8   Conclusions

SCL has implemented and installed the system as shown. The presented iterations for evaluation target test scenarios to see those parts under realistic and
simulated conditions. One of these scenarios, realized by using an acceptance
test, tries to evaluate the interaction between driver and DAC. This test takes a
closer look at GUI layout, the amount of shown information and usability. The
results are used to optimized the DAC and to fit drivers needs as best as possible. The other scenario is focusing on data analyzes and getting feedback about
how exact the range estimation model will work in case of different parameter
sets and in case of small, medium and large learning data sets.

The realized tests have shown some weak points. As seen in the acceptance
tests, participants can face problems regarding appreciation in case of descriptive scenario simulations. They have to suggest the logistic scenario by adapting
the instructions and answer through related questions about usability and client
acceptance. Unfortunately, it is hard to use EVs and corresponding hardware
installations in large scales to create test situations as realistic as possible. Apart
from that, tests within the Eltrilo cabin generates data as required and can be
modified to match any logistic scenario. The realistic visualization and handling
within this cabin helps participants to navigate within those scenarios and proceed in a similar manner compared to the use of EVs. However, those tests don't
compensate the real test beds which have to be done within SCL as well. The
simulated environment help to integrate a larger amount of participants than
the test bed could yield.

Concerning the integration of knowledge base technologies, there are still
open issues regarding the particular description language or logics specification.
By now, we implemented the runtime assistance in the form of a Prolog rule
base. The thereby implied closed world reasoning results in a good applicability
of the knowledge base assistance, as well as a well-anticipated scalability with the
integration of large databases. But the expressiveness of Prolog is really limited
regarding the use of full description logic ontology used as top level domains. So
by now, there is some kind of semantic gap between the conceptual description
of higher ontologies and the until now used Prolog logic rule base. We will try to
narrow this gap by testing the implementation of DL ontologies and open world
based reasoning without losing the functionality, applicability and scalability.

The results about architectural drafts, analysed related projects, as well as
embedded existing system landscapes in combination to the range estimation
model and knowledge base for this particular domain, will be transferred into a
reference architecture. This architectural documentation should help to design
and implement future systems which have to be used in addition to existing
logistic systems. Using a reference architecture within related projects can help
to get more EVs until 2020 as intended by the German national development
plan for electro mobility.

Acknowledgements. We would like to thank all members of the SCL research team here at FSU Jena there are too many to name them all in person. We would also like to extend our gratitude to our partners within the research consortium, end users as well as research institutions and industrial developers. This project is supported by the German Federal Ministry for Economic Affairs and Energy in the IKT-II fur Elektromobilitat program under grant 01ME121(-33).

References

1. Bundesregierung Deutschland: NEP Elektromobilität (2012). Internet http://www.bundesregierung.de/Content/DE/Infodienst/2012/10/2012-10-12-elektromobilitaet/2012-10-12-elektromobilitaet.html. Accessed 21 Oct 2015
2. Bundesregierung Deutschland: IKT für Elektromobilität II (2013). Internet www.bmwi.de/BMWi/Redaktion/PDF/Publikationen/Technologie-und-Innovation/ikt-elektromobilitaet,property=pdf,bereich=bmwi2012,sprache=de,rwb=true.pdf. Accessed 21 Oct 2015
3. DAKO: Website for the SCL project (2015). Internet http://smartcitylogistik.de. Accessed 21 Oct 2015
4. Schau, V., Rossak, W., Hempel, H., Späthe, S.: Smart city logistik Erfurt (SCL): ICT support for managing fully electric vehicles in the domain of inner city freight traffic. In: Proceedings of the 2015 International Conference on Industrial Engineering and Operations Management, Dubai (UAE) (2015)
5. INNOMAN: Projektidee (2015). Internet http://smartcitylogistik.de. Accessed 21 Oct 2015
6. EnBW: iZEUS - Projektziele - intelligent zero emission urban system (2015). Internet http://www.izeus.de/projekt/beschreibung-ziele.html. Accessed 21 Oct 2015
7. VISPIRON CARSYNC: Website for the ACM project (2015). Internet http://www.adaptive-city-mobility.de. Accessed 21 Oct 2015
8. Navimatix: Website for the eTelematik project (2015). Internet http://www.etelematik.de. Accessed 21 Oct 2015
9. Beikirch, S.: Mit Blaulicht und Schokolade (2015). Internet http://144.76.35.217/joomla/media/OTZ_11.03.2014_mit-blaulicht-und-schokolade.pdf. Accessed 21 Oct 2015
10. Technische Hochschule Deggendorf: E-WALD news - Technische Hochschule Deggendorf (2015). Internet https://www.th-deg.de/de/forschung/projekte/e-wald/e-wald-news#nav. Accessed 21 Oct 2015
11. Conradi, P.: Reichweitenprognose für Elektromobile. In: Siebenpfeiffer, W. (ed.) Vernetztes Automobil. A, pp. 179–184. Springer, Wiesbaden (2014). doi:10.1007/978-3-658-04019-2_26
12. Apel, S., Schau, V., Rossak, W.: Darstellung branchentypischer Abläufe und Wechselwirkungen in der innerstädtischen logistik. Technical report Math/Inf/06/2015, Friedrich-Schiller- Universität Jena, Institut für Informatik, Jena, Germany (2015)
13. Chopra, S., Meindl, P.: Supply Chain Management, vol. 3. Pearson Education, New Jersey (2007)
14. Arnold, D., Isermann, H., Kuhn, A., Tempelmeier, H.: Handbuch Logistik. Springer, Heidelberg (2002)
15. Busch, A., Dangelmair, W., Pape, U., Rüther, M.: Marktspiegel Supply Chain Management Systeme. Gabler, Wiesbaden (2003)
16. Die Qual der Wahl. Logistik Heute, vol. 5, pp. 36–37 (2005). https://www.wiso-net.de/document/LOGI_LOGI20050500131814263010211131427

17. Pirron, J., Kulow, B., Hellingrath, B., Laakmann, F.: Marktübersicht SCM-Software. Logistik Heute **3**, 69–75 (1999)
18. Faber, A., Ammerschuber, O.: Transporte im Griff. Logistik Heute **11**, 35–37 (2007)
19. Gamma, E., Helm, R., Johnson, R., Vlissides, J.: Design Patterns: Elements of Reusable Object-Oriented Software, 1st edn. Addison-Wesley Professional, Boston (1994)
20. Buschmann, F., Meunier, R., Rohnert, H., Sommerlad, P., Stal, M.: A System of Patterns, Pattern-Oriented Software Architecture. Wiley, Hoboken (1996)
21. Lian, P., Park, D.W., Kwon, H.C.: Design of logistics ontology for semantic representing of situation in logistics. In: Second Workshop on Digital Media and Its Application in Museum Heritages, pp. 432–437 (2007)
22. Jinbing, H., Youna, W., Ying, J.: Logistics decision-making support system based on ontology. In: International Symposium on Computational Intelligence and Design, ISCID 2008, vol. 1, pp. 309–312 (2008)
23. Anand, N., Yang, M., van Duin, J., Tavasszy, L.: Genclon: an ontology for city logistics. Expert Syst. Appl. **39**, 11944–11960 (2012)
24. Prinz, T., Kretzschmar, J., Schau, V.: A knowledge base for electric vehicles in inner-city logistics. In: The Tenth International Conference on Software Engineering Advances (ICSEA) (2015)
25. Rogge, M., Rothgang, S., Sauer, D.: Operating strategies for a range extender used in battery electric vehicles. In: Vehicle Power and Propulsion Conference, Beijing, China, pp. 1–5 (2013)
26. Ondruska, P., Posner, I.: The route not taken: driver-centric estimation of electric vehicle range. In: 24th International Conference on Automated Planning and Scheduling, Portsmouth, NH, USA (2014)
27. Gebhardt, K., Schau, V., Rossak, W.: Applying stochastic methods for range prediction in e-mobility. In: 15th International Conference on Innovations for Community Services, Nuremberg, Germany (2015)
28. Stolcis, C., Buchholz, J., Schau, V.: Evaluation of a driver assistant client in the context of urban logistics. In: Culén, A.L., Miller, L., Giannopulu, I., Gersbeck-Schierholz, B. (eds.) ACHI 2016: The Ninth International Conference on Advances in Computer-Human Interactions, pp. 235–239. IARIA XPS Press, Venice (2016)
29. Navimatix GmbH: Website of Navimatix GmbH (2016). Internet http://www.navimatix.de. Accessed 30 June 2016
30. Prümper, J.: Die Evaluation von Software auf Grundlage des Entwurfs zur internationalen Ergonomie-Norm ISO 9241 Teil 10 als Beitrag zur partizipativen Systemgestaltung - ein Fallbeispiel. Teubner Verlag, Stuttgart (1993)
31. Prümper, J.: ISONORM 9241/110-S: evaluation of software based upon International Standard ISO 9241, Part 110. HTW Berlin (2010). Manuscript Questionnaire
32. Website of Eltrilo (2016). Internet http://www.eltrilo.uni-jena.de. Accessed 30 June 2016

Analysis and Possible Mitigation of Interferences Between Present and Next-Generation Marine Radars

Gaspare Galati, Gabriele Pavan[✉], and Francesco De Palo

Department of Electronic Engineering, University of Rome "Tor Vergata",
Via del Politecnico, 1, 00133 Rome, Italy
{gaspare.galati,gabriele.pavan,
francesco.de.palo}@uniroma2.it

Abstract. The maritime traffic is significantly increasing in the recent decades due to its advantageous features related to costs, delivery rate and environmental compatibility. For this reasons it requires a high degree of control and an adequate assistance to the navigation. The related systems are the *Vessel Traffic System* (VTS), mainly using radar and the *Automatic Identification System* (AIS). In the recent years a new generation of marine radars with a lower cost of maintenance is being developed. They are based on the *solid-state* transmitter technology and uses coded *"long pulse"* in transmission, i.e. high *"duty-cycle"*, with *"pulse compression"* in reception. The main drawbacks of these apparatuses are the interference effects that they might cause on existing marine radars, becoming critical when the traffic density increases. The AIS data (identity, location, intention and so on) can be useful to estimate the mutual distances among ships and the mean number of surroundings vessels, that is the number of marine radars in visibility. Using suitable models it is shown that the high duty-cycle of solid-state marine radars can generate severe interference to all marine radar sets in visibility with a significant reduction, well below the international regulations, of their detection capability. The mitigation of these damaging effects, not an easy task, can be achieved by changing the radar waveforms, i.e. resorting to Noise Radar Technology.

Keywords: Vessel traffic model · Radar visibility · Statistical analysis · Sea traffic model

1 Introduction

Maritime traffic is strictly connected to economic growth: the international shipping industry is responsible for delivering about 90% of all trade worldwide (with 7 to 9 billion of tons loaded per year), and it is vital for the bulk transport of raw material, oil and gas. So, marine transportation is an integral, although sometimes less visible, part of the global economy. The marine transportation system includes a network of specialized vessels, as well as the ports they visit and transportation infrastructure from factories to terminals to distribution centres to markets. It is a necessary complement to other modes of freight transportation, and has the peculiar advantage of lower

M. Helfert et al. (Eds.): SMARTGREENS 2016 and VEHITS 2016, CCIS 738, pp. 296–322, 2017.
DOI: 10.1007/978-3-319-63712-9_17

damaging emissions. In fact, shipping is emitting about 2.7% of the global greenhouse gases (GHG) (versus 93.7% of road). For many commodities and trade routes, there is no direct substitute for waterborne commerce. On other routes, such as some coastwise or short-sea shipping or within inland river systems, marine transportation may provide a substitute for roads and rail. Other important marine transportation activities include passenger transportation (ferries and cruise ships), national defence, fishing and resource extraction as well as navigational service, including tugs.

The number of vessels in the world commercial fleet is about 110000 (for comparison, the number of operating commercial planes are is about 19% of this figure: roughly one commercial plane for five commercial vessels), 41% are cargo (general cargo, tankers, bulk/combined vessels, containers vessels), 42% *"non-cargo"* (fishing, passengers, tug boats etc.) and 17% military, for a global gross tonnage of the order of 650 millions [1]. A much larger number of leisure (or pleasure, recreational) boats is sailing near the shores.

Since the marine navigation is a potentially dangerous activity for the people involved as well as for the environment, a more efficient and a more controlled navigation is required to lower the risks and to increase the overall maritime safety.

To get these achievements, the *Vessel Traffic Service* (VTS) has been introduced by the *International Maritime Organization* (IMO) in 1985 and then updated in 1997 with the Resolution A.857 [2]. The VTS is a service implemented by a Competent Authority, designed to improve the safety and efficiency of vessel traffic and to protect the environment [2].

Unlike the *Air Traffic Control* (ATC) which directs aircrafts through controlled airspace [3], VTS only provides guidelines for procedures and manoeuvres in a crowded marine area, as well as information requested by the crew. Hence, outside the harbour waters the VTS has no any authority to impose speed and route to follow which are demanded to the captain's decision.

In addition to being a "VTS target", all ships of 300 gross tonnage (or more) engaged on international voyages and all cargo ships of 500 gross tonnage (and upwards) even if not engaged on international voyages, and finally all passenger ships, are required to carry on an *Automatic Identification System* (AIS) transponder [4, 5] capable of automatically exchange relevant information about the ship with other ships and with coastal stations, providing a kind of Automatic Dependent Surveillance. The primary use of AIS is to permit each equipped ship to *"see and be seen"* by other ships. Concerning the related radio link, AIS uses the VHF region: Channel A 161.975 MHz, Channel B 162.025 MHz, with a particular *Self-Organized Time-Division Multiple Access* (SO-TDMA) to the radio channel. The maximum distance in this ship-to-ship radio communication is limited by propagation over sea of the used waves and, depending on the environment and VHF antenna height, it is about 20 nm (nautical miles, one nautical mile equals 1852 m), while marine radars, operating in the microwave region, are generally propagation-limited to about half this figure. The aforementioned autonomous operation of vessels, however, does not help to achieve a well-organized marine traffic and, based on raw AIS or radar data, little can be said – in general – about the overall way in which ships are positioned in a given area and about the distribution of their mutual distances. The type of ship, and its destination, are only available for AIS-equipped vessels. The model proposed in this paper is aimed to infer some characteristics of all marine traffic for every type of vessels, including non-cooperating ones whether they are VTS targets or coastal radar targets.

The knowledge of the distances between pairs of ships can be useful to evaluate the minimum safety separation as well as, more important from the scientific point of view, the mean numbers of marine radars [6] in visibility that can interfere with the on-board radar of a given ship [7]. These visibility results can also be useful to evaluate the load of the AIS radio channels for applications such as performance analysis and installation planning of coastal AIS stations.

Even in the *Global Navigation Satellite System* (GNSS) era, the on-board radar sensor remains of fundamental importance to avoid obstacles such as non-cooperating (e.g. small) vessels and to visually acquire the coastline and the islands. Based on the IMO regulations [8, 9], the main characteristics of marine radars are: frequency band from 9300 to 9500 MHz in the X-band and 2900–3100 MHz in the S-band, and for the acceptable values (worst case): range accuracy 30 m; angular accuracy 1°; range resolution 40 m; azimuthal resolution 2.5°; minimum distance of detection from 5 nm for small ships to 20 nm for high coasts (60 m); probability of detection 0.8; probability of false alarm 10^{-4}.

The traditional marine radar systems are based on the low-cost commercial magnetron technology with relatively high peak power levels (up to 25–50 kW) [6] and a small duty-cycle, of the order of $2 \cdot 10^{-4} \div 7 \cdot 10^{-4}$. The simplicity and low-cost of these magnetron radars is, unfortunately, associated with the short life of the magnetrons themselves, of the order of one (or a very few) thousand hours, therefore calling for a frequent and expensive maintenance.

In the recent years a new generation of marine radar is being developed using the *solid-state transmitter* technology. These radar systems have a lower cost of maintenance, an operational life of the order of 50000 h and the absence of high voltage circuitry. They work with low peak power levels (hundreds of W) using *pulse compression* (coded pulse in transmission and *matched filter* in reception) with a variable duty-cycle up to 10%. A basic drawback of the use of *"long pulse"*, i.e. high duty-cycle, has been known for many years, but not yet seriously considered till now, excluding a single paper, [10] (Sect. 7, p. 163), where it is clearly stated: *"the interference effects that such a radar might cause on existing marine radars may be catastrophic"*. These effects become critical when the traffic density (number of ships per nm^2) increases. Although today the solid-state marine radars still have minimal diffusion, they are expected to represent the future solution for marine radar systems and several companies are introducing them on the market. For this reason, it is very interesting to study the damaging effects of the mutual interferences among different marine radars, a topic which in our opinion has not received enough attention, yet.

The aim of this paper is to evaluate the degradation of detection capability when more radars operate in mutual visibility conditions. This study starts from the definition of a statistical model for the distance between pairs of radars, derived using real data on six areas of the Mediterranean sea (see Fig. 1). The model has been derived from real-world AIS data kindly provided by the Italian Coast Guard for the week Feb. 23rd–Mar. 1st, 2015.

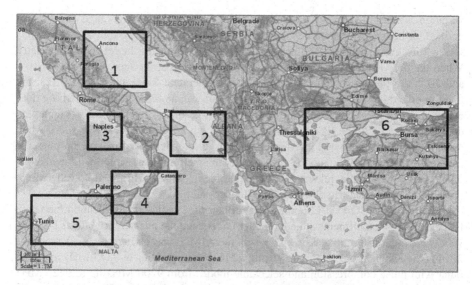

Fig. 1. View of the six Mediterranean areas.

Section 2 describes the present and the future relevance of the interference problem, reporting some first experimental results obtained in Germany [11].

In Sect. 3 the AIS data are presented with the related statistical analysis in which the parameters of the Gamma and Generalized Gamma models are estimated.

Section 4 considers the truncation of the distribution of the mutual distances in order to evaluate the mean number of ships in a given region, for example for radar applications. A simplified truncated model with only one parameter has been developed for the mutual distances. The relationship between the model parameters and the topology of the traffic has been investigated.

In Sect. 5 the degradation of detection capability, when more radars operate in mutual visibility conditions, will be evaluated.

2 Present and Future Relevance of the Interference Problem

Marine radars of various dimension and quality, between the consumer and the professional class, are produced by about ten medium or large international companies worldwide, from Japan to USA to UK to New Zealand and Italy. Presently, nearly all marine radar use *magnetron* transmitters, mostly in the X band (9375 or 9410 MHz with 20 to 30 MHz tolerance) with a pulse width selectable from very short – about 50 ns – for short-range operation to the order of 0.9 or 1 μs for maximum instrumented ranges. As the interfering pulses coming from nearby radars are asynchronous, they are suppressed from the operator's view by a simple *Interference Rejection* (IR) circuit, which analyses two successive sweeps of radar video at constant *range* and detects any sharp variations of its level, provided it is well above noise level. The rationale for that is the strong correlation of valid pulses in the dwell time. A sharp sweep-to-sweep variation is attributed to an interfering pulse, and the pertaining range cell is suppressed, or better, its content is changed into another one, e.g. the one of the previous sweep (of course, without adding any information about the target to be detected). When the duty cycle of marine radar is that of the magnetron ones, i.e. between 10^{-4} and 10^{-3}, the pertaining detection loss may be tolerated. Since the early 2010's, the main marine radar suppliers are selling radars with *solid-state* transmitters, whose duty cycle is about one hundred times the magnetron ones, making unacceptable the detection loss due to the IR circuit. The problem will arise in the next few years, when these new type of radar will interfere the much more widely used magnetron ones. Of course it is not possible to modify the so many magnetron radars which will operate for many years, hence the relevance of this problem, which will be followed by the problem of solid-state to solid-state interference later on.

By the Joint IMO/ITU Expert Group on maritime radio-communication matters a first example of experiments aimed to better understand the interference effects between *solid-state* radar (SS) and classic *magnetron* radar (MG) was carried out on October 21, 2014 at the Kiel harbour (Germany) using a MG radar operating at 9375 MHz and a SS radar with pulse compression and selectable modes from 9200 MHz up to 9420 MHz in steps of 20 MHz [11]. It resulted that for distances lower than 0.5 nm the MG radar is sensitive to SS interference, even if the interferer's frequency is far (with a difference of 55 MHz and up to 135 MHz) from 9375 MHz. this means that the classical interference rejection technique available on MG radar is not capable to suppress the interference due to SS radar. This effect decreases with the distance increasing, still remaining present up to 2 nm. Therefore, the operation of the standard marine radars (MG) and pulse compression radars (SS) in the same area seems to be problematic, and the interfering radar does not get an indication that it is causing interference to another radar. IMO/ITU EG suggests further studies to be carried within ITU-R.

Similar problems are expected in the automotive sector with the exponentially increasing diffusion of 74 GHz radars, whose available spectrum, 5 GHz wide (74 to 79 GHz), could be extended to the 81 GHz band [12]. In the automotive application area of radar, the interference problem has been treated by the European Union's *"More Safety for All by Radar Interference Mitigation"*, MOSARIM project [13]: further details can be found in http://cordis.europa.eu/project/rcn/94234. The MOSARIM's presented results only suggest well-known and trivial things such as time, frequency, polarization or code diversity: an example of how money from the European Union tax payer goes to the profits of large Corporations and their supporting entities, not to the benefit of the European citizen.

3   The Marine Traffic Model

In this section the statistical model for the mutual distances is derived from the AIS data. The General Command of the Italian Coast Guard kindly provided the AIS data for the week February 23rd–March 1st, 2015 related to six areas: (1) Central Adriatic, (2) Otranto Canal, (3) Central Tyrrhenian, (4) Messina Strait, (5) Canal of Sicily and (6) Dardanelles/Bosporus (see Fig. 1). For more details see Table 1. Each area was sampled at regular intervals of four hours from midnight [7, 14].

Table 1. Main characteristics of the six areas.

Area	Point N-E (DMS)	Point S-O (DMS)	Total surface [nm²]	Sea surface [nm²]	Sea [%]
(1) Central Adriatic	44°10′18.40″N 15°55′16.71″E	42°09′26.58″N 12°43′13.25″E	22632	13600	60
(2) Otranto Canal	41°12′57.47″N 20°01′18.74″E	39°31′42.97″N 17°12′28.32″E	17712	12300	69
(3) Central Tyrrhenian	41°07′27.98″N 14°40′34.17″E	39°46′07.02″N 12°55′19.09″E	8455	6700	79
(4) Messina Strait	38°55′08.47″N 17°33′00.99″E	37°13′27.60″N 14°10′22.01″E	20384	13700	67
(5) Canal of Sicily	37°56′26.98″N 14°14′01.89″E	35°59′03.12″N 09°56′44.44″E	30186	22800	75
(6) Dardenelles Bosporus	41°21′26.79″N 31°32′03.49″E	39°05′16.24″N 24°09′53.99″E	60112	21700	36

3.1   Analysis of the AIS Data and Their Distribution

From the first analysis of the AIS data, we derived the time slot with maximum number of ships in each area, as shown in Table 2. In the following we refer to the area with the highest traffic as the area with the largest number of ships.

Table 2. Maximum number of ships per each area and their density z. Data for the week February 23rd–March 1st, 2015.

Area	Day and time (in May, 2015)	Max number of ships, N	Ships' density $z\left[\frac{ships}{nm^2}\right] \times 10^{-3}$
(1) Central Adriatic	Tue 24th 04:00	285	20.88
(2) Otranto Canal	Tue 24th 08:00	46	3.74
(3) Central Tyrrhenian	Fri 27th 08:00	45	6.72
(4) Messina Strait	Fri 27th 16:00	74	5.40
(5) Canal of Sicily	Fri 27th 08:00	104	4.56
(6) Dardenelles Bosphorus	Thu 26th 12:00	53	2.44

The density z of en-route ships is calculated as the number of ships over the percentage of sea in the highest traffic condition. We extrapolated ships' positioning information from the AIS data related to Table 2 (i.e. highest traffic condition) for each area. We used the flat earth approximation for distance due to the small-sized areas (max distance is about 370 nm in Area (6)). Figure 2 shows the AIS positions of the vessels for Central Adriatic.

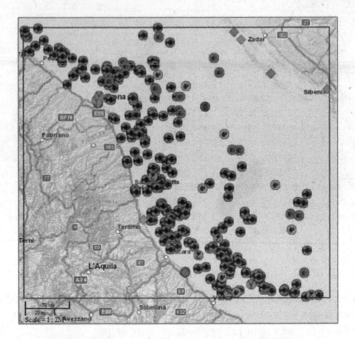

Fig. 2. Distributed traffic of Area (1) Central Adriatic.

It is known that the traffic in Central Adriatic in early morning is mainly made of fishing boats (88%) whose positions are someway randomly distributed, while in the Canal of Sicily are present cargos (20%) following some well defined (non random) routes.

If n indicates the total number of ships in the area in a specific time slot (e.g. the highest traffic condition), the number of mutual distances is:

$$N = \frac{n \cdot (n-1)}{2} \tag{1}$$

It is worth to note that the N distances are not statistically independent because they are *"mutual"* among ships: given n ships, if only one of them is moved, $n - 1$ distances do change.

3.2 Statistical Analysis of Inter-ship Distances

The ship-to-ship random distance R can be fitted with a probability density function $f_R(r)$ having the following properties: $f_R(r) = 0$ when $r \leq 0$ and $\lim_{r \to \infty} f_R(r) = 0$.

A suitable candidate for this positive random variable is the *Gamma* model whose parameters may be related to the density of ships. According to the performed *"Goodness of Fit"* analysis the Rayleigh distribution (or *"one parameter"* Gamma) does not provide the best fitting because of the very different traffic conditions difficult to be modelled with only one parameter. On the other hand, the Gamma density function [15]:

$$f_R(r) = \frac{\lambda^b}{\Gamma(b)} r^{b-1} e^{-\lambda r} \quad r \geq 0 \tag{2}$$

where $\Gamma(b) = \int_0^{+\infty} y^{b-1} e^{-y} dy$ is the Gamma function, having two-parameters (i.e. the scale parameter λ and the shape parameter b), can better match the empirical data. In order to improve the model of the AIS data, a third parameter μ can be added in Eq. (2) obtaining a Generalized Gamma model [16]:

$$f_R^{GEN}(r) \frac{\mu \cdot \lambda^{b\mu}}{\Gamma(b)} r^{b\mu-1} e^{-(\lambda r)^{\mu}} \quad r > 0 \tag{3}$$

The quantities b, μ are the shape parameters. These parameters can be estimated by the Maximum Likelihood (ML) method, which leads to a system of non-linear equations whose solutions are the values shown in Table 3 for Gamma model and Table 4 for Generalized Gamma. For the Gamma model the ratio $\frac{m_R}{z} \left[\frac{\text{nm}^3}{\text{ships}}\right]$ gives an idea about the topology of the traffic on the considered sea surface (e.g. en-route or randomly distributed): a low ratio values correspond to a distributed, or random, topology (i.e. Central Adriatic, Area (1)), while higher values are related to a route, more regular topology (for example, in Otranto Canal (2), Messina Strait (4) and Canal of Sicily (5)).

Table 3. Estimated parameters of the Gamma model for the six areas.

Area	Gamma Model		$\widehat{m}_R = \frac{\widehat{b}_{ML}}{\widehat{\lambda}_{ML}}$ [nm]	$\widehat{m}_R/z$
	$\widehat{b}_{ML}$	$\widehat{\lambda}_{ML}$ [nm^{-1}] $\times 10^{-3}$		
(1)	2.1542	38.7	55.66	2.66
(2)	1.9371	47.2	41.04	11.0
(3)	2.0472	62.4	32.80	4.88
(4)	2.4059	42.9	56.08	10.4
(5)	1.8674	34.7	53.81	11.8
(6)	1.5753	27.4	57.50	23.5

The sample size for each area is varying from 990 distances (with sample mean of 32.81 nm, Area 3) to 40470 distances (with sample mean of 55.64 nm, Area 1); day and time are listed in the above Table 2. In both Tables, using the estimated parameters $\widehat{b}_{ML}, \widehat{\lambda}_{ML}, \widehat{\mu}_{ML}$, the mean values $\widehat{m}_R$ (in nm) are also shown. They are very close to the sample means.

Moreover we observe that the ML estimation of μ leads to a system of three non linear equations where the μ-th power of the sample values (i.e. the measured distances) is present. Therefore it is necessary to find that value of μ whereby the derivative of the Likelihood function, $f(\mu)$, is equal to zero (see Fig. 3). However, as shown in Fig. 3, the values of $f(\mu)$ in the field of practical interest, i.e. $0 < \mu < 3$, are close to zero, i.e. there are sub-optimal solutions (values of $\widehat{\mu}$) that can be considered, including $\widehat{\mu} = 1$.

Table 4. Estimated parameters of the Generalized Gamma model for the six areas.

Area	Generalized Gamma model			$\widehat{m}_R = \dfrac{\Gamma\left(\widehat{b}_{ML} + \frac{1}{\mu_{ML}}\right)}{\lambda_{ML}\Gamma\left(\widehat{b}_{ML}\right)}$
	$\widehat{b}_{ML}$	$\widehat{\mu}_{ML}$	$\widehat{\lambda}_{ML}\,[\mathrm{nm}^{-1}] \times 10^{-3}$	
(1)	0.6061	2.287	11.9	55.63
(2)	0.8303	1.709	19.1	41.01
(3)	0.3334	3.576	16.5	33.04
(4)	0.3939	3.525	10.6	55.89
(5)	0.3848	3.03	10.3	53.63
(6)	0.7918	1.559	13.1	57.63

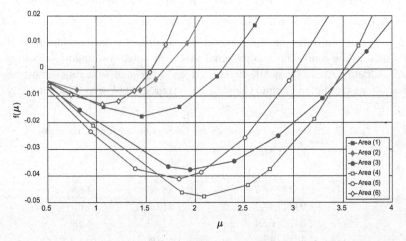

Fig. 3. The derivative of the Likelihood function for the estimation of the Generalized Gamma parameter μ. The $\widehat{\mu}_{ML}$ is obtained posing $f(\mu) = 0$

The use of $\widehat{\mu} = 1$ simplifies the model leading back to the Gamma model that looks more convenient than its generalization (see also in the following).

In order to validate the estimated parameters $\widehat{b}_{ML}, \widehat{\mu}_{ML}, \widehat{\lambda}_{ML}$ the Kolmogorov-Smirnov test and the χ^2 test [15] should be applied with the null hypothesis being (respectively for the Gamma and the Generalized Gamma distribution):

$$H_0\colon F(r) = F_R(r) \text{ or } H_0\colon F(r) = F_R^{GEN}(r)$$

However, since the N distances are not independent, the tests reject too often the null hypothesis H_0 [17], and cannot be effectively applied in the present case. Anyway, a visual inspection gives a fairly good idea of the goodness of fit of the measures mutual distances with these distributions. In fact, in Figs. 4 and 5 the histograms of distances are presented with the overlapped Gamma and Generalized Gamma models.

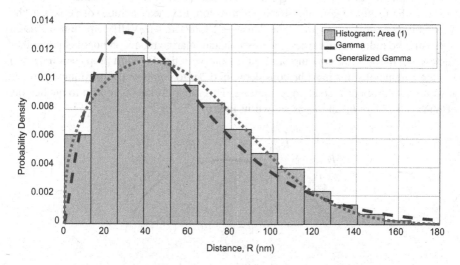

Fig. 4. Histogram and densities of R for Area (1).

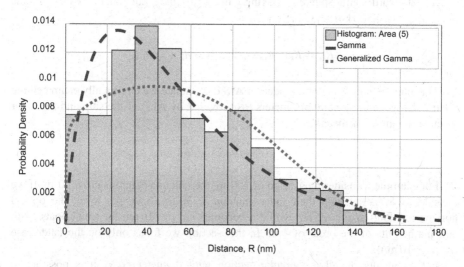

Fig. 5. Histogram and densities of R for Area (5).

In some cases, e.g. Areas (3) and (5), the Generalized Gamma model is not the best fit because the third parameter μ improves the fitting only locally. Hence, the Gamma model with parameters λ and b will be used in the remaining part of this paper.

4 Radar Visibility

We have shown that the distances between pairs of ships can be modelled with a random variable R distributed according to a Gamma model with parameters b and λ.

It can be useful to consider, for a generic ship, the mean number of vessels in the surroundings within a specific area. This need refers to the VHF communications as well as to the radar interferences due to solid-state marine radars on board nearby other vessels [7]. In the radar case the optical horizon (with the 4/3 earth propagation model) and the heights of ships must be considered in order to compute the maximum distance at which two on-board radars may interfere. This radar horizon is related to the heights of on-board radars h_k and h_i as shown in Fig. 6.

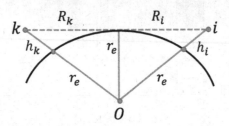

Fig. 6. Radar visibility between ships k and i.

In standard atmosphere, making use of the equivalent earth radius $r_e = \frac{4}{3} r_{earth} \cong 8500\,\text{km}$, the horizon R_{ki} is:

$$R_{ki} = R_k + R_i \cong \sqrt{2r_e} \cdot \left(\sqrt{h_k} + \sqrt{h_i} \right) \tag{4}$$

The antenna height is not included in AIS data, hence we empirically estimated the relation between the length x in meters (as provided by AIS) of the ship and the radar antenna height h (in meters) [7]:

$$h = 0.7825 \cdot x^{0.728}\ [\text{m}] \tag{5}$$

For example, considering a cargo of 150 m, the antenna height is *circa* 30 m. If we consider two cargos with their radar antenna at 30 m above sea level, the optical horizon is about $r_{MAX} = 35$ nm, while it becomes $r_{MAX} = 10$ nm for small boats, with antenna heights of the order of 4 m. In this section we focus only on the latter case ($r_{MAX} = 10$ nm).

Let's consider an all-sea circular section with diameter r_{MAX}. It is possible to calculate the average number of ships randomly distributed in this circular sea surface through the probability that the mutual distances among them should not exceed r_{MAX}:

$$P\{R \leq r_{MAX}\} = \frac{1}{\Gamma(b)} \int_0^x e^{-t} t^{b-1} dt = \gamma(b, x) \tag{6}$$

where $\gamma(b,x)$ is the Incomplete Gamma Function [18] with $x = \lambda \cdot r_{MAX}$. The parameters b and λ have been estimated with the Maximum Likelihood method for each area (Table 2). Multiplying the probability in Eq. (5) by the total number of ship in the area we obtain the expected number of ships inside the related area.

The probability density of the random variable R, i.e. the mutual distance among the n_{ships} vessels in the area (with $0 \leq R \leq r_{MAX}$), is given by the conditional density function of Eq. (2):

$$f(r|R \leq r_{MAX}) = \left| \begin{array}{cc} \frac{f_R(r)}{F_R(r_{MAX})} & 0 < r < r_{MAX} \\ 0 & r \geq r_{MAX} \end{array} \right. \tag{7}$$

This conditional density function can be computed using the already described Gamma model. Using Eq. (7) to compute the conditional density model from the Gamma model with parameters b, λ it is readily obtained:

$$f(r|R \leq r_{MAX}) = \left\{ \begin{array}{cc} \frac{\lambda^b x^{b-1} e^{-\lambda x}}{\gamma(b, \lambda r_{MAX})} & 0 < r < r_{MAX} \\ 0 & r \geq r_{MAX} \end{array} \right. \tag{8}$$

In Eq. (8) we have added the third parameter r_{MAX} named *truncation parameter* which considers the maximum distance at which the model should be considered (e.g. the optical horizon).

To estimate b and λ in Eq. (8), having fixed the value of r_{MAX}, a closed-form solution such as the well-known one for the Gamma and Generalized Gamma distribution does not exist. The problem of finding the maximum for the Likelihood function has to be solved by a non-linear optimization method. In particular, we have used the Nelder-Mead algorithm [19]. This estimation often gives very low values for λ, as shown in Table 5 for Areas (1)–(3).

Table 5. Estimation of b, μ, λ for $r_{MAX} = 10$ nm.

Area	Truncated Gamma		Truncated Generalized Gamma		
	$\widehat{b}_{ML}$	$\widehat{\lambda}_{ML}[n.m.^{-1}]$	$\widehat{b}_{ML}$	$\widehat{\mu}_{ML}$	$\widehat{\lambda}_{ML}[n.m.^{-1}]$
(1)	1.46	9.3×10^{-12}	1.46	1	9.5×10^{-14}
(2)	1.58	2.7×10^{-12}	1.59	1	2.7×10^{-12}
(3)	1.25	3.6×10^{-12}	1.26	1	3.7×10^{-12}
(4)	1.02	0.012	0.19	5.25	6.9×10^{-4}
(5)	0.99	0.017	1.21	0.82	0.015
(6)	1.74	0.078	0.22	7.10	0.09

Therefore, a different model with $\lambda \to 0$ has been considered for the *"short range"* (i.e. $r < r_{MAX}$, having set $r_{MAX} = 10$ nm) distance between a pair of vessels.

If $\lambda \to 0$ in Eq. (8), the only remaining term is x^{b-1} multiplied by a constant c depending on b. Posing $\beta = b - 1$ we obtain:

$$f(r|R \leq r_{MAX}) = c \cdot x^{\beta} \tag{9}$$

the unity area condition for Eq. (9) leads to: $c = \frac{\beta+1}{r_{MAX}^{\beta+1}}$. Therefore, the conditional density function for truncated distances with a single parameter β is:

$$f(r|R \leq r_{MAX}) = \begin{cases} \frac{\beta+1}{r_{MAX}^{\beta+1}} \cdot r^{\beta} & 0 < r < r_{MAX} \\ 0 & r \geq r_{MAX} \end{cases} \tag{10}$$

Normalizing with respect to r_{MAX}, i.e. posing $\hat{r} = \frac{r}{r_{MAX}}$ in Eq. (10) and multiplying for r_{MAX}, it results:

$$r_{MAX} \cdot f_R(r|R \leq r_{MAX}) = \begin{cases} (\beta+1) \cdot \hat{r}^{\beta} & 0 < \hat{r} < 1 \\ 0 & \hat{r} \geq 1 \end{cases} \tag{11}$$

If $\lambda \to 0$ (see Table 3) the Gamma model leads to Eq. (11) and if $\beta \to 0$ the model of Eq. (11) converges to the uniform-like distribution. Figure 7 shows Eq. (11) for different values of β between 0 and 1.

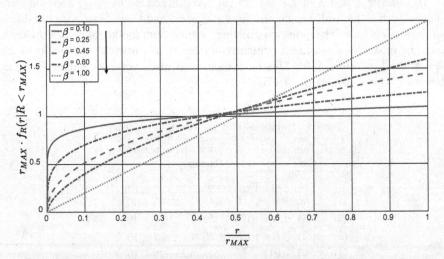

Fig. 7. Normalized Conditional density model $r_{MAX} \cdot f(r|R \leq r_{MAX})$.

In the following, we show the results related to Central Adriatic and Canal of Sicily. It is known that the traffic in Central Adriatic is mainly due to fishing boats whose positions are someway made of a large number of randomly distributed clusters, while in the Canal of Sicily the vessel traffic can be classified in: traffic near the coast, where fishing boats are the majority with some possible localized clusters of boats, and traffic along the sea routes where cargos, containers and tankers prevail.

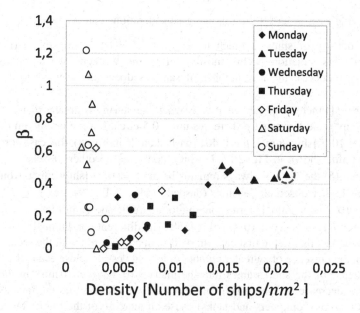

Fig. 8. Estimated values of β for Area (1) Central Adriatic.

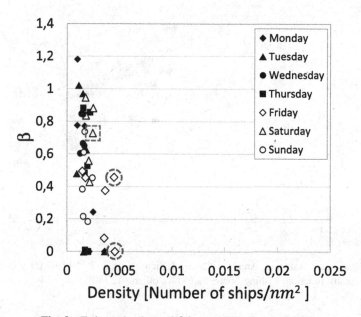

Fig. 9. Estimated values of β for Area (5) Canal of Sicily.

In particular Figs. 8 and 9 show the estimated values of β using all data during the week Feb 23rd–Mar 1st, 2015 (seven days, six values per day, 42 values in total) versus the ship's density (number of ships per unit area) for Area (1) and Area (5) respectively.

Observing Figs. 8 and 9 the following considerations can be done.

- If the density of ships is much lower than 2.5×10^{-3} [ships/nm^2] (in Central Adriatic this situation occurs mostly during the weekend when the fishery is strongly reduced), the low number of samples does not allow us to estimate β correctly.

- For Area (1) increasing the density, i.e. when the density is greater than 2.5×10^{-3} [ships/nm^2], the estimated β increases up to 0.5 circa. For the maximum density of 20.88×10^{-3} [ships/nm^2], β is 0.461 (dashed circle in Fig. 8); this case corresponds to the traffic shown in Fig. 2 (251 fishing boats and 33 other vessels).

- For Area (5) the density always remains below 5×10^{-3} [ships/nm^2]. Considering the two higher observed densities (dashed circles in Fig. 9), i.e. 4.56×10^{-3} and 4.47×10^{-3} [ships/nm^2], corresponding to the traffic shown in Figs. 10 and 11, the estimated β results 6.1×10^{-8} and 0.4558. The different conditioned distribution is due to the fact that in the first case (h: 08:00), in comparison with the second one (h: 00:00), the presence of a greater number of fishing vessels (close each other) implies an increase of the short ranges into the interval (0, $r_{MAX} = 10$ nm). In the second case the decrease of fishing boats in few localized clusters and the increase of the others (cargos, containers and tanks) cause an increase of the higher ranges.

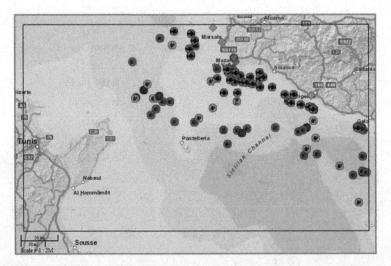

Fig. 10. Distributed traffic of Area (5) Canal of Sicily, Friday 27th h: 08:00 and estimated truncated density function. Fishing boats: 62 (60%), others: 42 (40%).

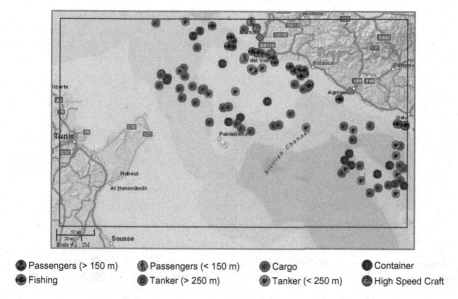

🔵 Passengers (> 150 m)	🔵 Passengers (< 150 m)	🔵 Cargo	⚫ Container
🔵 Fishing	🔵 Tanker (> 250 m)	🔵 Tanker (< 250 m)	🔵 High Speed Craft

Fig. 11. Distributed traffic of Area (5) Canal of Sicily, Friday 27th h: 00:00 and estimated truncated density function. Fishing boats: 31 (30%), others: 71 (70%).

- For the Canal of Sicily a third case (Saturday 28th h: 08:00) is shown in Fig. 12 when cargos, containers and tanks are predominant in comparison with the fishing boats. The density of ships is low, $z = 2.46 \times 10^{-3}$ [ships/nm²], and no clusters of fishing are present. The other vessels, i.e. cargos, containers and tanks, are more uniformly distributed along the routes. It results $\beta = 0.7265$.

Table 6 reports the ML estimate of β for the six marine areas considering the maximum observed density of ships for each area with $r_{MAX} = 10$ nm.

From Table 6 we can find very low values for β in areas (4) and (5). It is worth to note that in Area (6) β is comparable with the one in Central Adriatic although the area provides a main route. This effect is due to the presence, in Area (6), of two different seas (Aegean Sea and Sea of Marmara) as well as of Dardanelles, with the likely effect of strongly distorting the behaviour of ships' distances with respect to the open sea. In general, the sea percentage in Table 1 also gives an idea about the reliability of the β values.

From the previous results we can assert that when the density of ships is high enough to validate the results, β are strongly dependent from the topology of the observed traffic and from the geographic area: β close to 0.5 represents the presence of many clusters of ships uniformly distributed over the sea, prevalently due to small boats near to the coast (fishing boats). Values of β close to zero denote the absence of grouping of small boats, i.e. in this case large vessels are present away from the coast along the routes.

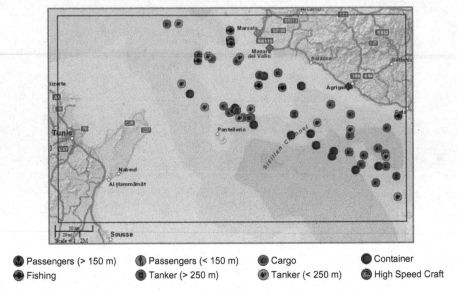

Passengers (> 150 m)   Passengers (< 150 m)   Cargo   Container
Fishing   Tanker (> 250 m)   Tanker (< 250 m)   High Speed Craft

Fig. 12. Distributed traffic of Area (5) Canal of Sicily, Saturday 28th h: 08:00 and estimated truncated density function. Fishing boats: 8 (14%), others: 48 (86%).

Table 6. Maximum Likelihood estimate of β with $r_{MAX} = 10$ nm.

	Area (1)	Area (2)	Area (3)	Area (4)	Area (5)	Area (6)
$\widehat{\beta}_{ML}$	0.461	0.589	0.257	1.9×10^{-6}	6.1×10^{-8}	0.455

5   Probability of Detection

To evaluate the effects of the interferences on the probability of detection, we define (Fig. 13) the time of overlap $T_{over} = \tau_i + \tau_k$ as the interval with no interfering pulses, where τ_k and τ_i are the pulse-width of the ship "k" (victim) and of the ship "i" (interfering) radars (independent radar operation is assumed) and t^* is the leading edge of the *"victim"* radar pulse.

The probability that n interfering pulses with repetition frequency PRF_i fall into the interval T_{over} is (*Poisson law*):

$$p_i(n) = \frac{(PRF_i \cdot T_{over})^n}{n!} e^{-PRF_i \cdot T_{over}} \qquad (12)$$

The probability that n interfering pulses with repetition frequency PRF_i fall into the interval T_{over} is a Poisson law:

$$p_i(n) = \frac{(PRF_i \cdot T_{over})^n}{n!} e^{-PRF_i \cdot T_{over}} \qquad (13)$$

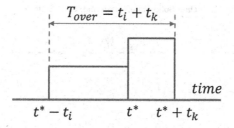

Fig. 13. Time of overlap.

Supposing that in an ideal condition (no noise, no clutter) the *"single hit"* probability of detection p_d is very close to 1. In the presence of N_I interfering pulses, p_d decreases as:

$$p_d(N_I) = \prod_{i=1}^{N_I} p_i(n = 0) = \exp\left[-\sum_{i=1}^{N_I} PRF_i \cdot T_{over}\right] \tag{14}$$

Supposing that all interfering ships are solid state type with same duty cycle (d_I), $PRF_i = 1000$ Hz and τ is variable from 10 μs to 100 μs (d_I up to 10%), while for the magnetron radar $\tau = 0.05$ μs, Eq. (14) when $N_I < 40$ can be simplified as:

$$p_d(N_I) \cong \exp[-a \cdot N_I \cdot d_I] \tag{15}$$

with $a = 1$ when the radar *victim* is a magnetron type, and $a = 2$ when the *victim* is a solid state type. Figures 14 and 15 show the reduction of the probability of detection, $p_d(N_I)$, when the victim radar is a magnetron type and a solid state one, respectively.

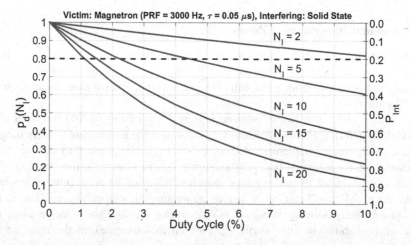

Fig. 14. Probability of detection $p_d(N_I)$ (left axis) and probability of interference P_{Int} (right axis) versus the solid state duty cycle, varying the number of interfering ships. Victim is a magnetron radar, interfering ships are all of the solid state type, $p_d(0) = 1$.

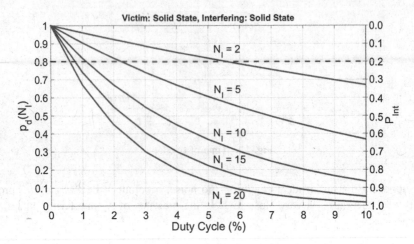

Fig. 15. Probability of detection $p_d(N_I)$ (left axis) and probability of interference P_{Int} (rigth axis) versus the solid state duty cycle, varying the number of interfering ships. Both victim and interfering radars are of the same solid state type (and parameters), $p_d(0) = 1$.

The number of the interfering ships is: $N_I = 2, 5, 10, 15, 20$. The axis on the right represents the probability of interference. We define the *"probability of interference"* P_{Int} as the probability of at least one interfering pulse in the interval T_{over}, i.e. the complement to 1 of Eq. (14). A few interfering ships, also for a low duty cycle, drastically reduce p_d under the IMO limit of 0.8, especially when the victim is a solid state radar as shown in Fig. 15. Note that the computation of these probabilities does not include the effect of the azimuthal integration of pulses, which will be discussed in the next Section. Moreover, the *"raw"* assumption was made that any interfering pulse *"blanks"* the overlapped valid pulse.

5.1 Azimutal Integration of Pulses

Considering the range of the typical antenna parameters for marine radar, i.e.: azimuth −3 dB beamwidth, rotation speed and PRF, the number of azimuthal pulses available for integration can vary from a few units to some tens (i.e. in most cases N ranges from 5 to 30 pulses).

The video integration is implemented in digital form using an A/D converter after the envelope detector. For the evaluations, we consider the simple case (widely used in the past for its ease of implementation) of a 1-bit converter, leading to a closed-form expression, i.e. the Binomial law, [20]. It corresponds to a threshold detector operating directly on the output of the envelope detector, followed by an accumulator which counts up to M "hits" out of N before generating an output alarm. This is the well-known binary Moving Window, MW extractor. In the case of noise alone the single hit probability of false alarm, p_{fa} (written in lowercase), at the input of the extractor, is:

$$p_{fa} = \exp\left[-\frac{T^2}{2}\right] \qquad (16)$$

where the threshold T has been supposed normalized to the *rms noise* value. Then the relationship between N, the detection thresholds (i.e. the primary, T, and the secondary, M) and the probability of false alarm at the output of the extractor, P_{FA} (written in uppercase), is (Binomial law):

$$P_{FA} = \sum_{k=M}^{N} \binom{N}{k} p_{fa}^{k} \cdot (1 - p_{fa})^{N-k} \qquad (17)$$

For each M, fixing P_{FA}, for example 10^{-6}, the probability p_{fa} is evaluated by Eq. (17) and the threshold T is estimated inverting Eq. (16). In the case of signal plus noise, the probability of detection on single hit, p_d (written in lowercase), depends on the target model. For a non-fluctuating (steady) target with a given Signal-to Noise-Ratio, SNR, it is [21]:

$$p_d = \int_{T}^{+\infty} v \cdot \exp\left[-\frac{v^2}{2} - SNR\right] I_0\left(v\sqrt{2SNR}\right) dv \qquad (18)$$

where $I_0(\cdot)$ is the modified Bessel function of the first kind. At the output of the extractor the probability of detection, P_D (in uppercase), is given by:

$$P_D = \sum_{k=M}^{N} \binom{N}{k} p_{d}^{k} \cdot (1 - p_d)^{N-k} \qquad (19)$$

The optimum threshold M is chosen by minimizing the SNR with fixed P_{FA} and P_D. Of course this way of integrating pulses causes losses with respect to a perfect (coherent) integrator exploiting the full dynamic range. For a steady target, $P_D = 0.9$ and a $P_{FA} = 10^{-6}$, the use of only 1-bit introduces an extra loss of $-1.6 \div -1.5$ dB which may be accepted because 1-bit A/D conversion offers significant protection against interference from random pulses of large amplitude. No matter how large the interfering pulse is, it can only add "1" to the count of first-threshold crossings.

It has been shown in [20] that the optimum threshold M (which minimizes the Signal to Noise Ratio, SNR), for a number of pulses of 10, 20 and 30 is $M_{Opt} =$ 6, 10, 14 respectively. For $N = 20$, $M_{Opt} = 10$ and steady target, the single hit probability of detection p_d and the probability of false alarm p_{fa} are 0.62 (0.72) and 0.0806 when $P_D = 0.90(0.99)$ and $P_{FA} = 10^{-6}$ respectively. The probability p_d in Eq. (19) should not be less than the previous values, but with interference, i.e. $P_{Int} > 0$, the p_d values decrease reducing the P_D and bringing it below the IMO requirement of 0.8 also for low probability of interference (less than 25%) as shown in Fig. 16 (solid line).

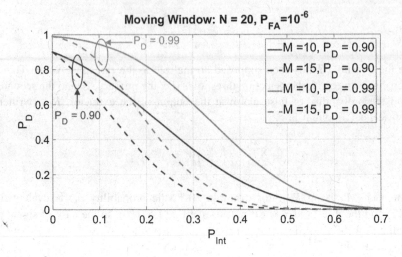

Fig. 16. Probability of detection after integration versus the probability of interference for N = 20, M = 10, 15. (Non-fluctuating target).

Substituting in Eq. (15) the probability $p_d(N_I)$ with $1 - P_{Int}$ and inverting this relationship, i.e.:

$$d_I = -\frac{1}{a \cdot N_I} ln(1 - P_{Int}) \tag{20}$$

reading in Fig. 16 the values of P_{Int} when P_D reaches 0.8, by Eq. (20) the maximum duty cycle tolerable can be evaluated as shown in when the victim and interfering radars are a solid state type ($a = 2$ in Eq. (20)). When the victim is a magnetron radar, $a = 1$ in Eq. (20) and the duty cycle doubles.

Increasing the threshold M up to 15 (leaving unchanged the SNR), the integration results more robust with respect to the effect of the interferences on the P_{FA}, however the probability of detection worsens as reported in Fig. 16 (dashed line). It can be concluded that the presence of interferences, also with low probability, strongly reduces the probability of detection when most vessels will use solid state radars, unless their duty cycle is kept low, i.e. generally below 1% and less than about 0.2% in high traffic as Area (1), see first row of Table 2 and second row of Table 7.

Table 7. Maximum duty cycle for $P_D = 0.8$.

MW: N = 20, M = 10, "victim" SS, "interfering" SS			
P_D	$N_I = 5$	$N_I = 10$	$N_I = 15$	$N_I = 20$
0.90	0.84%	0.42%	0.28%	0.21%
0.99	2.36%	1.18%	0.79%	0.59%

6 A Possible Mitigation Method

As a matter of fact, while in marine magnetron radars (having a duty cycle much below 10^{-3}) the mutual interference can be easily managed using simple techniques as the above-referenced Interference Rejection (IR) circuit, in solid state marine radars (whose duty cycle is typically of the order of 5% to 15%) the opposite is true. Pertaining solutions are not easily found. In the general radar (and radio communications) context, the interference problem is dealt with diversity in one or more parameters: frequency, space, time, polarization, code. For the problem at hand, the limited band allocated to marine radars, associated with the relatively wide band of their high-resolution and short-range operating modes, and with the lack of coordination between vessels concerning radar operation, does not show many potential for frequency multiplexing. The same applies of course to the emission time. Concerning the space parameter, the usage of ultra-low side lobes antennae could limit interferences to the main lobe, but the cost of these antennae is likely out of the budget of the marine market. Polarization diversity only permits to radiate pairs of orthogonal signals, and the same applies to Up and Down Chirp codes, while the traffic analysis presented before underlines the need here for N-ples (with $N \gg 1$, order of tens), not pairs, of orthogonal signals.

6.1 Noise Radar Technology as a Possible Solution

Noise Radar Technology (NRT) is a way being investigated to try to mitigate the problem presented in this paper, see [22–24]. However, the related costs are probably beyond the affordable costs for simple radar sets on board of fishing or leisure boats; therefore we are studying some innovative marine radar architectures to be presented in future works.

The problem of solid-state radar interferences must be handled by considering separately the effect against magnetron and against solid-state radars. The main reason driving this way to study the problem is the technological background behind the two kinds of radars: magnetron has no big possibilities to be re-designed since its main components are quite the same from many decades, while new solid-state radar is almost flexible in its high power chain as well as in its digital signal processing. As previously stated, the upcoming problem is mostly referred to the interference against magnetron, but it must not be neglected the problem among solid-state radars.

However, not much can be done to mitigate interferences against magnetrons since the magnetron radar design is not highly capable of implementing sofisticated interference rejection techniques; limited duty cycle, lower antenna side-lobes, low transmission power and frequency orthogonality are the only parameters available in solid-state radars to mitigate the problem.

Due to the flexibility of solid-state radar, same methods could be implemented on it to mitigate the interference against radar of the same type. In few years many solid-state radars are expected to operate in the same area, bringing with themselves the possibility to interfere as well as that to be interfered. Since the allocated available spectrum is the same for all radars vendors, it makes very difficult a strong frequency orthogonality, as it is unbelievable to implement a sort of time-coordination among them for obvious operating reasons; then only signal domain could be exploited to overcome the problem. One of the most promising way to design signals at will is the NRT [24]. Since solid-state radars use pulse-compression techniques, the main requirements for this type of signal are related to the output of the matched filter. The signal coming into a radar receiver might saturate it, or it might be a valid target return or it might represent an interference. Without considering the saturation case (because of the relative low power involved), the remaining two behaviours are respectively related to the autocorrelation and to the cross-correlation. The key parameter is represented by the level of their sidelobes w.r.t. the autocorrelation peak: the lower the sidelobes level, the higher the compression gain, so the higher the immunity to the interference. This last statement is possible because the noisy signals are inherently orthogonal to each other. In the literature signals with ultra low autocorrelation sidelobes have been proposed [25], to discriminate, after the matched filter, a valid return from a random interference. The requested level for autocorrelation sidelobes is about -60 dB which is comparable with the antenna gain (about 30 dB for transmission and 30 dB for reception). Many algorithms have been proposed, especially in [26], aimed to suppress the sidelobe region. Although they are very powerful from the point of view of sidelobes suppression, most of them do not take into account the bandwidth limitation of real radar systems. By accounting this issue, it becomes very hard to suppress sidelobes both in auto and in cross-correlation without reducing the suppressed area. The trade-off between the depth of suppression and the suppressed sidelobes region length comes as the limiting key point of all algorithms. Though a couple of algorithms such as Multi-CAO and Multi-SCAN, also with related applications [26], have been presented in [27] to generated a set of M signals with low sidelobes and limited bandwidth. A third powerful algorithm has been developed by the authors called Band Limited Algorithm for Sidelobe Attenuation (BLASA), which is an enhanced version of cyclic algorithms in [26].

BLASA is able to suppress sidelobes both in auto and in cross-correlation for a set of M signals starting from the level of noise sidelobes, i.e. $10 \log_{10}(BT) - 13$ dB, [24], where B is the bandwidth and T the pulse length, which is however optimal if very long pulses (large T) are used since solid-state NRT allows very long pulses. An example of the suppression sidelobes using BLASA is shown in Fig. 17 for BT = 256 with a bandwidth of 20 MHz. Figure 18 shows the spectrum of the signal. For large BT the computation complexity is very high and the algorithm BLASA has to be optimized.

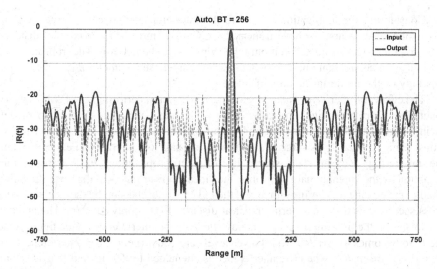

Fig. 17. Autocorrelation with suppression sidelobes (continuous line) in comparison with the input signal (dashed line).

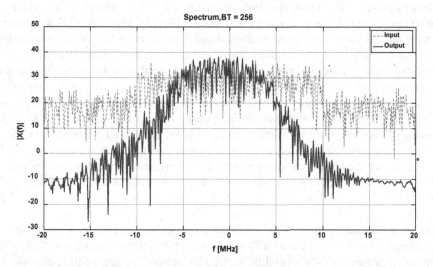

Fig. 18. Spectrum of the signal with suppression sidelobes (continuous line) in comparison with the input signal spectrum (dashed line).

7 Conclusions

The empirical analysis of the AIS data has led to a Gamma model for the mutual distances among ships, with the Generalized Gamma model being not the best solution to fit the data. We estimated the parameters of the models through the ML method.

Considering the application related to the interferences between marine (naviga-tion) solid-state radars, we have truncated the Gamma model to a maximum distance r_{MAX} in order to take into account only the ships inside the horizon. The truncation has led to a more convenient one-parameter distribution whose parameter β is related to the topology of the traffic in the area of interest.

The effects of interfering radar signals on the detection performance of solid state or magnetron marine (navigation) radars depend on many variables difficult to model, mainly related to the environment and to the specific conditions of the vessel traffic. Considering two radars (assumed equal just for the sake of simplicity), i.e. the own and the interfering one: in clear space, line-of-sight propagation, ideal transmission/reception by the antenna main lobe only, the "ideal" power ratio - in the same operating band - between the interfering signal and the radar echo of the ship having a given radar cross section σ and the interfering radar at distance R is simply $4\pi R^2/\sigma$. The antenna sidelobes and the filtering in reception may attenuate the interference by the figure A, so the ratio becomes $4\pi A R^2/\sigma$. Both power levels are equal (i.e. echo = interference) for $\sigma = 10$ square meters when the interference is attenuated by 60 dB and R is less than about half a nautical mile, or when the interference is attenuated by 90 dB and R is less than about 15 nautical miles, a value close to the radar horizon, or above it, in many practical navigation radar installations. Even including the attenuation by the antenna sidelobes (say, 50 dB considering both antennae), the needed additional 40 dB atten-uation can be achieved in principle by frequency selectivity. However, the scope would be very limited due to the narrow available band width (200 MHz) and to the relatively wide band needed for the required range resolution (i.e. 20 MHz needed for the requested 7.5 m resolution), not to mention the wide band occupied by the magnetron transmitters (normally, from 9.38 to 9.44 MHz for the "nominal" 9410 MHz com-mercial magnetrons), leaving not more than four frequency channels (e.g. at 9310, 9340, 9450 and 9480 MHz) to solid-state marine radars and two (at 9375 and 9410 MHz) to the magnetron ones. Anyway, a detailed analysis of the radar interferences in the various domains (frequency, space, time, polarization, signal coding) is beyond the scope of this work, in which we limited ourselves to consider the presence of interfering radar pulses (Poisson process) assuming that they simply negate the radar detection of overlapped, valid echo pulses, with no increase of the false alarm probability. This operation is typical of the widely used *"interference blanking circuit"* between successive radar sweeps. With such a model, the effect on the "victim" depends only on temporal considerations (pulse-width and PRT) and the probability of interference is related to the number of vessels in radar visibility, to the PRF and to the sum of the pulse-widths (interfered and interfering). Summing up, the driving factor is the integrated duty cycle of the radars in the visibility area of the "victim" radar, as well as its pulse-width.

The analysis has shown that the increasing diffusion of the solid state marine radars could represent a critical and relevant problem for the sea traffic when the percentage of operating solid state radars will reach a few percent.

Finally, the results shown here will be refined in future studies adding a more complete model of the "victim" radar receiver, the antenna patterns and the multipath effects. Such studies could lead to suggest new regulations (e.g. posing a duty-cycle limit) as well as new architectures for the next generation marine radars. Mitigation methods based on Noise Radar Technology are another active research field.

Acknowledgements. Special thanks are due to Italian Coast Guard for kindly providing AIS data of traffic.

References

1. Bosch, T., et al.: World Ocean Review. Hamburg, Maribus (2010)
2. IMO: Resolution A.857(20) - Guidelines for Vessel Traffic Services (1997)
3. ICAO: Air Traffic Service - Air Traffic Control Service, Flight Information Service, Alerting Service, 13th edn. ICAO (2001)
4. SOLAS: Regulation 19 of SOLAS Chapter V - Carriage Requirements for Shipborne Navigational Systems and Equipment (2002)
5. IMO: Resolution A.917(22) - Guidelines for the Onboard Operational Use of Shipborne Automatic Identification Systems (AIS) (2001)
6. Briggs, J.N.: Target Detection by Marine Radar. The Institution of Electrical Engineers, London (2004)
7. Galati, G., Pavan, G., De Palo, F. Interference problems expected when solid-state marine radars will come into widespread use, Salamanca, Spain, pp. 1–6. IEEE
8. IMO: Resolution MSC.192(79) on Adoption of the Revised Performance Standards for Radar Equipment, 12/2004 (2004)
9. ITU-R: Recommendation M.1313–1. On Technical Characteristics of Maritime Radionavigazion Radars (2000)
10. Harman, S.: The performance of a novel three-pulse radar waveform for marine radar system. In: Proceeding of the 5th EuRad Conference, Amsterdam, The Netherlands, pp. 160–163, October 2008
11. Joint IMO/ITU Experts Group on Maritime Radiocommunication Matters: Observed interference on marine radar. IMO/ITU EG 11 Meeting Agenda Item 6, 25 September 2015. https://imo.amsa.gov.au/secure/papers/2015/imo-itu11/6.pdf
12. Goppelt, M., Blocher, H.L., Menzel, W.: Automotive radar – investigation of mutual interference mechanisms. Radio Sci. **8**, 55–60 (2010). doi:10.5194/ars-8-55-2010
13. Kunert, M.: The EU project MOSARIM A general overview of project objectives and conducted work. In: Proceeding of the 9th EuRad Conference, Amsterdam, The Netherlands, pp. 1–5, October 2012
14. Galati, G., Pavan, G.: Mutual interference problems related to the evolution of marine radars. In: Intelligent Transportation Systems (ITSC), Las Palmas, Gran Canaria, Spain, pp. 1785–1790. IEEE (2015)
15. Papoulis, A.: Probability and Statistics. Prentice-Hall, Englowood Cliffs (1990)
16. Stacy, E.W.: A generalization of the gamma distribution. Ann. Math. Stat. **33**, 1187–1192 (1962)
17. Gleser, L.J., Moore, D.S.: The effect of dependence on chi-squared and empiric distribution tests of fit. Ann. Stat. **11**(4), 1100–1108 (1983)
18. Abramowitz, M., Stegun, I.A.: Handbook of Mathematical Functions. Dover Publications, New York (1970)
19. Nelder, J.A., Mead, R.: A simplex method for function minimization. Comput. J. **7**(4), 308–313 (1965)
20. Galati, G., Guargaglini, P.F.: A mathematical model for the binary moving window extractor analysis. Alta Frequenza **XLVI**(N. 4), 187-97E–191-101E (1977)
21. Skolnik, M.I.: Introduction to Radar Systems, 3rd edn. McGraw-Hill, New York (2001)
22. Galati, G.: Coherent Radar. International Patent PCT/IB2014/061454, 15 May 2014

23. Kulpa, K.: Signal Processing in Noise Waveform Radar. Artech House, Norwood (2013)
24. Galati, G., Pavan, G., De Palo, F.: Generation of pseudo-random sequences for noise radar applications. In: Proceedings of 15th IRS 2014, Gdansk, Poland, vol. 1, pp. 115–118 (2014). doi:10.1109/IRS.2014.6869189
25. Ge, Z., Huang, P., Lu, W.: Matched NLFM pulse compression method with ultra-low sidelobes. In: Proceedings of the 5th European Radar Conference, Amsterdam, pp. 92–95, October 2008
26. He, H., Li, J., Stoica, P.: Waveform Design for Active Sensing Systems - A Computational Approach. Cambridge University Press, Cambridge (2012)
27. De Palo, F., Galati, G.: Orthogonal waveform for multiradar and MIMO radar using noise radar technology. In: Signal Processing Symposium (SPSympo), Debe, Poland, pp. 1–4, 10–12 June 2015

Author Index

Printed in the United States
By Bookmasters